Women in the Irish Film Industry

STORIES AND STORYTELLERS

Women in the Irish Film Industry

STORIES AND STORYTELLERS

Edited by Susan Liddy

CORK UNIVERSITY PRESS

First published in 2020 by
Cork University Press
Boole Library
University College Cork
Cork
T12 ND89
Ireland

Library of Congress Control Number:2019955667
Distribution in the USA: Longleaf Services, Chapel Hill, NC, USA

ISBN-978-1-78205-373-6

Typeset by Alison Burns at Studio 10 Design, Cork
Printed in Poland by BZ Graf
Image courtesy of shutterstock.com

For the Sunday dinner crowd:
Eamonn, Chloe, Stef, Shane,
Milo, Evie and Da. For those in
transit and those yet to make an
appearance. But especially for
Eamonn, for getting me here.

CONTENTS

Changing the Conversation:
Education, celebration and collaboration

Text and Context: Documentary, fiction and animation

Conclusion

Acknowledgements

I am thankful for the support and interest of my colleagues in the Department of Media and Communication Studies in MIC, Limerick. I also acknowledge the financial support of the Research Office, MIC, which enabled me to undertake my research. I am grateful for it.

Thank you to the women who shared their time, experiences and reflections with me and, indeed, with many of the contributors in this book. You know who you are. This project would not have come to fruition without your input.

I would like to pay tribute to my colleagues in the Writers Guild of Ireland and in the EAC, the Equality Action Committee of the Writers Guild and Screen Directors Guild, with whom I first embarked on this journey. Thank you to my fellow board members on Women in Film and Television Ireland for their moral support and shared vision. A further thank you to the many female practitioners who continue to share their thoughts, defeats and triumphs, big and small. Needless to say, there has been great camaraderie and many laughs along the way.

There are individuals within organisations who have worked hard to create a more equitable industry and their contribution is noted and valued. However, here, I want to particularly salute those individuals and groups who devote time and energy to what is, quite often, voluntary work driven by a passion to embed gender equality in the Irish film industry.

We are travelling through interesting times. Hopefully, the best is yet to come.

Notes on Contributors

LAURA AGUIAR is Community Engagement Developer and Creative Producer at Making the Future, a joint project between The Nerve Centre, PRONI, Linen Hall Library and NMNI in Northern Ireland. She is a multimedia storyteller, with works including the documentary films *The Battery* (2018) and *We Were There* (2014) and the online interactives the 'Prisons Memory Archive' and 'John Maynard Keynes: The lives of a mind'. Laura has also worked as a freelance journalist in Brazil and Sweden and is the founder of the Rathmullan Film Festival. She has lectured at Queen's University Belfast and University College Cork.

CIARA BARRETT is a University Fellow in Film Studies at NUI Galway, where she lectures in film and visual culture, theory and practice. Her research interests lie in female performance and representation in contemporary audio-visual media.

RUTH BARTON is Associate Professor in Film Studies at Trinity College Dublin and author of numerous books and articles on Irish cinema, including: *Jim Sheridan: Framing the nation* (Liffey Press, 2002), *Irish National Cinema* (Routledge, 2004), *Acting Irish in Hollywood* (Irish Academic Press, 2009), *Rex Ingram: Visionary director of the silent screen* (The University Press of Kentucky, 2014) and *Irish Cinema in the Twenty-first Century* (Manchester University Press, 2019).

LAURA CANNING is a Lecturer in Film and Television at Falmouth University. She holds an MA in Film & Television and a PhD (which explored the industrial and textual history of quasi-independent American cinema, 1990–2005) from Dublin City University. Her research interests include media industry studies, production studies, gender and representation, and sports broadcasting, as well as the Irish media landscape, and she has previously published work on Irish women filmmakers including Neasa Ní Chianáin and Kirsten Sheridan, as well as Gerard Barrett and John Michael McDonagh.

MAEVE CONNOLLY is a Lecturer in the Faculty of Film, Art & Creative Technologies at Dún Laoghaire Institute of Art, Design & Technology (IADT), where she co-directs the MA in Art & Research Collaboration. She is the author of *TV Museum: Contemporary art and the age of television* (Intellect, 2014), a study of television as cultural form, object of critique and site of artistic intervention, and *The Place of Artists' Cinema: Space, site and screen* (Intellect, 2009), on the cinematic turn in contemporary art. She is also a contributor to several edited collections, including *The Blackwell Companion to British and Irish Cinema*, edited by John Hill (Wiley-Blackwell, 2017), *Exhibiting the Moving Image: History revisited* (JRP Ringier, 2015).

EILEEN CULLOTY is a post-doctoral researcher at Dublin City University's Institute for Future Media and Journalism. She has a PhD (2014) from DCU on the production and distribution of Iraq War documentaries. Her research examining fictional and documentary representations of conflict has been published in *Critical Studies on Terrorism*, *Studies in Documentary Film*, *New Uses of Bourdieu in Film and Media Studies* (Berghahn, 2016) and *The Visual Politics of Wars* (Cambridge Scholars, 2017).

ANNIE DOONA is President of the Dún Laoghaire Institute of Art, Design & Technology (IADT). She is Chair of Screen Ireland, and is a member of Women in Film and Television Ireland.

SARAH EDGE is a Professor of Photography and Cultural Studies in the School of Media, Film & Journalism at Ulster University where she teaches photography and film/media and gender studies. She has published a number of articles on feminism and film and post-feminism and the peace process in Northern Ireland, including the often cited 'Women Are Trouble, Did You Know That, Fergus?, Neil Jordan's *The Crying Game*', *Feminist Review*, no. 50, Summer 1995.

KARLA HEALION has a background in media, having worked in print publishing for many years. She is currently working as Associate Producer with independent production company Still Films, and is the current Office Manager at Deadpan Pictures. She has worked on various shorts and features including *Lost in France* (Niall McCann, 2017), *Kevin Roche: The quiet architect* (Mark Noonan, 2017) and *Frida Think* (Maya

Derrington, 2018). Karla was the founder and director of the Dublin Feminist Film Festival for four years, and has been involved in many grassroots, artistic and feminist campaigns. She is a board member of Women in Film and Television Ireland.

ISABELLE LE CORFF is Senior Lecturer in English and Film Studies at the University of Western Brittany, France. Her research focuses on film theory. An expert in Irish film studies, she has published *Le Cinéma irlandais: Une expression européenne postcoloniale* (PUR, 2014) and *Cinemas of Ireland* (CSP, 2009), and is co-editor of *Les Images en Question: Cinéma, télévision, nouvelles images: Les voies de la recherché* (Presses Universitaires de Bordeaux, 2011), *Biopics de Tueurs/Biopics of Killers* (Alter Editions, 2015), and *Penser les Emotions: Cinémas, series, nouvelles images* (L'Harmattan, 2016). She also created and is now Chief Editor of the Society of French Film Studies' online journal *Mise Au Point* (http://map.revues.org/).

SUSAN LIDDY lectures in the Department of Media and Communication Studies in Mary Immaculate College, Limerick (MIC). Her research interests and publications relate primarily to gender issues in the Irish film industry and the representation of, and participation of, older women in film. She is editor of *Women in the International Film Industry: Policy, practice and power*, to be published by Palgrave Macmillan in 2020. Susan is Chair of the Equality Action Committee (EAC) representing the Writers Guild of Ireland and the Screen Directors Guild of Ireland, and is Chair of Women in Film and Television Ireland. She is also a member of the Advisory Board of Women in Film and Television International (WIFTI).

ANNE O'BRIEN is a Lecturer in the Department of Media Studies at Maynooth University. She has published articles on the representation of Irish women in radio and television for *Media Culture & Society* and *Irish Political Studies*, on women workers in media production industries for *Television and New Media* and on women's leadership in media sectors for *Feminist Media Studies*. She has also examined why women leave careers in screen production in *Media, Culture and Society*. She has worked as a television producer, is a member of Screen Producers Ireland and was an appointee to the Broadcasting Authority of Ireland.

DÍÓG O'CONNELL is a Lecturer in Film and Media Studies at the Dún Laoghaire Institute of Art, Design & Technology (IADT). She is the author of *Irish Storytellers: Narrative strategies in film* (Intellect Books, 2010) and co-editor of *Documentary in a Changing State: Ireland since the 1990s* (Cork University Press, 2012). She has written extensively on Irish television drama and Irish cinema.

AILEEN O'DRISCOLL is Assistant Professor in Media and Communications at the School of Communications, Dublin City University. Her interests are in the cultural and creative industries, with her current research focused on gender, media and advertising, with an emphasis on the gender discourses articulated by advertising students. She is one of the organisers of the Dublin Feminist Film Festival (DFFF).

JENNIFER O'MEARA is Assistant Professor in Film Studies in the School of Creative Arts, Trinity College Dublin. Her research is concerned with the intersections between film and digital media, as well as between critical theory and creative practice: these include audio-visual essays, using digital tools for experiments with screen aesthetics, and film festivals as teaching sites. She is one of the organisers of the Dublin Feminist Film Festival (DFFF).

LANCE PETTITT (Professor) is Associate Tutor in English and Film at Birkbeck, University of London, and formerly Director of the Centre for Irish Studies at St Mary's University in London. He has published widely on Irish film and television and his work includes *Screening Ireland: Film and television representation* (2000) (2nd edition in progress) and *Irish Media and Popular Culture* (2008). He is series co-editor (with Beatriz Kopschitz Bastos) of 'Ireland on Film', whose most recent title is *The Road to God Knows Where* (2016, Alan Gilsenan), and co-curator of the 'Irish Lives' festival in Brazil (May 2016). He is the recipient of a British Academy/Leverhulme Research Grant for 2020.

KATHERINE STONE is Assistant Professor of German Studies at the University of Warwick and has published on various aspects of feminist culture and media studies. She was previously one of the organisers of the Dublin Feminist Film Festival (DFFF).

Introduction

Setting the Scene:
Women in the Irish film industry

SUSAN LIDDY

Over the last couple of decades, feminist film historians have re-discovered and re-evaluated women's contribution to the industry.[1] The obstacles facing women in the film industry cannot be relegated to the past, however. Based on the findings of a cross-cultural study, Smith et al. found that 'Gender inequality is rampant in global films. This was demonstrated by the percentage of female characters on-screen, the lack of girls and women as leads or co-leads in movies, and the few females behind the camera.'[2] As Wreyford and Cobb have observed, feminist research across all disciplines 'has championed the need to hear and include those whose voices have been excluded from history and marginalized in the present'.[3] The processes and practices that can foster and normalise such exclusion are important to excavate, analyse and challenge, and that is the purpose of this collection. By doing so, it is hoped that the contribution and experiences of women in the contemporary Irish film industry, which has until relatively recently evaded focus, will be recorded and not lost to future film histories.

The following chapters are concerned with both female absence and presence – historical and contemporary. They offer a spotlight on the work of specific female practitioners, explore representations and provide a critical evaluation of the ways in which women can be sidelined and their exclusion explained away with reference to a deficit of some kind: skill, talent, confidence or sheer persistence in a 'rejection industry'. While not all contributors necessarily self-identify as feminist, the work here has a feminist thrust in its inquiry and seeks to assess and evaluate cultural and ideological impediments to gender equality in the Irish film industry.

The underrepresentation of women in the film industry, both in front of and behind the camera, is an international problem, and this introduction will begin by contextualising the discussion. This will be followed by an analysis of the factors that led to the emergence of activism around gender equality in the Irish film industry since 2014 and which challenged the discourse of meritocracy in a number of significant ways. Such challenges range from targeted research into the procedures and funding decisions of Screen Ireland (formally the Irish Film Board); the changing social and political landscape within which demands for gender equality surfaced; and the enduring importance of the explosive 'Waking the Feminists' campaign, which led to the re-emergence of a strong feminist voice in Irish culture and created a space for equality demands to be heard across a number of sectors.

Important also is the role that social media played in the diss-emination of debates around gender equality and gender research, the ongoing robust pursuit of the equality agenda by lobbying/advocacy groups, the public debates that challenged, and continue to challenge, the status quo, and the response of funders such as Screen Ireland (SI) and the Broadcasting Authority of Ireland (BAI) to growing demands for gender equality. Finally, the chapters in this collection will be introduced. Contributors explore a range of issues pertaining to film history, representation, screenwriting, direction, production, cinematography, animation, features and documentary film, drawing on textual analysis, historical analysis and a production studies approach.

Women in the international film industry

Writing about 'the invisible woman' for the British Film Institute, Braughan suggests that 'it is now impossible to claim ignorance of the gender inequality that runs rife through the film industry'.[4] Indeed, there is a growing body of research (though very little of it relates to Ireland) that points to a serious international problem. For instance, between 2000 and 2015 women directed just 14 per cent of UK films and wrote or co-wrote only 20 per cent of produced screenplays; a mere 7 per cent of UK films had a female cinematographer and 17 per cent had a female editor.[5] The UK is not the exception but the rule; drawing on comparative research from seven European countries, Aylett finds that 'there is a significant under representation of female directors at all levels of the industry even though there is an almost equal share of women graduating from film schools'.[6] Across the world, in the Australian film industry, during the five-year period 2012/13–2016/17 the figures for female directors and screenwriters were 15 per cent and 22 per cent respectively.[7] In the US, research into the 1,100 most popular films between 2007 and 2017 found that just 4 per cent were directed by women. In addition, the career span of female directors is shorter than their male colleagues: women directors are far more likely to be 'one and done', i.e. to make only one feature film, to direct fewer films during their career, and to direct more lucrative genres such as sci-fi, action, horror or thriller. On top of this, less than 1 per cent of all top-grossing filmmakers during this period were women of colour and they were largely absent as screenwriters also.[8]

Internationally, women of all ages are significantly underrepresented as protagonists and central characters in film.[9] Female characters are often 'symbolically annihilated' and wilt on the margins in the vast majority of feature films.[10] The vista is altogether bleaker for female characters over the age of forty, when the intersection of gender and age can create a 'double jeopardy' for female actors, particularly in the representation of female sexuality.[11] However, the percentage of girls and women on-screen is significantly higher when at least one female is involved in directing or screenwriting. There is also evidence that more women directors will result in the hiring of more female crew: in the top 500 Hollywood films of 2018, where a film had at least one female director, greater percentages of women were hired as writers, editors, cinematographers and composers compared with films with exclusively male directors.[12] The link, then, between female filmmakers, the images and stories circulating in our culture and the opportunities for female film crew is well established. The presence or absence of women in key creative roles in the film industry is highly significant in determining the kinds of stories, perspectives and characters that audiences will see, or fail to see, on-screen. Indeed, Smith et al. suggest that more women in key creative roles will 'impact on the very nature of a story or the way in which a story is told'.[13]

Though outside the scope of this introduction, over the last few years a number of countries have taken action to rectify the serious imbalance in their industries. Sweden, under the leadership of Anna Serner, CEO of the Swedish Film Institute, first threw down the gauntlet internationally, implementing progressive gender policies and ambitious targets. Others have followed with varying degrees of success, including the UK, Norway, Australia and Canada. However, it is important to be mindful of the distinction between enlightened national funding bodies with gender policies in place and the wider film industry, which may not be as supportive of gender parity. For instance, Coles identifies a range of impediments for female directors in the Canadian film industry, including 'exclusionary networks, fiscal cliffs, negative stereotypes about women's leadership, systemic bias and informal, opaque hiring decisions'.[14] Yet, in 2016, the National Film Board of Canada (NFB), Canada's public film and digital media producer and distributor, committed to full gender equality in key creative roles by 2020. As early as 2019 the NFB announced that it had already hit its target for women directors, who now direct half of its productions, and, crucially, half of all its production funding is allocated to female-directed projects. A similar pledge to gender equality was made by Telefilm Canada, which primarily funds feature films. However, in 2018 it expressed concern that an ongoing gender gap is still in evidence in higher-budget films – from 2.5 million CAD upwards – a sober reminder of the risk-averse nature of the film industry and the disproportionate consequences for female filmmakers.[15]

The pattern of gender inequality in the Irish film industry has much in common with the position internationally. Ireland has been comparatively progressive in adopting a gender policy – an intriguing development in light of the status of women in Irish society more generally. Before going on to discuss the Irish film industry and its gender journey, a brief overview of women's role in Irish society will now be undertaken.

Women in Irish society

Despite the many social and cultural changes that have occurred in Irish society over the last twenty years, Irish women 'often find themselves lagging behind when it comes to equal opportunities and income', with outstanding issues including violence against women, the reconciliation of work/life balance and gender balance in decision-making and positions of power.[16] Indeed, the 'uniquely misogynistic' article 40.3.3, known as the Eighth Amendment, was inserted into the Constitution following a referendum in 1983 and resulted in women being unable to avail of abortion services in the state unless in prohibitively restricted circumstances.

Following a referendum on 25 May 2018 the electorate voted overwhelmingly in favour of repeal and for provision to be made for the regulation of abortion services.[17] On 13 December 2018, the Regulation of Termination of Pregnancy Bill passed through all stages of the Oireachtas and was signed into law by President Michael D. Higgins a week later.

Women are still underrepresented in a range of decision-making sectors in this country, according to the National Women's Council of Ireland (NWCI), including the public sector, politics, the diplomatic service, state boards and non-state boards.[18] In Ireland, to give just two examples, only 14 per cent of CEOs or Head of Operations and 16 per cent of corporate board members are women. Even after the implementation of the candidate selection quota in the 2016 general election women only comprise 22 per cent of TDs in the Dáil, ranking Ireland seventy-sixth in the world for women's representation in the lower or single house of national parliaments.

As a result of occupational segregation women are clustered in a narrow range of jobs or professions and constrained by the 'glass ceiling'. The gender pay gap, as of November 2017, is 13.9 per cent, and women are found in primarily low-paid, part-time, 'precarious' employment, clustered in a narrow range of jobs or professions in which they are less likely to reach the level of senior management, a fact that also impacts on rates of pay.[19]

Given that the 'overwhelming number of those in positions of authority, whether elected or appointed, continue to be men', it is hardly surprising that women's representation in the arts would also be problematic.[20] As Walsh et al. have shown, women's voices are significantly underrepresented on primetime radio shows on RTÉ, Newstalk and Today FM in terms of on-air content, as news subjects, or as 'experts', guests, journalists, reporters and presenters.[21] In Irish theatre, 'women are poorly represented in all roles except costume design' and Donohue et al. suggest that the higher the funding an organisation received, 'the lower the female presence'.[22] In the Irish film industry, Liddy found that between 1993 and 2013 only 13 per cent of produced live action screenplays funded by Screen Ireland had an Irish or Irish-based female screenwriter.[23] If co-productions and animated film are included, that figure rises to 19 per cent for both writers and directors.[24]

Celtic Tiger, austerity and gender equality

Before 'Waking the Feminists' and the resurgence of widespread feminist activism and debate, there were a number of years during the Celtic Tiger and austerity period in which discourses of gender equality were sidelined. The post-feminist discourse of the 1990s and beyond was predicated on the belief that continuing gender inequalities were the result of individual women's choices and preferences. There were few challenges to the prevailing neoliberal orthodoxies in Celtic Tiger Ireland, though, as Barry and Conroy argue, prior to 2007, across the EU, Ireland was acknowledged as a country with 'strong and comprehensive equality legislation covering a broad range of grounds in relation to both employment and services backed up with an Equality Authority and enforced by an Equality Tribunal'. However, after 2007 with the financial downturn and austerity measures in place the 'entire architecture' of public and statutory bodies set up to support, monitor and promote equality collapsed.[25]

Davies and O'Callaghan hold that austerity is an ideological system, as well as a fiscal one, promoting values that include profit, competition and individualism.[26] These are in sharp contrast to the values and goals of feminism, which privilege gender equality, social justice, and inclusion. The result was the marginalisation of equality, anti-discrimination and gender issues within a 'crisis management' approach to the Irish economy.[27] Budget cuts and funding restrictions impacted on 'frontline advocacy and support', seriously reducing the ability of women's organisations to protect and advance the rights of women.[28]

Murphy distinguishes between defensive and offensive feminist agency during this time. Defensive agency was concerned with campaigning against the introduction of measures such as lone parent cutbacks, often framed as sectoral or anti-austerity campaigns.[29] Offensive feminist agency related to campaigns challenging structural power inequality such as equality proofing campaigns and the emergence of the 50/50 lobby group that campaigned successfully for gender candidate selection quotas in politics. While feminist agency was 'injured by the crisis', it was, according to Murphy, 'still very much alive'.[30]

This was to become clear with increasing calls from groups such as the Abortion Rights Campaign (ARC), which sought the repeal of the Eighth Amendment and the provision of abortion services in Ireland – calls which intensified after the death of Savita Halappanavar in October 2012. At that time, few were articulating any concern about the male-dominated nature of the Irish film industry and its output, though a couple of short articles were published in *Film Ireland* between 2013 and 2015 signalling the existence of the problem.[31]

Screen Ireland is funded with public money and administered through the Department of Culture, Heritage and the Gaeltacht. It has defined itself as 'the national development agency for Irish filmmaking' and functions as a cultural gatekeeper with the power to award or deny financial support to projects at a development or a production stage.[32] As 'the only source of public funding for feature films directed towards a cinematic release' it occupies a position of great importance not only in Irish filmmaking but in Irish cultural life generally.[33] However, prior to 2015, Screen Ireland was unproblematically calling for 'Irish stories' and seeking Irish 'creative talent' despite the majority of our stories being about men and told by men.

Liddy's 2014/15 research interviews with Screen Ireland decision makers sought to understand how gender inequality was made sense of and how the organisation could justify the lack of statistical data in the public domain. With some notable exceptions, the reality of women's underrepresentation was evaded or deflected.[34] This ranged from explaining away the absence of statistics which would reveal the reality behind their proclaimed 'gender-neutrality' to minimising the role of the organisation to that of a 'funding body' exclusively, rather than the national film development agency with a broader remit. A strong merit-driven ideology permeated the majority of accounts; project-led development was deemed ungendered in a system that prioritised 'quality'. That the concept of quality could be subjective was not widely acknowledged at that time.

In some cases, the scarcity of women screenwriters or screenwriter/ directors was made sense of in terms of personal choice – implicitly women's own 'fault' – in as much as they were just not applying in enough numbers to an organisation that is unbiased and concerned only with the merit of the project. A neoliberal choice discourse had the effect of glossing over the gendered nature of Irish society and justifying the low numbers of women applicants. O'Toole identifies what she calls 'the logic of lack' as explaining the dearth of women in theatre prior to 'Waking the Feminists': 'Irish female artists of sufficient quality and national importance weren't excluded from the centenary program, they simply didn't exist: they were lacking.'[35] Such a position, whether in theatre or film, effectively serves as a justification for maintaining the status quo and continues the cycle of female exclusion.

'Waking the Feminists'

As already argued here, the male-dominated nature of the arts in Ireland and in the Irish film industry specifically went, for the most part, publicly unchallenged for many years Screen Ireland had already started to be called out behind the scenes (Liddy, 2016) and at public events such as the Galway Film Fleadh 2015. But more widespread anger was eventually ignited by 'Waking the Feminists', which arguably marked the resurgence of widescale feminist activism here, as has been recorded extensively elsewhere. In brief, when Ireland's national theatre, the Abbey, launched its programme, Waking the Nation, to mark the centenary of the 1916 Rising – an event that led to the foundation of the Irish state – only one out of the ten plays selected was written by a woman. Lian Bell, a freelance Dublin-based set designer and arts manager, denounced the exclusion on social media, triggering a surge of anger and recognition; a public outcry erupted. A campaign entitled 'Waking the Feminists' gathered momentum over the course of a number of days and kick-started an interrogation of women's place in the arts and beyond.[36] Animated debate filled the airwaves, television and print media. Journalist Una Mullally articulated the outrage many were feeling in a rousing column for *The Irish Times* on 4 November 2015;[37] letters to the editor of that paper quickly followed over the coming days with academics Brenda Donohue and Susan Liddy citing research relating to Irish theatre and film respectively which supported the emerging accusations that women were being sidelined in the arts.[38] Feminist demands for gender equality in the Irish film industry accelerated quite rapidly, galvanised by social media.

Social Media

Social media played, and continues to play, an important role in consciousness-raising and the dissemination of gender research around women in the international film industry. Murphy points to the increased use of Facebook and other social media during and after the austerity crisis.[39] Certainly, the use of social media was central to the debates and exchange of information during the period marked by 'Waking the Feminists'. While acknowledging that digital spaces can be highly problematic and that 'hashtag feminism' has its limitations, Turley and Fisher argue that feminist social media campaigns are indeed political actions.[40] Issues that are first debated on social media are often subsequently spotlighted by mainstream media, garnering further exposure and increasing the audience.

Increasingly, technology is being used by marginalised groups to represent themselves and to organise transnationally: to form networks that can 'overcome time/space constraints, potentially leading to movement spill-over'.[41] Whether it can actually provide tools to fundamentally alter power relations in society is still contested, but social media can be used, and was in the case of 'Waking the Feminists', 'as a means of mobilisation in the crucial task of "getting people on the streets"'.[42] As Lian Bell describes it, 'All of a sudden, a huge number of people were saying "hold on" – this isn't good enough. Definitely, social media played a huge role … particularly because people were connecting, meeting peers and being able to see who was saying what.'[43] The grassroots movement gathered thousands of supporters, including international celebrities such as US actress Meryl Streep, and impacted on national and international news coverage.

After a public apology by the Abbey, its stage was made available for a mass public meeting on 12 November 2015 during which the concerns and demands of 'Waking the Feminists' were aired to a packed audience: 'sustained policies in achieving female inclusion in the arts, equal championing of female artists by Irish arts institutions, and economic parity for women working in the sector'.[44] That same morning, the acting chair of Screen Ireland, Dr Annie Doona, issued a statement acknowledging that the film board 'recognises and accepts that major underrepresentation of women exists in Irish film'. She further declared that Screen Ireland had a 'strong and heartfelt commitment to gender equality and diversity as a strategic priority'.[45] Doona's personal commitment to feminism, her awareness of gender politics and her desire to create changes for women within the film board and the wider industry has previously been noted.[46] Plans to introduce gender equality measures in Screen Ireland were likely to have been discussed internally during 2015. However, this hasty public announcement shortly after the publication of Liddy's letter to *The Irish Times* and on the same morning as the 'Waking the Feminists' public debate in the Abbey is suggestive of the power of activism and, arguably, concerns within the organisation about 'public shaming' in light of the Abbey debacle. Screen Ireland's gender policy, the Six Point Plan, was announced on 22 December 2015 and included a commitment to publish and monitor statistics and the introduction of a 50/50 target to achieve parity in funding over three years.

The pursuit of gender equality: from there to here

Certainly, there was a shift by Screen Ireland by the end of 2015, from a 'gender-neutral' position in which the importance of gender was discounted, to the publication of a gender policy on 22 December 2015.[47] The policy was eventually followed by targeted gender initiatives, announced in late 2017, with a view to offering specific support to female writers and directors – arguably positioning Screen Ireland, at least potentially and for now, as comparatively progressive. However, despite a reconfigured, more gender-aware organisation in 2019, considerable work remains to be done. Gender statistics for produced films from 2011 to 2017 reveal that women still comprised only 21 per cent of screenwriters, 17 per cent of directors and 59 per cent of producers. While gender statistics for 2018 indicate an improvement, progress is slow, suggesting a more proactive approach may be necessary to embed change.

The Broadcasting Authority of Ireland has also reviewed its policy and practices, albeit at a slower pace than has Screen Ireland. During a colloquium on gender equality in MIC, Limerick, in 2016, it emerged

that the BAI had a g
with little or no ready a
funding was being distrib
with stakeholders and volunt
Gender Action Plan (2018) and
round in November 2017, a mecha
will be published annually going forv

A number of lobbying/advocacy gro
in 2015. Their impact has been considera
in a voluntary capacity for gender equality
Women in Film and Television Ireland (WF
informally in advance of their eventual launc
2015[49] and the Equality Action Committee (EAC
Writers Guild and the Screen Directors Guild began to meet formally
in November of the same year.[50] Through a combination of advocacy,
negotiating with major funding bodies and broadcasters, awareness-
raising and heightening female visibility in the industry, groups such as
these continue to vigorously pursue gender equality.[51] To date, Screen
Producers Ireland have been far slower to engage with gender issues and
the organisation does not, as yet, have a gender policy.

The boards of the Writers Guild, the Screen Directors Guild, and
Women in Film and Television have supported the introduction of
gender quotas, arguing that quotas will accelerate the rate of change in
the industry and cultural change will follow. Screen Ireland chair Annie
Doona had voiced her personal view that the introduction of quotas
may need to be looked at in time. However, during a robust discussion

Irish film industry 'knows and describes
the ongoing, vigorous international debates
arth of women screenwriters, writer/directors, producers,
d cinematographers. They interrogate both feature fiction film
documentary film, reflect on emerging fields such as animation, and
explore the contribution of, and the challenges for, individual female
practitioners within the industry.

An interdisciplinary approach gives rise to a combination of
production studies and traditional film studies approaches. While a
traditional film studies approach interrogates the text, production studies
scholars could be said to 'examine the cultural producers, [and] the
organisational sites and practices they inhabit and through which they
exercise their power'.[53] However, as Banks et al. observe, while producers
may wield considerable power within the media industries, they 'do not
distribute that power to all producers equally'.[54] Contributors utilise a
range of methods – empirical (interviews, questionnaires and surveys),
textual analysis and archival research – but all are underpinned by a
feminist analysis of an industry that has marginalised women, and this
underpinning provides the coherence in the collection.

O'Connell and Edge seek to reappraise and reclaim, respectively,
different contributions to Irish film history. Historically, Ellen O'Mara
Sullivan has been accorded merely a supportive role in the Film Company of Ireland but an excavation of her life and work paints quite a
different picture, albeit one with unanswered questions and, as yet,
historical 'gaps'. Sarah Edge revisits two important films from the 1980s
and suggests that the sociopolitical meanings of feminism and the

Maeve Connolly spotlights two Irish female cinematographers and their work, Suzie Lavelle and Kate McCullough, and argues for their 'double invisibility': as women in a male-dominated profession and as professionals rarely credited as the author of a film.

Director and editor Emer Reynolds discusses her career with Susan Liddy and reflects on what needs to change for women in male-dominated professions. She shares stories about her two great loves, science and film, and how her award-winning documentary *The Farthest* is 'the quintessential Emer film'. Staying with documentary, Anne O'Brien's work focuses on the perception that this is a more gender-inclusive genre. How does that square with the reality that budgets are smaller, crews are smaller and documentary films, in the main, enjoy less prestige?

Strategies for fostering change are given consideration by a number of authors. Annie Doona is concerned with the role of education in encouraging young women into the film industry. She argues for a coherent multi-agency approach to film education in which issues of gender inequality are addressed. Karla Healion, Aileen O'Driscoll, Jennifer O'Meara and Katie Stone discuss the potential for activism in an event like the Dublin Feminist Film Festival. This 'grassroots' festival is an example of 'cultural activism' which showcases the work of women filmmakers and encourages debates on gender issues in a range of accompanying panel discussions. Laura Aguiar evaluates the possibilities inherent in collaborative filmmaking for female empowerment. Working in post-conflict Northern Ireland, she proposes a model of filmmaking that shares authority and authorship, making women 'the heroes' of their own stories.

Contributors also engage with a range of texts to appraise questions of content, form and representation in the work of specific filmmakers. Lance Pettitt offers a retrospective analysis of Pat Murphy's body of work and her development as a filmmaker. From *Maeve* (1981) to *Tana Bana* (2015) Pettitt contends that Murphy has retained a feminist concern for intersectional gendered inequalities of power. Eileen Culloty explores documentary-maker Dearbhla Glynn's work on wartime sexual violence. Foregoing 'the politics of pity', she argues that Glynn's use of 'proper distance' allows her to weave individual and local stories of suffering with a sociopolitical understanding of context. Isabelle Le Corff offers a postcolonial analysis of the Irish film industry and Juanita Wilson's place within it. Le Corff unravels the influences, content, structure and aesthetic of Wilson's work – 'a master of adaptation' who draws upon stories from around the world, often unknown to Irish audiences.

Ruth Barton is concerned with the ways in which recent Irish cinema has reflected on the gendering of place, particularly the place of women. How does Irish cinema and society 'interrelate'? How does film construct its social world? Barton reviews a number of recent Irish films, by both male and female directors, that problematise, in varying degrees, familiar binaries. Finally, Ciara Barrett's chapter asks whether gender parity has been achieved in the Irish animation industry. Combining a production studies approach with a textual analysis, Barrett explores whether increasing numbers of women in the industry has translated into a more progressive politics of representation in animated film.

All the chapters in this collection argue for women's greater involvement in the Irish film industry, particularly in the key creative roles that can impact on the stories and images on-screen. All are concerned with women moving from the margins to the centre and focus on some of the most pressing political issues relating to gender and the film industry. Important questions about gender and the politics of knowledge are also raised. Hence, *Women in Irish Film: Stories and storytellers* can be viewed as a critical feminist intervention at a particular historical moment both nationally and internationally.

Revisiting the Past

Ellen O'Mara Sullivan and Her Role in Early Irish Cinema

DÍÓG O'CONNELL

Introduction

By the time *Knocknagow* and *Willy Reilly and his Colleen Bawn* graced the Dublin screens in 1918 and 1920 respectively, nearly two hundred women had already taken part in the 1916 Rising as couriers, gunrunners, nurses, doctors, armed combatants, commanders, and ghosts (persons prepared to assume the duties of a dead leader), and many were to continue in these capacities during the ensuing fight for independence.[1]

This paper explores the story of Ellen O'Mara Sullivan, who lived at the turn of the twentieth century in Ireland and was connected to the work of the Film Company of Ireland, set up in March 1916, a month before the Easter Rising. In the spirit of biographical recovery, this project is about giving Ellen O'Mara Sullivan agency, voice and identity by creating a narrative of part of her life, both public and private. This is not to underestimate 'the often-insurmountable limitations of knowing a life characterised by silence and omission',[2] but an attempt to piece together, from a limited source and base, the contribution of O'Mara Sullivan to early Irish cinema. As Michelle Staff outlines, one of the key challenges of this broader project is to 'find the balance between making their voices heard and framing the life within a "faithful" narrative that incorporates a sense of broader issues and themes'.[3] The excavation of Ellen's story takes place, therefore, in different strata of Irish history. These include the rise of nationalism against colonial forces, the rise of the suffrage movement and the emergence of the new technology of film, with all its potential. This project is lodged firmly within the history of Irish cinema, while sharing many of the challenges that women's history has faced as it evolved, particularly since the 1980s.

While researching women screenwriters in Ireland for *Women Screen-writers: An international guide*, edited by Jill Nelmes and Jule Selbo, a consideration that maybe Ellen O'Mara Sullivan was more central to early Irish film than was previously acknowledged took root. The first indigenous Irish feature film produced by the Film Company of Ireland in 1917–18, *Knocknagow*, credits as its scriptwriter a woman called Mrs N.F. Patton. However, little is known about Mrs N.F. Patton and the few references to her are contradictory. An American print of the film mentions Ellen O'Mara Sullivan as writer and, even though some historical records see this as just a legal technicality of copyright, it got me thinking. Is Mrs N.F. Patton a pseudonym for Ellen O'Mara Sullivan, and is the wife of James Mark Sullivan the true writer of the script for *Knocknagow*? Even though the results of this research to date cannot conclusively prove that Ellen O'Mara Sullivan is the scriptwriter for *Knocknagow*, it has recovered many aspects of Ellen's story and events around women's history, Irish history and Irish cinema history that add to the knowledge base of the period. The case for Ellen O'Mara Sullivan as central to the production of *Knocknagow* is not in dispute. Donna Casella in her article for the Women's Film Pioneer Project at Columbia University confirms Ellen's active role within the company. According to Casella, 'sources such as the James O'Mara Papers at the National Library of Ireland ... acknowledge both O'Mara Sullivan and her husband as working company directors', but in what specific role she was active needs further investigation.[4] While some histories are about understanding a figure and what she/he did, this history is attempting to reassign focus where there was little focus beforehand. In the history of Irish cinema, we are missing Ellen's voice.

The wider context for this paper is women's film history. According to Donna Casella, 'indigenous silent feature filmmaking was born out of [a] critical period of political and social change [in Ireland] ... Irish silent film was a male-dominated industry with a nationalist agenda that perpetuated gender stereotypes.'[5] If this is an adequate description, it makes Ellen O'Mara Sullivan's role in early Irish film history particularly significant. Because women were involved in the revolutionary movements as stated above, it is likely that they were also involved in wider cultural and public life. There is evidence that women 'wrote, directed, edited and set designed early Irish films'.[6] It is within this context that Ellen O'Mara Sullivan is examined as a key figure in the Film Company of Ireland.

Methodology

Trawling the archives at the Irish Film Institute, National Library, Military Archives, Limerick City Archives, online sources and the census of 1901 and 1911 reveals snippets of detail about Ellen O'Mara Sullivan, mainly through association with others. Firstly, she is known through her famous Limerick family, the O'Maras of the hugely successful pig and bacon company, and secondly through her husband, James Mark Sullivan – Irish-American lawyer, diplomat and journalist. These pieces of information, gleaned in this way, are akin to putting pieces of a jigsaw together as crumbs of information emerge. Filling in the gaps with other sources helps to further enlarge the picture. Writing women's stories back into history involves less conventional approaches to evidence, because of absence and omission from the archives. As Staff states, 'Using personal archives as an alternative to the traditional archives from which women were largely excluded, a focus on the "silenced" individual helped to restore women's agency and create a core complex historical picture.'[7] Much of Ellen's story detail is contained in such archives.

In *Doing Women's Film History*, Michele Leigh cites the term 'central paradox', which describes 'historians as prisoners of sources'.[8] She argues that historians can make meaning out of sources and make sources meaningful, an approach to history that is particularly relevant here. The first step is to identify sources, the second is to establish them as valid and the third is to derive meaning. And even after these stages are complete, the narrative will be incomplete. But this is always the case and should not be any less significant in this context. In writing about Russian film history, Leigh suggests that sometimes 'uncertainty and idiosyncrasy is all the historian has to work with', a further parallel to this Irish context. She tells us, 'What researching Russian cinema from 1908 to 1917 has taught me is that sometimes histories must be pieced together and told, not through a chain of primary sources and personal documents but rather through a mindful attention to a series of asides and offhand comments'.[9] Part of the biographical recovery project involves recovering stories that have 'largely been forgotten and consigned to a fragmented and incomplete source base', as in this instance.[10]

Documentary evidence in the form of letters written by Ellen during her time in America are kept by her granddaughter, Mary Rose Callaghan, the novelist and writer, in her private collection. These documents, together with the oral histories passed down through the generations and remembered by Callaghan, represent an interesting mix: solid, tangible sources alongside the memories and feelings of those who lived with the family legacy, an approach that might be described as an 'illegitimate source of history'.[11] Connecting and identifying with one's subject might not be accepted as 'legitimate' on the record, but it is what historians and writers do all the time off the record. In dealing with incomplete source material, other ways of making the subject heard must be found, as a way of activating agency, individuality and voice, collected from a range of sources which have been enhanced in the digital age. Approaching these sources, at the same time, comes with a degree of caution.

In establishing timelines, locations and dates, the cross-referencing of information often pointed out contradictions rather than establishing certainties in Ellen's life. In a rather counter-intuitive way, this is reassuring. Because this narrative is crafted from a variety of archive sources in the form of personal letters, genealogical digital sources, newspapers files, photographs and personal histories, these sources are both academic and non-academic. This raises questions around already established and/or perceived truths. For example, Ellen and James' wedding notice, which appeared in the American press, reveals more about culture and society in the US at the time than the lived reality of either Ellen or James. In a newspaper notice titled 'LAWYER WINS HEIRESS', a headline tapping into a narrative of myth and fairy tale, *The New York Times* on 19 September 1910 announces that 'James M Sullivan's friends hear he'll wed Irish manufacturer's daughter'. According to the notice, Ellen was the daughter of Stephen O'Mara, 'said to be the wealthiest button manufacturer and importer in Ireland ... highly educated, a great beauty and a social favorite'.

Once information appears in print and is then archived in a context, the reader and researcher are positioned to adopt it as a legitimate and accurate source. Yet this notice is full of factual errors. The hierarchy of evidence places the written record as more reliable than other sources. In researching women's history, the written record is treated the same. New knowledge can be established in the unwritten records when they are appropriated in less conventional and mainstream ways. This project crafts a narrative of a woman's life, manoeuvres it into place in a bigger narrative – that of early Irish cinema – and presents a logic and coherence that clearly is influenced by all these approaches – legitimate, illegitimate, conscious, unconscious, rational and instinctive. In the shadows of conventional sources and combined with more unconventional sources, this history of the individual in a wider context and structure is written. As Michelle Staff writes, the 'notion of telling the story of a person left out of the pages of history is a recurrent theme in what has become known as "recovery history"'.[12] Giving Ellen agency and a voice is a feminist project.

Ellen O'Mara's family life

Ellen's early life appears solid and stable; she was provided with a good education, and was part of a highly successful business family and one centrally placed within nationalist politics. This can be established through archive documents about the O'Maras of Limerick.[13] Ellen (Nell) O'Mara was born on 6 June 1882 in Roches Street in the city. Circumstantial evidence suggests that, like her sisters, she was educated by the Sacré Coeur nuns in Highgate, London, while her brothers went to Clongowes, a long-established Irish boarding school for boys. It is interesting that the O'Mara daughters were sent to London for their education, given that the family were staunch nationalists, suggesting a privileged family that placed value on education for all their children. Ellen's father, Stephen O'Mara (born in Limerick in 1844), a Parnellite MP who was friendly with Isaac Butt, a very influential MP and Home Ruler, and Michael Davitt, founder of the Land League, would have been a frequent traveller to Westminster, and therefore had a broader experience beyond the provincialism of Limerick. Revealing the ambitions her parents had for their children, and daughters notably, puts Ellen's later life in perspective: well-read and well-travelled despite her untimely death.

Stephen O'Mara served two terms as mayor of Limerick, elected on a nationalist ticket and therefore agitating against British rule in Ireland.

His criticism of the running of the Athenaeum – 'the Athenaeum is for the general benefit of the citizens … not a closed borough'[14] – suggests he would combine a position of privilege with a sense of equality as a politician. While he was mayor, the Prince of Wales (later to be King Edward VII) visited Ireland. One source, a book written by Ellen's aunt Patricia Lavelle titled *James O'Mara: The story of an original Sinn Féiner*, records that the luggage train was sent on ahead to be met by Ellen's father, who informed the equerry that there would be no civic ceremony in Limerick and sent them on their way. However, not everyone was happy with his actions. His wife, also called Ellen, realising that the lace-makers of Limerick, the other big local industry, had laboured over garments to present to Queen Victoria's family, bought the lace from them. This shows her empathy for women and their work, and the influence she could exert. Family lore has it that the lace was kept as an heirloom and served as the wedding veil for some of the daughters, recorded in family photographs.

Ellen's family, staunch nationalists, were also very successful business people. The O'Maras ran the famous Limerick Bacon factory, and Stephen's regular trips to London provided him with opportunities to expand the business. He travelled frequently to America too, his sons later developed links with Russia and Canada, and Stephen and his wife Ellen spent some time in Mexico. By 1893 the O'Maras had established a lucrative export trade and, according to *The Old Limerick Journal*, 'the volume of business with the English market called for a permanent agent in London'.[15]

The picture of Ellen's parents and their marriage, gleaned from various archive sources – including newspapers, personal letters, historical journals, family lore and genealogy is one of unity and support. Ellen senior gave birth to twelve children as well as being involved in the family business. Tragically, in September 1872, the first three children died of diphtheria, aged four years, two years and eleven months. The other nine were born between 1873 and 1889. At this time, Stephen needed to travel a lot, often abroad, while Ellen worked in the business at home. Some of the letters from Stephen and his diary entries reveal a devoted husband and a couple very much united. The historical sources, which are private correspondence, give an insight into the relationship. Difficult to frame within the context of public histories, it is a valuable source that helps ascribe details of emotional histories, creating a portrait of the wider family context for Ellen O'Mara Sullivan's earlier life. The nature of business and politics must have meant long periods apart for Stephen and Ellen, and their letters provide an insight into how they endured these separations. Stephen writes affectionately to his wife in July 1875: 'I love you so well, that I can imagine nothing that would cause me a sigh as long as God leaves you to me, unless it be the loss of your love or regard ... I am still unworthy of so good a wife ... You are my first, my only, and my last love please God, your own stout.'[16]

Ellen senior was centrally involved in the family business, at home particularly in her husband's absence, and abroad while travelling with him. All these bits of evidence point towards a family with strong work and business ethics, supporting later discussions in this paper about Ellen junior and her involvement in the business life of the Irish film industry, through the Film Company of Ireland. These details of Ellen's early life and family background provide a context for the choices made later when she meets Irish-American lawyer James Mark Sullivan. This narrative helps to make sense of what is to happen as Ellen and James embark on what must have been an unconventional life together in the second decade of the twentieth century.

Ellen meets James Mark Sullivan

Ellen was twenty-eight when she married James Mark Sullivan. Her husband, known commonly as Jim, was born in Ireland, near Killarney in County Kerry in 1870, and was twelve years her senior. He had moved to America at a young age – the records are conflicting, some say he was three while others suggest he was about fourteen. He was educated at Yale, qualifying in his late twenties, and was registered as a lawyer in New York between 1904 and 1916. It was on a visit to County Clare, to deal with land ownership, property deeds and an inheritance case for a US-based client, that James Sullivan met Ellen O'Mara. By this time the O'Maras had moved to their substantial dwelling, Strand House, in Limerick city, and James records his first sighting of Ellen as riding side-saddle down the avenue of the house on Strand Street. According to Ellen's granddaughter Mary Rose Callaghan, their story is remembered in the family lore as love at first sight, a romantic narrative ascribed nostalgically to the couple.

The married life of James and Ellen, although short-lived (she died prematurely and tragically in 1919), would be highly adventurous, involving transatlantic travel, the movie business and American politics – incorporating opportunity and controversy, and unconventional for the times. By 1912 James had returned to America, campaigning for the Democrats in New York and continuing his law practice, developing links with Tammany Hall and keeping in with the Irish nationalist community in the city. His networking paid off, and when in 1913 he was appointed United States ambassador to Santo Domingo in the Caribbean, a new adventure for the couple and their small family beckoned.[17]

What combination of experience, support and opportunity combined to set Ellen and James on this adventure? According to Felter and Schultz, Sullivan probably secured the post based on his religion rather than his political skills, going as far as to suggest that his lack of diplomatic experience proved an embarrassment. Sullivan's reasons for applying for the post, he says himself, were financial; securing the post meant a good salary. Their first child, Dónal, was born in 1912 and the second, Stephen, a year later just as James was taking up his post in Santo Domingo. At some point after Stephen's birth, Ellen travelled to the Caribbean to join her husband. However, the post did not last long and by 1915 James had left under a cloud. Following a congressional investigation, it was found that Sullivan was guilty of 'deportment, cronyism, misrepresentation to superiors of the Dominican situation and biased interference in local politics'.[18]

How did the conversation go between the couple, one wonders, faced with no post or income for James, and Ellen thousands of miles from home with two very small children to look after? She was highly educated, from a successful business family, used to a comfortable life, and probably not afraid of hard work or challenges. Letters exchanged between Ellen's parents reveal that her mother worked in the family business alongside her husband, and also when he was away from home. What did Ellen do between leaving school and marrying at the age of twenty-eight? If her mother worked in the business, might she also have been expected to, gaining experience that would be very useful in setting up a film company later?

Ellen and James returned to Ireland in 1916 and we know that James Mark Sullivan partnered with Henry Fitzgibbon in setting up the Film Company of Ireland. Or is there more to the story? The conventional history accepts that the Film Company of Ireland was established by Sullivan and Fitzgibbon, although Casella sees Fitzgibbon as appearing to serve only as a financial advisor. Ellen O'Mara Sullivan is not mentioned in the historical references to the company's formation but is described as co-director. Establishing her role in more detail is difficult in the absence of sources. Yet later activity, which is documented, places her centrally in the decision-making activities once the film company has a slate of films for distribution.

1916 and the Film Company of Ireland

Ellen's role in the Film Company of Ireland in 1918–19 is documented through her letters written from the Unites States when she and James were negotiating distribution and exhibition for their films, including *Knocknagow*. However, there is a case to be made that she was part of the project from the start and not just through association as the wife of James Mark Sullivan. Dr Michael Rynne, in a letter to Proinsias Ó Conluain in RTÉ, describes how he visited the Film Company of Ireland offices on Dame Street in Dublin 'practically every other day between 1917–18' as a youngster, says that 'apart from Mr. Sullivan and his wife, Ellen ... most of the Company's Directors took little active part in the actual production and distribution of the pictures'.[19]

Did Ellen discuss the possibility of setting up a film company with her husband, before their return from Santo Domingo to Ireland? Ireland had already experienced film production through the Kalem Company. The Lumière brothers and Pathé News were two of many production companies coming to Ireland to record events and screen to Irish audiences at the time. A letter from Ellen's time in Santo Domingo reveals a woman who likes the theatre, and in later letters she mentions books she bought in New York. As well as being well educated and coming from a successful business family, Ellen had a keen interest in the arts, suggesting that it is likely she was aware of these films and film activity. With her wealthy family background, steeped in an established and successful business, linked to nationalist politics, with contacts in the United States, and probably aware of the entrepreneurial value of the new medium of filmmaking, she was likely to have been more central to the discussions on the setting up of the Film Company of Ireland than we have material documentation for.

Even though the history books record that James 'painted rosy pictures of the money to be made in film, and interested a group of public men, who between them, put up £5000',[20] it is possible that Ellen played a significant role, by having a shared vision and facilitating contacts, although there are no material sources for this. She certainly played a role in enabling the project to take off. She was well connected in Irish society, through the family business and their political involvement, and her husband was well connected in America. While her letters suggest a pragmatic approach to life, James comes across as convivial, a 'people person' in today's parlance.[21] When *Irish Limelight* describes the Film Company of Ireland as having a mission that 'was to make Ireland known to the rest of the world, as she had never been known before, to let outside people realize that we have in Ireland other things than the dudeen, buffoon, knee-britches, and brass-knuckles', it suggests a vision arising from the collision of a romantic and pragmatic approach to the new medium.[22]

Returning to Ireland in 1916 with two small children and a third on the way meant that Ellen and James would need somewhere to live and a means of providing for the family. This would pose a challenge, but the backdrop of the Easter Rising and the upheaval that Dublin was going through added to the challenge and makes the achievements of film production even more noteworthy.

Ellen and *Knocknagow*

Between 1916 and 1920 the Film Company of Ireland produced almost thirty films, mainly short one- and two-reelers, and a mixture of comedy, romance and historical stories, few of which have survived to be archived. Best known among these include *Knocknagow* (1918) and *Willy Reilly and his Colleen Bawn* (1920). *Knocknagow* was based on the Kickham novel of the same name, 'a novel about absentee landlordism, evictions of peasant farmers, their relationship to the land, starvations and emigrations'.[23] Felter suggests that picking this story for dramatisation considering the public opinion shift in post-Rising Ireland reveals James Sullivan's business acumen as sharp. But what evidence suggests that it was James who chose the source material for the film?

Although Mrs N.F. Patton is credited with scriptwriting *Knocknagow*, other sources suggest that the key influence and direction of the company came from Ellen. References to Mrs N.F. Patton are limited: she is described as an 'Ulster romance writer' in one source[24] and as 'Mrs. Patton, a Dublin lady' in another[25] and then the trail runs dry. However, the US print of the film *Knocknagow* suggests another writer: 'the author and copyright holder of the screenplay is identified in the opening title as Ellen Sullivan, James Sullivan's wife'.[26] To what extent Ellen was part of the decision to adapt Kickham's novel for the screen, or that she was even the writer of the screenplay under a pseudonym, is difficult to prove without hard documentary evidence. Consequently, most scholars, including Donna Casella and Kevin Rockett, do not support the idea that she was the scriptwriter for *Knocknagow*. However, circumstantial evidence does suggest that she had a major role to play, details of which will be explored later. Ellen Sullivan most likely had read *Knocknagow*, which would become the most popular Irish novel up to the mid-twentieth century, running to twenty-eight editions between 1873 and 1966.[27]

Looking to other sources to glean the significance of this novel in a wider context of Irish history and women's literature is revealing. Dr Caitríona Clutterbuck explores how Kickham offered a renewal of the ideal of nationalism and placed it within a female-centred space. 'This vision of nationalism is grounded in the complex role in *Knocknagow* of women and the feminine zone generally. [Kickham] wants to re-focus our attention on women and on female values as a means to achieving the right balance of elements that will create and sustain true Irish independence.'[28] This may well have been the appeal for Ellen. The daughter of a Parnellite MP and member of the Irish Parliamentary Party, she would have been immersed in nationalist politics through her family, Home Rulers turned Sinn Féiners, and she had direct personal experience of the 1916 Rising when her husband was arrested and imprisoned during Easter week.

A female-centred narrative, Kickham's *Knocknagow* is described as having, unusually for romantic fiction of the time, 'no fewer than four strong female characters: the physically weak but spiritually powerful consumptive Norah Lahy; the queenly and ideally beautiful Mary Kearney; her friend, the precociously intelligent Grace Kiely; and the "keen-witted and ambitious" Bessy Morris, beloved of Matt the

Thrasher',[29] a multi-protagonist narrative not unfamiliar to modern-day popular drama targeted at a female audience. Framed in this way and described by Ó Cathaoir as approaching 'an ideal of feminist liberation', it makes for an interesting choice as the source for the first Irish independent feature film and adaptation for screen by a female writer. While the documentary and archival evidence is scant, the circumstantial evidence is very strong. Taking these viewpoints together, it is suggested that the female interpretation of these stories, rather than simply re-stating the dominant discourse of nationalism, within the over-arching frame, portrays a slightly different view of the world. It doesn't become a narrative that elides the female experience, but rather seeks to incorporate it.

As Casella argues, the colleen character ('colleen' is the Irish word for girl but with much wider cultural resonance) was a company staple for the Film Company of Ireland (FCOI), which produced social melodramas and romantic comedies in addition to the historical melodramas such as *Knocknagow* and *Willy Reilly and his Colleen Bawn*.[30] While these are viewed as traditional characterisations, they are also often considered traditional female narratives. In the hands of female screenwriters, they get a slightly alternative treatment. Clutterbuck, writing about the novel, says that 'this vision of nationalism is grounded in the complex role in *Knocknagow* of women and the feminine zone generally. [Kickham] wants to re-focus our attention on women and on female values as a means to achieving the right balance of elements that will create and sustain true Irish independence.'[31] Did this strike a note with Ellen, leading to the adaptation of this novel by the FCOI, scripted by her and filmed around parts of Ireland that she was very familiar with, the county of Tipperary bordering her native Limerick?

'We will have to sell our scenic negatives': Ellen and James in America

There is tangible evidence of Ellen's role in the Film Company of Ireland in her letters from 1918/19, kept in the private collection of her granddaughter, Mary Rose Callaghan. Ellen's letters, written to her niece Hazel and Hazel's husband Karl, who lived in Cleveland, Ohio, provide us with first-hand detail of the time she and James spent in New York trying to market their films and also – according to Felter and Schultz and further explored by Donna Casella – trying to incorporate the FCOI in America. The trip to New York wasn't without challenges: Ellen's letters reveal the difficulties at a business level, including the seizing of the films by customs, and at a personal level, the wrench she felt being away from the children.

In a letter dated 27 July 1918 Ellen writes:

> We won't get our pictures out of the customs house until Monday at the earliest … We have the pawn ticket for my rings from Henry Fitzgibbon and we are getting the money to redeem them – he came to New York and phoned James here, he also gave us back the two films which have never been used. I think Karl's letter must have frightened him – he is doing well, he is a broker in Boston.[32]

It appears that the films were seized on arrival in New York by the Customs House and would be held until a tax was paid on them. As they didn't have the money to pay the tax, Ellen's rings were pawned. There is some tension between Ellen and James and Henry Fitzgibbon, co-founder of the FCOI. Why did Karl's letter frighten him? Was he holding on to the pawn ticket and the films? Something affects the relationship between Henry Fitzgibbon and the Sullivans at this time, although Fitzgibbon does continue to have a role in the Film Company of Ireland later, as other sources suggest.

On 14 August, Ellen writes that they are nine days waiting for 'our pictures' from the Customs House and mentions that Pathé want to see the films. She refers to them as 'our films' throughout her letters and is central to a lot of the decision-making and planning as they strategise about distributing them. 'We will have to sell our scenic negatives for what we can get and send the money home,' she writes.[33] What do they need the money for? To cover the expenses of the family being looked after back home or is it to do with the company? By mid-August, the films are out of customs and Ellen is very excited about them. 'Looking at Knocknagow from this side our picture stands up better than the rest – the scenery and photography is beautiful.'[34] However, it is some months still before they begin to see results, moving between New York and Boston, staying with friends and relatives and in hotels. While it was an exciting time for the couple and they clearly had a shared mission, the distance from the children began to take its toll. Having arrived in New York sometime in July, they spent almost five months trying to sell the films until finally, in December, there was a breakthrough.

Ellen, in a letter to Hazel, tells her that the films will be screened at Tremont Temple in Boston on 9 December. Revealing her central role in the decision-making of the FCOI, Ellen describes how the company decided against taking a percentage of the box office takings but instead opted to pay a rent to the theatre, and notes the risk involved in this decision. On 19 December Ellen writes that their pictures are 'an assured success and the takings are splendid for the worst theatrical week of the year', Christmas week, so much so that James got more films printed. However, although the films had finally got a screening and according to Ellen were doing very well, connecting with the Irish emigrants in Boston, her concern for her children is more frequently expressed and the anxiety about getting home is more intense. Writing sometime between November and December, Ellen says that if 'neither Jim or myself is allowed home of course there is nothing for us to do but go ahead and get our children', and in mid-December, still in America and facing Christmas away from home, she writes, 'We are so lonely for our little family that we can't bear to think of Christmas at all.'[35]

According to Ellen's family, despite being centrally involved in the business of selling the films and clearly part of the decision-making process, as an equal in many respects to her husband, she was not happy about living in America and is sometimes quite critical of the places in which she finds herself: 'I spent 2½ hours at the passport department on appointment today and at the end of that time they took my name and address – wonderful nation – they are not for freedom of anything or anybody, anywhere.'[36] Each letter now reveals the impatience and almost desperation she feels as she tries to get home, and how frustrated she is with the process. She has her passport by 4 December but still must wait a full month for her visa: 'Our great news is that my passport has been *visé* – I am to go for it on Monday and I suppose answer more questions – but thank God I can get back to the babies and there is a chance of Jim getting away too.'[37] Ellen and James had hoped to get home for Christmas but in January she writes, 'We go to Boston on Monday for the Company meeting on Wednesday and then I hope to leave the end of the week from New York.' The tone of this letter is much more upbeat. 'Jim is making arrangements today with Shubert's for theatres all over the country for the showing of our pictures. The picture in Boston was really a success – and everything depended on that.'

Although Ellen reveals that James cannot get a visa back to Ireland, made more difficult in the context of the First World War, she still holds out hope. At the same time, their stay is prolonged much more than they planned for and he is anxious for Ellen to return home. The story emerging from these letters is of a couple on a very exciting mission, completely united in a common goal, sharing the burden and decision-making as they try to get their films out to an American audience. At the same time, they are three thousand miles from home, having left a young family behind, now with four children under seven years, and no doubt the feelings of loneliness and anxiety for their children must have run deep. According to Staff, the 'use of imagination in the writing of a person's life diverges from traditional historical writing and its commitment to the facts, yet can nevertheless present itself as a method for reaching an authentic understanding of the subject'.[38] In what is called biographical recovery and in relation to women's history, the use of imagination and the evoking of emotional truth in constructing narratives has a methodological value relevant here. Ellen O'Mara Sullivan's story is about her private and public life, and writing this narrative is hindered by coming from a very low source base. This is where imagination as a tool to construct a narrative becomes valid.

Going home

Ellen left New York sometime in January 1919, arriving in Ireland early February, leaving James trying to get a visa. Although the details are vague, James kept working on the distribution of the films, but his main concern was to return to Ireland, to Ellen and the children. Sadly, tragedy was to strike the family some weeks later when the eldest son, Dónal, aged seven, who had contracted typhoid, died on 10 April 1919. It seems that, although advised against it, Ellen nursed her sick son, when maybe he should have been quarantined; she caught the disease and became infected also. Arriving home to a sick child after an absence of six months must have been very worrying and heartbreaking for Ellen. Throughout her absence she consistently wrote about her children and how she missed them. When James eventually made it back to Ireland, he was met at Cobh by his father-in-law with the news that Dónal had died, and Ellen was very ill. James made it to her bedside at her family home in Limerick just in time, before she passed away a month later.

Ellen O'Mara Sullivan died on 17 May 1919, only thirty-six years old. According to a letter from her uncle, Dr Michael Rynne, Ellen was accorded 'an almost national funeral with the tricolour of the new republic and representatives of the First Dáil [present]'. Such honour would not have been bestowed purely for family association and so must be connected to events in Ellen's life. Although Dublin Castle (the security headquarters during British rule in Ireland) kept a file on James Mark Sullivan between 1907 and 1919, a file that now lies in the British National Archives and runs to over two hundred pages, the records for Ellen's life are few and far between. In the search for her story the re-searcher is constantly pushed towards her husband's story – her identity, her history and her life are entwined in the record of his life.

And yet his story is very much entangled with hers. Felter and Schultz wonder what happened to James Sullivan after Ellen's death.

> Did he sell the company or work from behind the scenes? Probably both – for a time. He and Ellen may have had dreams of 'making it big' in the movies, but without Ellen by his side, perhaps he sold the company or at least put it in the hands of people who could take his vision to audiences in America.[39]

Widowed and left caring for three surviving young children, James departed Ireland for America in 1922 and left the world of film for law and journalism. Casella quotes a writer working for the British trade paper *The Bioscope*, who 'predicted that [Ellen's] death would interrupt the company's production'.[40] Only three more films were released after her death and, as Casella notes, all were in preproduction or production before she died (*Dáil Bonds Film*; *Willy Reilly and his Colleen Bawn*; and *Paying the Rent*). The gravestone in Dublin's Glasnevin cemetery records the burial of Ellen with her son Dónal in 1919 and reveals that, although James died in Florida in August 1935, his body was returned to Ireland and interred with his wife in Glasnevin a year later.

Conclusion

Ellen was a key player in the Film Company of Ireland. Her letters reveal that she had the contacts, the money, the family connections, the business sense, the talent and the inspiration to be a significant player in the organisation. However, she remains hidden in the shadows of history. Piecing together from a variety of sources – which the process of recovering women's histories entails – helps construct this narrative. This is about giving a flavour of a complex life when conventional narratives attempt at constructing simple lives. It is not just about deviating from the traditional focus of history, which centres on 'big names' and public lives. It is not about re-writing history or even about recovering lost histories. This is about giving agency, voice and identity to a historical figure we know existed but who is not written about in either their public or private life. This paper records Ellen's contribution to early Irish cinema as we can know it, by drawing on a range of different perspectives, from a variety of sources and evidence, against the backdrop of a broader context of early-twentieth-century Ireland. As in archaeology, the excavation of Ellen O'Mara Sullivan's life reveals gaps in the accepted story, but the process at least allows a new narrative to emerge.

Feminist Reclamation Politics: Reclaiming *Maeve* (1981) and *Mother Ireland* (1988)

SARAH EDGE

In a recent academic text that plots the emergence of contemporary cinema in Ireland, in the section on first-wave indigenous film, two films by female directors were included. One was *Maeve* (1981), directed by Pat Murphy and John Davies, and the other *Hush-a-Bye Baby* (1989), directed by Margo Harkin. Both of these concerned themselves with Irish women's experiences of the Troubles in Northern Ireland. The history suggests that by doing this they entered the 'dialectical quagmire' of 'the relationship between women's politics and nationalist politics', opening up the topic but then closing it down as an inexplicable quandary.[1] This chapter returns to one of those films, *Maeve*, and adds the television documentary *Mother Ireland* (1988), directed by Anne Crilly, in an attempt to enter these murky depths. It considers in detail how these two productions engaged with the intersectional subject of feminism (women's oppression) and Irish nationalist politics (Irish oppression).

There are other productions by female directors from this period that deal with the relationship between feminist issues and Irish nationalism. These include the aforementioned *Hush-a-Bye Baby*[2] and *The Visit*,[3] directed by Orla Walsh in 1992. However, to concentrate my discussion I am going to limit my review to *Maeve* and *Mother Ireland* because they deal explicitly with the republican movement and its – sometimes violent – aspirations for equality, and the political movement of feminism during the Troubles in Northern Ireland. This is in contrast to the Troubles functioning as an important backdrop for wider feminist storytelling.[4]

This chapter also aims to test the historical and academic positioning of these two productions to reclaim them as significant examples of feminist cultural interventions that interrogated the intersectional relationship between feminism and nationalism in the 1980s.[5] To do this it will draw upon theoretical approaches to the study of media discourses, and in particular reception studies, to examine how the social and cultural environment of the 1980s gave meaning to the interface between feminism and Irish nationalism at the time of their release. It will also examine how these socio-historical readings have gone on to inform how the productions are remembered within the history of (Irish) feminist film and media studies.

This return is, I believe, timely. The close of 2017 has been noted for mainstream media coverage on what is positioned as the modern questions of feminism:[6] government-led examinations of equal pay in the UK and celebrity culture's exposure of sexual harassment within their industry[7] has fuelled something akin to a media panic. However, there is something disconcerting in this exposé of selective types of female inequality,[8] as well as the publicity given to certain types of 'feminist' action exemplified by the 'post-feminist'[9] strategy of dressing up in your little black dress as a form of protest – a neoliberal action that resulted in the policing of less privileged women's bodies.[10] A return to these 1980s productions can remind contemporary readers that modern twenty-first-century feminism needs to be attentive to how patriarchal structures impact on the lived experience of women while also conceding the intersectional power between women (race, nation, class and location) that has perhaps been overlooked.[11] It also raises questions on how patriarchal culture will interpret feminist political actions.

Feminism, film and the 1980s: Irish feminist production in Northern Ireland

The 1970s and 1980s is recognised as a moment when dialogue opened up between feminist film theorists, filmmakers and the grassroots movement of feminism. Kuhn locates feminism as 'a political practice' but explains how 'the linking of feminism with cinema in itself raises a series of questions, some of them analytical or theoretical, others more obviously political'[12] in which these two sets of knowledge 'might provide a basis for certain types of intervention in culture'.[13] Theorists also identify how the intention for an action or work to be interpreted as a feminist challenge does not guarantee it will be. Janet Wolff offers a useful example drawn from a 1980s Irish feminist protest: a group of women swimming unclothed protesting against the exclusive male use of a naked bathing area in Sandycove, Dublin. The Irish press recorded the event, and Wolff notes how the reporting was inevitably caught within the traditions of patriarchal culture, concluding that, 'Without having been at the event, one can only assume that female nudity achieved nothing more than male lechery. The lesson (or one of them) is that there are problems with using the female body for feminist ends.'[14] This chapter will relocate the work of these two feminist directors back into this analytical and theoretical moment to highlight the complexity of their work as feminist projects that I am suggesting has been undervalued.

Reception studies, feminism and Irish nationalism in the 1980s

Reception theory is an approach to the examination of meaning in film that complements the more structuralist readings that have more readily been used to commend or condemn these two productions. The approach grew from television studies to suggest that a concentration on the structure of the text undervalues how in most instances 'categories and their relationships are not inherent in the text ... they are meaning-making processes of the reader',[15] and that those meaning-making processes are not fixed but are linked to the social, cultural and historical environment in which the reader's 'ideas' on a subject are formed.

To rebuild how Irish nationalism and feminism were made sense of by the audiences of these two productions, it is crucial to move beyond the actual productions. Carol Coulter has researched how the 'wider' feminist movement interpreted women's involvement in the republican movement during the Troubles. She concludes that this can be linked to wider intersectional differences in which 'Western feminism has a problem with nationalism'.[16] Coulter's research notes how the forceful drive for a unifying women's movement in the 1980s, the sisterhood, was challenged by the 'large number of women in organizations linked ... to the republican movement'. This was deemed divisive. Coulter summarises how this essentialist-based feminist position argued that 'feminism and nationalism are incompatible' and 'women who claim to be able to combine their feminist convictions with nationalist ones are, at best, deluded',[17] a position that implied that such women were 'hijacking' feminism itself in an Irish–Northern Irish context.[18] Moreover, because this difference between women was based on what was perceived as a more localised or regional problem, women's concerns with this intersectional power could be interpreted as parochial rather than part of the uniting voice of international feminism. It was this socio-historical receptive field that informed how these productions would be interpreted on their release in the 1980s.

Due to limitation of space, I cannot offer an in-depth explanation of the conflict in Northern Ireland. However, some context setting is required to explore how these feminist productions acquired meaning not just framed by dominant discourses on feminism but also in relation to the way in which an expression for an Irish identity in Northern Ireland was interpreted. Media research has illustrated how, during the Troubles, this was primarily expressed via representations of the IRA (man).[19] Other research has widened this out to rebuild how it functioned internally within Northern Ireland, whereby any active expression of 'Irishness' via music, sport, religion or even name could be read as disputing the 'naturalised' status of Northern Ireland as British. In this context such expressions could be conflated with the actions and aspirations of the IRA, making attacks on such expression 'legitimate'.

These two productions had to navigate these interrelated discourses summed up as: how the conflict within Northern Ireland (a desire for an Irish identity) was being made sense of both externally and internally, and the powerful place of essentialism within the 1980s feminist movement.[20] On a more structuralist level, they also had to consider how meaning was communicated via dominant patriarchal (popular cultural) signifying systems and storytelling traditions.

Before turning my attention to the productions, I would also like to offer a more personal experience to validate the importance of recognising the extra-textual setting for these two productions. In 1991, I took up a post in media studies at Ulster University with the remit to teach feminist media and film studies (an indication in itself of the importance feminist film theory held in academia at the time). I employed these two films as significant examples of the complex feminist film strategies that resonated in the 1980s. It became clear that students read the films informed by the varied social and cultural backgrounds I have outlined. Students who identified as Protestant or British tended to be unreceptive to the films, interpreting them as apologists for IRA violence; while students who identified as Catholic or Irish, in a pre-ceasefire environment, tended to be apprehensive and guarded in their opinions. In contrast, non-home students read the films as examples of feminism, feminist reclamation histories and wider international politics around identity.

In 1994 I also became aware of how this positioning impacted on Anne Crilly when she recalled how the interpretation of *Mother Ireland* as 'sectarian'[21] and un-feminist influenced her later work.[22] These two factors led me to start the tentative research I can now return to in this chapter,[23] research that allowed me to experience first-hand just how difficult it was to raise these intellectual issues in the 1990s.[24]

In the opening of this chapter, I suggested that the historically specific reading of the two productions has continued to influence academic writing on Irish film and television and I will examine this more fully. A review of writing on the two productions can be summarised as follows: *Maeve* was, and is still, celebrated as part of the first wave of indigenous Irish filmmaking with the focus placed on the avant-garde and experimental counter-cinema technique.[25] *Mother Ireland* has not been so well-received, located in opposition to *Maeve* in the tradition of a documentary – closed, uncritical and partial.[26] For a contemporary readership the two productions are acknowledged as examining the relationship between feminism and nationalism within the conflict of Northern Ireland; however, a detailed examination of how they did this is sidestepped by overemphasising the counter-cinema techniques in *Maeve*, while *Mother Ireland*, even in more supportive writing, is still described as 'very community specific, and unashamedly sectarian'.[27]

Maeve as feminist counter-cinema

Maeve is located as drawing upon 1970s political avant-garde filmmaking, 'which set out to challenge and question film as a symbolic practice, especially cinema as a patriarchal symbolic code, and to interrogate the political and ideological implications of representation itself'. This is then linked to the content of the film where 'ambitious politics is woven into an interrogation of Irish nationalism/republicanism as another patriarchal symbolic code'.[28] A number of key scenes and moments where this dual aim is achieved are well-rehearsed in academic texts on the film.[29] In summary: Maeve's father's reminiscing and his position as a nationalist storyteller is interrogated in the scene when Maeve's mother, Eileen, begins to tell a story about the Troubles and her father, Martin, takes over the storytelling, breaking convention and closing with Martin talking directly to the camera. These visually 'fracturing devices' are also employed by Murphy to comment on Maeve's relationship with her republican ex-boyfriend, Liam, as a symbol of 'the successive generations of patriarchy' (a reading I will examine as this chapter develops).[30] The anti-realist and jarring counter-cinema techniques used in the extended political discussion between Maeve and her ex-boyfriend Liam on 'Cave Hill overlooking Belfast (renowned for its United Irishmen connections)',[31] where the camerawork breaks with the traditions of male point of view and verisimilitude, as well as its disruption of characterisation and non-naturalistic dialogue, are widely cited by critics. In these readings the character of Maeve is interpreted as alienated from the debates on Irish nationalism, exiled from them, and the voice, therefore, of an outside 'international' feminism. While I am not in dispute with these readings, I am interested in how such a 'selective' reading might impact on contemporary (feminist) appreciation of the complexities of how the film actually deals with the intersectional politics of feminism and Irish nationalism.[32]

It is my aim here to rebuild Pat Murphy's wider and more ambitious intentions for the film. This is possible by revisiting a detailed interview she gave to the feminist film theorist Claire Johnston, first published in 1981, in the key academic journal of the time, *Screen*.[33]

Johnston opened the article in a manner that endorses the socio-historical positioning I have outlined by suggesting, 'There is no autonomous women's movement in the North of Ireland at the present time', citing 'the Troubles' as paralysing 'attempts to build such a movement'.[34] The film, Johnston proposed, lays down a challenge to the 'frequent uncritical support which English feminists have given the republican movement'.[35] Secondly, she employed a quote from Derry Women's Aid, taken from the feminist magazine *Spare Rib* 1980, which proposed that this support served 'to divide women along the traditional "Orange and Green"', resulting 'in a lack of attention to feminist issues'.[36] Johnston acknowledged that *Maeve* is a film that 'reflects these debates within feminism and makes its own unique contribution'. Her extraordinary detailed academic interpretation of the film paves the way for subsequent readings emphasising how, 'Like much feminist film-making of the last decade, *Maeve* has an experimental narrative structure which works within and against the operations of the classic narrative *vis-à-vis* the spectator.'[37] She reviews many of the key scenes noted above, and, again, I have no issue with these readings; however, in the interview with Pat Murphy that followed there is a slight tension between this emphasis and Murphy's expressed intentions, and this deserves further examination.

In the interview, Murphy verifies that one of her objectives was to offer an informed discursive challenge to the media's representation of the IRA and the conflict in Northern Ireland that 'casts Republicans as criminals and refuses to give credibility to the IRA as a coherent political group' and 'isolates their activities as dislocated criminal events'.[38] In this respect the film was not just intentionally dealing with dominant modes of representing women, but also the representation of the violence of the Irish, linking it to other well-respected academic writing of the period.[39] The tendentious drive was to examine the dual oppression of Irish women during the Troubles in 1980s Northern Ireland. *Maeve*, Murphy notes, was 'very much about a Catholic woman's experience. Protestant women don't come into that much so the film reflects that. Their exclusion is not a conscious sectarian act on our part.'[40] It is significant that even though Murphy made it her intention to deal with the intersection of such identity politics, film histories still have difficulty in acknowledging this.[41]

In 2009, Christine Gledhill, among others, called into question the academic prioritising of a structural intervention as the official mode of feminist filmmaking,[42] calling instead for wider feminist cultural studies that could relate 'commonly derided popular forms to the condition of their consumption in the lives of sociohistorical constituted audiences'.[43]

If we return to *Maeve* with this in mind, it is clear that it draws from both these academic propositions. Outside its avant-garde techniques *Maeve* is best described as a women's film or a melodrama. Its content is centred on the domestic, the family, love and relationships and how the Troubles impacts on this. Melodrama, as feminist theorists note, is a popular genre 'in which the fissures and contradictions' of patriarchal culture are often made visible for a female audience.[44] In *Maeve*, the avant-garde filmmaking techniques make audience identification with Maeve's character almost impossible, and this was intentional. In contrast, Murphy placed the more factual intersectional examination of the experience of being female and Irish Catholic into the conventional (melodramatic) sections of the film. Murphy confirmed this visual control: 'The relationship between the women … is rooted entirely in the realistic sections.'[45] This is represented by the relationship between Maeve, her sister Roisin, and their mother Eileen. In this context and within the tradition of melodrama, audience identification is more settled and secure. Roisin is established as a more positive and 'realistic' role model. She is constructed as a well-rounded character, likeable and set within the material experience of the often frightening and harrowing harassment of Catholic women in Northern Ireland by the army. She demonstrates humour, determination and power in the face of this oppression.

Once again, the interview highlights just how controlled and thoughtful Murphy was in terms of this intentional use of traditional melodramatic form and content. She notes that, while the 'film provokes' audience 'identification with and criticism of the main character', Maeve, Roisin offered the audience a quite different identification. 'For me,' she explained, 'the oppression of women is the fundamental oppression, but at the same time, I do see the only way forward as being through a united Ireland.' She goes on to further explain that, 'The women who saw *Maeve* in Belfast identified the lack of a republican woman's voice as a problem. I felt that, in a sense, the character of Roisin fulfils that role. Her strength is such that she doesn't have to articulate herself in the way Maeve does. She doesn't experience that kind of alienation.'[46] In 1981 Murphy felt the need to apologise because her intention for Roisin was not 'coming across'. However, I would argue that the failure to read this complexity was not a fault of the actual film text or Pat Murphy as a director, but a consequence of the limited socio-historical meaning available to the 1980s audience.[47]

To further this argument, I suggest the film should also be credited as an examination of Irish masculinity. The place of the storyteller of the Troubles is firmly located with Maeve's father – a point well-rehearsed in other texts. Nonetheless, the film concedes that both Maeve and Liam are dissatisfied, via their mutual desire to change the old patriarchal myths of the Irish nation. Murphy confirms how part of the disruptive use of conventional cinema in the much-cited Cave Hill scene was to highlight how 'Liam doesn't represent an orthodox republican position

... [He] speaks of the differences between him and his father. He moves from an alienation from the kind of belief which had sustained his father, to a conviction that those beliefs can be mobilised in the service of a more progressive politics.'[48] In this respect Murphy began to open up discussions that are explored in more recent academic research on Irish masculinity.[49]

The character of Maeve was located within these alienated and disruptive cinematic techniques not to articulate a 'positive' feminist voice for Irish women in opposition to patriarchal Irish nationalism, but rather to serve as an example of the danger of prioritising any essentialist understanding of feminism. In this respect Murphy employed the structural alienation of Maeve to emphasise the 'unrealistic' position of a feminist, or feminine politics, that fails to acknowledge the lived (intersectional) experience of being a woman (Roisin) in Northern Ireland in this historical moment. This suggests a reading of Maeve as an unattainable subject position, a position alluded to in the key scene when Liam (Murphy's expression of a different type of masculine nationalist politics) states, 'What you're proposing is no history at all.'

It could be argued that Murphy plays with the idea of a feminine voice outside the traditions of patriarchal culture as examined by theorists such as Julia Kristeva.[50] What I believe has been undervalued in the reviews of *Maeve* is that Murphy intended Roisin to be a more 'credible' female voice that counteracted Maeve's unattainable separatist ideals, offering an internal critique of the failure of 1980s essentialist feminism to acknowledge interrelational differences between women. This was consciously expressed in the content of the film and crucially also within its formal structures: realist for Roisin and anti-realist for Maeve. Following the conventions of melodrama, it is in those moments of discussion between the alienated, unattainable voice of idealised feminism and the embodied voice of Roisin that the viewer gets privileged information in relation to their mother's feminist 'resistance' to patriarchal Irish nationalism. A key scene in which this topic is discussed by Maeve and Roisin concludes with Roisin telling Maeve how she went to some of her feminist meetings and they ended up 'sounding just like Mammy with men as the enemy and taking advantage of you, that's what I've been hearing since I was five', offering commentary on the problems of this essentialist separatist feminist position represented by Maeve that has a contemporary resonance.[51]

Mother Ireland as feminist documentary

Mother Ireland has a different genesis to *Maeve*. Produced in 1984 by the campaigning community group Derry Film and Video Collective, its form is more conventional as a documentary and for this reason it has received less academic attention than *Maeve*. Nonetheless, feminist film theorists have argued that documentary can be a mode of storytelling that lends itself to a feminist project. In 1978 Julia Lesage identified how feminist filmmakers, as part of the second wave of feminism, were drawn to documentary as a storytelling device that could be mobilised to tell the missing and powerful 'ordinary details of women's lives'.[52]

Mother Ireland fits within this tradition. Feminist documentary filmmaking, in this instance, was often made by untrained women taking up the camera for the first time, allowing, as Kuhn identifies, for different modes of documentary storytelling to emerge whereby 'methods and philosophy were appropriated in a rather selective manner, and transformed to meet the requirements of a feminist film practice … to produce certain codes and modes of address which constitute a specific set of signifiers for feminist documentary cinema'. She identifies these as autobiographical discourses in which the 'enunciating voice of these films belongs to the female protagonists themselves';[53] personal stories are made political by the 'naming' of women's experiences. The use of oral histories to insert groups 'into the mainstream of historical discourse' signifies that 'women can be subjects in history'.

Kuhn explains how the critical edge of feminist documentary productions in this period was 'the fact that they unite two forms of verisimilitude: … [one] emerging from the transparency of documentary realism itself … [and another] from the notion underpinning the practice of oral history that there is a "truth" in accounts of the lived experience of members of certain social groups'.[54] These are the formal characteristics of *Mother Ireland*. While media-studies critics have begun to acknowledge this,[55] the content of *Mother Ireland* is still interpreted as operating against such feminist credentials in which McIlroy maintains that its 'Achilles heel' was 'to raise women's consciousness by denying or "writing out" the history of a quarter of Ireland's women'.[56]

Channel 4 funded *Mother Ireland* as it attempted to meet its remit of representing diverse and underrepresented communities and areas of the UK. Hill notes how this funding allowed the Derry Film and

Video Collective group to begin to make 'short documentaries on strip-searching ... urban redevelopment ... before embarking upon its narrative feature, *Hush-a-Bye Baby*'.[57] The group had a majority of women members, all from a feminist and nationalist political position, and while it was inexperienced in filmmaking, this cultural background informed the intentions for its productions.[58] Kuhn's proposition that this mix allowed a new type of documentary to emerge is verified in Crilly's recollection: 'When we first got the video equipment we literally did not know how to use it, but we decided that instead of just doing a training exercise for the sake of it we would pick a project and do it no matter how it turned out. There was a very strong campaign around strip searching of women prisoners in Armagh, so we took that as the topic.'[59]

In terms of the intention and control of the project, it is also valuable to counteract any 'amateur' positioning of *Mother Ireland* as a 'community' video. Crilly had a background similar to Murphy, having just completed an MA in Anglo-Irish Literature and Drama at UCD, and this academic cultural awareness informed the making of *Mother Ireland*. The production fits well within the remit of feminist reclamation histories undertaken in other mediums in the 1980s. In Ireland, the publication of Margaret Ward's *Unmanageable Revolutionaries: Women and Irish nationalism* represented a forceful challenge to the established history of Irish nationalism and provided evidence 'that women had also been politically active, and that they too warrant serious consideration by historians',[60] but the history for women that this text rebuilds stopped short of the Troubles. Ward explains how 'the contradiction between nationalism and feminism continues to overwhelm us',[61] and one way to address this 'is to see what happened to our sisters of another generation'.[62] In other words, Ward invited the type of socio-historical contextualisation I have undertaken here.

Mother Ireland had a comparable aim to Margaret Ward's literary quest to offer visual and factual evidence of women's interests and investment in Irish political resistance to British rule. However, in the socio-historical environment of the 1980s it came 'unstuck' by carrying this historical reclamation into the present day. The documentary's opening contextual setting immediately disputes readings of it as community specific; instead it connects it to the creative and intellectual terrain of concurrent academic discussion within postcolonial studies, feminism and cultural theory. It opens with personal views given by Bernadette

Devlin, Margaret MacCurtain, Pat Murphy and Mairéad Farrell, an active member of the IRA. The documentary employs film clips, paintings, newspapers and photographs as 'evidence' of the past. Visually, this imagery moves the viewer across the well-established terrain of the construction of a specific type of femininity within Irish nationalist culture via the feminisation of the land and the problematic place of Catholicism. This first section reinstates women as active participants in the military fight for Irish independence from the first modern articulations of this desire in the early nineteenth century, evident in the Ladies' Land League, Cumann na mBan, and the Suffragettes.

The production is quite traditional in its use of evidence; however, the claim to authority of the documentary tradition is often, amusingly, exposed as deceptive by the testimonials of the Irish women interviewed by Crilly. This happens within the terrain of popular culture when the Peppard sisters knowingly discuss how Fáilte Ireland used an image of one of them as a stereotypical Irish colleen. And it is also evident in the minor differences between the testimonies given by republican women from the early twentieth century, from those in Cumann na mBan and from historical writing where, as McIlroy also notes, their 'own personal memory of the events resist strongly any suspicion that the women's organization was a glorified tea-serving activity'.[63] It is this present and past interplay that gives *Mother Ireland* its critical edge. Irish female voices from the 1980s, contemporaneous with the viewer, comment on these historical and selective representations of their past. But it was also this interplay that was to prove problematic by giving a platform to current and varied Irish nationalist female voices. My suggestion is that if *Mother Ireland* had restricted its examination to the past, its feminist documentary credentials would have been unquestioned. However, once it moved on to the contemporary conflict, the socio-historical meanings I have rebuilt conflated all these voices into a sectarian and un-feminist position, limiting how the audience could receive it and subsequently how it is still critiqued.

Channel 4 did not screen *Mother Ireland* on its completion on 19 October 1988 because the British government had introduced the British broadcasting ban.[64] Crilly has explained how five days after the programme was finished, Mairéad Farrell was shot on 'active service' by the SAS in Gibraltar. Subsequently Channel 4 held back until the inquest. Crilly recalls that they 'didn't disapprove it or ban it, but they didn't give it the go-ahead to be screened either, and they just held onto it'. The broadcasting ban impacted on the content and form of the documentary: testimonials from Mairéad Farrell, Rita O'Hare from Sinn Féin and the women from Cumann na mBan could no longer be broadcast. The ban 'also applied to archive footage – so the archive footage of Maud Gonne that was taken in the 1930s at a rally couldn't be screened'. The documentary was shown in other locations such as women's film festivals. It was finally broadcast in 1991 as part of Channel 4's 'banned' season.[65] Under the broadcasting ban the voices of many of the women had to be dubbed with those of actors. This went through various versions; the version that was broadcast 'allowed Mairéad Farrell's own voice in the opening piece, but imposed an actress's voiceover for the latter section where she talks about getting involved in armed struggle and being imprisoned'.[66]

In the opening of this chapter I identified how the act of generating a feminist message is a complex process because the act of interpretation or reading a contesting message will be restricted by the form and content of patriarchal communicative structures. My aim in this study has been to identify how even though *Maeve* and *Mother Ireland* are usually positioned as polar opposites in their use of formal strategies, on closer inspection their similarities are confirmed. Both are innovative and complex in how they use established traditions of gendered filmmaking to expand rather than limit how feminists can 'use' popular cultural forms to articulate feminist messages.

My opening also raised the problem of intention, exampling how the desire to communicate a feminist message does not guarantee its interpretation as such. These two productions illustrate this crucial point, confirming how interpretation is always based on the changing sociopolitical environment. This is never fixed and requires constant vigilance from feminist activists.[67]

To illuminate this, we can return to *Mother Ireland* and the act of officially censoring the voice of Mairéad Farrell to unpack the interrelational power structures that can inform feminist appreciation of the subject position: Irish women. The broadcasting ban was officially directed at the IRA in an attempt to silence their message in a 'postcolonial' propaganda war. However, when it is used in a documentary that challenges the silencing of women in the official history of Irish nationalism, the alliance between patriarchal nationalist history and 'colonial' power structures is exposed because the figure of the 'IRA' woman is intrinsically disruptive to patriarchy and conventional patriarchal nationalism. I have argued elsewhere in a different context that

> women's involvement and interests in national identity struggles ... disrupts traditional and dominant ideologies surrounding femininity on a number of levels. Women who are involved in violence disrupt dominant ideologies of the feminine as passive and peace loving. Similarly, women's involvement in the public world of politics disrupts ideologies surrounding women's space in the private world of home and family. In nationalist/cultural identity struggles, women's demand for a national/cultural identity dislocates the place and right of patriarchal authority to define such an identity for her.[68]

The aim of this chapter has also been to identify how the sociopolitical meanings of feminism and the Northern Ireland conflict in the 1980s functioned to position these two productions in specific ways: firstly as 'sectarian' or 'un-feminist' in the case of *Mother Ireland* and as almost 'selectively feminist' in the case of *Maeve*. I have also argued that this original positioning continues to inform subsequent readings of the productions, obscures how they engaged with the important field of intersectionality, and masks the relevance they have for a wider history of feminist filmmaking.

To conclude, it is worth acknowledging how courageous Crilly and Murphy were in their aim to deal with this configuration of identity politics in the tense environment of 1980s Northern Ireland. The reception impacted on them, with Crilly recalling how 'one of the worst things about what happened to *Mother Ireland* is how ... this whole thing affected me ... I went into self-censorship mode. And I just really nearly pulled away from it all.'[69] Anne Crilly and Pat Murphy both made further productions that examined the relationship between Irish nationalism and feminism; however, they did not return to the highly contested space of the Troubles.[70]

Practitioners and Production Culture

'Where Are the Women?'
Exploring perceptions of a gender order in the Irish film industry

SUSAN LIDDY

Introduction

Ongoing research confirms that, like many other sectors, the international film industry is male-dominated and characterised by occupational segregation, discrimination and unconscious bias.[1] In Ireland, and across the world, women are underrepresented behind the camera in key creative roles; as film crew and, on-screen, as protagonists and central characters.[2] This has implications for the kinds of stories being told, the employment and creative opportunities open to women, and for 'innovation' in the audio-visual industries.[3] However, what distinguishes Ireland from many other countries is the relatively early introduction of a gender policy by Screen Ireland, formally the Irish Film Board (IFB). The Six Point Plan was announced in December 2015 and unveiled in early 2016. In addition to 'softer' equality initiatives including mentoring, training and education was the inclusion of a 50/50 gender funding target over three years aimed at increasing the numbers of female screenwriters and writer/directors. Crucially, for the first time, Screen Ireland undertook to collate and publish statistics relating to applications and funding decisions. The importance of statistics and data monitoring in making gender issues visible cannot be overstated, for without such information, the extent of women's underrepresentation can be, and was, denied or evaded.[4] The Six Point Plan held out the promise of reconfiguring the gendered landscape of Irish film, though as I will go on to discuss, it failed to do so within the designated timescale, for a number of reasons.

Despite the introduction of this potentially radical gender policy, applications by women have been lower than anticipated and female writers and directors remain underrepresented in funding awards (though there are tentative signs of improvement in late 2018), with the notable exception of the short film funding schemes. Indeed, in early 2018, Annie Doona, chair of Screen Ireland, described progress as 'glacially slow'.[5] In a series of discussions with female practitioners this chapter will explore why that might be the case and what measures could be implemented to encourage greater engagement going forward. Film plays a major role in reflecting and shaping perceptions of the world and our place within it and the absence of women as storytellers is of serious concern. The importance of women in key creative roles cannot be underestimated; their input can help to shape the characters and narratives in the films we see. However, an exclusive focus on women is not to suggest that male writers always and inevitably experience the industry, or Screen Ireland, as supportive and encouraging. Indeed, a comparative study may well be an interesting project in the future.

It is widely recognised that the film industry is extremely competitive, described by respondents here as 'a rejection industry'; one in which 'women have to be more talented and work harder than men'. However, given that the underrepresentation of women is stark enough to merit the introduction of a gender policy by Screen Ireland, it seems appropriate and timely to interrogate the absence of women by focusing exclusively on their experiences and the sense they make of their own underrepresentation. A feminist perspective informs the work, centring on the standpoint and experience of female writers and writer/directors.[6]

Cynthia Enloe coined the expression 'the curious feminist' to denote an inquiry-based approach that aims to unravel and unpack structures of power, starting with the fundamental question 'Where are the women?', an approach that is adopted here.[7]

Methodology

A feminist methodology provides a critique of prevailing knowledge and assumptions and can be understood as the point where 'philosophy and action meet'.[8] It is an approach that contributes to the creation of new knowledge and to women's experiences of exclusion by mining the 'subjugated knowledge' that can otherwise be obscured.[9] To that end, a questionnaire was devised to build a profile of Irish women screenwriters and writer/directors by eliciting demographic information and to tease out their experiences in the Irish film industry and, specifically, with

Screen Ireland (as the Irish Film Board was renamed Screen Ireland on June 18, 2018, respondents refer to the organisation by its former name). Questionnaires were then emailed to respondents. This is primarily a qualitative piece of work and questions were open-ended, resulting in detailed discursive responses which were followed up by email correspondence.

In order to identify potential respondents, an examination of the online Screen Ireland funding awards was carried out. Women screenwriters and writer/directors who were awarded funding for development and/or production finance were contacted either directly or through their production company. The research was also publicised by the Writers Guild, the Screen Directors Guild, and Women in Film and Television Ireland. A total of fifty-five female writers or writer/directors took part; 27 per cent of the interviewees have had one feature produced with funding from Screen Ireland and 9 per cent have had a second feature produced. Over half the respondents (65 per cent) have received development funding once, or multiple times, as an individual writer or through a production company.

Interviewees were assured of anonymity so they could speak freely without fear of giving offence and perhaps damaging relations with executives with whom they wish to remain on good terms. The acquisition of data online ensures ease of access, and the ready availability of transcripts is helpful in gathering and processing material effectively. De Vault and Cross's reservations that 'email exchanges lack the contextual cues and linguistic nuances of face-to-face conversation' was only of minor concern.[10] The chosen method offered participants time and distance to reflect on and review their contributions and was well suited to this project. A small number of contributors articulated a preference for face-to-face or telephone interviews and that was subsequently undertaken.

Building a Profile: Irish female writers and writer/directors

BACKGROUND

Before exploring the experiences of female practitioners in the Irish film industry a demographic profile follows which identifies their educational and training background, age, and geographic location.[11] With regard to educational qualifications, the vast majority of these women (85 per cent) have acquired an undergraduate degree, with most being wholly or partly related to communications, film or the film industry, i.e. film studies, filmmaking, or performance. Others have, alternatively or additionally, obtained diplomas in specific areas such as camera or editing. Over half (60 per cent) have postgraduate degrees and, again, many pertain to screenwriting and/or directing for the screen.

The commitment of participants to the industry is evidenced in the numbers (84 per cent) who have attended a range of specialist courses: 'I've done every Screen Training Ireland course going' (Screen Training Ireland was rebranded Screen Skills Ireland on November 19, 2019). Many continue to extend and develop their skill base by attending workshops/training courses such a multicamera, editing, and advanced film directing. Pipe-line theories are not adequate to account for the small numbers of women working in the industry. Across Europe, Aylett found that there was a significant difference between the proportion of female directors graduating from film schools (44 per cent) and the proportion who are working in the industry (24 per cent): 'The talent exists but the potential is not exploited.'[12]

Nearly three quarters of the interviewees are over forty years of age (70 per cent), with the highest number (30 per cent) in the forty-five to fifty year age bracket. Lisa French's findings from the Australian audio-visual industry appear to have some resonance in an Irish context also; the female population in the industry has aged.[13] Indeed, some age concerns emerge in a number of these accounts, including the observation that reaching 'middle-age' has consequences for funding awards because you are no longer, even potentially, the next 'big thing':

> If you are a former hot 'one to watch' hitting middle age it becomes very hard … I feel they favour younger film makers on the rise, and older film makers, especially women, are put on some red menopause alert list …

This age profile may well have implications for women going forward in a culture in which age discrimination in recruitment, selection and promotion has been identified in other employment sectors[14] and within the film industry in on-screen representations.[15] This is particularly important when many respondents are still struggling to gain a foothold in the industry and others have not built up the experience necessary to cancel out the perceived disadvantages of age.

Over half the women (53 per cent) are Dublin-based and a quarter (25 per cent) live in cities or towns around the country. A sizeable group, 22 per cent, now reside wholly or partly outside Ireland, mostly in London or New York, and for some this brings its own liberation, 'reminding one that the Irish Film Board and RTÉ aren't the be all and end all of one's career'. Most respondents (64 per cent) believe that it is an advantage to live in Dublin or in the city that is central to the film industry in their adopted country. They speak about the dangers of not being 'in the loop' in 'a people industry', missing events and gatherings that usually take place after 6 p.m. when 'building relationships' is crucial and fraught for those who don't know 'how to navigate the system'. Indeed, one Dublin-based writer expresses concern for 'those women in Leitrim or Cavan ... or anywhere outside of Dublin really for whom writing for the screen seems impossible'. Such concerns have some grounding. Research into gender inequality in the British film industry suggests that informal networking plays a powerful role in maintaining such inequality, particularly given the freelance nature of much of the industry.[16] Informal recruiting is commonplace, despite the industry's insistence that it is driven by a meritocratic culture[17] and 'market-led decision-making'.[18]

This is a profile of a highly educated, committed group of women who have demonstrated their commitment by regular upskilling. The overwhelming majority are, or have been, active in other creative areas – as short filmmakers, documentary filmmakers, visual artists, novelists, television writers and directors and playwrights and producers. Additionally, some have taught, or currently teach, a younger generation of film students while also working on their own creative projects. Most respondents (95 per cent) define themselves as feminist, though a small number had caveats attached such as: 'but I don't support protest or shouting' or 'but it should never be us and them'. It would seem that such a group would be well placed to avail of a gender policy that specifically targets women. However, the perceived existence of a gender order, expressed in the stories and characters that attract funding – the myth of 'male genius' and the identification of a gendered organisational culture informed by unconscious bias – impacts on personal confidence and confidence in established practices, which may account for a lack of engagement with the system.

STORIES AND CHARACTERS

Women are subordinate to men structurally in the patriarchal gender order, where O'Connor has defined patriarchy as

> culturally constructed ideas about male supremacy and privileging that are embedded in procedures and processes inside and outside the workplace, as well as in attitudes about what is 'natural', 'inevitable', 'what women want'.[19]

Lantz's research on the Swedish film industry suggests that within such a gender order, in which the male is norm, men's stories are more likely perceived as universal and women's stories as niche.[20] Her work points to the concept of quality being 'gendered to male advantage' as men dominate the decision-making and gatekeeping positions and have the 'preferential right of judgement' as to how quality is defined.[21] Moreover, male-driven projects are more often associated with 'quality', having, for instance, a named director or a reputable producer, or by long-standing collaborations between writers, directors and certain production companies, all of which can impact on how a film project will be assessed for funding.

In this piece of research, many female participants question the extent to which personal taste and 'quality' become conflated. Screen Ireland has, at least up until 2014, unproblematically supported 'project-led decision-making' in what was deemed to be a 'gender-neutral' organisation.[22] And many of these practitioners question how a 'good' project is assessed. One respondent reflects, 'With public money you don't get to choose your favourites', while another says, 'I think sometimes funding decisions can be based upon personal taste, influencing a funder's idea of what is quality and what isn't.'

Irrespective of how quality is defined, there is widespread agreement that the decision-making process has excluded women and their work. Respondents are emphatic that 'women's stories' and female protagonists are not valued and consequently fail to get funded.

> Perhaps not consciously (biased) – but certainly in relation to what they consider 'good' or 'valid'. This applies to both male and female decision-makers as we've all been formed by the same experience of male-heavy screen stories.

The dearth of female protagonists and, indeed, female characters generally has been identified as an international problem. For example, Smith, Choueiti and Pieper have suggested that the percentage of female speaking characters in top-grossing Hollywood films 'has not meaningfully changed in roughly a half of a century'.[23] More specifically, in 2018 Lauzen found that while the number of female *protagonists* in Hollywood films increased to 31 per cent in that year, only 35 per cent of films featured ten or more female characters in speaking roles while 82 per cent of films had ten or more male characters in speaking roles.[24]

The imperative to get stories about women on-screen in Irish productions emerges in the majority of the accounts here. One writer/ director spoke of making 'a pure political choice' to write female characters when there are so few produced films headlining women. Yet industry experience has demonstrated to these practitioners that there is 'an unspoken preference for male protagonists'. Interviewees are 'tired of looking at tepid, one-dimensional female characters', seeing women represented 'in diminishing ways'. The 'toning down' of female characters is often referenced by development executives, script readers and production company personnel. These observations substantiate Jacey's contention that 'heroine softening' is commonplace in script development[25] and throws light on the male reader with Screen Ireland who advised one writer to 'make the young female character less streetwise and more naïve'.

Industry perceptions of what is 'likeable' or 'relatable' in female characters is deemed to hinder creativity and diversity among female screenwriters.

> They find the strong female character unlikeable. They find sexually active and subversive women unlikeable. They often question how broad their appeal is …

Reflecting on her own observations as a development executive, one respondent says that 'there are deeply rooted psychological issues around female characters' with female executives as well as male keen to 'water down' strong female characters. In contrast, reports of ill-ease at the sidelining of male characters emerges many times: 'Male development people always want you to put more emphasis on the male characters.' One writer/director recalls the barrage of questions about female characters at the time of her film's release: 'Journalists actually asked the question, "How come there are so many women in your film?"'

Scripts featuring older female protagonists were met with particular resistance from development executives and producers. It was suggested to one screenwriter that her protagonist, who was conceived of being 'an ordinary woman' in her early forties, might work better as 'thirty-five and pretty'. Another writer/director acknowledges the challenge of bringing a film to production with an older female lead: 'A 49-year-old protagonist – that took/takes a lot of battling for in a mostly male-dominated commissioning world.' These experiences are borne out by Lauzen, who found that female characters remain consistently younger than their male counterparts in Hollywood film.[26] Issues also emerge in Liddy's work about the tentative expression of older female sexuality on-screen.[27] Such representations support Imelda Whelehan's contention that post-menopausal women are assumed to disappear into 'a dismal neutered future',[28] as the experience of this screenwriter illustrates :

> One that comes to mind – a grieving woman seeking escape in sex with her ex-lover. Happens to be fifty-five. I was told cut at the kiss – who wants to see old people having sex, specifically the woman.

Respondents bemoan the way in which character-based, female-led drama is devalued, but there are other concerns. A number of practitioners voiced reservations about 'the totalitarian focus on the hero's journey' model. Others argue that development executives and producers can harbour rigid, stereotypical perceptions of the kinds of narratives and films most appropriate to women writers. These writer/directors want to distance themselves from the perception that women are innately 'more lyrical, more intimate, curiously often taken as more artistic (for which read low-budget)'. Women can write genre too and they variously express a love of war movies, thrillers and the desire to tell 'large-scale, cinematic stories with strong narrative drive'.

THE MYTH OF THE MALE GENIUS

Hesmondhalgh and Baker (2015) observe the persistence of the stereotype of 'masculinist creativity' across a range of cultural industries, where 'associations of various modes of masculinity with creativity serve to marginalize women from the more prestigious creative roles and even sectors in the cultural industries'.[29] The accounts offered here identify a hype surrounding male filmmakers that can often be unrelated to previous achievement.

> I had one male exec in the film board tell me a certain young filmmaker was the bright shining new star of Irish film. He had not made a single film, not even a short. But he was twenty-five, upper middle class, very attractive and confident as hell and got funding for two feature documentaries.

Whatever the reality, respondents articulate a belief that fears of 'risk' are associated primarily with female filmmakers – fears that have been cited extensively in international research.

> I think funders are more nervous of female directors. They seem comfortable up to the point of production but then there seems to be a lack of support to back the projects.

> They'll have to invest in projects that are a bit risky … a lot of the things they have invested in haven't been working anyway so actually there isn't that big a risk. They're not a studio.

The nature of men's relationships with other men is widely seen as a key factor in sustaining such patterns, resulting in the unchallenged continuity of the 'male genius' myth. The freelance, project-based nature of the film business seeks to minimise risk, and to that end 'trustworthy' individuals are identified and hired during the informal networking that characterises the industry. Jones and Pringle have argued that those chosen are expected to 'fit in immediately and are seen as competent'.[30] Through homosocial reproduction men recognise other men as 'like themselves', sharing similar, desirable traits. For Grumble et al., 'leaders effectively "clone" themselves in their own image, guarding access to power and privilege to those who fit in, to those of their own kind'.[31]

The accounts provided here attest to a perception that homosociability underpins relationships between men in the wider Irish film industry, to the disadvantage of women. There are references to 'a crowd of middle-class white boys, mostly from the Pale, talking to each other' in an industry in which 'mountains of cronyism' is believed to exist. This writer/director reflects, 'I've watched as my male contemporaries were championed: their films, their careers.' Indeed, the notion of 'a boys' club' surfaced multiple times, with one respondent observing that 'most of the producers and commissioners all went to the same school'. Such relationships may partly explain an industry in which the perception is that men have the proverbial inside track, as 'lesser talented men have moved up' and men 'have a right to fail' without penalty.

However, the privileging of the male is not the prerogative of men. Many women executives have internalised the myth of male genius, and male directors are perceived to be 'looked after' by women – 'there's a big history of that in Irish film'. They are guided through the process by producers and development executives 'literally drooling at young male talent' while their female contemporaries are passed over, in some cases for many years.

> At festivals, there are so many young guys all telling the same story … you'd see all the female actresses trying to woo them. Kinda gross really.

In such a culture it is perhaps understandable that women would 'downsize' their ambition: 'The odds are stacked. How long can any sane person keep persevering before finding some other avenue of expression?' Fels suggests that in order to sustain ambition, women must feel rewarded or well regarded in some way. A lack of recognition for their accomplishments leads to 'demoralization' and women 'lose their convictions about their own abilities and talents'.[32]

ORGANISATIONAL CULTURE

Organisational research offers some useful concepts with which to theorise the operation of bodies such as Screen Ireland and make sense of the lacklustre reaction of many respondents to the new gender initiatives. Organisational culture has been defined as 'the complicated fabric of myths and values that legitimate women's position at the lower levels of the hierarchy'.[33] Transparency and accountability are key areas of concern. For instance, women can have difficulty accessing masculine structures of influence; many accounts provided by participants point to the perceived ongoing experience of stonewalling by Screen Ireland project managers whose brief it is to identify 'quality' and 'talent' and to sanction or deny funding.

> Simply ignored … I have not found it supportive, welcoming or encouraging in any way, unfortunately.

Concerns are also expressed about transparency – how the funding process operates – even by those who have applied over many years; and the vagaries and legitimacy of readers' reports and the lack of engagement with project managers, especially when a project is rejected. It is also unclear why it is that some individuals can obtain face-to-face meetings or have phone calls returned and others cannot.

> I think a lot of people give up before they even begin because the industry seems so impenetrable to them. I think a lot of great people fall at that first hurdle.

Appearing to validate the unease at the lack of transparency in Screen Ireland, one script editor, who had been an external 'reader' for them, notes:

> There are people who are never refused, and as someone who has been privy to many of their scripts, it remains a mystery to me. I do think it's very political.

Issues of transparency also emerge in relation to the practice of sending scripts to such 'readers' and the role they may play, or not play, in the funding process. It is unclear whether the project managers even factor the content of such reports into their decision-making. In any event, the 'reports' receive mixed reviews, with the majority not finding them useful or constructive. One respondent says, 'I was always gobsmacked at the negativity … it tended to infuriate me and affect my confidence going forward.' Many challenge the credentials of readers and the rigour with which they make their assessment, arguing that they are paid poorly and not professionally invested or publicly accountable.

The reports were, for the most part, unprofessional, openly subjective, often mean-spirited, superior in tone, unimaginative in terms of narrative and possibility, and similar in taste, preference and decision.

There is also widespread disapproval that a script is not sent 'blind' to readers, resulting in the writer being identified but the reader remaining anonymous. Moreover, the vast majority of applicants never have direct contact with a project manager after rejection and have to pursue reader reports, sometimes quite vigorously, before gleaning something of the perceived deficiencies in the script that has led to a refusal.

I would like to see a more active engagement regarding the projects. At the very least, feedback to take from a refusal and apply successfully to the next submission.

Each of these grievances may appear trivial in isolation. However, as Acker remarks, 'practices that generate gender inequality are sometimes so fleeting or so "minor" that they are difficult to see' but the cumulative effect is a jaundiced perception of Screen Ireland's commitment to real change.[34] What might be read as disinterest or apathy about new opportunities for women can, perhaps, be better understood as a distrust of the system. Over time a disengagement can occur, which Kanter has described as 'a social means of coping with "blocked opportunities"'.[35] Traditional ways of working in organisations, discriminatory attitudes and practices, 'pure gender bias at work' and a lack of support mechanisms can dishearten women and discourage them from applying. A proactive approach is essential if women are to be persuaded that the culture that alienated them is embracing change.

Sexism is identified as a problem by a number of respondents – accounts of 'blatantly misogynistic' producers and an on-set culture in which a female director comes to work 'ready, armed and prepared to fight'. However, the overwhelming majority (84 per cent) believe that unconscious bias, in the film industry as in many other sectors, is the real issue. A Higher Education Authority (HEA) report in relation to female academics echoes these concerns and observes that 'women face barriers to progression that men do not have to contend with: systemic barriers in the organisation and culture which means talent is not always enough'.[36] Respondents identify unconscious bias as underpinning many aspects of the film industry: the driving force behind perceptions of a 'good' project; what a director should look like; and how an organisation is 'naturally' run.

> They subconsciously believe that a script by a male writer will be more successful/marketable and make decisions on that basis.

> I had a former (male) executive of the film board tell me recently: 'You can't get romantic comedies funded anymore, no chance.' I wasn't even pitching a romantic comedy, I was pitching a coming-of-age drama with a love element in it but it's clearly a drama. I think the assumption was because I was a woman, naturally that's what I'd want to make.

The problem does not lie with women's talent, as their education, training and achievements testify. Rather, it is the mechanisms of assessment that must be reviewed – 'perceived merit-based selections cannot rectify this disparity on their own; they must be coupled with proactive efforts specific to gender'.[37] Indeed, a range of gender initiatives designed to incentivise female writers, directors and producers to apply to Screen Ireland for funding were launched in 2018, which I will return to shortly.

CONFIDENCE

A number of studies relating to women in a variety of different sectors have identified a lack of confidence and self-belief, a lack of ambition, and a reluctance to self-promote and 'market' themselves. Some respondents here reject explanations that rely on women's lack of 'confidence' and perceive it as a convenient get-out clause by an industry that will not support women filmmakers in any concrete way: 'I have had nothing but interference and intervention.' For these women, it is solely about 'funding and hidden biases in how things are judged and what stories are deemed important or marketable'. However, despite the existence of unconscious bias and stereotypical preconceptions which disadvantage women, many respondents also identify a lack of personal confidence 'to unearth my own voice'. This chimes with the experience of one development executive who observes, 'The women undersell themselves.

The men oversell themselves. A generalisation but an observation.'
Male confidence, on the other hand, is 'fed by the industry'.

> The way they openly and with confidence talk about their ideas –
> there is no room for doubt. The way women talk about theirs, quietly,
> hushed tones and generally not openly in front of men. This is not
> just an issue of personal confidence, this is a symptom of an industry
> that puts value on the male storyteller and male-orientated stories.

Women's lack of confidence can be seen as 'reflecting an androcentric
cultural reality'[38] in a society in which they have less social power, are
paid less, are poorly represented in civic, political life and cultural life
and did not, until the Regulation of Termination of Pregnancy Bill
was signed into law on 20 December 2018, have full bodily autonomy
under law in Irish society.[39] A lack of confidence can also result from
'the perception of one's choices of success in the current environment'
and the expectation that they will not be selected.[40] In a corporate
context, Grace, Leahy and Doughney found that women's choices
were shaped by the prevailing gender inequality.[41] They do not seek
senior positions because they know they are less likely to get the job.
Additionally, Taylor has observed that, broadly speaking, 'women have
a lower sense of entitlement and lower expectations in the workplace
than do men'.[42] Following that logic, women may appear to assess their
chances of success in an organisation like Screen Ireland, which has not
traditionally acknowledged or supported them, and effectively 'opt out'
from being active players, at least temporarily.

Conclusion

The existence of a gender order in the Irish film industry is implicitly
identified in the widely held belief that women and their work are not
valued and are routinely sidelined either by commissioners, development
executives, producers or financiers. Pipeline theories are discounted as
providing an explanation for the small numbers of women in the field,
which research in other sectors supports: 'Solving the pipeline issue
and even reaching an over-supply stage offers no guarantee that gender
equality will automatically be achieved.'[43] The perception exists that

unconscious bias is still in operation in Screen Ireland and elsewhere within the wider industry and continues to disadvantage women.

The overwhelming majority of respondents reject what Edley and Wetherall call 'a progressive view of history'[44] in which society will move inexorably towards greater equality and articulate support for a range of affirmative action measures, particularly Screen Ireland's 50/50 gender funding target. Indeed, many (73 per cent) believe that it does not go far enough and is taking too long to implement, and they express the wish to see gender quotas put in place. That said, there is also a concern among a small number, bolstered by the lack of progress since the Six Point Plan was announced in December 2015, that Screen Ireland will never deliver on its stated goal and is paying 'lip service' with 'no intention of changing the status quo'.

There is widespread support (82 per cent) for incentivising producers to increase the number of female-driven projects – something which Screen Ireland could initiate by withholding funding from producers who do not meet gender targets themselves. In a period of growing gender awareness, an already produced writer/director was surprised to receive only one response (which took six weeks) to ten 'query emails' sent to Irish production companies requesting a reading of her screenplay. She speculates, 'I think perhaps I've been boxed into some category and I'll probably have to fight my way out.' Indeed, another writer/director with multiple television drama directing credits and a number of feature film projects in development puts the onus primarily on the 'production company executives, the private equity financiers and the distributors', all of whom play a significant role in determining where, and to whom, money will be directed. This, she argues, is where 'the naked, unvarnished sexism takes place'.

A small number of respondents (3 per cent) reject a structural explanation for women's position in the industry. Instead, they exhibit the individualism Budgeon has identified in a post-feminist climate where 'women are encouraged to adopt a view of themselves as fully autonomous individuals, free to wield power in the pursuit of personal goals'.[45] Here, in such accounts, respondents were wary of being 'unfair' to men; felt that women 'would catch up' in time; were unaware of Screen Ireland's gender policy – 'haven't read it' – and adopted personal strategies such as 'Be brilliant. Be positive.'

Going forward, transparency and accountability must be key; a transparent organisation will ultimately convince women that gender initiatives are embedded and projects will be enthusiastically and fairly assessed, providing women and men the same opportunities for development, visibility and reward. It is the culture of organisations that must change 'in order that talented women and others who do not automatically benefit from the status quo are fully recognised and rewarded'.[46] As French has suggested in relation to the Australian film industry, 'assisting women as they navigate these obstacles and sensitizing decision-makers' must be prioritised.[47] This respondent is clear that practices need to change:

> They should set up a system whereby women writers can work their way through the funding minefield in a supportive rather than an adversarial way ... staff should be open to discussion of script issues that arise and positive ways of addressing those issues.

It is not sufficient for equality to be a stated goal; it must be enacted and monitored with tangible targets and reviews. It is imperative that unconscious bias is addressed and a rigorous review of talent assessment procedures is undertaken. Unconscious bias may blinker male and female decision-makers to the potential of women screenwriters and directors. Such bias is so pervasive that it can also affect how women perceive themselves – 'from assuming you need to take on more "masculine" characteristics to succeed, to doubting your abilities and strengths'.[48]

Women's perceived relegation to second class, expressed in the devaluing of narratives about women's lives, the showcasing of the male 'star' director, the ubiquitous 'boys' club' and a gendered organisational culture, has very real consequences for women continuing to invest in the Irish film industry. Organisations that seek to introduce gender initiatives, such as Screen Ireland and the Broadcasting Authority of Ireland, need to be alert as to why women may resist measures that seek to include them. Only a transparent, accountable and proactive approach, what Kamberidou refers to as a move from 'gender fatigue to gender energy',[49] in which policy is translated into action and women are encouraged and supported in line with that policy, will allay fears that systemic barriers in the organisation and wider film industry are resistant to change.

Irish Production Cultures and Women Filmmakers: Nicky Gogan

LAURA CANNING

C o-founder of Dublin/New York-based production company Still Films, and founder of the Darklight Film Festival, the digital film festival which became a mainstay of the Irish new media calendar during the early millennium, Nicky Gogan is a filmmaker and curator/programmer who has worked across a range of media including features, shorts and animation. She is perhaps best known for feature documentary work such as *Seaview* (Nicky Gogan and Paul Rowley, 2008), *Pyjama Girls* (Maya Derrington, 2010), *Build Something Modern* (Nicky Gogan and Paul Rowley, 2011), and *Lost in France* (Niall McCann, 2017). As such, her tendency both to elide simple categories of production roles – saying 'I call myself a filmmaker, so I don't really see the distinction [between director, producer and editor]'[1] – and to work outside of the dominant 'fictional feature film' paradigm may contribute to her relative lack of visibility outside of the industry.

Gogan has been chosen for this study on two grounds. Firstly, her career, spanning a range of roles including producer, director, editor and curator, serves as an exemplar of the kind of 'portfolio' career which characterises much employment in the sector and, considering it longitudinally, provides a record of the strategies one woman has employed in navigating the Irish media industry – particularly in the context of the 'systemic barriers' identified by Susan Liddy here and in other writing.[2] Secondly, her role as a producer marks her as a member of an under-examined cohort of contributors to film culture, in Ireland and internationally; while lack of academic attention to producers is not an Irish-specific phenomenon, it is significant when we consider Screen Ireland's (previously known as the Irish Film Board, IFB, until June 2018) acknowledgement that 55 per cent of completed Irish productions during the period 2010–15 had a female producer attached.[3]

While film authorship is notoriously difficult to attribute, it has traditionally tended to be identified in the axis of writer and director. Auteurist frameworks centralising the film director may serve in the context of textual analysis, but considering the producer *as* a filmmaker allows us to move away from masculinist–auteurist frameworks and centre instead, by revealing underlying themes and patterns within the gendered practices of the industry, the unexamined work of women who have built sustainable careers in Irish film. This chapter examines Gogan's work as per Mayer, Banks and Caldwell, 'tak[ing] the lived realities of people involved in media production as the subjects for theorizing production culture'.[4]

Methodologically, foregrounding the idea of the producer as occupying a central creative role also allows us to consider the importance of state funding routes outside of the direct purview of Screen Ireland; in particular Arts Council funding, as well as the ways in which informal networking practices dominate Irish production, the possibility that collectivist approaches may problematise notions of the individualist auteur, and Irish tendencies towards transnational production. It derives in large part from a 2017 interview with her, conducted following several informal conversations in the preceding years, and takes as a methodological basis Mayer's caution that practitioner interviews 'must be put in the context of an ethnographic stance'[5] if they are to avoid inadvertently replicating promotional discourses.

A graduate of Fine Art (Sculpture) at the National College of Art and Design where she developed related interests in video and computer technology, Gogan moved to San Francisco in the mid-1990s, where she engaged with the artistic and communicative possibilities of digital culture in its earliest public incarnations. This link between technology and art informs her approach to both curatorial and production work and was central to her return to Dublin to study Creative Multimedia at the then recently launched media arts centre, Arthouse. It was central, too, to her establishment of the web design and digital media company Sink Digital Media in 1996,[6] and the founding in 1999 of Darklight. Emphasising both technological innovation and art, exhibiting a combination of experimental and commercial digital work – games, graphics, gallery pieces, CG and 3D animation, drama and documentary alongside symposia, workshops, and multimedia club nights – Darklight occupied a symbolic location in the Irish dotcom era, less about the contentious politics and technology of convergence than a marker of notions of Irish creativity and 'transcendence' of an agrarian, 'underdeveloped' past.

While Darklight was the project of three enthusiasts, the sometimes labyrinthine connections between state policy of the time, private enterprise, neoliberal currents in international economics, and the development of Ireland's technological infrastructure underpinned the notion of the 'digital economy' as connecting art and technology in ways that made Darklight very much of the *zeitgeist*. It found financial support from quasi-state institutions of culture, such as Arthouse and the Arts Council; the former was linked to Gogan's employment as an instructor at Arthouse, and her engagement with informal local cultural networks that had an understanding of the potential and scope of digital technology. However, the latter happened more formally and required greater contextual framing for the institution. As Gogan describes it

> After the first festival in 1999 we went – I think someone suggested it – 'You know, the Arts Council sponsor film festivals' and we were like, 'Oh, really?' We went to have a chat with them about the digital revolution and they didn't know what we were talking about.

Her note that they subsequently became 'a huge backer of Darklight' indicates the extent to which state frameworks for cultural support were 'recalibrating' their understanding of the contemporary contexts of fine art production.[7] Gogan sees Darklight as a product of her desire to

> run an art collective, do something collaborative. I wanted to be part of a community of some kind, making work. I didn't know at the time it was going to be filmmaking, I didn't even really think about that … it was about collaboration, working with people.

This engagement with the potentially democratising possibilities of technology, and her development of networks within film culture – crucially, funding sources like the Arts Council as well as practitioners – contributed to Gogan's movement into production. Having met Dublin-born visual artist Paul Rowley in San Francisco, Gogan first collaborated with him on Super 8 film in the mid-1990s. With the addition of Maya Derrington, whose background in television made her the only experienced producer in the group, and composer Dennis McNulty, their production collective, Still Films, was established initially to produce the feature-length documentary *Seaview* (2008). With Gogan and Rowley credited as co-directors, *Seaview* explores the use of the former Butlin's camp at Mosney, County Meath, as a long-term holding centre for refugees whose asylum applications awaited processing by the Irish state.

While Gogan notes experiencing no specifically gendered barriers to entry, she sees this as a function of what she describes as Still Films' 'outsider-y' status. This she attributes to the collective's tendency to work in 'marginalised' genres such as documentary, experimental film, and animation. However, it may relate to her curatorial work as having constituted a type of accidental 'pre-qualification' for the industry. By saying 'I'd learned a lot about the language of film, and I could talk about filmmaking, and talk about storytelling, and talk about [the] contemporary and pushing boundaries, from Darklight', she describes having developed linguistic and social 'mastery' of the informal networking practices that Jones and Pringle outline as characterising the industry.[8] These are irrevocably gendered practices, reliant on communicating in particular – perhaps 'masculinized' – ways in order to 'demonstrat[e] that you are "good"'[9] as if this networking was 'somehow a simple, transparent and objective process, without bias'.[10]

The funding of this film, a combination of Arts Council and Irish Film Board resources, bears examination, as it illustrates some key points in relation both to Gogan's work, and to Ireland's film production culture. A small grant from the Arts Council facilitated early development of the work, and demonstrates the extent to which Gogan had developed her understanding of the availability of funding, crucially, still outside of the IFB 'regime'. Secondly, it was a chance encounter, considerably later, with an IFB executive which resulted in more formalised access to IFB resources. As she outlines it,

> We were sitting in [a Dublin restaurant] and [we met Victoria Pope] who worked in the Film Board, and we were chatting and she said 'What are you doing?' and we told her, and she goes, 'Why don't you come into us for some funding?' We were like, 'Really? Oh, is that not for … Jim Sheridan? Does this belong to us?' We didn't really – I mean we *knew* [about IFB funding opportunities] but we hadn't put two and two together.

While Darklight had screened IFB-funded shorts previously, and indeed launched the Irish Flash programme,[11] it is interesting to note the bemusement with which Gogan – a highly experienced film curator and festival runner – greeted the invitation to apply for funding. This is suggestive of the kind of psychological barriers which may inhibit emerging talents, particularly women and minority entrants, from engaging with established structures of support and funding, as evidenced in Susan Liddy's work here.[12] It may replicate

the IFB argument that the issue is not so much that it is hard for applications from women for funding to succeed but rather that it is hard for female creative talent to reach a point where they feel they can credibly apply for such funding in the first place.[13]

However, it also reflects Gogan's perception that the IFB prioritised drama over documentary (particularly the kind of experimental or creative documentary favoured by Still Films). Therefore, genre may constitute a factor in considerations of the relationship between filmmakers and film funders; this inflects the gender question further when one notes the preponderance of female makers in the documentary and experimental fields, nationally and internationally.[14] In fact, the IFB awarded Still Films €83,000, which facilitated the production of *Seaview* over the several years it took to make.

Also noteworthy is the significance of informal female-focused networks. In interview with Gogan, one thread which emerges throughout her account of her work to date is the importance which female executives have assumed in the establishment and development of her career, outside of her own collaborators and business partners. Gogan cites Aileen McKeogh and Aoibheann Gibbons at Arthouse, Laura Magahy, Eve-Anne Cullinan of MCO (founders of the Digital Hub), Emma Scott, Teresa McGrane and Sarah Dillon at the IFB, Grainne Humphries of the Irish Film Institute and Dublin Film Festival, Grainne Bennett and Helen McMahon of Screen Training Ireland, Eileen Bell from Enterprise Ireland, and Mary Hyland, Jane Dooley and Fionnuala Sweeney at the Arts Council as having been instrumental to the formation of her professional and creative practice. This suggests a potentially positive – or even transformatively counter-institutional – instance of what Smith et al. (2012) describe as 'homosocial reproduction'[15] in film production contexts, particularly in light of the IFB's 2015 acknowledgement that women are 'not fully represented either in terms of accessing funding for film or in public recognition of their talent'.[16]

Gogan notes that her work with Darklight meant that

> I already had a bit of cred[ibility] before I went into [the IFB] … Paul, as well, had a lot of credibility. He had a career as a very successful visual artist … so the two of us together [were] coming into that kind of film space from our art space and our technology space.

The significance emerges both of local networks to production culture in Ireland, and ideas of 'credibility' in permitting access to these cultures. Caves' work on the creative industries discusses the industrial 'gatekeeper' within each creative realm, describing the 'set of intermediaries who select artists … many are excluded at the gate, although they would gladly sign the contract that the gatekeeper offers to those who pass'.[17] The cultivation of local networks of gatekeepers, while clearly open to accusations of nepotism, facilitates the development of the kind of reputational capital which allows any aspiring filmmaker 'to pass'. As Conor, Gill and Taylor note, in cultural labour markets characterised by informal working environments and equally informal hiring practices, 'reputation becomes a key commodity, and networking and maintaining contacts a key activity for nurturing it'.[18] The idea of female filmmakers mobilising female networks of administrative power therefore – while not without its own ethical issues – offers at least the possibility of a kind of corrective to the notional 'old boys network'.

While *Seaview* was critically well-received, following its premiere at the Berlin Film Festival (Forum), screening at festivals internationally and earning an IFTA (Irish Film and Television Award) nomination, for Gogan the experience had been emotionally complex.

> The people who ran Mosney at the time … were quite upset about it. I guess it showed a side … they might have been in denial, that there were people that were so unhappy there, because they really felt that they were doing a good job. And they *were* doing a good job, we say it in the film a few times, and at the end … they felt that the representation of Mosney was unfair … We were very upset about that.

The film's title – originally *Mosney* – was changed to *Seaview* in order to deflect their response, but the Mosney staff's reaction to the film affected Gogan deeply, and at the time she did not believe she would direct again. This may link to Díóg O'Connell's point that surmounting barriers to entry for debut filmmakers does not necessarily imply further engagement with the Irish industry, as 'relatively few progressed to a second or third feature, thus limiting the potential for nurturing and developing talent'.[19] However, O'Connell argues that this issue 'was addressed in 2002 through policy changes and the introduction of the low-budget fund, the "Micro Budget Scheme"', itself the resource which supported *Seaview*'s production.[20] This suggests that there can be many reasons why a debutante director might not progress further. However, the experience of many women in film production, as per Jones and Pringle's assessment of a 2008 UK Skillset report on women in film, implicates a punitive culture of ingrained sexism, long hours and family-unfriendly working practices. Problematically, these are often framed as reflective of 'individual qualities and choices … whereby women are the problem, and they must change their own characteristics to solve it'.[21]

In this context, I argue that it is the nature of Still Films' specifically *collective* approach that facilitated Gogan's retention in the industry. Where Gogan and Rowley had co-directed and co-edited *Seaview*, and shared producing credit with Maya Derrington, Gogan confirms that Derrington 'got involved with the company with a view to directing … It was kind of her turn, you know?' Therefore, Gogan was able to take a step back – whilst still remaining engaged with the business and the wider industry – by confining her role on their next documentary feature, centring on the friendship of two working-class Dublin teenagers, *Pyjama Girls* (2010), to that of producer, with Derrington as director and Rowley as editor. The collective nature of the Still Films model thereby enables its members to immerse themselves in creative film work as their interests, desires and other responsibilities dictate, or to provide support which facilitates the work of their partners. This approach may assist in mitigating a problem clearly identified by several studies: that the creative and cultural industries are 'better at recruiting women than at keeping them'.[22]

Gogan and Rowley took directing and editing roles with *Build Something Modern* in 2011. Funded through the Arts Council 'Reel Arts' initiative, a project administered by the Dublin Film Festival and (recently defunct) Filmbase,[23] the scheme was designed 'to provide film artists with a unique opportunity to make highly creative, imaginative and experimental documentaries on an artistic theme'.[24] This emphasis on the 'artistic' approach materialises the tensions inherent in the Irish film industry; as O'Connell notes, 'Aspirations towards a small, radical, auteurist, artisanal cinema inevitably clash with the economic imperative to produce films fitting a model of multiplex distribution modes: a tension facing most small indigenous cinemas.'[25] Arts Council funding, while small in scale, positions itself to 'complement, rather than replicate, the documentary and other funding programmes provided by the Arts Council, broadcasters and funding agencies in Ireland'.[26] As such it can provide a valuable alternative to Screen Ireland funding for emerging filmmakers – provided that their creative intentions dovetail with the specific criteria outlined for such funds.

Build Something Modern is in one sense the product of a deliberate search for an idea to fit the funding available. In another sense, it is rooted in Gogan's allied interests in documenting the processes and (often collaborative) practices of creativity, and in technology. Conceived with design historian Dr Lisa Godson, it explores the work of mid-twentieth-century Irish modernist architects and missionaries in designing churches in Africa – often churches they never saw in person. Central to the film's narrative and structure are animations of slides and architectural drawings, which both produce a distinctively stylised underpinning to the film's more documentarian approaches, and place it squarely in Reel Arts' remit of prioritising projects that offer 'visually engaging, creative and experimental approaches'.[27] A collaborative project in that 'me and Paul [Rowley] directed it and shot it, and then we cut it together', Gogan describes this film as vital to her learning process, particularly in terms of developing editing skills. She also emphasises the importance of cooperative enterprises like The Factory.[28] This is particularly the case in relation to the way in which, following the completion of *Build Something Modern*, Gogan began actively driving to 'expand the collective' as she puts it, with Rowley in New York and Derrington on a family-based career break.

Over the next several years Gogan produced experimental, documentary, and animated shorts and features, and her involvement as co-producer on an experimental animated feature documentary, *Last Hijack* (Tommy Pallotta and Femke Wolting, 2014), introduced her to international coproduction. It also provided an opportunity to build on her interest in animation technology and her desire to harness technological innovation in order to make 'directing animation more creative, more intuitive'. The project's origins demonstrate the industrial significance of the international festival circuit, as well as of informal network-building and reputational credibility, in sustaining a career in the Irish film industry. As Gogan describes it, she was at the 2012 Sheffield DocFest screening *Build Something Modern*, and pitching a film project at its Meetmarket event. At the same event, Alan Maher, the IFB's representative, received a pitch from a Dutch company, headed by Femke Wolting and Tommy Pallotta.[29]

> And basically they were like, 'We want to do this animated documentary,' and he said, 'Well, I know one producer in Dublin, in Ireland, who's produced a lot of animation, and also documentary, and is also interested in technology … I had had a standing invitation to Tommy Pallotta to Darklight for over ten years … I didn't meet them in Sheffield but they went back to Amsterdam and … were chatting about it and he was going, 'I know that name' and he looked at my resume and was like, 'Ah, I know Darklight.'

Gogan also brought the services of Dublin-based commercial content production, animation and visual effects studio Piranha Bar onto the project, signalling the increasing importance of animation to the Irish production environment.

This episode also highlights the fact that in the contemporary Irish film industry, many productions are not strictly dependent on national state funding structures – they are increasingly part of the circuitry of Irish cinema as a *trans*national phenomenon which is the result of the globalised circulation of capital: a possible 'third wave' of Irish cinema as Tracy and Flynn term it,[30] or as per Higbee and Hwee Lim: as 'a subtler means of understanding cinema's relationship to the cultural and economic formations that are rarely contained within national boundaries'.[31] For Gogan, this meant working with Section 481 funding for the first time, raising a proportion (€400,000) of the film's overall €1.2 million budget in Ireland, with the remainder coming from sources in Germany, the Netherlands and Belgium. This experience, and that of learning about the mechanics of leveraging international pre-sales, which provide potential avenues for filmmakers to capitalise on alternative sources of funding such as the MEDIA programme, was one which Gogan says she found extremely valuable. It also illustrates the extent to which IFB funding has become merely one source among many others for filmmakers; the IFB slate for the last decade shows that many productions now take a 'patchwork' approach to financing which combines private capital with state support. This tendency – which complicates the nature and purpose of state funding – may in theory provide opportunities for women filmmakers to step outside of the strictures of the IFB's organisational culture. However, it may also simply reinforce the kinds of occupational segregation and discrimination identified by studies in the field.[32]

2017's *Lost in France* (Niall McCann) illustrates Gogan's increasing use of complex international funding arrangements, financed as it was by the IFB and Creative Scotland, using Section 481 funding as well as UK tax credits, funding from Curzon Artificial Eye and private investment. It picks up familiar threads for Gogan; here, the creativity focused on is that of the Glasgow music scene of the 1990s, with labelmates from cult indie label Chemikal Underground reunited on a trip to the location of a 1997 gig in Brittany. As much about the decline of the welfare state – and the vital lifeline that dole money gave to those engaged in creative practice – as about memories of post-industrial Scotland, Gogan immediately knew, on meeting McCann as a co-panellist at the Cork Film Festival, that she wanted to work with him.

> The film unfolded before my eyes as he told it to me for the first time, you know that way? It doesn't happen very often, where you're suddenly just ... you can see it.

McCann was not a first-time filmmaker, having written and directed the Luke Haines documentary *Art Will Save The World* in 2012. However, Gogan's relationship with him foregrounds the role of the producer as mentor, one which can be obscured by the work of the producer as organisational and funding manager. For Gogan, despite McCann's status 'outside' of the collective, the film remains identifiably part of the Still Films body of work.

We thought *Lost in France* was going to be much more mainstream than it was until we made it, and then it turned into a Still Films film … Maya and Paul had lots to say about *Lost in France* when we were making it … As collaborators we do kind of all like to stick our beaks into everything we produce, and that's not for everybody, obviously.

Gogan sees McCann as fitting into the existing dynamic of collective filmmaking, describing a 'kind of even-handedness [in] collaboration between us three, and I feel Niall was able to flow into that … I think it's about choosing the people that you work with as well, that can fit into that.' She describes him as 'not a particularly egotistical man, he's very sweet and sound', in a manner which suggests that auteurist power dynamics – arguably themselves gendered – within the producer/director relationship can be mediated by a collective approach. The mediation of tension between problematic rival myths of the director as (masculine) creative controller and the producer as (feminine) bureaucrat does not, in a collective approach, have to be negotiated with each new producer/director pairing. A caveat is that this possibility is qualified or 'bounded' by the personalities involved, and determinedly self-perceived auteurs will likely sidestep production approaches which privilege collective working practices.

Gogan corrects herself slightly when describing how she has (in her role as producer) worked repeatedly with first-time and second-time directors. 'That's what Still Films says our mission is, to encourage new talent … I've definitely had, I think, a thing as a producer, kinda taking … directors under my wing, or not under my wing, but … it's an excitement to help people kind of achieve their dreams.' That idea of having a director 'under one's wing' suggests a kind of maternal – or at least protective – approach which may also, in its expression if not in its performance, be gendered, and which may reinforce existing gender-based norms in the industry or challenge them, but cannot necessarily be regarded as 'neutral'.

When pressed on whether she has experienced gender discrimination or overt sexism in the industry she indicates not, apart from noting a tendency for men in meetings to speak over her.

We joke about it … men, they don't do it on purpose, they don't mean to do it … it's just the way that society has, that culture has, brought them up … once you establish yourself on an equal footing in terms of the volume at which you speak [laughs] or what you're talking about, your intellectual input or your creative input into the conversation …, then it's fine, it's never a problem.

Gendered emotional and social labour aside, however, she does have experience of what she describes as 'antagonism' or 'disdain' for producers. While the role of the producer has, historically, been under-theorised at an academic level, Gogan's experience of 'producer bias' offers some useful points for us to consider. She says that producers

have a bad reputation, similar to agents or something … As a producer, in a way you're trying to give something, but the person you're giving it to often feels like you're taking something away from them. It's a very unusual dynamic.

This is an observed phenomenon as well as an experienced one, and she describes in detail her experiences of seeing the work of producers discursively minimised by other creatives – specifically writers and directors – including their own collaborative partners.

Gogan's sense is that while 'the US is very producer-led … the ideas are generated by the … producers and writers, and the directors are somebody that gets attached afterwards', the Irish model of production and funding tends to privilege a more auteuristic framework of self-perception on the part of creatives. As she says, 'I think what it is again is the auteur thing, that people who write feel they have to direct their own work in order to get the film made, and in order to get paid for it.'

She identifies some historical inconsistencies in script draft funding which may bear further investigation, but primarily sees it as an issue of structural power and film workers' self-positioning. This is, firstly, in the privileging of the writer/director as the creative 'owner' of a project; as she says, 'All the writers are directing their stuff because that's how it's set up here, it's the auteur model, and I think that feeds into the suspicion of producers.' It is, secondly, in terms of the relative lack of power of writers (as opposed to writer/directors) within that model. She sees this as an issue which has a significant impact on the wider industry.

There's great writers and there's great directors but the two are not necessarily the same, they're not the same discipline. I think if writers had more … power in the system here, as they do in America, there's great writers here …. There are potentially writers who maybe should be writing more and not directing at all, just focusing on their writing. But if there was some [better] financial framework for them to do that, it would be really good. We're not in that situation yet, though there's a real drive with the Film Board to encourage writing more.

This perhaps speaks to Liddy's discussion on 'the unchallenged continuity of the "male genius" myth'[33] which may account for a tendency for male writers to believe that they have a 'right' to direct their work, and vice versa. The historical Irish tendency to privilege literary culture over screen culture – and therefore to regard writing for screen as a 'second-best' form – may also play a role. The extent to which the systematic application of a collective approach may insulate Still Films from problems of cultural capital, of auteurism, or indeed of producer bias, is not quantifiable, but it seems reasonable to suggest that it is their collective approach which allows Gogan to identify them *as* problems.

The trajectory of Gogan's career is emblematic of the shifting conditions of the Irish media environment, as the movement towards increasingly technologised and globalised production continues. Darklight, having shifted from an annual to a biannual event a few years prior, ran for the last time in 2014. In part this is due to the increasing demands of filmmaking work on Gogan's time.[34] But while Gogan sees some future potential for Darklight outside of a strictly 'festival' context, she also sees contemporary technology as 'on a plateau now … in 2014 we did a big VR thing, but to be honest VR is still the "next big thing" … unless there's another big shift'. Darklight's current hiatus is also indicative of the extent to which digital technology and the digital world no longer represent innovation, having been 'mainstreamed' as part of our daily life and cultural practices. Where, at the beginning of the dotcom boom, festivals like Darklight were a unique opportunity to experience works exemplifying the emergence of a distinctive technological–artistic intersection, these now constitute the fabric of our everyday digital existence.

Interestingly, none of Gogan's more recent or forthcoming work directly engages with female writers or directors; she has executive produced several works which fit clearly within the Still Films profile, such as Niall McCann's most recent film *The Science of Ghosts* (2018) – another idiosyncratic music documentary, about Dublin musician Adrian Crowley, funded under the Reel Art programme – and *Kevin Roche: The quiet architect* (Mark Noonan, 2017), with its clear conceptual link to *Build Something Modern*. She is also in the planning phase of some potential projects which would reunite herself and Paul Rowley more directly as a producing/directing/editing team. This perhaps indicates that, in the absence of a deliberate focus on 'bringing through' female screenwriters and directors, once a producer has become embedded within the film industry, it has a tendency to hermetically 'self-seal' and reproduce existing gender dynamics. Where Gogan does appear to have taken on a 'mentor' role is in the introduction of Karla Healion to the Still Films collective; perhaps best known as founder of the Dublin Feminist Film Festival, Healion has since worked on *Lost in France* and produced Paul Rowley's 2017 short *The Red Tree*. This dual curatorial/production role is reminiscent of Gogan's own trajectory. Taken together, these points suggest that while collectivist production approaches may offer opportunities for entry, 'pipeline' theories of diversity cannot alone counter the industry's tendency towards homosocial self-replication – therefore, the presence of women producers in the Irish industry may result in the emergence of more women producers, but not necessarily more women writers or directors.

However, Gogan is currently focused on a different role, with Still Films temporarily taking a backseat. Having initially taken on contracts and financing work for them, she is now Head of Development with Gavin Kelly and Dave Burke's Piranha Bar, a position which emerged – somewhat circuitously – from their experience of working together on *Last Hijack*. It is this which most clearly points to Gogan's position somewhere between 'outsider' experimental documentary-maker and explicitly mainstream corporate producer. As Piranha Bar have moved to expand out of commercial advertising, visual effects and postproduction services, they have made a distinction between 'branded content' and 'original content'. This linguistic transition – indicating a movement from form- and platform-based distinctions such as 'film' and 'television' to ones which privilege the commercial, creative, and functional contexts of a particular text – speaks to the central issues of contemporary production: those of shattering the boundaries between media, and the erosion of traditional patterns of screen viewing.

This role continues Gogan's interest in the intersection of visual arts and technology, negotiating the boundaries between and across film, television, animation, gaming, and online delivery, such as in a link with Epic Games designed to transform production pipelines for animation through 'creating really high-end, high production values for lower budgets, because we're using the [Epic Games 'Unreal Engine'] game technology to make the work'. It also exemplifies the transition to transnational coproduction described by Tracy and Flynn (2017), linking Piranha Bar with state and commercial partners in Spain and Canada, and with current works in progress budgeted at figures ranging from €3 million to €7.5 million. In Gogan's opinion, the globalised industry leaves few options to practitioners who wish to scale up their operations.

> We're a small island, if we want to have ambitions past anything that costs about a million or so euros, really, we have to [go outside Irish funding opportunities], we have no choice. We need to go to a coproduction model for that.

Examining the role producers play in the Irish film industry, given their comparative invisibility and yet relative power, can assist us in identifying some of the wider – spoken and unspoken – conditions of production, and in illustrating the importance of non-Screen Ireland resources to the emergence of new women filmmakers as well as in wider film culture, as curators and production workers. Where Screen Ireland has, historically, marginalised women, bodies like the Arts Council have been crucial in supporting them, albeit within specific formal and thematic boundaries. It is also vital to understand the role that (formal and informal) women's networking plays in the network of Irish film, both in negotiating gatekeepers and in mobilising reputational capital. At the same time, the myths both of the gender-free 'meritocracy' and the auteur continue to dominate approaches to Irish film. The flexibility and support that a collective model like Still Films offers may provide a stable ground from which to operate and has, notably, allowed its members to pursue careers across different media and genres. This does not mean that they are removed from the circuitry of inequality's reproduction, but that collective approaches may mitigate its impact on women excluded by a masculine–individualist mainstream industry.

Women Cinematographers and Changing Irish Production Cultures

MAEVE CONNOLLY

Introduction

The work of the cinematographer is characterised both by visibility and invisibility.[1] Even when the images on-screen are celebrated in scholarly or popular discourse, whether because they are formally distinctive or technically innovative, the cinematographer is rarely regarded as the author of a film or television work in the same sense as screenwriter, director, or even producer. In practice, the cinematographer typically functions as part of a larger team, using expertise in image composition, camera movement and placement, lighting and colour to serve, and articulate, the director's 'vision'.[2] Consequently, within the realm of textual analysis, it can be difficult to determine the individual contribution of the cinematographer. At least one professional association – IMAGO (the European Federation of Cinematographers) – has sought to assert a legalistic model of authorship in order to protect the intellectual property rights of its members, within a rapidly changing media economy. IMAGO has devised a guide for cinematographers to use in negotiating contracts, which draws particular attention to the expansion of digital technologies for distribution and exhibition of moving images, encouraging its members to ensure that they are properly compensated for every use of 'their' images.[3]

Yet IMAGO itself has been relatively slow to address the double invisibility of women cinematographers, often tacitly reinforcing the perception of cinematography as a male profession, both within the industry and the public realm. In 2003, the organisation published a lavishly illustrated book celebrating one hundred years of European cinematography and, of the hundred films profiled, not one was shot by a woman. In her contribution to that publication, Cathy Greenhalgh seeks to justify this omission, stating, 'In Europe and at world level there are a growing number of female cinematographers, some of whom ... are

IMAGO members. However, developing a consistent body of work at a level high enough to get seen is not easy, quite apart from the number of years and sacrifice in other areas of life it can take to succeed. Here, too, a good partnership with a director, male or female, is very important.'[4] So, instead of directly acknowledging sexism within the industry, or within IMAGO itself, Greenhalgh implies that women either have not made the sacrifices needed to excel, or have been unable to form the alliances and partnerships needed to progress. It was not until 2016 that IMAGO actually established a Gender and Diversity Committee, in response to 'a recent surge of research on female representation in cinematography',[5] which highlights 'firstly the structural problem of unconscious bias in employment, and secondly the perception of what a DP looks like and who can be one'. Yet even though the committee welcomes initiatives to make women behind the camera visible, its members insist that 'No cinematographer wants to be called a "female" cinematographer, rather just "a" cinematographer.'

Making the work of women cinematographers 'visible' is clearly fraught with difficulty, not least because of the fact that accurate data on the number of women working (or educated) as professional cinematographers is difficult to access. The Irish Society of Cinematographers, which forms part of the IMAGO federation, lists twenty-two members, of whom only one (Suzie Lavelle, discussed below) is female. Its UK counterpart, the British Society of Cinematographers (BSC), lists ninety-eight members in the 'full accredited category', of whom only five are women (and they include Suzie Lavelle). These numbers demonstrate the marked underrepresentation of women within professional associations, if not within the field at large. The photographs accompanying the BSC membership list are also worth noting, since the vast majority depict (white) men posing beside large cameras,[6] underscoring the value placed on technical skill by many of those working in this field. This emphasis is not new, but rather long-established and deep-rooted, as evidenced by Michelle Citron and Ellen Seiter's analysis of sexism in film schools, originally published in 1981. Drawing upon their experience as filmmakers and educators at New York University's Tisch Film School, Citron and Seiter highlight the specific obstacles faced by female students of camerawork, noting that production classes in film schools have tended to 'treat filmmaking as pure technology'.[7] This approach, they argue, discourages 'women who believe that their talents are verbal and visual, but not mechanical, from entering the field. Women's hes-itation is further aggravated by the widespread belief that women cannot handle heavy and often clumsy equipment.' While education is not my primary concern in this text, there is little doubt that film schools are integral to the formation of production cultures, and play a key role in challenging (or confirming) gender stereotypes.

Although Citron and Seiter primarily sought to disseminate practical strategies for combating sexism in the film production classroom, their text also communicates their own isolation within the film school, and their 'lack of job security as women teachers'.[8] Duncan Petrie concurs that women were often underrepresented (in both the student body and staff) at the major US institutions, but he suggests that this situation began to change in the early 1980s, following the emergence of some prominent female independent filmmakers, including Susan Seidelman.[9] Petrie's comparative critical history of film schools, co-edited with Rod Stoneman, encompasses Europe as well as the US, and charts a growing convergence between education and industry. Although Petrie does not focus directly on the issue of gender, he is attuned to the marginalisation of women and minorities within the UK education context. According to Petrie, it was the arrival of Channel 4 in the early 1980s – an organisation mandated to represent marginalised constituencies – that prompted the National Film School (NFS) to introduce 'equal opportunity training for women and ethnic minorities'.[10] It would seem that, historically at least, film schools have sometimes functioned as hostile environments for those seeking to critique (rather than reproduce) the norms of industrial production culture, with schools occasionally following rather than leading 'industry' when it comes to addressing inequality.

In this chapter, I consider some of the strategies developed by women cinematographers to increase their collective, and individual, visibility. Taking up Cathy Greenhalgh's point about the need for cinematographers to establish partnerships with directors, I explore some of the specific cultural and social challenges faced by women in securing and sustaining advantageous professional connections and partnerships. To date, relatively little scholarly attention has been paid to the working culture and practice of cinematography (or to the specific experiences and practices of women in this role, either in the present or historically). Evan Lieberman and Kerry Hegarty have, however, challenged a prevailing tendency within national cinema studies to frame the 'director as the primary conduit of his or her national culture',[11] through a comparative study of two acclaimed cinematographers, Gabriel Figueroa and Gregg Toland. Lieberman and Hegarty examine not only the formal strategies and production techniques used by Figueroa and Toland, but also their professional trajectories, long-standing collaborations with particular directors, and negotiation of contractual, cultural, economic and political constraints. While their analysis is not specifically concerned with gender issues, Lieberman and Hegarty usefully advance a model of 'multiple authorship',[12] which recognises the complexity and diversity of interactions between cinematographers and other film workers.

Informed by Lieberman and Hegarty's expansive analysis of Figueroa and Toland, I develop a comparative approach to the practices of two Irish women cinematographers: Suzie Lavelle and Kate McCullough. In addition to discussing a selection of film and television works shot either by Lavelle or McCullough, I seek to understand their respective processes of research and collaboration, and I also consider the labour of professional self-representation, which includes securing agents in various territories, professional networking, updating promotional materials, making proposals and pitches for new projects, negotiating conditions of employment via agents, and participating in public promotional activities. While Lieberman and Hegarty are primarily interested in expanding definitions and models of authorship in national cinema studies, my primary objective is to understand how multiple forms of change (cultural, economic, social, technological) directly impact upon the work of Irish women working within the field of cinematography. I also consider how prominent practitioners such as Lavelle and McCullough can, through their contributions to public discourse, as well as their work behind the camera, help to change the dominant culture of production.

Lavelle and McCullough have both worked as cinematographers across a range of genres, within and beyond the Irish context. Significantly, both were educated either wholly or partly outside Ireland. In 2003, McCullough completed a BA in Film Production at the Irish National Film School in Dublin, followed by postgraduate studies in cinematography at the Polish National Film School in Lódz. Lavelle was awarded the Freddie Young Scholarship (2005–6) to study at the National Film and Television School in the UK, where she also completed a master's in cinematography in 2007. She also received a

Kodak scholarship to attend Budapest Cinematography Masterclass in 2010–11. My discussion in the latter half of this chapter references a small selection of the short and feature-length works, including film and TV documentary and drama, advertising, music promos and artists' films, shot by Lavelle and McCullough. I also draw upon interviews, documentation of public discussions, industry reports, policy documents, and materials produced by professional associations.

Changing professional identities, roles and workflows

Before discussing the trajectories and practices of both Lavelle and McCullough, I want to briefly explore some key transformations in production culture, which are relevant to the situation of the cinematographer. The first transformation worth noting is the generalised, but unevenly distributed, disruption to established work practices wrought by the introduction of digital technologies, particularly since the early 2000s. In their discussion of the classical era, Lieberman and Hegarty usefully enumerate the extensive responsibilities of the cinematographer, both before and after shooting begins:

> (1) devising a lighting strategy and supervising its implementation; (2) making choices regarding lenses, filtration, film stock, camera, and lighting equipment; (3) determining exposure, contrast, focus, and depth of field; (4) orchestrating and executing (or supervising the execution of) camera movement; (5) collaborating with the director on framing and all aspects of shot composition as well as on the breakdown process in which the scene is divided up into individual shots; (6) participating, oftentimes, in positioning the actors on the set and blocking their action; (7) placing, moving, or removing set dressing; and (8) consulting on wardrobe, makeup, location choice, and production design.[13]

The well-defined hierarchies and lines of communication, implied in Lieberman and Hegarty's description, are still a feature of media production, but since the early 2000s cinematographers have had to grapple with the introduction of new techniques of image capture, management, storage and processing, and acquire expertise with a diverse array of shooting formats and media.

It can be argued that technological change is a constant for cinematographers, since they routinely seek out (or indeed develop) new processes and techniques, but the transformations associated with the use of digital media have been notably disruptive, involving conflict over standards, and the reorganisation of long-standing workflows. Writing in 2004, Stephen Prince observes that 'traditionally, cinematographers have had minimal involvement with postproduction, with the exception of the lab timing [in the processing of film stock]. Now, however, as more and more of the components of cinematography are altered or even created once principal filming is finished, cinematography is becoming a postproduction process in ways it has never been.'[14] This means that cinematographers must consult (and collaborate) more closely with a wider range of personnel, including colour graders and those involved in visual and special effects processes, while also considering the demands of multiple distribution platforms. This expanded role is outlined in textbooks,[15] but relatively little scholarly research seems to have been published on the changing role and situation of the cinematographer within the field of production studies. Studies have instead tended to focus on the experiences of less senior (and perhaps less enfranchised) workers such as production assistants, runners, visual effects workers, or self-employed videographers, as distinct from professionally accredited cinematographers.[16]

Within this shifting culture, workers rely heavily upon professional networks (including union memberships and more informal industry affiliations) to secure opportunities and defend their perceived rights and traditional territories. John Caldwell has studied the expression of professional anxieties and grievances ('worker blowback') in industry-focused blogs and forums, noting a tendency to assert the value of expertise that has been gained 'on the job', rather than in film school.[17] Workers may also express concerns about declining standards, appealing to abstract artistic (or craft) values assumed to be under threat. These cultural tensions have a long history, but Caldwell's research under-scores the intertwining of social and professional affiliations, and the growing use of online networks to seek and secure employment. This intertwining of social and professional networks can serve to exclude specific groups, including women. In a publication from 2013, Rosalind Gill finds evidence of ongoing 'unmanageable inequalities in film, media and other cultural and creative industries',[18] citing statistics that chart a decline in the number of (US) features shot by women. According to Gill, gender inequality has become 'not only unmanageable but actually unspeakable, even for those profoundly affected by it', particularly within 'creative and media work, where there is a significant investment in notions of meritocracy and egalitarianism'.[19]

It is possible, however, that the lived experience of inequality and sexism within the media industries is no longer entirely 'unspeakable'. As is well known, specific abuses of power by individuals in the media industry became highly public in late 2017, via the viral #MeToo movement. This was followed (in January 2018) by the Time's Up campaign, which funds and supports legal action against sexual harassment. Interestingly, however, these movements were preceded by several lobbying and networking initiatives within the field of cinematography, aiming to combat sexism and gender inequality. For example, 2016 witnessed the formation of two US-based networking organisations seeking to represent the interests of women: the International Collective of Female Cinematographers (ICFC)[20] and Cinematographers XX (CXX).[21] The latter organisation was formed by female members of Local 600, the (US-based) international cinematographers guild. Prominent founders of CXX include Rachel Morrison, the first woman ever nominated for the Best Cinematographer Academy Award, but the organisation also supports women in less senior roles, such as camera operators and assistants. In addition to increasing the visibility of women within Local 600, CXX has targeted industry decision-makers and the general public, publishing an advertisement in Hollywood trade journals with the names of female DPs and camera operators, organising meetings with studios and producers, and showcasing the work of women on its website and through other media.[22] A similar ethos is apparent in illuminatrix DOPs, established in November 2016, which includes Suzie Lavelle as a member. Intended to function as an 'industry resource' and a 'private network', this organisation is a collective of female cinematographers (each with over five years' professional experience) based in the UK and working internationally.[23] All three networks can be described as strategic responses to the specific challenges faced by women within the field of cinematography, and all aim to foster solidarity among peers, while also increasing the visibility of women, among media audiences as well as within the industry.

Gender and Irish production culture

In 2016, the Irish Film Board (IFB), now renamed Screen Ireland, announced a series of measures intended to increase the representation of women within the Irish industry, particularly in the key roles of writer, producer and director. These measures, which were not fully implemented until 2018, include gathering and publicising production statistics on gender diversity, incentivising female-led production and development, female-focused mentoring, training schemes that highlight unconscious bias, and lobbying initiatives aimed at industry organisations. According to Gill, the direct impact of formal measures to 'protect equality of opportunity'[24] can be somewhat limited in the media industries, because employment practices are difficult to regulate. But as the Irish film and television industry continues to be supported by state subsidies (from grants to tax incentives), often directly aimed at job creation, there may be greater scope to effect change in employment practices, in specific areas of production. Screen Ireland has not produced any statistics on the representation of women in the camera department, but a glance at the 2016 production catalogue suggests that there is room for improvement, particularly within feature drama. The catalogue lists thirteen films categorised as 'Irish Features', along with seven 'co-produced' features, and only one of these twenty features (*Unless*, dir. Alan Gilsenan) was shot by a woman (Celiana Cardenas). In the same year, the IFB funded seventeen feature documentaries, five of which were shot by women. While this sounds positive, four of the five – *The Farthest, The Queen of Ireland, Blood Sisters, It's Not Yet Dark* – are partly or wholly credited to McCullough. Although her prominence in this category is welcome, it inevitably skews the statistics, making it possible to state that almost 30 per cent of Screen Ireland-funded feature documentaries in 2016 were shot by women.

It is difficult to know for certain if the extension of gender-based incentives to include cinematography would actually increase employment opportunities for women in the Irish industry. A quota system might require Irish productions to actively recruit female cinematographers who are based elsewhere, simply because the current cohort in Ireland is so small. In 2017, McCullough contributed to a masterclass on cinematography hosted by the Irish chapter of the organisation Women in Film and Television (WFT), during which she described herself as one of only three women cinematographers actively working in the Irish context.[25] The second is (presumably) Frida Wendel,[26] a Swedish cinematographer based in Ireland, who also contributed to the masterclass session. McCullough did not name the third cinematographer, noting only that she is based mainly in the UK, but this unidentified individual is most likely Suzie Lavelle. The WFT session directly addressed the issue of gender in Irish production culture, and the discussion encompassed not only employment opportunities but also experiences of film school and workplace behaviour. In response to a question from the chair about the existence of 'laddish behaviour' on set, McCullough elicited input from an audience member, the writer and director Emer Reynolds, with whom she worked on the feature documentary *The Farthest* (2016), discussed below. Interestingly, Reynolds stated that, during the making of *The Farthest*, McCullough occasionally had to explain her rationale for specific set-ups, justifying her decisions to gaffers and lighting crew. Reynolds also observed that an overtly 'alpha' culture on set could sometimes overwhelm a 'quieter story'. This is a significant point, since it suggests that the culture of production has a direct impact upon the form of the finished work. From one perspective, this seems obvious, and yet it is difficult to quantify. Both Wendel and McCullough argue for a more egalitarian environment, with the latter stating that she specifically favours a mixed set (neither all female nor all male) and identifying a 50/50 split as ideal, because it reflects society at large. In order to move toward this ideal ratio, however, it is necessary to both quantify and analyse the current gender balance more fully. The quantification process alone would require a significant expansion of the existing Screen Ireland data-gathering measures, to encompass all roles on funded productions.

The formation of CXX suggests that professional associations can support women to develop gender-based networks, perhaps more effectively than film schools, and this is borne out by comments from Wendel. Reflecting on her experience of film school in the WFT masterclass, Wendel admits that she initially found herself competing with other female students. As she became more established, she consciously changed her own behaviour, increasing her engagement with female peers through groups such as the women's section of the Swedish Society of Cinematographers. Within the Irish context, professional associations could also play a key role in expanding research on gender equality, particularly in relation to employment on advertisements, which are outside the funding remit of Screen Ireland. Wendel notes that women rarely have the chance to shoot commercials. These lucrative opportunities are often secured through informal channels, in keeping with the economy described by Gill. Wendel also suggests that women are less likely to be offered action-centred narratives, although this may be changing. At another moment in the WFT discussion, McCullough states that she routinely receives scripts for projects centred on children, or female-led pieces, even though she does not necessarily seek out this kind of subject matter. So it is worth remembering that (unless they are also writers or directors) cinematographers generally do not develop or initiate projects. Instead, they rely largely on the material that they are offered, complicating the analysis of their artistic concerns and authorial intentions.

The work of Suzie Lavelle and Kate McCullough

Describing herself as an 'Irish DOP' with bases in both the UK and Ireland, Suzie Lavelle is represented by agents in the US as well as in the UK and Europe. Her professional online profile lists her as shooting drama, documentary and promos, emphasising her experience with both film and HD. In the years immediately following completion of her cinematography studies, Lavelle worked on two relatively low-budget projects by Still Films, a Dublin-based production company with a reputation for critically engaged filmmaking across various genres, including several films developed by artists. The first project was *Divestment* (dir. Paul Rowley, 2008), a short and highly stylised drama that used the language and social conventions of the board meeting to explore corruption in Irish financial institutions. Lavelle subsequently shot the Still Films documentary *Pyjama Girls* (dir. Maya Derrington, 2010), which focuses on the experiences of young women growing up in an urban Dublin community affected by drug abuse, who assert a kind of territorial claim by wearing pyjamas in public. Picking up on the patterns in the pyjama fabric, Lavelle uses saturated colour and graphically compelling compositions to articulate spatial and social boundaries, contrasting claustrophobic interiors with static, formally detached shots of the urban environment, treating apartment balconies as intermediate spaces between inside and outside. These formal compositions suggested an attempt to observe the city from a vantage point – young, urban, working class and female – largely underrepresented in Irish cinema.

A focus on claustrophobia is even more integral to Lavelle's first feature film, *One Hundred Mornings* (dir. Conor Hogan, 2010, Blinder Films), which received the Irish Film and Television Award (IFTA) for Best Cinematography. *One Hundred Mornings* is a tense study of two couples forced to share a small wooden cabin, located somewhere in the Irish countryside, following a sudden and unexplained collapse in the social order. Somewhat unusually for an Irish feature drama, the narrative is visually led. The dialogue is minimal and there is almost no reference to the detail of life before these people were forced into close quarters. Working with a small crew, Lavelle's approach to the cinematography is subtle and restrained, although she makes occasional compositional use of vertical forms – particularly when shooting the interior and exterior of the cabin – to explore divisions within the dwelling and articulate the pressures of social isolation. Her palette is muted (in keeping with the autumnal tones of the countryside) and the camera remains at a distance from the characters, often observing them in natural light, diffused through faded curtains.

Lavelle was nominated for the Best Cinematography IFTA in 2012 for her second feature, *The Other Side of Sleep* (dir. Rebecca Daly, 2011, Fastnet Films), a psychological thriller with a rural setting and a sleepwalking protagonist, but since the early 2010s she has primarily worked in UK television drama, rather than features. Lavelle has shot several Tiger Aspect productions for Channel 4, including multiple episodes of the comedy *My Mad Fat Diary*, and has also worked on numerous crime and legal dramas, including the BBC productions *Silk* and *Silent Witness*, and various crime or horror-themed dramas with a period setting, including *Ripper Street*, *Endeavour*, and *The Living and the Dead*. As already stated, partnerships with writers and directors are crucial for all cinematographers, and it is worth noting that Lavelle has worked on several productions involving Mark Gatiss as either actor, writer or creator, including a feature-length episode of *Sherlock: The abominable bride*, 2016, discussed below.[27]

Feature film dramas are typically credited to a single cinematographer, who plays a key role in the development, as well as technical realisation, of the image – in keeping with the model of 'multiple authorship' elaborated by Lieberman and Hegarty. In television dramas, however, a cinematographer may have to replicate the in-house shooting style established by someone else, to ensure that relatively consistent visual language is maintained from one episode to another. Consequently, it can be difficult to determine signs of authorship. For example, Lavelle shot episodes three and four of the British drama *Jamestown* (2017), which is set in the seventeenth-century colony of Virginia. But much of season one was shot by others, including John Conroy, who (like Lavelle) has also worked on crime dramas such as *Silk* and *Silent Witness*. She also shot several episodes in the 2017–18 season of *Vikings* (2013–) but at least one of these episodes also credits regular *Vikings* DP Peter Robertson, again complicating the attribution of authorial decisions.

Lavelle's involvement in *Vikings* is also notable because the show is primarily action-driven (a genre dominated by male DPs), with high production values and significant postproduction demands. Each episode of *Vikings* typically involves a camera department of approximately twenty, in addition to visual effects on set (as well as outsourced crowd effects and computer-generated imaging). 'The Prisoner', an episode of *Vikings* on which Lavelle receives a co-credit with Robertson, features a technically complex battle scene with animals, a large number of extras, and multiple visual effects. It is possible that Lavelle's role was to oversee the shooting of an entirely different (less action-focused) storyline in the same episode, shot and set in a desert location remote from *Vikings*' Irish production base, but she receives sole credit on a subsequent episode, 'The Message', which includes a mix of action-led and character-focused scenes, including several shot at sea. Significantly, 'The Message' also incorporates a disturbing scene in which an established female character is subjected to protracted sexual violence, and it is conceivable that this content might have informed the choice of DP, although such scenes are not unusual in this type of drama.

In at least one instance, Lavelle worked on an award-winning production where another cinematographer's contribution was recognised above her own. She shot the second half of the six-part television mini-series *The Living and the Dead* (2015–16), set in rural England with a dual timeline (moving between the late nineteenth and early twentieth centuries). The narrative becomes progressively darker and more violent in the final three episodes, shot by Lavelle, and this is underscored through the use of deep tones of red. Lavelle also makes extensive use of candlelit reflections in mirrors and windows to evoke a Victorian gothic aesthetic. Matt Gray, who shot the first three episodes of *The Living and the Dead*, was nominated for a British Society of Cinematographer (BSC) Television Drama award for his work on this series. Subsequently, however, Lavelle was nominated for a Primetime Emmy for Outstanding Cinematography for a feature-length special episode of *Sherlock: The abominable bride*, 2016, written by Mark Gatiss.

Not unlike *The Living and the Dead*, this feature episode of *Sherlock* incorporates a dual timeline and deploys stylised references to the gothic horror tradition, early cinema and stage magic. But the narrative of *Sherlock: The abominable bride* is very explicitly structured around illusion, centring upon a hallucinatory journey into the protagonist's interior 'mind palace'. Lavelle references several 'trick' effects associated with early cinema, and these are combined with more contemporary techniques, such as 'bullet time' sequences in which actions (described by witnesses) are recreated and viewed in 360 degrees, so that they appear to be frozen in time.

In addition to her work in film and television drama, Lavelle has shot music videos (including one for Hozier, featuring *Game of Thrones* actress Natalie Dormer), concert videos, advertisements and several artists' films. While an in-depth discussion of artist–cinematographer collaborations lies beyond the scope of this chapter, it is worth noting that both Lavelle and McCullough have primarily shot films by women artists.[28] Although often modestly resourced in terms of crews and technology, these projects are frequently scheduled around the availability of the cinematographer, creating opportunities for formal experimentation and (in the case of McCullough's work with artist Sarah Browne, discussed below) critical reflection on the production of images.

Like Lavelle, Kate McCullough works on film and HD, and has received numerous awards, including a prize at the Aspen Film Festival for the UK short *Hibernation* (2003), made while she was studying at the National Film School in Lódz, Poland. She also subsequently shared the World Cinematography Award at Sundance for the feature documentary *His and Hers* (dir. Ken Wardrop, 2009).[29] Like Lavelle, McCullough has worked in feature film drama – including *Snap* (dir. Carmel Winters, 2011, Samson Films), but she is more widely known for her documentary work, including a number of long-running collaborations. For example, McCullough has worked repeatedly with Ken Wardrop, Emer Reynolds, and also Patrick Farrelly and Kate O'Callaghan, often on films that might loosely be described as biographies, sometimes focusing on creative practitioners, such as architects, filmmakers and writers, which are typically structured around interviews to camera.

McCullough's particular aptitude for interviews is evident in the WFT discussion of her approach to shooting *The Farthest*, a film that explores the history (and ongoing cultural and scientific significance) of NASA's Voyager space exploration missions. Prior to each interview, McCullough arranged volumes of sequined fabric out of shot to create a kind of diffuse glitter, which could be perceived in the eyes of her subjects. She also seems to have approached the bodies of her subjects as though they might be planets, letting light fall dramatically off to the side. Although ostensibly a biography, the feature documentary *Kevin Roche: The quiet architect* (dir. Mark Noonan, 2017) also touches upon relatively abstract themes, such as the importance of public space. Using camera focus to direct attention, McCullough keeps the background pin sharp, while blurring the foreground and middle ground. At other moments, she directs attention towards the sky, visible beyond the glass rooftops of atria, in multiple shots marked by lens flares.

McCullough has also played a key role in several documentary features that were shot by multiple contributors.[30] *It's Not Yet Dark* (dir. Frankie Fenton, 2016), for example, is based on the autobiography of Simon Fitzmaurice, a writer and filmmaker with motor neurone disease, and it incorporates footage shot by him, his family members and many others. In approaching this project, McCullough decided to focus on 'three main motifs: interviews would be an intimate portrayal, reconstructions [would] be abstract and nuanced, observations [would] be economical and honest'.[31] Relying primarily upon her own camera equipment for budgetary reasons, McCullough used tracks in the interview sequences, allowing the camera to move slowly (almost imperceptibly) around the subjects, who are lit from the front, as though emerging from deep darkness. The film features recurrent dreamlike drone shots of the natural world, including lakes, rivers, seashores, forests, with particular attention to boundaries between land and water, communicating a sense of disembodiment, and, at a key moment, McCullough uses a simple close-up of water bubbles in a jug to communicate the profoundly disorienting effect of Fitzmaurice's diagnosis.

In 2014, Kate McCullough both shot and appeared briefly in *Something From Nothing*, a film by the Irish artist Sarah Browne.[32] This film, which was shot by McCullough on a smartphone camera, examines the creative work of women, exploring both historical and contemporary practices of multi-tasking and the labour of self-presentation. As part of this project, Browne sought to make the work of art and film production – which can be social and communicative as well as technical – manifest on-screen. So Browne herself is shown scrolling through files on a microfiche reader, while McCullough is briefly pictured behind a smartphone mounted on a tripod. While many aspects of this film invite further discussion, I cite it here specifically as evidence of McCullough's capacity, and willingness, to reflect upon her own practice and the changing conditions of labour.

Conclusion: Gender, representation and cinematography

Even though the number of women actually working as cinematographers in the Irish context remains low, it is clear that Lavelle and McCullough have both established strong professional reputations. They have also contributed actively to the formation of new peer networks, which are intended to support women working in cinematography by increasing their visibility both within the industry and more broadly among media audiences. These networks often seek to counter a tendency (perhaps fostered in education) for women to be placed in competition with each other. These emerging professional networks should be understood not simply as a strategic response to long-standing forms of sexism within the field of cinematography, but also to the specific pressures and demands faced by media workers since the early 2000s as a consequence of digitisation and the associated reorganisation of traditional hierarchies, communication channels and workflows. Some of the women-only peer networks I have highlighted here were established within, or alongside, pre-existing union or guild structures, but others belong to a less formally organised reputational economy, which prioritises the development and management of professional partnerships with directors and producers.

Further research is clearly needed on the experience of women working in the field of cinematography, in Ireland and elsewhere. This research could explore how organisations such as CXX, illuminatrix DP or WFT can assist in peer networking by marginalised and underrepresented groups of women. It might also investigate the specific obstacles faced by women cinematographers seeking to work within action-led productions or in those areas of media production that tend to fall outside the scope of Screen Ireland funding, and data-gathering, such as advertising. As already indicated, Screen Ireland statistics on employment provide only a partial picture of women cinematographers' participation in the Irish industry. A fuller picture could be developed through a more qualitative investigation of Ireland's production culture(s), encompassing analysis of industry-oriented education and training, as well as activities and practices within the professional sphere. Peer networks are certainly integral to the ongoing formation of this production culture. When constituted publicly, in the case of CXX, illuminatrix DP or WFT, they can be highly effective in changing perceptions and practices. But it is also important to acknowledge the value of smaller-scale, less formal, networks. They too are crucial to the creation of a working environment where women can assert their creative agency and authority. This is evidenced by Kate McCullough and Emer Reynolds' account of shooting *The Farthest*, which demonstrates that partnerships between cinematographers and directors can be especially significant, helping to foster a production culture that is open to new and diverse forms of storytelling.

A Cut Above:
In conversation with Emer Reynolds

SUSAN LIDDY

Introduction

Emer Reynolds is an Emmy- and Grierson-nominated, multi-award-winning director and feature film editor, based in Dublin, Ireland. Over the last two decades, her editing work has spanned TV drama and documentary and many notable feature films. She has written and directed four short dramas and has also directed television drama. *The Farthest* (2017), her award-winning feature documentary on the trail-blazing Voyager spacecraft, was described as 'dazzling' by *The New York Times* and lauded by critics and audiences worldwide. It won the George Morrison Best Feature Documentary at the Irish Film and Television Awards (IFTAs), 2018. It also won an Emmy for Outstanding Science and Technology Documentary at the 39th News and Documentary Emmys, 2018. TV versions of the film have been broadcast in the US, Britain, Ireland, Europe, Asia and Australia. Previously, Reynolds edited and directed *Here Was Cuba* (2013), a feature documentary on the Cuban Missile Crisis, which garnered widespread international acclaim and was described by the *Hollywood Reporter* as 'a real-life end-of-the-world-thriller'.

SL: Tell us something about Emer Reynolds before the film industry.

ER: I grew up alternating between Dublin and Tipperary, where we lived on a farm with beautiful dark skies overhead and I was obsessed with space. Obsessed with the night sky. I wanted to be an astronaut. That was my fevered desire. In fact, I only tempered that a tiny bit because my uncle Paddy told me if you want to be an astronaut, you really need to learn how to fly so for a while I wanted to be a pilot. But that was only ever a secondary plan to becoming an astronaut. That was my main goal all the time – until I joined the film society in school when

I was about fifteen. The very first film they showed was *Twelve Angry Men*. I thought my world had spun on a twopence. I couldn't believe … I just literally fell in love. I thought: film can change the world, it can give you a window into a world that you didn't have any idea was there. I came home and I had a cross between a row and a massively brilliant conversation with my father. About the story of the film, about prejudice; we weren't talking about filmmaking, we were talking about the film. We talked about it for hours. Astronaut was gone and I wanted to work in film.

SL: When you told people you wanted to become an astronaut did anyone try to put you off because you were a girl?

ER: Everyone said that, apart from my own family. I didn't get that at home. I grew up in a family with four girls with my dad on his own. My mother died when I was four, sadly. I don't know did he raise us as though we were boys but it was a kind of totally gender-neutral environment. We were always fixing plugs, you know, mending punctures, really into sport. I don't know if that was any machinations on his part but we just assumed we were the same as him. I don't want it to sound like a cliché, we weren't trying to be little boys, you know, it just never occurred to us in our house that there were any gender issues. But outside of that, in school, they certainly did. They weren't even sure women could be pilots – it was like, 'Really?' I think there was one female pilot in Aer Lingus at the time. In my school, if you were good at maths you went into engineering and if you were good at anything else you went to secretarial college. There didn't seem to be any other route.

SL: So, at that stage in terms of your desire, you were sold on film as a career?

ER: I wanted to work in film but actually knew nothing about it. This was the eighties, I had no sense of there being an Irish film industry. I had one cousin who was a cameraman in RTÉ, but knew of no-one else. I decided to study film but my dad didn't really think film was an appropriate degree – he thought you needed to get a *proper* degree. That makes him sound like an ogre but he was just the opposite. He was wonderful: warm, inquisitive, inspiring – a real intellectual. So I went to

Trinity to study for a proper degree in physics and maths and then was going to somehow segue into film after that – I'd no idea in what role or how that would work.

SL: Opting to study physics and maths was a non-traditional choice for a woman at the time?

ER: Yes, I think in my class of fifty there were about four women. I joined the film society in Trinity when I was in first year, everyone else I met was in third or fourth year. They were all more advanced than I was. I was doing continuity, carrying the camera, whatever. Seeing what all the different jobs were. They were making a short film, *Sheila*, on Super 16, borrowed little bits of film and it actually starred Anne Enright who went on to win a Booker. Directed by Alan Gilsenan who's a very close friend of mine and still a frequent collaborator of mine. I met a few people and I kinda got into it. Went on shoots and things and thought it was really interesting. I probably thought I'd be a director but I didn't know what it was or how you'd even do that. I had no clue about any of it. I was kinda figuring it all out. The short was being edited by an editor in RTÉ. I went out to the edit to see what was happening. From the day and hour I walked in there, it was like a lightbulb going off. I thought editing was just magnificent.

SL: What was it about editing that gripped you?

ER: My old boyfriend used to say they'll carve on my gravestone: 'She was nothing if not contrary' and I suspect some of those choices are to do with seeking the contrary. Going into a non-traditional degree for women, there's a little bit of 'what's that all about?' Inquisitive or contrary, I don't know. But from the minute I walked in I thought editing was a form of storytelling that was so free. The idea, and literally I remember it from the very first moment, the idea that one shot placed beside another shot created a meaning that didn't exist before. There's this alchemy, this frisson you couldn't know was there and to reveal it you had to be brave. You had to be open and ready to ask a question, ready to experiment and capable of deconstructing it and interrogating it. That shot beside that shot *means* something. But what does it mean? Is that meaning the meaning I mean? The meaning I want? And that shot now placed beside that shot, with this new inherent meaning, what is it causing in the rest of the film? The idea that every single cut in a film, maybe there's fifteen hundred or maybe there's three thousand, whatever, that they're all making these new universes of meaning and alchemy, I couldn't get over it and I wanted to learn it. On day one, it was like somebody just lifted up a curtain and I peeped in and I thought, the joy of it! The joy of the creation.

SL: You call it contrariness, this inquisitive side of you. Was there any formal understanding of gender politics at that stage?

ER: I was a feminist and I remember reading *The Handmaid's Tale* and, like a lot of people, having another one of those lightbulb moments. I remember being emotionally struck by the voice of the female, something I hadn't understood up to that point. Most of the books I was reading were from another voice and I hadn't really discerned that. I had probably fallen into the mythology that the male voice is universal and that the female voice, perspective and experience was 'other', even though I was a woman. I can see that, even now, when I talk to young girls so it's very, very pervasive and very, very hard to pull it apart. So I sought out Susan Sontag, and Betty Friedan, and Germaine Greer, books about feminism. I was probably trying to figure it out, I didn't have any formal understanding of it. I don't think I ever thought: I wonder are there women astronauts? I wonder are there women physicists? I wonder are there women filmmakers or editors? I don't know that I ever actively asked those questions, I just probably belligerently thought, I'll do it, if it strikes me.

SL: So, once you realised editing was for you, how did you carve out a career?

ER: That was a time, thankfully for me, when editors trained their assistants. A glorious time, when you got a job working with a specific editor. Initially it was with Martin Duffy, who edited *Sheila*, and had subsequently become freelance, and then with the wonderful Sé Merry Doyle, and they trained me up in the art of being an assistant and ergo being an editor. Because you were in the room with them, involved with the whole machinery. You saw what they did creatively, you saw what they did practically, you saw their relationship with their director, with the producer, with the audience. The whole journey was revealed. I trained on the job with them and with other editors. I was seven years as an assistant editor, until I got offered my first feature as an editor myself. I never perceived any resistance. I knew quite a number of assistant editors that were women but I didn't know any editors that were women.

SL: In 2015 women were 17 per cent of editors in UK films and in the top 250 Hollywood films of 2017 they were 17 per cent. Why do you think there aren't more women editing?

ER: I'm actually surprised at that statistic, I thought it was even lower. But there's a dearth of women across the board, in all the creative areas. Like, I was looking around at the IFTAs this year (2018); I'm not saying that's a reliable sample, but there were no women nominated in design or sound or cinematography or music. There was one woman, Úna Ní Dhongháile, in editing, and there were women in costume but there were no women in sound recording, on the floor. There's a massive demarcation. In fact, I think editing, statistically, is doing slightly better than some of the other crafts. I think, although I don't see it like this myself in any way, shape or form, I think editing is perceived as slightly passive. A support role, which couldn't be further from the truth, but that may account for the slight statistical bump for editing. Why the lack? I wonder if women, young women, are a little put off by how 'techy' it might be perceived to be? That's about both editing and, in fact, all the other crafts, cinematography, everything. They have to learn a lot of gizmos, machines and computers. I'm wondering if that's part of it?

Also lack of visibility. I'm also very, very conscious about visibility. You know, growing up when you're not seeing women doing this thing. And that's across the board, that's science as well and, having directed *The Farthest*, that's a constant conversation about women in science. You say you love the women in the film, that was a very conscious effort to make sure women were in there. And when women and young girls come to the screenings, that impression is rippling out. 'If you can see it, you can be it.' You're seeing women are scientists, you're seeing that women are top scientists, you're seeing that women are filmmakers. Young girls are writing to me – you won't believe this, Susan – every single week for a whole year now, I get letters from young girls saying,

'I'm going to go into film.' Or, 'I saw your film and I'm going to go into science.' It's extraordinary and that's a great privilege for us to be an influence. That's just one film, so the more films that women make, the more editors that are women, the more scientists that are women, the more times women get out there and start talking, the more young girls will say, yes, actually, that could be a role I could play. So maybe a little put off by the technology, maybe a lack of visibility, historically, all those ways.

SL: How do we go about challenging that resistance?

ER: There's some statistic I read about what happens to girls when they go into film school and I don't know how to explain it. They come in full of the joys of spring about being directors and screenwriters and cinematographers and by the end of the course they're all taking more support roles in production, or whatever. I don't mean that production is *just* a support role; it's an exceptionally creative, influential powerhouse of action and choice in the business, but it's not the lead creative voice. Women are choosing to be the secondary voice and allowing the alpha males to take the lead. So that's some nefarious, trickle-down thing that's happening in women's lives, in women's understanding.

The other thing worth asking is – are women not brave enough? It's hard to be the lead director, sticking your head out, taking the good reviews and the bad reviews on the chin, putting yourself forward; I'm naturally quite shy. Having to go out doing TV interviews, taking the stage, it's tough. I don't know, I think it's a whole load of things. And maybe a little bit of not knowing how important our experience is, the female gaze, in the real sense. Our gaze needs to be articulated. Maybe women … a bit like me as a child, reading all these books and not perceiving that I was being fed a diet of male experience and being peddled it as being universal. Maybe young girls aren't quite deconstructing it.

Right now, in this moment, it's about changing and challenging those assumptions. So even if it's going to take time and even if it's causing bumps and even if it's not quite right, it's actually chipping away at preconceptions. Maybe we, as women, don't think our stories are worth telling. And the culture, the film industry culture, is not a happy environment for women, in the main. On a set, it's quite male, it's quite macho. You go into production-pitching sessions – they're quite aggressive, quite cut-throat, you know? That misogyny is still in there, in the culture. Maybe women sniff it out. I'm not suggesting that women are little teeny frail things but we might happily invent a different culture, that's not quite as aggressive, if we were given the option. One that was a little bit more respectful and a little more room to talk in a different way. I find it hard with these pitching things, 'hit me in fifteen seconds'. I mean maybe we should be doing it a different way, shouldn't we? At least ask that question.

SL: What are your experiences as a female editor in a predominantly male industry? Did your gender have an impact on your career?

ER: I don't know if it impacted on the work …

SL: You've had such a hugely successful career, I think we can agree that it didn't!

ER: When you think about being in the editing room, it's very, very intimate. You're pretty exposed; it's you, a director, a producer. These people have worked hard, developed the film for a long time, and you're really carrying their baby. There's always been an awful lot of respect and thoroughness once you get in there. Have I not gotten jobs because I'm a woman? That's harder to discern. I do know that my husband – who is also an editor – gets offered more money than me for equivalent jobs. If you ask the question, they'd probably say oh he's won a BAFTA or he's got more experience. I don't know how else to deconstruct that other than to put a question mark over it. Maybe he's worth more than me, we don't know.

So being a woman in that environment … I started to really query it when I became aware of how few women directors I was working with and how few women writers I was working with, over time. I cut my first film in 1993 so at the beginning I was just delighted to be editing, to be meeting directors, getting scripts and working on films. Then over a couple of years I was like, 'Where are the women?' In fact, in over twenty years of editing feature film drama just one director was a woman. TV drama was better, documentary was slightly better again. But very few writers, very, very few. And quite a number of shorts but not actually coming on up to the next level. That was part of my motivation for getting out from behind the chair myself. We have to do this, force ourselves out of our comfort zone. Take the microphone. After a while it wore me down, the type of stories, the type of genre I was being sent.

SL: Was it a conscious decision to transition to directing?

ER: Yes and no. I directed a number of short dramas and I wanted to explore that. For various reasons, some personal and some creative, and some to do with the quality of the work I was being offered as an editor, I didn't keep pursuing that. I kept doing the shorts and going back to editing. Maybe trying to figure out was it what I wanted to do. So, yes and no, in that I was trying and then getting distracted or not one hundred per cent committing.

When I started directing documentaries … *The Farthest* was my second documentary, I co-directed the first one which was called *Here Is Cuba*; it was John Murray, who was my co-director on that, who asked me would I consider co-directing. Up to that moment I had never considered it, which is hilarious to me now. I had never considered directing documentaries. I don't even really know why but I loved it, from the minute I started. I thought, why wasn't I doing this all along because it really suits my personality. It's extremely intellectual, stimulating, challenging. It's all the good stuff but I had never really thought that through. I don't know why I thought that it wasn't for me. So it's been a conscious decision now with *The Farthest*. I directed this one on my own – John was one of my two producers. I want to continue to direct if I can, and I'm developing a number of documentaries and I'm also developing a number of dramas to direct.

SL: Let's talk about *The Farthest*. Firstly, what was the difference between co-directing and directing, was it quite a different experience for you?

ER: John and I had worked together for a number of years as director and editor so we already had a very strong relationship and we are very complementary in terms of our skill set. So in some ways we parachuted that across into *Here Is Cuba* in terms of how we worked that film. We were co-directors and discussed everything, but we looked after different areas. I developed the visual side and the storytelling style. He was very strong on the practicalities, the shooting, and he interviewed all the characters, so we already had a very nice knit, a nice sharing and collaboration. Then when I solo directed *The Farthest* he was one of my producers, so in some ways that relationship then travelled across into that.

How it was different was that I did feel the weight of being the sole director. I hadn't probably understood how wonderful it had been on *Here Is Cuba* to have another person who was up there, standing at the front with me. Suddenly to be solo, wearing that on my own, that was a bit of a shock. A wonderful shock in some ways but a bit of a shock. Bit of a baptism of fire the last year. Finding it hard then, knowing what I have to do. I have to do the Q&As, I have to do the interviews. Directing itself, I loved doing it on my own. I loved figuring it out, but I had ongoing wonderful support from John, who was still a huge voice on the film with me, as was Clare Strong, my other producer. As were, indeed, all my other core collaborators. Kate, my cinematographer, Tony Cranston, my editor. All the people you surround yourself with and I loved drawing on them, listening to them, draining them, I'm sure, for all their input. I found it really stimulating, empowering, all the good stuff.

SL: When talking about women and directing, one of the issues that often comes up is women's traditional domestic and familial responsibilities. Could you talk a little about that? Do you think the rules of the game need to change?

ER: It's a complex one. I don't have children so I have been free in editing and in direction to travel wherever the jobs are, to pick up and go. My husband's also in the film business. Tony cut *The Farthest* and he's a brilliant editor. Never asking any questions really – you're gone for six months. I've been free to live as a single man in some ways. If I'd had children it would have been a hugely different conversation. And Clare, my producer on *The Farthest*, she subsequently has had a daughter who's nearly one. How she's been working in the last few months with a daughter in the frame has been completely different for her. Your priorities, in a good way, have shifted. You don't have twenty-four hours a day to devote to the film.

What has to change about film is that it shouldn't require that level of commitment – and it's a macho thing as well. If you really care you'll be at the editing desk until two in the morning because it's the north, south, east and west of the whole thing. Whereas when you've got a family, it's not. It might be really important to you as well, of course it is, with all the money at stake, with everybody's livelihood and creativity and all that. But, actually, that macho thing about 'really show me your worth', hanging in there half the night, that would have to change. And the structure of how shoots go would have to change. I mean the director, if you have children, and you're going away for six weeks, how's that going to work with a two-year-old, or a five-year-old, or someone in school? They're all conversations to do with class, to do with nannies and money and budgets. If you were doing a big film, I presume they could fly all your family out there, wherever you're going. So there's complicated questions about how does it work? How could it work? And I don't know the answer. Do films, if they're going to have key women, do they have to have creches on site? We have to have the conversation about how it would work.

SL: We do have to have this conversation but we don't want to put young women off.

ER: I wouldn't want to make this a headline but I think part of the conversation I had in my life not to have children was an awareness of the impact it would have. That makes me sound like career over everything, but I knew … I thought to myself that's going to be a whole other life, a whole other thing. I'm trying to think of all my female friends who are at a top level in the industry and their family circumstances are all very complex. Some of them have stay-at-home partners so there's an inversion of the role, one hundred per cent. A lot of them don't have children; a lot of them maybe had children quite young and then came into their own when they were in their forties. But the men I know at the top level, they're not having that life – they're doing children and home and career all at the same time. But we're not, we're not able to.

SL: Could you have made *The Farthest* with women involved who had children? Could you have provided childcare for people?

ER: Hard to say but probably not. In most of the roles I would have needed two people, if people weren't able to do the swinging from the chandeliers at midnight for the emails. Or the chaos that descends. Maybe it's a part-time thing. You need a kind of job sharing … and even that's complicated for film because there's so much to do, so much detail – a researcher for example that was job-sharing has to then communicate with the other person and they'd be spending a third of their day prepping, for that other person. Could I have? I'd love to think I could, I don't know. I don't think I could have directed if I'd had children, or young children.

SL: It's a hard call if we can't imagine another way, isn't it?

ER: And we don't want it set in stone that this is *our* conversation to have. We actually want everyone to be part of it. I think I can imagine a model on feature drama sets where maybe there is some kind of childcare provision. There's even an editing room I can imagine, maybe a longer editing period, that didn't require having to stay late into the nights. Some of the structures, I think, can be addressed and some of them possibly can't. Maybe lower-budget stuff or feature documentaries that work on tiny crews, maybe. There's ego in part of that as well. Women producers should maybe be leading that charge but they don't want to be written off as that touchy-feely. They want to be as hardcore as everyone else.

SL: Why do you think there are more women directing documentary than feature films?

ER: Less money. Less money at stake, less money being paid. Less risk. More of a chance to be taken a chance on.

SL: Groups like Women in Film and Television Ireland (WFT) and the Equality Action Committee (EAC) representing the Writers Guild and the Screen Directors Guild are lobbying for change and working to increase the visibility of women in the industry. Do you believe enough is being done to change the landscape for Irish women in the film industry?

ER: Bit like Fianna Fáil – lots done, more to do. I think it's a fantastic moment in time and it's all due to all the noise and all the initiatives and all the cage-rattling. But absolutely more to do. The gender parity initiatives at the IFB [now Screen Ireland] and the BAI; schemes like POV [a Screen Ireland production and training scheme to support female creative talent] directed solely at women; all of these are huge in terms of turning the ship around. Producers are now looking carefully at projects for gender balance, in a way they wouldn't have done before. But is there enough being done? Never, until there are so many women directing, producing, editing, doing cinematography that I don't even *notice* who's directing and who's writing what story. I want it to be so ubiquitous, so normal. Until we get there, there won't be enough done. But everything that's being done now, I'm hugely thrilled about.

SL: What are your thoughts on positive discrimination?

ER: I'm in favour of positive discrimination until such a point that there is no need for it. You absolutely need to turn the tide and sometimes turning the tide involves doing something dramatic that maybe, outside of war time, you wouldn't want to do. I know young men and male directors and writers who feel right now that it's a very hard time for them. That they're being discriminated against. They'll probably not be able to make the stuff they want to do and I feel sorry for them. I have real empathy for them, and I agree that finding their stuff is getting sidelined may be a really difficult and unfortunate side-effect. However, the reason for that is because there's an attempt to positively rise up women's talent, women's voices, women's stories, women's crafts and actually encourage women in. And if the only way to do that is to open these doors by force, I think that that has to be done. And it has to be borne. And perhaps it's been, you know, the opposite for years for women who have felt their voices haven't been supported. Maybe it hasn't been positive discrimination towards men but it's been the equivalent of that. Unconscious bias towards male stories, male talent, male everything. I think it's unfortunate that it's needed.

SL: What about quotas?

ER: The same as positive discrimination. Quotas are more troublesome for me, while I'm in favour of them, philosophically. When I hear political parties talk about quotas I wriggle – that's tokenism of the worst sort. I hate the idea that they're going to shoehorn in this fake statistic, it troubles me terribly. However, is it how change happens? Possibly. So it's a deal with the devil, it just is. There's no easy solution. Quotas are necessary for a period of time, with reluctance.

You have to ask yourself: why does it matter? Why does it matter at all that women are behind the camera or on-screen? It matters for two huge reasons. It matters because our lives, our stories, our taste, our tone, our way of seeing, is *worth* seeing. Because we do see and experience the world in a different way and our reality is part of the experience of being human. Bit like how *The Farthest* has a sense of awe and wonder that, perhaps – *perhaps* – a male director wouldn't have done with a film about science.

The second reason is maybe the male version of the world, or the reality we are living in, hasn't worked, hasn't given us a world we're proud of, happy to be in. Maybe women's vibe, and taste, and way of running the universe, would be different. Maybe it wouldn't – Margaret Thatcher and Golda Meir and all that. But it's at least possible that if our voice, our experience, our reality was louder, then we would be in a different world than we are in now. Am I blaming men? I don't know if I am, but the world that has been set up in that image is an ugly place and that's why women's voices are needed, and not to be seen as 'other'. It's also incumbent upon women to stand up and grab the mic. So we're not only being oppressed – or are we even being oppressed? – we're shirking responsibility. Some desire for someone else to look after it. You have to step up and drive the thing, you might crash but …

SL: What advice would you give young women entering the industry?

ER: I'd say to my younger self, take the risk, you have to. Don't hang back. Because it's important to be part of the conversation. It took me all that time to direct and I'm not a shrinking violet, I had a loud voice as an editor. I'm sure all my directors would say I'm a presence in the cutting room. Hopefully for the better. Now I'm actively pursuing directing again. In fact, I've a meeting on Friday about what I think will be my next film, another feature doc. Hopefully it'll be thumbs-up and it'll be all go. I'm also in development with other feature docs and a number of feature dramas as well.

However, I'm not ready to call time on being an editor, formally or even probably. I have relationships with directors, collaborations I'd love to still continue and still plough in that field. I would like to think I could. However, momentarily, at least, I'm taking the chance to carry on being a director. So we'll see. I don't even know if the two can co-exist. I don't know mostly because of the amount of time. If I take an editing job, I'll be gone for six months. This might be my limitation but when I'm editing, I become completely absorbed, immersed in the film, and that's what your director needs and deserves. They want you right at the machine, drowning in everything that you're seeing, living and breathing it. So that person then going home and planning their next film may not be complementary. I don't know.

SL: When you're editing a film do you have to physically go where the shoot is or can you work from your home base with new technology?

ER: If the film you're editing is on location, you probably would go there for the shoot. Or at least best practice is that you'd go there for the shoot, to be close to the director and to be part of the environment where the filming is happening. While in the editing phase proper the director, the editor, and the producer at times, in the same room, working the material together, responding as they are seeing it. There's very fluid and fertile cross-pollination happening between the set and the cutting room when you're shooting.

Sometimes these days, for money reasons, they won't have the editor going with them so they have you working in your home base. It's a TV model but it's also a changing technology model. Some of that is now happening remotely, over Skype. The editor could be in Dublin, the director is in London and they're sending links. I send you a link to the new cut, you ring me. That's developing but I don't like it, at all. Ultimately, it changes the conversation. The editor becomes somebody who is given a whole load of notes and then just executes, sends them back and says, 'What do you think now?' Whereas if both of you are in place together, in the room, in the environment together, it's not so much 'I execute and you respond', it's 'We progress together.' Now maybe it's in a teething stage so that's still being figured out. I don't like it, but maybe that's not to say it can't be perfected.

Visibility is the biggest thing. I don't think we're doing enough in women's groups to deal with this. As far as I'm concerned, we should be going into schools. I was suggesting to WFT these kinds of 'pods'.

Let's say a director, a cinematographer, these little kinda roving gangs, targeted all the colleges. And we'd say to these young girls, you know, she's a designer, she's a stunt woman, we present ourselves and we chat. I know none of us has the time, it's all voluntary and this business is really intense. Maybe we should make something that schools could use. Maybe a website or an hour-long film? I'd love to go into Dún Laoghaire on week one of their four years and say to the women in the room, hold the line. How do you communicate that? And the thing about having families is certainly part of that conversation.

SL: You talked about the maleness of certain situations. Have you come across situations where the culture of the film industry was off-putting for you?

ER: Absolutely, sets can be very off-putting, even when I used to turn up as an editor. The amount of men, nobody wants to be in that kind of swamped environment. What I've experienced recently more is the culture coming down from funding and pitching that can be quite tough. It's quite combative. I don't even want to be hanging around. And you're going, why would a young girl want that? But if I'm going to direct, I guess I have to learn that language. Learn how to grow in that, swim in that pond.

SL: Have you experienced sexism yourself?

ER: I did have a bad experience with some producers and I believe it was because I was a woman. It was sexist bullying. Absolute, old-fashioned misogyny. The more I resisted, the more their ego was challenged, the worse it got for me. I'd have had a better outcome had I submitted. Definitely, I'd have had a better outcome. An uppity woman having a view did not fly. When I suggested to one of the associates that it was sexist bullying, he said, 'Oh, no, no. We treat everyone like this.' Imagine that for a defence.

SL: The young Emer looking up at the night sky and the Emer who started that degree in physics and maths and Emer who went on to make *The Farthest*, there seems to be a thread connecting all of them.

ER: Space was the absolute natural fit for me. The absolute place I wanted to set my next film. And Voyager, through conversations, became the vehicle through which I could make a film about space and science, that is exactly the way I feel about space and science. It was to tell a science story, that had science chops, some serious science chops, but is opened out into a story about wonder, a story about awe, a story about inspiration. A philosophical story about the nature of being human; all the mysteries that define our existence so that is absolutely the film I was always going to make, even though I never knew it before it happened. In some ways, that makes me sad because maybe I'll never make that again. I absolutely have made the quintessential Emer film. It's pure me. It's pure me, straight out of my childhood, it's pure me out of my dreams, all the books I read, all the thinking. Absolutely, I'm so happy with it, I'm so proud of it. And I'm so glad that the team went out so far for it, and I'm so grateful to the producers, the funders, the Irish Film Board, to everyone who encouraged me. Because it was a risk. A lot of films about space are very dry, they're very scientific, very cold. This was hoping to take a kind of emotional tilt at space and science.

It was kind of conceived as three stories weaving about each other: the central scientific story of the spacecraft and what it discovered and what it did; its curious passenger on the side of each spacecraft – the Golden Record – which is this kinda weird, mind-expanding adventure, about how would we communicate with aliens if we ever encountered any; and, finally, this epic philosophical frame for the whole thing, the cosmic questions that the contemplation of space kicks off in me. I think it kicks off in everyone. We look up at the moon, we look up at the stars, and have this consciousness-expanding experience where we go: Am I alone? What's out there? What's it all for? How did it all start? And I was really lucky that I had the support of John and Clare and the support of our funders, to make that emotional, philosophical, poetic film. It absolutely is the film I always wanted to make.

SL: You've managed to unite your two great loves, space and film.

ER: I would happily make films about space for all time. You're talking first love, you're talking real love, and you're actually talking first great love meeting second great love. Space and film and art and aesthetics and emotions and awe and all that. I used to lie on the grass in Tipperary at night clinging on to the grass, aware that the earth tumbles at a massive speed and rotates round the sun at a massive speed. I used to literally hold onto the grass thinking we're hurtling through space. And I was dreaming this place up. When I watch *The Farthest* that's what I see. Wow, I think. That's me, the young girl. My mother died when I was four and I used to lie there staring out thinking: Is she out there? Is there somebody out there? Is there anyone watching me? I'm an atheist but space became a kind of a church or a place where I could have that kind of conversation. And film is, in fact, a church too. A place where you can have conversations about existence, about your own humanity, your own mortality. So yes, *The Farthest* was a joyous coming together of all my loves.

Susan Liddy was in conversation with award-winning director/editor Emer Reynolds.

Documenting Documentary:
Liberated enclave or pink ghetto?

ANNE O'BRIEN

Introduction

Documentary has always been loosely defined and is most simply understood as non-fiction programming. It is defined partly according to subject matter, for example nature, history or education; partly by style or formal elements, such as the 'voice' of the text, a point of view that organises and presents material to the viewer; but also by its purpose, or intention 'to achieve something in addition to entertaining audiences and making money'.[1] Documentary has a long international history in the form of feature-length production for distribution to cinema theatres.[2] Since the beginning of television, documentaries have also been a central element of programming, in particular meeting the public service broadcaster's remit to entertain and inform.[3] In recent decades, documentary has been somewhat usurped by reality television, where the 'reality' documented is one heavily staged, managed and manipulated. Documentaries have lost ground to reality formats largely because the former are more expensive to produce and to market. As 'one-off', hour-long programmes, the capacity to build ratings over a series is lost, while at the same time, the cost and effort of promotion is more prohibitive for documentary than for long-running reality series. In addition, formatted reality shows can potentially be sold on international markets to recoup costs and generate revenue, which again puts traditional television documentary at a disadvantage. Corner has gone so far as to claim a post-documentary culture consisting of 'the relocation of the documentary project within revised, expanded and often considerably "lightened" terms for portraying reality'.[4] Simultaneous with the rise of reality formats and the decline of broadcast documentary there has been an increasingly wide-ranging dispersal of documentary viewing practices. New media services such as internet television, curated bundles of streaming television channels, and low-cost online subscription services all offer documentary-makers the potential to tap into a new form of documentary production that bypasses the traditional gatekeepers, and which instead facilitates documentary production directly for global platforms, such as Home Box Office (HBO) and Netflix. The latter, with 86 million subscribers in 190 countries, has licensed hundreds of documentaries, acquired new originals for distribution and developed an integrated process of production 'from pitch to premiere'.[5] In 2014 Netflix invested $US 3 billion in original content and 'issue-driven docs that drive international viewership'.[6] Netflix's entrance to the market as a major buyer, with an increased budget of $US 5 billion in 2016, was presented as encouraging for producers, 'offering big budgets, artistic freedom and access to a massive audience of subscribers'.[7] This new platform was presumed to make the genre more sustainable in terms of work and earning a living. But the use of data or an algorithm to detect audience interest, Netflix's favouring of big-name issue-documentaries, and a lack of pricing transparency are all potential downsides to the model for programme-makers.[8]

As audiences for low-cost multiscreen subscription services have continued to expand, so too the market for new media productions and overseas trade in documentary has become more significant – and complex. Newly interconnecting distribution flows have emerged across platforms – from internet television networks to cinema distribution and even film festivals, when online platform productions want to qualify for awards. As these productions become more established, with increased festival and award nominations, the question becomes how women will fare in the increased competition to produce for this more lucrative global audience. To begin to understand the future for women in documentary production it is important to map their current position and this is not an endeavour that has been undertaken extensively to date, either in an Irish or an international context. It is to that lacunae in knowledge about women's gendered experiences of contemporary documentary production in Ireland that this chapter is addressed.

Documentary and women

A number of authors have noted that media production is not gender-neutral.[9] Women account for only 25 per cent of directors, writers, producers, executive producers, editors and cinematographers in US documentary production.[10] US festivals screened twice as many documentaries directed by men than by women, and in terms of awards only eleven women have ever won Oscars in the documentary director category.[11] In the Irish case, as Liddy notes, 'the central role of the IFB (now rebranded as Screen Ireland) is to invest in Irish creative talent', but a review of the Film Board's funding decisions with regard to gender 'tells another story'.[12] According to Screen Ireland statistics, 'Combined figures for 2010 to 2015 show that 16% of production funding applications came from projects with female writers attached, 14% came from projects with female directors attached and 36% of production funding applications came from projects with female producers attached.'[13] In response to these low rates of female participation in the sector, Screen Ireland made a public commitment in 2015 to address the issue. They announced a Six Point Plan that would publish information on gender and funding, would stimulate applications from women, would offer training and mentorship for women filmmakers, would intervene in gender patterns in education, would work with state agencies on entrepreneurship schemes and would partner with other funding agencies so that 'gender equality is embedded within the decision-making process in screen content'.[14]

More recent statistics on women's participation in documentary in Ireland are positive. In 2016, Screen Ireland received twenty-three applications for documentary funding of which eleven, or 46 per cent, had female directors attached, and of thirty-four producers attached sixteen were female, a 47 per cent rate. Of those applications thirteen were successful, with 36 per cent participation from female directors and 75 per cent participation by female producers.[15] These statistics reflect a sense in both media and academic circles that the world of documentary production is more gender-inclusive and less sexist than other areas of film production. Historically, a number of women participated in early forms of international documentary production. 'Ruby Grierson made films in the 1930s and 1940s and a few women participated in experimental documentary in the 1950s and early 1960s ... but it was not until the late 1960s and 1970s that documentaries by women began to become more common.'[16] Elsewhere, there are a number of other reasons to be optimistic about women's more equal role in documentary. There are a number of key female commissioning editors working in the broadcast and online documentary sectors, such as at HBO and Netflix. In addition, women filmmakers have garnered dedicated audiences for compelling and important stories of neglected issues and lives on television, in cinema and online (Smaill, 2007).

However, other reasons remain for documentary to be perceived as female 'unfriendly'. The genre generally has poorer budgets, smaller staffs, lower barriers to entry and less prestige than other areas of filmmaking. Thus, women are caught between competing discourses of documentary as a feminist enclave of equal engagement and the lived reality of it being something of a pink ghetto, where women's contributions are still marginalised. Despite, or perhaps because of, the competing discourses, very little research has been conducted on the lived working experiences of women documentary filmmakers in Ireland. This chapter aims to contribute to such a study by exploring women's labour position in documentary-making in Ireland. It examines the extent and nature of both their engagements in and exclusions from production during the commissioning process, in preproduction, during production and at postproduction stages.

The key findings are that women have a dualistic – both positive and negative, or 'push and pull' – relationship with documentary that is evident at all stages of production. On the one hand, women are 'pulled' into documentary because they bring social and emotional skills to projects, such as a capacity for empathic engagement, but, on the other hand, they are also 'pushed' out as a minority. Their approaches to narrative and to directing are questioned, in gendered ways and in ways in which men are not challenged. Women are less likely than men to be present at meetings with commissioning editors. During preproduction, respondents propose that they are often overlooked for roles in ways that they believe are gendered, and their ability to fully inhabit certain roles are sometimes questioned. However, women are also clear that, when the opportunity presents itself, women would recruit other women in ways that negate gender stereotyping. During production, women acknowledge a gendered affinity with the social, emotional and organisational skills required to produce documentary but this does not necessarily create a 'female advantage' for them, as they can often be burdened with this work whether they want it or not, and their skills are oftentimes questioned by co-workers.[17] Finally, during postproduction, respondents have experiences of being 'pushed' out by having to fight for credit for their work, but a corresponding 'pull' dimension of that process is that the women particularly valued the collaborative nature of their work in documentary, where they are happy to share credits.

Methodology

The data was gathered through semi-structured interviews with a snow-ball sample of twenty filmmakers. Their contributions were anonymised and some details of their descriptions were changed to protect their identities. This is important because the Irish industry is small and highly networked and many of the women expressed concerns about reputational damage that might accrue if they were seen to 'cause trouble' about gendered issues. Documentary-making refers, in this chapter, to both feature and television production. This does not intend to negate key differences between the approaches, such as their diverse commissioning processes, but the study does focus on documentary as a genre in both of these modes of production. The study does not look specifically at production for online platforms as this was not something in which respondents were widely engaged. In addition, the study focuses on women who are freelance, working for, or owners of, independent companies. The research does not include women working in broadcasters' own in-house documentary units. This is largely because the in-house production of documentaries within Irish broadcasters that do not come under the remit of news and current affairs is relatively small and most commissions are channelled to the independent sector.[18]

The women interviewed were reflective with regard to their production practice and careful not to essentialise gender as a category, nor to see it as a strict binary. They were clear that it was difficult to isolate gender as an absolute variable of analysis. As one respondent put it, 'It's hard to describe the gender thing sometimes because it's your day-to-day reality. It's only when you start opening up the topic and look at men your age and see how things are going for them and think, "hang on now".'[19] Gendering is defined in this chapter as 'practices that are perceived, interpreted and/or intended as being about gender' that contribute to the social institutionalisation of gender.[20] Findings from a small snowball sample that focused on subjective and qualitative experiences of work within a specific screen genre and in a single nation state are not generalisable beyond those terms. Nonetheless, the study offers a detailed and nuanced account of the ways in which the experiences of gender are operationalised for women in documentary production. The findings that follow are structured according to four key phases of documentary production, those being commissioning, preproduction, production and postproduction.

Commissioning

In the broadcaster–publisher system, commissioning editors hold most of the power to decide on programmes in a very competitive context, where small independent producers offer a surplus of ideas. Commissioning editors frequently exercise substantial creative and editorial control over commissions and over choosing the production team to fulfil any contract awarded. During the commissioning phase a documentary producer selects a specific issue for media attention. As Zoellner notes, 'During the development phase decisions about the content, narrative structure and presentation for new programs are made that are crucial to the successive production process, concerning for instance the selection of topic, contributors and presentation.'[21] Often to increase their chances of getting contracts, on which a small independent production company often depends for survival, producers tailor proposals to match commissioning editors' requirements, known interests and tastes. 'Perceived genre traditions and professional standards and conventions combined with personal preferences, therefore, influence the judgement of documentary ideas in the development process, both at the broadcaster and in independent production companies.'[22]

While Zoellner's work expertly outlines the nature of the broadcast commissioning process, she does not consider the manner in which that process may prove to be gendered. Nor does she examine the processes through which feature films are funded. I argue that the perceived genre traditions as well as the professional standards and conventions and indeed the overarching perspective on topics, contributors and presenters that pertain to commissioning can all be gendered. By this I mean that they are normatively masculine, derived from a tradition that has always favoured and privileged male ways of thinking, perspectives on topics and patterns of working. While women participate in these traditions of production, they do so in a gendered way. On the one hand, women bring particular strengths and insights to projects, such as emotional insights and a capacity for empathic engagement. On the other hand, as a minority their approaches to narrative, their inclusion in decision-making processes and their capacity to execute commissions can all be fundamentally questioned, in gendered ways, in which men are not challenged.

Respondents observed women's capacity to engage with narrative in a highly empathic manner. As one director noted, 'I think producers look at women as more empathetic. They're good at emotional stories and social justice … Observational is about the moment, being there, and women are quite good at that, they're generally quite good at those conversations.'[23] Another director concurred that her empathic approach to narrative inspired her approach to documentary. 'I'm attracted to stories of real life, because women share a lot with each other, I'm inspired by going on emotional journeys … And putting a narrative around that attracts me.'[24] The emphasis on connection and engagement that women valued in their approach to narrative and to documentary was not something that was necessarily valued by the industry, however, and oftentimes women questioned whether their idea of narrative 'fit' within industry convention and (normatively masculine) standards of narrative, when it came to commissions or funding agencies. As one producer-director put it,

> The idea of narrative is gendered (in the sense of a patriarchal culture) because I come up all the time against more mainstream funding bodies and they say that my stuff isn't narrative enough and I say it's just a different kind of narrative but that's seen as not correct … So some women in a patriarchal culture will tell stories in that correct way and some men will not and indigenous cultures will tell stories differently but identity definitely comes into it, women and different traditions have different ways of thinking.[25]

Another dimension of the commissioning phase that respondents experienced as gendered was their exclusion from decision-making processes that occurred in meetings with commissioning editors. Women's presence in meetings with commissioning editors did not seem to be in proportion to their presence in the industry generally. As one respondent noted, 'The executive producers are mainly men, I've only worked with a couple of female-led companies.'[26] As one director put it,

> I haven't dealt that much with commissioning editors, which is interesting ... it's all about power and control because if you go into those meetings, you might get notions about yourself, you become more empowered, think you're of more value to the company, and maybe want more money or a title. So sometimes the producer will monopolise those meetings to hold you back, I'm not sure how much of this operates at a conscious level ...[27]

Gendered dynamics can result in women being disproportionately excluded from discussions with commissioners about how topics will be treated, who will contribute and how programmes will be presented, all of which is decided at commissioning phase. 'We know those conversations go on behind closed doors. "Who are you getting to direct this? Or produce this? And no, I wouldn't get them."'[28] If not actually excluded from the space, pitching for commissions was also described as a very gendered experience. As one producer-director recounted,

> It was all men in a room that we had to pitch to ... and we didn't get it. It went to a male director ... the man had never directed documentary before ... There was a level of flirtation that went on ... It was so off ... You're just not being taken seriously.[29]

Commissioning of broadcast documentaries and the greenlighting of features are premised on a perception of generic traditions, standards and conventions, which centre on particular ideals of and approaches to narrative that are not gender-neutral. Rather, these normative standards are derived from a long and continuing history of male domination in media and documentary production. While the women interviewed state that they valued alternative, feminine or empathic approaches to narrative in their own work, this was not necessarily a dimension of documentary that was overtly valued by commissioners or funders within industry, which questioned their fit with conventional mainstream narrative approaches that dominate in screen production. Thus, while women participate in those conventions, they do so from a minority position, and from a space of disproportionate exclusion in terms of their absence from senior decision-making positions in the Irish media industry.[30] While women bring expertise to projects, because of their gender and minority status within industry that expertise can be fundamentally questioned.

Women and preproduction

In the second phase of documentary-making, preproduction, recruitment of crew and participants occurs. This process was also experienced in gendered ways that were sometimes inclusive and sometimes excluded women. Respondents argued that they were overlooked for roles in production in ways that they believed were gendered and their ability to assume those roles was often questioned. However, they were also clear that, when given the opportunity, women would hire other women, oftentimes in an overt attempt to redress gender imbalance in the industry.[31] One producer-director stated that men were slow to give women a chance or opportunity as crew. 'I think that there's men who give each other jobs and they don't particularly see women at all … I've always found it amazing that nobody's given me work …'[32] Another camera operator noted, 'I've gone for meetings and men with one third of the experience I have were given the job. I don't think it's very equal.'[33] In addition to being overlooked, many women recounted having their ability questioned. A producer observed, 'I did a job for five years and then I had to interview for it, and it was given to a man. There's an automatic higher reverence for men.'[34] A researcher similarly noted the apparently automatic assumption that men could perform as crew and that women would not necessarily perform, and were automatically 'placed' in production rather than technical roles. She comments,

> I believe some gender bias exists, the belief that men are better at the more physically demanding production roles, for example camera operators, sound technicians and lighting. Most of the crews

I worked with were made up of more men than women. I think women are assumed to be better in the production or office side of the programme.[35]

This tendency was evident from the outset of women's careers, during traineeships or in entry-level roles. As one director pointed out,

At the very beginning of my career I watched very young men come into the office and be given opportunities before me. It did feel like they were trusted because they were male. I knew for a fact they weren't as experienced as me and I'd be sitting there available do to whatever it might be and they'd get given the job. And nurtured in a way around technical things, shown how to use a new camera that might have come in or given more opportunities to go out and shoot things and presumed that they could do it ... It's like I had to go out and prove myself first ... I saw men winging it until they knew what they were doing.[36]

Even an Emmy-nominated producer, Porter, noted that women experience a bias during production: '... when working with a crew you aren't familiar with – you get people challenging you in ways that I'm positive they don't challenge guys. For instance, they think you never shot an interview before.'[37]

Perhaps because of the discrimination against hiring women or maybe as an adaptation to that situation, Mortimer notes the attractiveness of feature-film documentary-making for women who do not want to have to negotiate the typical hierarchies of screen production and instead actively avoid the pecking order of crew and of 'male egos that dominate the film industry' by working alone or predominantly with other women.[38] She notes that 'when you are making a documentary you can set out on your own – you don't have to impress people, or assert authority; you can just be you'.[39] In addition to having the freedom to avoid hierarchy, a further interesting feature of increasing women's participation through practices of recruitment and crewing is that 'Both in film and in television, when you have a woman in a position to hire others, she tends to hire women at a greater rate than a man does in the same position ...'[40]

Women respondents were clear that they tend to hire other women.

> I suppose I consciously try to hire women myself, which is correcting something. There are very few women in technical roles. I know women who have gone into them and not lasted because it's so hard, so I do have a natural bias towards women, but only if they're good. It is about their merit and whether they're competent.[41]

Another director concurred.

> I've directed stuff myself and mostly worked with women ... I'm not getting paid a lot of the time for the work that I'm making, so I tend to try to do it my way with the resources that I have. So I try to work with other great people ... I get on quite well with women and we end up working together, so it's a good choice for me.[42]

Gipson, the national director of SAGindie Outreach Program, reframes the preproduction challenge of recruitment in terms of a problem inherent to men rather than one of deficiency in women. She argues, 'We have to educate our men to maybe stop looking exactly for themselves and maybe start looking for people with potential and talent.'[43] The central challenge for women was clearly articulated by Edwards: 'Making documentaries is tough all over, but ... ultimately the first people who get what they need to get going are white dudes ... The only way it's going to change is to talk about it and hire more women.'[44]

Women and production

In the production phase of documentary-making Nicholson proposes, in somewhat essentialist terms, that

> Women naturally possess the traits that you need to make a great documentary. You have to be really organized, compassionate to a fault, passionate about your subject matter, tenacious, tireless, willing to talk to pretty much anybody from any walk of life and be willing do pretty much anything to finish.[45]

Despite the tendency towards gender essentialising, nonetheless many respondents did acknowledge that women brought strong social, organisational and emotional skills to the production process. As one respondent commented,

> The team that I worked with were very strong, very independent women, so they were a great education, a great team for me to be around, in terms of everything, in terms of how to deal with people, how to brush people aside, they were a great bar for me to aspire to …[46]

Another producer-director observed, 'I think women can sometimes negotiate their way into situations that might be easier for them than it might be for men and I don't mean using their feminine wiles, but that the fact that a woman is less threatening can be an advantage.'[47]

However, the presumption of a gendered affinity with the social, emotional and organisational skills required to produce documentary does not necessarily translate into a valued 'female advantage' for women working in production.[48] Their obvious skills were something of a double-edged sword, in so far as they could often be burdened with this emotional work, whether they wanted to or not. As one director commented, 'Male directors sometimes have female researchers who do that emotional work …'[49] Another producer-director agreed: 'I think women have to take on this role of being a "mothering" type within the team … The people organising the social and supportive components of the team's life are usually the female assistants.'[50] Or as another wryly noted, 'Often men don't realise that there is any emotional labour to be done …'[51]

As well as getting left with emotional labour, which was not necessarily valued in production, in addition women were frequently questioned in the production roles that they held.[52] Directors recounted how 'the cameraman kept trying to direct all the scenes'[53] or even actively undermined them: 'I worked with cameramen occasionally in the early days and I felt like they were looking at me going, "That's a stupid shot." I felt quite undermined by them.'[54] And, 'I did run into problems with camera or sound operators giving me a bit of lip, and they probably wouldn't have said those things to men.'[55] Similarly, presenters could undermine directors in ways that were gendered. As one director notes,

Working with an older male presenter I noticed that when I was with him and a female camera op, he just didn't listen to what we were asking. He would steamroll us and then he would miss focus or walk out of shot in the wrong way. So it became a self-fulfilling prophecy because he had no faith, didn't do what we wanted and did it all in a way that would not work and we had to do it again and again.[56]

Sometimes this questioning of their ability turned into outright bullying. As one respondent recounted, 'One man was very biased against women to the point of bullying, it was very underhand, he'd treat you like you hadn't a clue … he'd never do that to any of the lads.'[57] While core social skills should result in an advantage to women during production, often it was a period in which their skills were not valued and, sometimes publicly questioned.

Women and postproduction

Finally, in the postproduction phase of documentary-making, industry literature observes the bias women experience in terms of credit allocation and their positioning with regard to awards. Two-time Oscar nominee Garbus recalls having to fight with a male production partner for a producer credit for work she had done in securing financing deals, self-financing, spending two years in production and a third in post to get the film finished.[58] Similarly, regarding awards and recognition, screenwriter Kernochan has won two Academy Awards for her non-fiction work, but notes,

> The Oscar didn't get me anywhere at all because it was assumed that Howard [co-director] did all the work and I was just the tag-along. The second Oscar, it had absolutely no effect. I think one person asked to meet with me. One! And it was just a meet and greet. It didn't lead to a job. That would have never happened with a man. Especially a young man.[59]

Irish filmmakers enumerated similar experiences with credit allocation and were clear that this was not something they believed their male peers experienced. Sometimes women were manoeuvred or written out of the jobs they had actually done on documentaries. A female camera operator did work that was beyond her assigned role but she got no recognition for it. As she recounted, 'I was shooting a documentary with a new producer, who didn't know what he was doing ... so I had to carry him, but he was credited as the producer-director and I had to shoot with no direction ... my complaints fell on deaf ears.'[60] Another woman described how she had worked as a producer-director on a programme but 'The Executive Producer would only give me a director credit and gave the producer credit to an absent man. I fully believe that was because he wanted a man to be seen to produce the series.'[61] As another producer-director recounted,

> If you negotiated the access, it was your idea and you handled all of the legal difficulties and managed the relationships, if you played a massive integral role in the production and you're given a credit that says you had a tangential role, it just isn't fair. It does seem to happen to my female colleagues more, it's never happened to my male colleagues ...'[62]

Another director had a similar experience: 'When it came to signing off there was a battle to get the credit I had understood I was getting ... in the end I almost felt maybe I don't deserve this credit?'[63] Another producer noted, 'I've produced work where people are fighting over credits; there were two instances where the women backed down.'[64]

Finally, respondents described feeling compromised when the credit due to them was questioned, but at the same time women often saw their work as fundamentally collaborative and suggested that credits could ultimately be shared. As Smaill observes in an interview with Longinotto, a feature documentary-maker, 'Perhaps more than any other contemporary film-maker, Longinotto chooses to work collaboratively on many of her projects, sharing co-direction credits with female colleagues.'[65] As Longinotto herself observes,

> I always think that if you're working with somebody very closely around a language, then it's fair to credit them as being 'co-director' because you wouldn't have been able to do it without them ... And also, it's quite good because it means they can go to the festivals with the films as well.[66]

Another Irish producer noted about her female peers, 'We have a different perspective and a different way of working. I think that women can collaborate properly … We share credits because it's a genuine collaboration not just because it's amorphous.'[67]

Conclusion

Media work is characterised by a number of patterns of gender inequality, which relate to informality, autonomy and flexibility.[68] O'Brien has shown how processes of gendering in Irish screen production operate by channelling women and men into different types of roles, where they receive differential rewards and opportunities from their work.[69] She also argues that gender impacts in complex ways on the routines of production, where it shapes the perspective applied to media content and expectations regarding the behaviour of staff.[70] The informality of recruitment and the distinct gendered challenges of networking, self-promotion and parenting while working in the globalising field further add to ongoing gender inequality.[71] Relatively little work has examined the phases of production and how gender manifests as an experience of inequality at various points in programme-making.[72] This analysis has started to explore production and the ways in which it can be experienced in ways that are ambivalent for women.

The key findings of this study are that women have a dualistic, both positive and negative, or 'push and pull', relationship with documentary that is in evidence at all phases of production. While women's emotional and social skills are valued, their presence at discussions with commissioning editors is less likely because male executive producers predominate in the industry, and during development women's capacities around narrative and directing are questioned in gendered ways that their male peers don't seem to experience. Similarly, women were overlooked for certain roles but were simultaneously more willing to recruit other women in ways that negated gender stereotyping. During production women did acknowledge a gendered affinity with the social, emotional and organisational skills required to produce documentary but this did not necessarily translate into a 'female advantage' for them as they could simply be left with this work.[73] Finally, during postproduction respondents had experiences of being 'pushed' out by having to fight for credit for their work, but a corresponding 'pull' dimension of that process was that the women particularly valued the collaborative nature of their work in documentary, where they were willing to share credits.

Many of the women interviewed offered evidence of the various ways in which they experienced an unconscious, or sometimes plainly conscious, bias against them, which was clearly gender-based. These women were largely and admirably pragmatic in their response to these biases and discriminations and were resilient and adaptive in finding ways to inhabit documentary production despite being 'pushed' out. However, because screen production is at core about the representation and reproduction of our culture, it behoves us to ensure that women have a central place on the team so that documentary production can be a feminist enclave for fair, accurate, imaginative and creative representations of women in all of their diversity and not merely a pink ghetto of marginal participation in screen production.

Changing the Conversation: Education, celebration and collaboration

Educating Gráinne: The role of education in promoting gender equality in the Irish film industry

ANNIE DOONA

The issue of the underrepresentation of women in the film industry is a topic of much debate internationally, with film industries from London to Hollywood via Sweden[1] raising the issue of the dearth of women in lead roles, both in front of and behind the camera, as actors, directors, writers, producers, editors and technical staff.[2]

The underrepresentation has been attributed to a number of factors, including conscious and unconscious bias on behalf of those, often males, working in the industry, lack of supports for women, lack of clear pathways into the industry, and the nature of the film set environment.[3] The subsequent waste of talent and potential and the lack of women's voices both on- and off-screen has also been highlighted. A range of solutions have been proposed, including positive action initiatives, women-only funding opportunities and a focus on zero tolerance of harassment or bad behaviour by those in the industry.

This chapter focuses on whether education has a role to play in addressing this underrepresentation. Can early intervention in the form of opportunities to engage with or study film through education have an impact on women's future careers in the industry? A report published by the European Women's Audio Visual Network (EWA) references film education as a factor in gender equality.[4] The EWA report showed that there are large differences between the proportion of female graduates on their way into the industry (44 per cent) and the total proportion of women who work in the industry (24 per cent). The report concluded that the high percentage of women graduating shows that the talent does exist, although not at 50 per cent, but that their potential is not being harnessed.

In Ireland, there are opportunities to study film at third level, i.e. higher education, in both the university and the institutes of technology sector and in a small number of private colleges. In 2018 there were fifteen higher education institutions offering film-based courses listed in the Central Applications Office (CAO).[5] Some of these courses are described as being primarily theoretically based, i.e. the study and analysis of films, for example Arts with Film at University College Dublin; others are described as having more of an emphasis on filmmaking skills, for example Film and Television Production at Dún Laoghaire Institute of Art, Design and Technology (IADT), or Film and TV Production at Dundalk Institute of Technology. Some higher education institutions, for example Trinity College Dublin, offer a hybrid approach with opportunities to create a short film as part of the course. Analysis of applications shows that there are gender differences in the number of applications to undergraduate film programmes, in the numbers graduating, and those working successfully in the industry.

In 2017, applications to third-level undergraduate programmes from females via the CAO ranged between 30 per cent and 70 per cent by course, although there were differences in the types of film course applications. In relation to film studies, the academic text-based and film analysis courses had higher female application rates than those that had an emphasis on practical film production. For example, between 2013 and 2017, the percentage of female applicants to Arts with Film Studies at UCD, described as a 'programme based on understanding and interpreting film', had 60 per cent female applicants. The Film Studies course at Trinity College Dublin, described as 'combining a cutting-edge intellectual environment with the opportunity to gain introductory skills in filmmaking', had 64 per cent female applicants. Courses described as having a more practical approach – more based on filmmaking – were lower in their numbers of female applicants. For example, IADT's Film and Television Production course, described as 'focusing on the advancement of practical filmmaking and television production skills, as well as developing strong and creative storytelling abilities', had an average of 36 per cent female applicants in 2013–19 while Dundalk Institute of Technology's practically based Film & Television course had an average of 43 per cent female applicants.

The policy context for film education

A report into the audio-visual industry in Ireland, published in May 2017, highlighted the need to make the film industry an attractive career destination to ensure the development of career pathways into the industry.[6] Largely absent from the report was any consideration of the gender issue, and the role education has played, and is playing, in both promoting the issue of gender equality in the film industry and in perpetuating inequality. The report does state that a detailed census should be undertaken around training and skills development and states that 'gender, disability and other diversity measures should be included'.

The recently published report by the Broadcasting Authority of Ireland (BAI), Screen Ireland (formally known as the Irish Film Board), and Crowe Horwath in respect of a strategy for the development of skills within the sector focused on the importance of education and training and the need to develop and train a multifaceted skills force which can continue to compete on the international stage.[7]

The Irish government's 2011 report *Creative Capital: Building Ireland's creative audio-visual industries* highlighted the need to develop digital and media literacy programmes for primary and post-primary education.[8]

The Irish government has placed creativity, and the development of culture in Ireland, high on the political agenda. The launch of an ambitious Creative Ireland Programme in 2017 outlined a commitment to developing creativity in every child.[9] Two key pillars of the Creative Ireland strategy, Pillar 1 and Pillar 4, are relevant to the development of the Irish film and audio-visual industry.

Pillar 1, 'Enabling the Creative Potential of Every Child', **states that** creativity begins in 'early years' education. The argument is that children flourish through creative activities such as imagining and creating roles, scripts and ideas, sharing stories and symbols of their culture, and using the creative arts to express ideas and make meaning.

Pillar 4, 'Ireland: A Centre of Excellence in Media Production', has an overarching, long-term objective of elevating the creative industries (including media, architecture, design, digital technology, fashion, food and crafts), drawing together, on an all-government basis, state agencies, industry partners and those engaged in fostering innovation in enterprise. As an initial project, the key focus will be on Ireland's potential to be a global leader in film production, TV drama, documentary, children's storytelling, and animation for the screen.

A Six Point Plan on gender equality, announced by Screen Ireland in 2016, does acknowledge and recognise the importance of education and training in addressing inequalities in the Irish film industry, articulating the need for 'early intervention in the education process', which it sees as 'an integral part of change of mind'.[10]

Therefore, a clear policy approach acknowledges that creativity in children is desirable and that education has an important role in this; film in education, with its potential to deliver creativity, digital literacy and storytelling, has a key role to play.

Previous studies have highlighted this need to develop film education formally in schools. The Irish Film Institute (IFI) produced a Screen Ireland-sponsored report on film education in schools in 2012.[11] The focus of the report was on the study of films and filmmaking, and a number of issues were raised which highlighted the need to introduce more filmmaking and content production. Some of the issues highlighted in that report, for example the lack of resources and time for teachers and the lack of understanding of film education, were raised as continuing issues by the respondents in this research; however, consideration was not given to the gender issue in this report.

My research draws on previous work that has proposed the further development of film education within formal education in Ireland, but with a particular focus on gender. I will be analysing the opportunities available to pupils and students to engage with filmmaking and production as part of their education in Ireland, both formal education and informal, and whether this contributes to the underrepresentation of women in both film education and the film industry in Ireland. Perceptions of the industry and the availability of role models are explored to assess their impact on women's intended career ambitions in film. The research will also address good practice, examining what educational bodies and the film industry can do to promote women's interest in film production and in enabling them to see film as a viable and exciting career option. Drawing on published data and using a quantitative and qualitative approach to elicit the views of educators, participants and stakeholders, the issue of how to increase opportunities to engage with film with a particular emphasis on gender will be addressed. Recommendations for educational policymakers will also be included.

Methodology

Key stakeholders across the Irish film industry were contacted to ascertain their views and understanding of the current situation in relation to filmmaking education; they were asked how gender inequality could be addressed to ensure a pipeline of successful women into the industry. A questionnaire was sent out which focused on a number of themes, including opportunities to study film in all levels of education, awareness of education-based gender incentives in film, and suggestions for how education could encourage and support gender initiatives. Respondents were also asked to identify barriers to women's full participation in the film industry.

The questionnaire was sent to key players and policymakers in film and film education. These included representatives from the key industry guilds, filmmakers, representative bodies, funding bodies, formal and informal education providers and policymaking bodies in the Irish education system.[12] The views of a sample of young women studying filmmaking and those considering a career in the film industry were sought. Responses are classified throughout by their sector and gender only, as respondents were informed that they would not be identified by name or specific organisation. In two cases, telephone interviews were conducted in lieu of a written response at the request of the participant.

Why are women underrepresented in the industry?

Initially, respondents were asked what they perceive to be the main reason for the underrepresentation of women in the film and television industry in Ireland. The responses dealt with a range of issues, many citing perceptions of the industry as male-dominated and a lack of female voices as key factors. The view was expressed that there is a hard-wired notion that men are better at creativity and that women are really playing at it. Respondents highlighted the view that the industry acts and feels like a 'boys' club', and that this is replicated on set, making entry and progression into the industry more difficult for women filmmakers. One female guild member expressed a belief that things were changing, citing her experience in Los Angeles where 'recently on a number of occasions when pitching talent to agents or streaming platforms, they only want to hear of female talent'.

Key decision-makers were perceived to be more often male than female and respondents felt that a combination of factors led to a male-dominated industry. One respondent (female informal film educator provider) did offer the view that things were beginning to change with the democratisation of the industry and the fact that young filmmakers entering the industry may be less affected by 'the old ways'.

The perception of the work involved in conjunction with the physical nature and demands of the industry were highlighted as relevant factors. Respondents suggested that the lack of women in technical roles might be a factor in many young women shying away from the technical roles on set, due to the large amount of heavy lifting and physical demand of these roles. Because of these demands, the technical areas such as camera, grip and lighting are predominantly male and this too is viewed as potentially unattractive to most females, who see it as a macho-driven environment. This was not felt to be necessarily intrinsic to the industry of the future, with the need for a modernisation of the film workplace raised, with one respondent (female director) citing the continuing 'macho environment affecting all' as an issue. The issue of caring responsibilities and the challenges of working in the film industry was raised by a male careers advisor, who suggested it was important to challenge stereotypes and gender positioning in terms of caring responsibilities, stating that 'This way there is a possibility of a ground up approach, a new cohort of graduates who will question and critically analyse this way of living and working, who hopefully will then endeavour to effect change from within.'

Three respondents proffered the view that the technical departments and other sections of the film industry are going to be the hardest culture to change. A number of the third-level students stated that they were aware of the demanding and sometimes physical nature of the industry, but as one said, 'As long as people were prepared for that then it should not be an issue.' One suggested that many occupations had similar tough regimes and long hours, citing hospital doctors as her comparator, but she was not aware that this was a reason for women not to consider those jobs.

Many respondents felt that industry itself has a responsibility to deal with this issue. The view was that men who work in the sector are obviously working under conditions that in the modern workplace are surely unacceptable, and that the industry needs to be more generally family and carer friendly. 'Anecdotally,' said one female project manager, 'I am reminded of a friend of a friend who missed his own father's funeral so as not to miss the first day of shooting a film – such was the long period between jobs and the fact that he would get pushed down the contact list for future work.'

Interestingly, three of the respondents referred to the role of women themselves in perpetuating gender inequalities. Two of them stated that women in the industry that have made it into the positions of power are partly responsible for not bringing others with them; one respondent suggested that some women in the industry might not even be aware of the issue. One female third-level lecturer quoted a friend who was wary of recommending female students as she knew the demands on them to be available day and night.

The lack of understanding by parents and teachers of the film industry and the opportunities and careers available within it was mentioned by most respondents as a barrier to young women entering the industry. It was stated by two members of guilds, one female and one male, that the film industry is still seen by many parents and indeed teachers as a male domain, partly due to a lack of role models, and partly because of the perception – sometimes accurate – of it being a hard and unforgiving industry.

Some respondents felt that parental reluctance to encourage their children to pursue a career in film centred on their lack of understanding of film and on perceptions of underlying uncertainty in income and career progression. The *Film Focus: New directions in film and media literacy* report from IFI/Screen Ireland highlighted parents as key influencers on young people's choice as to what to study at third level. Other influences, including career guidance counsellors, were also seen as not having knowledge of the film courses available. One female third-level student pointed out that her parents and career advisor had no real clue about filmmaking courses: 'My careers advisor at school thought I wanted to do film studies; she did not seem to be aware of film production courses at all.'

A variety of reasons were therefore given as to why women are underrepresented in the film industry. I was interested next in how third-level providers viewed film in education, and what could be done to encourage more women into film courses and into equal participation within the industry.

Third-level film education

Respondents were aware of the range of film courses available at third level and also of the limitations on studying film prior to entering third level. My focus with third level was about ascertaining the views of respondents as to what could be done in relation to gender awareness and facilitating women's entry into the industry.

Staff in third-level institutions that offer practical filmmaking programmes were asked if they were involved in any gender-specific initiatives to encourage women into film. While most said that they were aware of the gender issue, only two reported that they were taking any gender-specific actions to encourage more women into the industry. Two projects were mentioned: one institution was a partner in a Creative Europe Project, Women@Arts, aimed at restoring gender parity to a number of areas including filmmaking, lens-based media and new digital tendencies using masterclasses. The second project cited was IADT's 'Young Women in Film and Television' – an annual event that works specifically with young women in schools, and uses women working in the industry as mentors and role models in a three-day filmmaking series of masterclasses.

Some respondents said they were aware of the issue and were considering how to proceed in relation to gender equality. Most believed that involving successful women currently working in the industry, sending them into schools to work with and motivate young women and to act as role models, would be helpful. Two third-level lecturers said that they would like to develop this area but were unsure how to and would welcome collaboration with other institutes of higher education across Ireland to develop a consistent approach to gender inequality in the creative industries.

Respondents raised the issue of access to and ease of use of technology, suggesting that it was important to break down the barriers of 'a male sphere' (female third-level lecturer). One suggested hanging pictures of women beside as much technology as possible to break down the bias of women not getting up close and comfortable with cameras. As one female third-level student said, 'The guys appear more comfortable with the technology and will tend to take it over.'

Staff attitudes, staff training and the actions of staff were raised as important issues, with the need for unconscious bias training being highlighted. One female lecturer stated, 'We are influencing the hearts and minds of young people, we have to be aware of the inequalities, accept that there is a problem and take steps to change.' Nearly all the respondents advocated the use of role models to promote women in the industry. Providing training in confidence-building was also suggested, with one female student stating, 'I used to be assertive but when working with men it has often fizzled out or I end up being made to feel stupid.'

Students also raised the issue of what and how they were taught, including offering consideration of the need for lecturers to 'shut down casual misogyny among students and be leaders' (female third-level student).

The content of student work and films shown to students were also felt to be important topics to address. Laura Mulvey's concept of the male gaze as a way of defining how visual arts and cinema depict the world from a male point of view is relevant here.[13] Students commented on the types of films shown to them in class, seeking an equal representation of women, both in front of and behind the camera. One male head of department also raised the issue of tackling the subject matter of student films and how women are represented, saying, 'I'm not going to accept another student film with a woman locked in the boot of a car.'

A number of specific and practical supports for women on courses were also suggested: some involved providing monetary help, supports or scholarships and mentor programmes, while funding young women to attend film festivals, and to travel abroad to markets and festivals were also seen as good ways of engaging women in the industry. As one female third-level lecturer said, 'Film festivals are a unique opportunity to talk directly with your target audience in large groups. Provide free workshops for them to attend and engage with them on a personal level in a more informal setting.'

Responses from some students, both male and female, were mixed in relation to women-only sessions. Most who had attended were positive about the sessions as being good for awareness-raising, offering a chance to share experiences and ideas. However, some articulated that they would rather be part of mixed groups so as not to feel 'patronised', or so that men would also become more aware of the issues around gender, suggesting that it was important to include men to find and create solutions to the problems in the industry. One female student suggested that she felt single-sex groupings 'only encourage us to segregate men and women further like a boys' and girls' club when it should just be one club'.

One female student, who had attended a women-only event with industry involvement, felt that a more positive approach needed to be taken: 'I like women-only sessions, but I want to hear success stories from women in the industry. In the end, everyone just complained how hard it was to be successful as women to make it for forty minutes.'

Respondents also felt that alumni success stories, graduate profiles, and news of awards related to female film graduates could all contribute to a stronger image of the role of women in film, and help to 'push through the glass ceiling or rise up from the sticky floor' (female head of department).

An issue raised by most respondents was the limited opportunities to study film at primary and second level, which if addressed would give young women more understanding of film, its career paths, and a better grounding in the subject prior to entering third level. This became the focus of a section of the questionnaire.

Filmmaking at primary level

Respondents were asked what their understanding was of the opportunities available to young people of primary school age to engage with filmmaking, both informally and formally. Most responded that they were aware that many young people are engaging with content-making from a young age. As one respondent said, 'Children now are engaging much more with audio-visual content creation and consumption across a range of platforms than previous generations. Access to creativity, digital learning and literacy are all-important' (female guild member).

Another respondent commented, 'The irony is that the children of today are already making small films on their phone from the age of six and are more film-literate than any generation gone before' (female guild member).

When asked what opportunities they were aware of through the primary school curriculum for engagement with film, most were not aware of formal opportunities in the curriculum, although many were aware that arts, music, drama and, increasingly, technology all did form part of most primary schools' work. Some respondents were also aware of the work of the Professional Development Service for Teachers (PDST), a nationwide support, staff development and training service, and they believed that the PDST did offer training in audio-visual skills, technology and filmmaking for teachers. Some respondents commented that, although there was potential to use film and to engage with content-making, there were a number of factors that could make this difficult. Feedback from schools and from those involved in developing education at primary level was that often the skills and interest of the staff, and the resources and technology available, are determining factors in how much a school engages with the potential of filmmaking. It therefore seems that children, whether boys or girls, do not have adequate access to filmmaking through the curriculum prior to third level.

When asked what would help to develop filmmaking in primary schools, the respondents had a range of ideas, some of which focused on curriculum content: one primary school teacher suggested that embedding technology in the classroom across all subjects would help develop digital and visual literacy skills. A female guild member suggested that the skilled merging of storytelling in the form of creative writing, drama, dance, photography, film and painting would develop creativity in children. Nearly all the responses stated that the best film education would start at primary level and include all these facets of film. This increased access to film education would potentially engage more young women and girls in film and visual literacy. As one male industry body member stated, 'If we were to develop any kind of future film industry, I would argue that an educational awareness of filmmaking needs to happen from primary school.'

Responses from representatives and members of the industry guilds indicated that they felt they would have a role to play in primary schools' development of film education, and in raising the issue of gender, with one female guild member saying, 'At our last board meeting, the issue of gender equality came up and the board agreed that visiting schools was the answer – primary schools.'

When asked about non-formal opportunities for filmmaking offered outside of the school classroom, respondents at all levels were aware of many opportunities for primary school children to engage with film and content-making. Among those cited were Film in Schools (FÍS) and the Young Irish Film Makers (YIFM) projects.

FÍS is a project that introduces teachers to the filmmaking process and embeds the creative use of technology in Irish primary-school classrooms. The primary-school filmmaking project is the cornerstone of the FÍS suite of initiatives, working with project partners, the PDST.

FÍS actively encourages schools to display their films in school, in their community, or in local or national festivals such as the FÍS Film Festival, and was commended by some respondents for raising awareness of film at an early age.

In terms of gender participation in FÍS between 2015 and 2018, more mixed or 'boys only' schools participated than 'girls only' schools. In terms of staff involvement, 47 per cent of teachers participating were male (male teachers comprise 13 per cent of nationwide primary-school teachers) and 53 per cent were female (female teachers represent 87 per cent of nationwide primary-school staff). Therefore more male teachers were actively involved proportionally in FÍS than female teachers. This could be important in perpetuating the view that filmmaking is a male domain. It also needs to be explored whether the lack of experience in using technology, highlighted earlier, could be a factor in the gender imbalance here.

Another project that respondents cited was Young Irish Filmmakers (YIFM), which offers a range of film and animation programmes to young people from ages eight to eighteen years. YIFM has dedicated film-training facilitators who offer countrywide programmes to schools, community groups and youth organisations. The majority of work in schools is carried out with Transition Year (TY) and School Completion Programmes, although some work takes place at primary level.

With regard to YIFM initiatives, the gender breakdown of participants over the past three years has been 40 per cent female and 60 per cent male. YIFM has made a conscious effort, at all levels of their programmes, to encourage gender diversity and participation, and has been a partner, at third level, in gender in film initiatives including the IADT's Young Women in Film and Television project.

YIFM state that gender balance, respect and equality have always been an intrinsic part of their work practice. Each year YIFM collects data around gender representation on all their programmes, both locally and nationally. This data is collated and reviewed, forming an integral part of an annual programme review and planning process. An example of a positive initiative is the National Youth Film School, which has

50/50 gender balance as a requirement for funding, which Screen Ireland provides. This funding requirement is a positive step towards gender parity in the sector. YIFM also state that they make every effort to reflect gender balance among the crew of film mentors working with the young filmmakers, providing positive role models for both genders. 'It is our belief that advocacy work of this nature, supported by gender balance funding requirements, will promote greater balance across the audio-visual sector for the future' (male, YIFM).

Several respondents did say that role models and diverse images should be used early in primary school in order to have an impact, pointing out that 'STEM [Science, Technology, Engineering and Mathematics] has recognised that this is important in terms of science and maths so we should be doing this in terms of the creative subjects too' (female education policymaker).

Three of the respondents did state that, in their view, gender might not be such an issue at primary-school level. Their view was that, in general, primary children might be more willing to work together, try out a variety of roles, and be involved in all aspects of projects than older students.

Respondents did, however, raise the issue of gender and access to technology: 'It's important to make sure that if technology is used in school, it is being used equally, and not being hogged by the boys' (male primary school teacher).

Second level

Respondents were also asked about opportunities for film study and gender initiatives at second level. The vast majority of pupils transfer to second level school when they have completed their full first-level course, generally at about twelve years of age. Schools are largely state-funded (with some fee-paying schools) and all follow the same state-prescribed curriculum and take the same state public examinations. The second-level education sector comprises a junior cycle and a senior cycle. The junior cycle engages students with a number of subjects, including art, craft and design, English, technology and visual art. Formal opportunities to engage with filmmaking at junior cycle as part of the examined curriculum are limited, although there are opportunities in the new English curriculum to study film.

The new junior cycle English curriculum has ten films listed under its recommended texts. Over recent years, films such as *ET: The extra terrestrial* by Steven Spielberg, *Life Is Beautiful* by Roberto Benigni, *Spirited Away* by Hayao Miyazaki, and *In America* by Jim Sheridan have featured.

For the Junior Certificate examination in 2018, none of the prescribed films were directed by a woman; in addition to the ten prescribed films, there were additional short films and of these additional short films, two out of eleven were directed by women.

Many respondents were aware of the limited availability of opportunities at junior cycle but there was awareness that informal education and projects similar to those available in the primary cycle were how most young people engaged with film. Most did not highlight any formal opportunities other than through English, although this was generally understood to be the study of films rather than film production or content-making.

Respondents were aware of a junior cycle short course in film studies available for teachers who are interested, which covers film appreciation, critical thinking and media literacy. Respondents were also aware that there had been the introduction of a Digital Media Literacy Short course in the junior cycle technology syllabus, although there was no indication from any respondent of a gender dimension to this. Respondents were also aware that there had been the introduction of Digital Media Literacy in the junior cycle short course technology syllabus.

Respondents also pointed out that the IFI, FÍS and Fresh Film Festival developed a short course in film. The course was created with guidance from the National Council for Curriculum and Assessment (NCCA), and appears to be offered purely as an online resource, i.e. there will be no taught/delivered element to it. Respondents could not identify any formal opportunities in the junior cycle that were specifically related to gender, again other than teacher-initiated projects if they had an interest in this area.

Senior cycle

At senior cycle, students normally study six or seven main subjects from a prescribed list. The English curriculum does reference the study of film, but again, this is a text-based syllabus. In the Leaving Certificate Applied

English and Communication module, Units 3 & 4 cover Television and Film, but this is more theoretical in content than practical or hands-on. The Leaving Certificate English curriculum references the study of film and scriptwriting but not the actual making/production of a film. The list of prescribed films for English Leaving Certificate texts for 2018 has six major titles, none of which was directed by a woman.

When asked about opportunities to study film as part of the senior cycle, respondents were clear that, although there were some opportunities, these were limited and did not focus on practical filmmaking skills. A new Moving Image module based around film appreciation and cinema visits was developed for TY students and piloted in 2005 and 2006. The results of an internal review of the module carried out by the IFI were very positive. While the teachers and students welcomed the opportunity to study films, one of the challenges of the project was identified as the lack of time and resources to carry out a practical element.

A number of TY initiatives were mentioned, but these were viewed as projects based on student and staff interest, and were not regarded as being part of the formal examined curriculum. As one third-level female student stated, 'In my school, we had a chance to make films and do drama as part of our Transition Year, which was great, but it was not part of the Leaving Cert as such.'

When asked about gender-specific initiatives around film at second level, most respondents stated that this was not a feature of the formal school syllabus. Two projects were cited: one was IADT's Young Women in Film and Television project and the other was the IFI Spotlight events on Women in Film, which, although not specifically targeted at second level, were seen to be good events at raising awareness on gender issues.

Respondents had a number of ideas in relation to promoting filmmaking and tackling gender inequality in film education at second level, with one saying that the Film in English syllabus needs reforming to be more *Hurt Locker* and less Steven Spielberg (female educational policymaker).

The view was that in order to develop a pipeline of women into third-level film courses and into industry, second level needs reforming. This would help to develop a more functioning audio-visual sector – in terms not only of gender but also diversity. Informal short courses in film, which include the subject matter of gender equality and representation, were seen to be desirable. A mix of film-watching, making and critical analysis in groups and individually through reflective writing was also proposed. 'The idea would be to develop a space where the young people question and critique the current "norms" in film today' (male informal film education provider). Respondents highlighted the importance of gender as a key component of this new approach.

Conclusion

Although around 40 per cent of students on filmmaking programmes at third level in Ireland are female, there are few opportunities to participate in filmmaking formally at primary and second level, and few projects based around women in film. Opportunities that do exist are largely informal and outside of the curriculum. Recent reforms of the curriculum responding to the needs of industry have placed digital and visual literacy as important skills in Ireland's development. Progress has been made in identifying the issues in relation to STEM; what has been absent is a clear recognition that filmmaking in education could contribute to the development of a number of key skills. Perhaps there is a need to follow STEM's example and have a strongly focused campaign to promote the technology-based nature of the industry, in order to capitalise on the government's stated intention to develop and support technology-based sectors through a series of policy frameworks.

Recommendations for policymakers

There are a number of recommendations for policymakers arising out of this study into gender and film education in Ireland:

• Introduction of audio filmmaking to young girls and women early in their education

• Introduction of audio-visual literacy and filmmaking as mainstream curriculum subjects

• Provision of training to enable staff to tackle issues of gender inequality and gender representation from a young age

• Provision of formal staff training and development in practical skills

- Provision of appropriate and additional technology and staff resource allocation

- Introduction of supported women-only projects and initiatives in schools

- Encouragement of the use of role models and mentors in education

- Provision of positive action visual displays for schools and third-level institutions

- Continued formal consultation with industry on how to tackle this issue

A seamless and coherent multi-agency approach to film education in Ireland is needed, led by Screen Ireland and Screen Skills Ireland in partnership with schools, educational policymakers, third level and the industry. If we can do this, then we can attract more young people, and specifically girls, to develop a passion for filmmaking at a young age that continues through their school and college career; and if we consistently tackle issues of inequality throughout film education, then perhaps we can help to change the gender imbalance in the Irish film industry.

Activism through Celebration: The role of the Dublin Feminist Film Festival in supporting women in Irish film, 2014–17

KARLA HEALION, AILEEN O'DRISCOLL, JENNIFER O'MEARA, KATIE STONE

This chapter will examine the activist potential of the annual Dublin Feminist Film Festival (DFFF). Launched in 2014, it was one of the first film events of its kind in Ireland to pursue an explicitly feminist agenda.[1] In the following, former and current members of the organising committee consider the origins and development of the festival in the context of other contemporary Irish women's activist movements, such as 'Waking the Feminists' and the Abortion Rights Campaign, as well as the festival's engagement with, and support from, the wider Dublin arts scene. Our contribution will outline the mission statement of the festival, which uses a programme of short films, features and special events to showcase women's diverse contribution to the film industry. During the 2017 festival, for instance, the DFFF brought a programme of ten international features and nine short films to a total audience of 415 people over three days. Although the festival includes offerings from diverse global locations, each programme to date has worked to highlight and celebrate the work of emerging and established Irish women in film. Through three case studies, the second part of this chapter argues that the DFFF provides a valuable space for working through issues related to women in cinema in terms of Irish productions, distribution, exhibition and criticism. These cases are chosen because they illuminate our conception of what is 'feminist' about film and 'activist' about our festival. First, we discuss the screening of Vivienne Dick's *She Had Her Gun All Ready* (1978) and *The Irreducible Difference of the Other* (2013) against the background of DFFF's objective to draw the attention of the Irish film-going public to lesser-known filmmakers. Explicating the experimental aspects of Dick's internationally renowned work and contextualising it provides a fitting example of DFFF's determination to programme avant-garde works. Secondly, chosen in part because its sold-out 2015 screening indicates a significant public interest in the film and its subject matter, we explain that screening Lelia Doolan's *Bernadette: Notes on a Political Journey* (2011) provided the opportunity to consider women's place in the male-dominated worlds of politics and film, as well as women's achievements in social justice movements. Finally, with the 2016 screening of Anne Crilly's *Mother Ireland* (1988), we emphasised the important role that film plays in shaping our ideas about femininity and women's social roles. Our screening of this film exemplifies DFFF's activist ethos in engaging with feminist topics that encourage reflection and review the changing material and symbolic status of Irish women, and is therefore an interesting case to consider. The accompanying panel discussion 'Women's Voices in Media Industries' reiterated that the production of more diverse and more complex stories is dependent on women's participation in high-level roles across the industry. To close, we reflect on the activist potential and limitations of feminist film festivals.

Our approach in this chapter is informed by scholarship on the relationship between feminist theory and practice. In her study of the New York Women's Video Festival, which ran from 1972 to 1980, Melinda Barlow examines the benefits of festival-based cultural activism. Referring to a similar question posed in the festival's 1976 catalogue, she asks, 'Why should women, who constitute more than half of the US population, need a special showcase for their work?'[2] Variations on this question remain one of the most frequent that we hear when publicising the DFFF in the mainstream media. Barlow offers an effective answer, explaining that 'a specialized forum' is more effective for bringing the work of women to public attention. The ongoing need for such women-focused fora is confirmed by a brief survey of the programmes from Irish film festivals. In the three years before the launch of the DFFF, for example, on average women directed only 18 per cent of the films shown at the Audi Dublin International Film Festival.[3] This figure mirrors the male bias in high-level creative roles within the film industry. According to Liddy (2015), between 1993 and 2013 only 13 per cent of Irish-produced screenplays were written by women.[4] Recent gender statistics published by Screen Ireland show, moreover, that in 2018 only 31 per cent of applications for Irish Production funding had a female director attached. Of the Irish Production films completed, 45 per cent had a female writer (up from 20 per cent the previous year), 36 per cent had a female director (an increase of 16 per cent), and 73 per cent had a female producer.[5] These figures suggest that the Six Point Plan on gender equality, introduced in December 2015, is bearing some fruit.

The DFFF symbolically alludes to women's historical lack of representation in and by the industry in its very form: the event does not take place in a cinema but in a small theatre. It has never used film or even DCP (Digital Cinema Package) files for screenings; rather, we play discs or high-resolution computer files from a projector. Notwithstanding the essentially grassroots structure, approach and tone of the event, or perhaps because of it, the founders of the DFFF hope to redress the gender imbalance in the film industry through an event that celebrates female artists. We thus share Claire Johnston's conviction that feminist film events help to open up spaces 'in which the transformation of the relationship between production, distribution, exhibition and criticism could be worked through and from which strategies could be forged'.[6] Since Johnston's influential article, which takes the 'Feminism and Cinema Event' at the 1979 Edinburgh Film Festival as its starting point, a growing body of literature on film festivals has emphasised the role that festivals play in film culture – and society more broadly – as circuits of distribution and exhibition. Of particular relevance is the volume *Film Festivals and Activism* (2012), edited by Leshu Torchin and Dina Iordanova, which conceptualises the specific nature and possibilities of advocacy in this context. The DFFF aligns best with what Torchin terms 'cultural activism', a form of advocacy that operates by providing venues and opportunities to filmmakers whose work might otherwise be marginalised by systemic imbalances of power in the film industry.[7] In this respect, women's and feminist festivals share motivations with festivals that screen media representing or produced by LGBT groups or people of colour. As Skadi Loist and Ger Zielinski note in their study of media activism and queer film festivals from the late 1970s onwards, 'Gay film festivals were established as much to re-present [sic] gays to an interested audience as to provide a showcase for gay filmmakers who had few, or no, other opportunities to screen their work publicly.'[8] The agenda of the DFFF is similarly two-pronged, focused on both representing a diverse range of women on-screen and providing a designated venue for short and feature-length productions by female writers and directors working in Ireland and abroad. The festival especially wishes to draw attention to Irish women filmmakers who have been overshadowed in recent decades by the international commercial success of directors like Jim Sheridan, Neil Jordan and Lenny Abrahamson. Beyond celebrating female filmmakers, we hope to inspire and empower others to get involved in filmmaking and production by creating a networking space for those who care about women's cinema, women in cinema and, of course, women in society. Furthermore, we donate all profits to a women's charity.

This affiliation allows the festival to marry theory and practice. As Johnston notes, the interplay between the two has been a priority of the women's movement, which has always sought 'to construct knowledge of the nature and causes of women's oppression in order to devise strategies for social transformation'.[9] Such transformation, she implies, is more likely when attention is paid to the relationship between text, subject and historical conjuncture, rather than analysing films purely in terms of the content of the film 'text'. The DFFF puts this idea into practice through panel discussions that foreground relevant cultural and political contexts. For instance, Jennifer O'Meara's introductory talk on 'The Achievements of Women in Film' at the 2015 festival purposefully included references not only to filmmakers but also to the various female film scholars working in Irish universities. Her aim was to draw attention to the bias towards male film critics in Ireland's popular media. Similarly, the programme notes for the respective festivals indicate any political issues that shaped the production of the films being screened. In 2016, for example, we showed *Margarita, with a Straw* (dir. Shonali Bose, 2014), a film about the sexual awakening of a bisexual young woman with cerebral palsy. As we explained in the programme notes, this film was 'one of the first Hindi films to get LGBTQ sex scenes past a strict board of censors'.[10] This aspect of the film's production served as a reminder of how far Ireland has progressed in relation to LGBT issues, particularly since the legalisation of same-sex marriage in 2015. It also reminded Irish audiences that such freedoms are not universal. The simultaneously local and global perspective of the DFFF was emphasised by the fact that *Margarita, with a Straw* shared the programme with Anne Crilly's *Mother Ireland*, which was censored by British television because of restrictions introduced by Douglas Hurd in 1988.

At this point, it is worth considering Sophie Mayer's discussion of what is 'new' about feminist cinema in the twenty-first century. For the

London-based film curator, critic and scholar, feminist cinema today is marked by 'its negotiation of a transgenerational feminist film history of four decades within a reflexive awareness of the interruption and re-vision of feminism, and interconnectedly of film cultures, in the new millennium'.[11] Mayer's summation relates well to the various components of the DFFF analysed here: the intergenerational dialogue created when featuring Irish women filmmakers from the past alongside those of the next generation(s); the connections the DFFF has established with other women's rights groups in Ireland, feminist film festivals (London), and distributors (the US-based Women Make Movies); the ways in which the identity politics and digital technologies of the twenty-first century have influenced the film and festival landscape in which DFFF operates. As well as allowing grassroots events like ours to stream films, new digital technologies enable filmmakers to submit their works to festivals online. For instance, in 2016 DFFF began using FilmFreeway to accept submissions to its Short Film Competition, receiving ninety-seven entries in the first year. Such platforms facilitate DFFF's attempts to create a programme that is inclusive and intersectional, one organised and publicised using digital platforms and social media, including a website as well as Facebook, Twitter and Instagram. The festival has also made use of mailing lists, not only to engage with attendees, but also to seek feedback after the festival. Thus, while Barlow identifies the importance of the New York Women's Video Festival using a 'graffiti booth' to record feedback from attendees,[12] digital technologies now allow for less obtrusive ways for attendees to provide anonymous feedback and suggestions for the festival. Social media channels have also allowed engaged attendees to provide unsolicited feedback immediately, or to share events with their friends and followers.

Such networks are a vital element of our ambition to bring feminist ideas to a wider audience. With a self-proclaimed nostalgia for the US mass feminist movement of the 1970s, Alexandra Juhasz criticises the insularity of theory-based feminist film studies that 'has steadily transformed into an expert's language that speaks almost solely to its own and other academic disciplines'.[13] She urges feminist scholars to 'reinvest' in feminist media practice and politics: 'Join a group; speak your specialist knowledge about feminism and media there, in a language your comrades can understand; use these political goals to locate or even produce new and relevant texts.'[14] A commitment to making specialist knowledge more accessible has intuitively underpinned our programming decisions. What is more, we have established a presence in the local cultural community, not least through our links with Trinity College Dublin, Maynooth University and Dublin City University, our annual fundraising feminist table quiz, as well as our sister gig 'Coup d'état', held at the Tivoli Backstage in 2016. By engaging with a variety of industry and academic stakeholders, we are a truly interdisciplinary festival that provides a variety of frameworks for the public to engage with art.

Through such collaborations, we believe that we can debunk the myth that women as creators and filmmakers must constantly reinvent the wheel by creating opportunities for networking and engagement between audiences, the film industry, and academia. In the past, we have worked with the noted short film programmer Eibh Collins, who hosted a panel with directors on our competition shortlist in 2016, and Cara Holmes, the only filmmaker whose work we have screened more than once. By creating opportunities for engagement with audiences and film industry experts, we also hope to help up-and-coming filmmakers to establish a reputation and develop links with industry insiders. For the 2017 festival, moreover, we selected the theme 'Feminist Futures' in a conscious effort to steer away from the canon and showcase fresh perspectives, limiting the programme to films released since 2010. We also invited Nora Moriarty to run a workshop entitled 'Make a Movie on Your Phone' with thirteen- to seventeen-year-old girls. As Mary Celeste Kearney recognises, women's film festivals can play a vital role in encouraging more girls and young women to become involved in the masculine world of filmmaking. Crucially, Kearney argues that girls-only workshops provide a safe environment for them to get to grips with equipment and feel empowered to make films that celebrate their experiences.[15]

Using her experience of attending the Seoul Women's Film Festival as an example, Juhasz explains that such yearly events allow women to 'use feminist films to better understand their lives, history and the role of cinema in these matters'.[16] Accordingly, our artistic vision prioritises films that challenge society to reject stereotypes, help us to understand our identities, desires, and relationships, and bring pleasure by celebrating (Irish) women's achievements. Writing about the Uist Eco Film Festival in rural Scotland, Torchin notes there can be a distinct value to festivals with such a 'local' focus that brings a community together, rather than primarily aiming to change the minds of audiences from further afield.[17] In that case, a festival with discussions partly held in Gaelic was particularly valuable for exploring questions of conservation in a community where individuals had suffered losses due to soil erosion and major weather events. In a similar manner, the DFFF caters to those segments of the Irish public that have a renewed interest in watching films that highlight the institutional struggles still facing Irish women today. It seems apt that the DFFF was founded two years after Savita Halappanavar died from sepsis at Galway University Hospital after being denied an emergency termination to end a non-viable pregnancy. Her death triggered renewed efforts to repeal the 1983 Eighth Amendment to the Irish Constitution, which affords equal right to life to a pregnant woman and her unborn child. In 2015, the year after the inaugural DFFF, the 'Waking the Feminists' movement in Irish theatre was born in response to the Abbey Theatre's announcement of a male-dominated centenary programme. Much as 'Waking the Feminists' has been described as 'a grassroots movement' that aims to 'put the spotlight on a new wave of female playwrights, directors and other creatives', the DFFF refocused attention on women filmmakers, both at home in Ireland and abroad.[18] What is more, the screening of Irish political documentaries like *Mother Ireland* and *Bernadette* can take on new meaning when reviewed in the context of Ireland in the second decade of the twenty-first century.

Torchin notes that while programming is an important aspect of any film festival, unique considerations determine the line-up of activist festivals.[19] A programme may choose to prioritise the representation of marginalised groups, to call attention to political issues, or to screen underappreciated works. These considerations are central to the programming decisions of the DFFF. In direct response to the film festival brochures we had been used to seeing, the criteria for film selection are simple: every film has to be directed by a woman. Our commitment to inclusive art is also reflected in our programmes, which are committed to showcasing documentary, fictional, and experimental films, as well as work by non-heteronormative women and women of colour. Secondly, political considerations informed our decision to screen films such as *Trapped*, Dawn Porter's 2016 documentary about the impact of TRAP (Targeted Regulation of Abortion Providers) laws in states such as Texas and Alabama, which was shown at the festival in 2017. Choosing to screen a film that tapped into the issues at the heart of the emergent Repeal the Eighth movement, we acknowledged that, to quote Iordanova, 'topical debates are probably the single most important feature' when it comes to a festival's potential for activism.[20] Thirdly, most years we commit to showcasing neglected works, often of an avant-garde nature, as well as films that have been forgotten or purposely marginalised. In 2016, therefore, we expanded the scope of the festival to include a non-traditional film experience. Local electronic musicians provided a live soundtrack to *The Seashell and the Clergyman* (1928), directed by pioneering (and soon forgotten) female director Germaine Dulac. This event allowed audiences to engage in modern and innovative ways with silent film. By including a mix of recent and older films in our programme, we provide opportunities for new generations to engage with classics of feminist cinema. To return to Torchin, such 'representational interventions may challenge the expected aesthetics'.[21] The following case studies demonstrate how our programmes seek to juxtapose films that portray a wide palette of female experience with works that develop a feminist aesthetic, thus challenging the norms and exclusions of the culture industry.

Case study one:
Vivienne Dick's *She Had Her Gun All Ready* (1978) and *The Irreducible Difference of the Other* (2013)

At the inaugural festival, we felt that it was crucial to recognise and appreciate the work of some of the most important female filmmakers in the country. For this reason, we decided to dedicate the closing event to Vivienne Dick, screening *She Had Her Gun All Ready* (1978) and *The Irreducible Difference of the Other* (2013) followed by a Q&A with the filmmaker. Dick has been lauded globally for her work and is revered within the artistic community, perhaps more so than in traditional film communities. In fact, Dick was one of the originators of the New York No Wave movement, which, as Eileen Leahy notes, 'brought avant-garde experimental film into bars and clubs, screening trash Super 8 short films alongside punk bands and performances'.[22]

She Had Her Gun All Ready, Dick's second film, cemented her avant-garde credentials. For Jim Hoberman, it is her 'most compact and accessible narrative'.[23] The film features underground icon Lydia Lunch in one of her first roles and depicts her antagonistic struggle against a passive foil, played by another fixture of the No Wave scene, Pat Place. As critic Karyn Kay résumés, the film 'speaks the contemporary unspeakable: women's anger and hatred of women at the crucial moment of overpowering identification and obsessional thralldom'.[24] *She Had Her Gun All Ready* is not merely about the dichotomous tension between these two exceptional female figures, it also tells the story of normal people and New York, the city so synonymous with Dick's early years. In so doing, the film draws on four traditions that Hoberman has identified as integral to narrow-gauge filmmaking, not least the psychodrama.[25] In addition, Dick fuses a gritty home-movie aesthetic with the perspective of a *flâneur* observing the city. The attempt to capture the megalopolis on lo-fi Super 8 produces an 'ironic spectacle, in which the filmmaker's visionary ambition is continually played off against the paucity of … her means'.[26] With an expressive style and wild edge, Dick's camera tracks the figures from the Lower East Side and New York's famous punk mecca, St Mark's Place, to Coney Island, where the confrontation between Lunch and Place reaches its violent climax. As Hoberman remarks in his review for *The Village Voice*, 'Dick's attempt to keep them in frame as the rollercoaster goes into its horrendous first drop ends the film in an exhilarating, totally kinetic jumble'.[27] Under the lens are not merely the sights and sounds of the prototypical US city but also the dark underbelly of American culture. As Connolly notes, references to stalkers and serial killers add a feminist edge to Dick's broader 'exploration of "Americana" through myth and popular iconography'.[28] Her critique of popular culture and its representation of women is reinforced by her choice of medium, which rejects the 'oligarchy' and 'prodigal values of the larger culture industry', as Hoberman eloquently summarises.[29] Not only is Dick's work uncompromisingly artistic, it seems to encapsulate perfectly theoretical conceptions of 'feminist film' as a kind of 'counter cinema'.[30] All of this makes Dick a formidable feminist filmmaker, of course, 'for the master's tools will never dismantle the master's house', as Audre Lorde famously claimed.[31]

The title of Dick's more recent film *The Irreducible Difference of the Other* (2013) contains an explicit nod to the work of feminist philosopher

Luce Irigaray. The homage expresses Dick's concern with the recognition of difference and otherness as ethical desiderata. It is also a clue as to the underlying feminist message of the film. Dick rebukes the patriarchal techniques of mainstream film by eschewing traditional narrative forms and instead using experimental techniques, which include Franco-Irish actress Olwen Fouéré inhabiting two personae, avant-garde dramatist Antonin Artaud and Russian poet Anna Akhmatova. Likewise, the film uses a wide palette of shots and sounds to emphasise distinctions between her subjects, from a roof-gardener in Cairo to the chief personae. As Leahy explains, the 'weaving together of disparate sounds and images posi[t] our interrelatedness as humans and challeng[e] the prevailing understanding of relationships in terms of power, where one group or individual affirms themselves through dominating another'.[32] In fact, the film includes references to the Iraq War, the Arab Spring, and recent protests against austerity in Ireland. Leahy perceives traces of the No Wave aesthetic in Dick's latest film, for example in 'some of the audio (the performed-sound sequence by Suzanne Walsh which focuses on a close-up of her mouth at a microphone)' and 'the party sequences in which a bright red colour dominates'.[33] Such echoes of earlier films bridge the past and present in a film that is fundamentally about the possibilities of connection and relation in a world dominated by conflict and alienation.

Case study two:
Lelia Doolan's *Bernadette: Notes on a Political Journey* (2011)

Similar to Dick, Lelia Doolan is a stalwart of independent cinema. It is not uncommon for evaluations of her contribution to Irish cultural and cinematic life to cite former Archbishop of Dublin John Charles McQuaid, who once described Doolan as 'mad, bad, and dangerous'.[34] Such a 'badge of honour' (as luminary of the Irish and international screen, Fionnula Flanagan, puts it) attests to Doolan's formidable character, unconventionality, talent and influence.[35] She was heavily involved in the early years of the newly established Irish public service broadcaster RTÉ, initially in acting and presenting roles before turning to producing and directing. Doolan is particularly credited for her work developing one of the first Irish soap operas, *The Riordans* (1965–79), as well as her involvement in the seminal current affairs programme *7 Days* (1966–76). Doolan went on to become artistic director of the Abbey Theatre from 1971 to 1973 before moving on to Queen's University Belfast to undertake a doctorate in anthropology, meanwhile becoming heavily involved in the social and political life of the city. In the 1980s, she moved to Galway. Her love for the city and appreciation of the power of art, culture and film to enrich people's lives led to her negotiating the terms of her role as chairperson of the IFB; among other things, she insisted to the then minister for culture, Michael D. Higgins, that the IFB be located in Galway. Doolan's role in this organisation and her involvement in setting up the now internationally acclaimed Galway Film Fleadh cemented her position as a figurehead for a changing and maturing Irish film industry.

This legacy was at the forefront of our minds when we put together the programme for DFFF 2015. Our decision to screen Doolan's 2011 documentary feature *Bernadette: Notes on a Political Journey* in part reflected our commitment to showcasing the best films made by Irish women alongside renowned and less well-known international work. Moreover, we relished the opportunity to remind the audience of the history of feminist and socialist activist Bernadette Devlin McAliskey, born in Cookstown, County Tyrone, who acted at the heart of the civil rights movement in Northern Ireland, which united Protestants and Catholics in the fight against poverty and discrimination.[36] She became the youngest woman elected to the parliament of the United Kingdom in 1969, having run as an independent 'Unity' candidate. In 1974, she co-founded the Irish Republican Socialist Party. | Less than a decade later, she survived an assassination attempt by the Ulster Freedom Fighters. Through all this, Devlin McAliskey witnessed first-hand, and played a part in, some of the pivotal events of twentieth-century history, including the Battle of the Bogside and Bloody Sunday.

As Jerry Whyte notes, then, the political journey evoked in the title of Doolan's film 'is both Devlin's and Ireland's'.[37] The documentary combines archival footage with recent interviews between Doolan and Devlin McAliskey spanning the decade prior to the film's release. These interviews shape the narrative of the film. Doolan astutely recognised that her intended focus on the political ideas and opinions of Devlin McAliskey would best be captured by allowing her protagonist to 'decide what she wanted to say, and I was merely putting it into place as we went along'.[38] Devlin McAliskey appreciated this sensitivity and generosity, which reflects the radically collaborative ethos of much feminist research and art. In giving Devlin McAliskey the opportunity to articulate and expand on the various strands of feminist, socialist and republican thought that underpinned her activism, Doolan affords the viewer an insight into this figure's deeply held beliefs and principles. Liz Greene emphasises the novelty of this approach, musing that 'it is still uncommon to make a documentary film about political ideas and not focus on personality'.[39] This observation especially holds true for biopics about noteworthy women from history, which all too often obscure the achievements of the women in question by instead focusing on titillating aspects of their private lives.

The filmmaker's own political ideology, rooted in an ethics of equality, fairness and justice, facilitates her incisive treatment of Devlin McAliskey's life and activism. Doolan uses montage sequences of the civil rights movement, Battle of the Bogside, and the Troubles to weave together complex ideas and social commentary. For Greene, these sequences bear the hallmarks of what she calls 'clashes'. That is to say, rather than adopting a wide-lens angle to observe street violence, the montages immerse the viewer in the action. They 'follow and track the protestors as they oppose State repression'.[40] Doolan underscores these 'clashes' effectively with music, using Leonard Cohen's song 'Everybody Knows' during a montage sequence showing a civil rights protest in 1968. The theme of retrospection is emphasised through this song, 'written about a position of looking back'. As Greene adds, however, there is a tension between this music and the tone of the film: 'Cohen's song is about defeat and pessimism and yet the film is centred on struggle and optimism.'[41] Nonetheless, ending in the present, with images of political candidates who espouse socialist principles, the film suggests the perseverance of the social struggles for which Devlin McAliskey first advocated in the 1960s, not least inequality and capitalist oppression.[42]

Similar tensions were reflected in the panel discussion that followed the screening, which offered the opportunity to discuss the joys and challenges of creating in an Irish context. Doolan was joined by Maeve Connolly (lecturer in Film and Animation, IADT), Jesse Jones (filmmaker and visual artist), Tess Motherway (documentary filmmaker and festival director at Dublin Doc Fest), and Maria Pramaggiore (Head of Media Studies, Maynooth University). The title of the panel ('Forms of Feminist Film: Fiction, Non-fiction, Experimental') reflected the fact that the programme of DFFF 2015 included a range of short and feature-length documentaries and experimental films, as well as more mainstream fictional narratives. Drawing on their own backgrounds, the panellists considered the relative merits of these forms in terms of funding and screening opportunities. Questions raised included whether, for women filmmakers, the decision to make a short or a feature is typically an artistic choice, or something determined by financial constraints, the kinds of challenges and opportunities that exist when recording women's real-life experiences in documentaries, and the impact of digital media (such as the use of crowd-sourcing, self-distribution, or streaming) on women filmmakers. The panel was conceived to allow the audience to reflect on the diverse range of feminist cinema represented at the festival and the importance of recording women's real-life experiences on-screen.

Case study three:
Anne Crilly's *Mother Ireland* (1988)

The cultural and political status of Irish women has always informed the decision-making process at the DFFF. Screening Anne Crilly's film *Mother Ireland* allowed us to marry these concerns with the theme for DFFF 2016: 'Othered Voices: The female voice on screen'. Produced by Derry Film and Video with support from Britain's Channel 4, Crilly's documentary offers a fascinating account of how the motif of a mythical 'Mother Ireland' (also known as *Kathleen Ni Houlihan* or *Sean-Bhean Bhocht*) served to marginalise women in public, political, social and cultural life. Crilly situates the historical roots of her film in nationalist culture of the seventeenth and eighteenth centuries, when, 'due to reasons of political censorship (Ireland's political situation couldn't be discussed), Ireland was personified as a woman – whose allies had to come from France or Spain to help her fight'.[43] This discourse conceived Irish women's rightful and dutiful place in the home as nurturers and carers of their men.

Centuries later, this mythical image continued to underpin a cultural imaginary that compressed the multidimensionality and complexity of female experience into the emblematic image of the stoic, suffering and silent mother. Crilly's film measures how this myth matched up to the reality of women in political life, above all in feminist and nationalist culture. *Mother Ireland* includes interviews with noted Irish women historians, journalists, filmmakers and activists. It thus gives voice to a mute icon, by allowing Irish women to express their relationship with the imagery. For example, one of the documentary's contributors, Mairéad Farrell, an IRA member shot dead in controversial circumstances months after filming was completed, reveals that she and fellow female inmates at Armagh prison would cynically joke, 'Mother Ireland, get off our back.' They rejected this figure because 'it didn't reflect what we believed in'. Furthermore, the 1980s witnessed a growing rejection and resistance to this motif amongst feminists.[44] Irish feminists well understood the need to step out of the shadow of 'Mother Ireland' in order to push back against reductive and constraining depictions of Irish womanhood. By way of illustration, filmmaker Pat Murphy claimed that, on balance, Mother Ireland

> is not a positive image, the associations I have with it are not positive ones, I actually think it's a wrong thing to do – to call a country after a woman – because it gets into those kind of areas where a country is to be won, or penetrated, or ploughed … And it means that women aren't seen for themselves.[45]

In other words, associating Ireland, Irishness and nationalism with a static set of feminised characteristics robs women of a framework that is flexible enough to allow them to express the diversity and multiplicity of their personalities, talents, sexualities, political persuasions and ambitions – in ways that would enable them to live full, empowered and dignified human lives. As A.K. Martin notes, the symbolic burden on Irish women 'involves very real material consequences for body, self, and nation', most notably sexual repression and abuse, and patriarchal double standards, not to mention the reproductive restrictions endured by generations of Irish women.[46]

These issues came to bear on the discussions that comprised the closing panel of DFFF in 2016: 'Othered Voices: Women's Voices in Media Industries'. The participants included writer-director-producers Nicky Gogan and Margo Harkin, as well as members of the Department of Media Studies at Maynooth University: Sarah Arnold, Anne O'Brien and Maria Pramaggiore. Iordanova notes that unlike Q&A sessions at mainstream festivals – which tend to focus on the film's making and message – discussions at activist festivals can 'go beyond the film and address the issues that the film is concerned with, as well as to influence the thinking of the audience'.[47] Accordingly, our panel incorporated ideas around the voice, literal and figurative, and how women's voices are heard, or not, in the industry. Such a focus on 'instances of control' aligns DFFF with other activist festivals discussed by Iordanova that are committed to renouncing censorship, which can undermine artistic creativity and potentially also interfere with a human rights agenda.[48] The censorship of *Mother Ireland* is a case in point. When originally broadcast, two segments were removed from the film, one showing human rights activist Emma Groves after she had been shot with a rubber bullet by a British soldier and one featuring Christy Moore's song 'Unfinished Revolution'. It is ironic that Crilly's production was the first programme to fall victim to the British broadcasting ban given the documentary's broader aim of underscoring how cultural and stereotypical images of Ireland as a woman have influenced an idealised version of femininity within Irish society.[49] At a moment when the country was poised for a referendum on repealing the 1983 Eighth Amendment, such a fully rounded recap of Irish women's current material and mythic position was certainly timely.

Conclusion

Factoring the relationship between film, subject and historical conjuncture into programming decisions has allowed the festival to benefit from, and provide a platform for, women working in Irish cinema and media. It is also a pragmatic set-up, given that events focused around international guests would be prohibitively expensive for a group with grassroots origins and fundraising aims. In our history so far, moreover, we have remained conscious of our commitment to offer celluloid reminders of how far Irish women have had to travel in a considerably short period, all the while acknowledging how far we still have to go in order to achieve full equality. Simultaneously, we endeavour to advocate for film's ability to explore issues pertinent to this complex. When considering the potential impact of activist festivals like the DFFF, Torchin makes two important arguments. First, she problematises the view that audiences can and should be immediately transformed upon viewing activist films, or that exposure to activist festivals 'inevitably leads to action'.[50] Secondly, she reflects on the phrase 'preaching to the converted', which is often directed at activist festivals or documentaries by the news media as a way of questioning – and, perhaps, undermining – film's activist potential. Even if festivals do preach to the converted, however, there is value in that process. As Torchin explains, festivals can serve as 'places for renewal of commitment' to a given issue.[51] What is more, even if those in attendance at DFFF screenings, talks and panels already make an effort to support media produced by women, a feminist film festival can function as what Torchin terms 'a performative platform'.[52] For the local and national media coverage received by festivals like the DFFF keeps the underrepresentation of women in the Irish film industry in the news. Our event serves as an annual reminder to organisations like Screen Ireland and the Irish Film Institute that more work must be done to achieve equality in production and exhibition.

What If We Had Been the Heroes of the Maze and Long Kesh? Collaborative filmmaking in Northern Ireland

LAURA AGUIAR

Introduction

The title of this chapter is taken from Sue Thornham's *What If I Had Been the Hero?* (2012) in which she suggests that if women are not put at the centre of their narratives, 'a single gender reversal of hero/heroine, activity/passivity, subject/object produces outcomes that self-evidently don't work'.[1] When women are the heroes, whether as characters or interviewees, they are the main subjects of the story, not its secondary objects, they are given agency and, as a result, may cease thinking like victims and become empowered. Being the hero is a state of being and action. For women to be the heroes, questions of agency, subjectivity, narrative, desire and the gendered ordering of space and time must be addressed throughout the filmmaking process and in the film itself.

This chapter explores how a collaborative approach to filmmaking[2] can not only address the power imbalance between filmmakers and participants, but also help place women at the centre of the male-dominated history of the 'Troubles' in Northern Ireland – the thirty-year period of political violence which left almost four thousand people dead and over forty thousand injured.[3] The chapter examines the practice-led methodology adopted, which consisted of making the sixty-minute documentary film *We Were There*, in collaboration with the Prisons Memory Archive (PMA), and writing a critical reflection of the process. The PMA was created by film scholar and practitioner Professor Cahal McLaughlin and is a collection of filmed interviews with people who had a connection with Armagh Gaol and the Maze and Long Kesh Prison during the Troubles. The former prison served as the only female prison, while the latter housed mostly male paramilitary prisoners, from

1971 to 2000. Some of the major events of the conflict centred on, originated from, and were transformed by prisons, turning these places into symbolic heritage sites.[4]

Drawing on literature on women and war, I begin with a discussion on how war history has been gendered and how this has influenced its cinematic depictions. As will be noted, women's active participation in the Troubles, particularly in relation to imprisonment, has been largely confined to the margins of historical and filmic discourses. I then explore how Irish filmmakers, such as Pat Murphy, Maeve Murphy and Margo Harkin, have questioned historical stereotypes and proposed alternatives that show the diverse, multifaceted and dynamic roles that women played during the conflict. Drawing on participants' and audience responses, I conclude with some of the lessons learnt in my research and demonstrate how the adoption of a gender-sensitive lens and a collaborative filmmaking framework is paramount to addressing the gap between media representations of women and their lived experiences of war.

The research

In the summers of 2006 and 2007 the PMA brought 175 men and women back to the empty Maze/Long Kesh Prison and Armagh Gaol sites to record their memories as prisoners, visitors and workers. Participants were recorded inside the empty prisons by a single camera operator who followed them while they walked and talked around the buildings. This way, they acted as co-authors of their stories. Co-ownership and the right to veto or withdrawal were also given to each participant. This ethical framework motivated me to conduct my research with the PMA. My work with them began in the postproduction phase, four years after all the interviews were recorded and digitised, and my task consisted of selecting some of the recorded material and turning it into a linear film. Motivated by the near absence of women's diverse lived experiences in cinematic depictions of the Maze and Long Kesh Prison, I selected ten interviews (out of twenty-three) which featured female relatives of prisoners and staff and female prison workers.

The research was divided into four phases (pre-editing, rough cut editing, fine cut editing, and screening) and in each phase I met the project's director Cahal McLaughlin regularly and carried out semi-structured individual interviews with participants to document our discussions of rough cuts and our aesthetic and ethical decisions. As '[r]ealistic parameters of participation are particularly critical in the editing stage' of films and often requires 'more time than most community collaborators have to contribute', I kept control of the technical part of it, that is the editing on the software Final Cut Pro.[5]

In our encounters we would decide the inclusion and exclusion of parts of the recordings and the addition of images of the prison, soundtrack, and on-screen text. This approach ensured that the participants' earlier role as co-authors during the filming process – they were recorded while they walked and talked with little probing from camera operators – was maintained throughout the editing as well. Hence, consent was ongoing and not a single document to be signed at the beginning or end of the project. On completion, participants were invited to attend screenings and take part in panel discussions in as many cases as was feasible.

Gender and war

Understanding the context within which wars take place and the cultural, narrational, linguistic and subjective implications for film production is paramount to any attempt to represent women's multiple relations to war. However, when exploring this relationship it is important to regard women not as a monolithic group, but as individuals whose experiences are influenced by a range of factors, including age, economic class, race, tribe, ethnicity, religion, sexuality, culture, geographic location and national identity.

Although relatively new, scholarship on gender and war has focused on four key areas: structural power relations, gendered identities, gendered institutions, and gender as a meaning system.[6] This scholarship has demonstrated that women's diverse experiences before, during and after warfare have often been relegated to absence, silence and marginality in historical discourse.[7] Indeed, one does not have to delve very far into war history or war cinema to uncover persuasive evidence that what has been mostly represented is 'the record of warfare – of conquest and revolution, of battles fought and treaties signed, of military and political tactics, of great leaders, and of heroes and enemies'.[8] As a result, men have often been represented as 'away and in danger' while women have been portrayed as the relative who 'waits and worries' about their loved ones.[9]

Institutions such as the military and the church have used gender as a way of mobilising identities and organising access to power, resources and authority, particularly in periods of war. The military, for instance, 'not only employ and manipulate ideas about masculinity to accomplish their ends, but are equally dependent upon manipulating ideas about femininity as well'.[10] Critical scrutiny of the connection between gender and military helps us understand why fighting has often been regarded as a male practice: with men being perceived as soldiers and the heroes of war, one way of protecting this masculinised view of war has been by reinforcing the idea of femininity. It comes as no surprise then that women, subsequently, have often been depicted as naturally compassionate and supportive to the male hero and as victims of armed conflict.

Women and the Troubles

While making *We Were There* it was also important to understand Northern Ireland's context and how institutions such as paramilitary organisations and the church have created myths and reinforced the dichotomy between feminine/passive/private and masculine/active/public in Northern Ireland. For instance, within nationalist areas Ireland's folk history of strong Celtic goddesses has contributed to public cultural representations of the nation as female while England is seen as 'the male aggressor, coming to rape and plunder this beautiful, tragic woman, this sorrowing mother-figure'.[11] Women, thus, as the eternal sufferers works as a metaphor for Ireland's oppression.[12] Femininity, particularly Irish motherhood, has often been identified with the Virgin Mary due to the Catholic Church's strong influence in everyday life. As Lorraine Dowler notes, '[Virgin Mary] can simultaneously embody a sense of the private (mother, nurturer and sacrifice), and of the public (victims, martyrs and casualties)'.[13]

Within loyalist areas, there 'is no equivalent symbolic role for women in Protestantism, where worship of the Virgin Mary is strongly condemned ... Unionism is associated with conquest and settlement, its imagery triumphalist and masculine.'[14] Unlike their nationalist/Catholic counterparts, there are no heroines; there is only the figure of Britannia, which has often been used as a symbol of British imperial power and unity. Nevertheless, the similarities between these two opposing paramilitary and religious myths lie in the saturated images of violent/active male and victimised/passive female. Moreover, women from all sides also share the marginalisation of the Northern Irish peace process which has been mostly 'all-male',[15] despite the efforts of many groups, including the Women's Coalition, a political party which played a key role in the inter-party talks that led to the Good Friday Agreement in 1998. Therefore, the narrative remained for the most part 'all about men' and domesticated the peace process even further rather than opening up discussions on the politics of class or gender within the family.

Challenging Troubles history and films

When sourcing literature on women and the Troubles, one strand that can be found is of studies examining women's experiences as victims of, for instance, domestic violence and imprisonment.[16] There is also a growing literature exploring the complexities of women's activism in various women's and community groups, such as the Relatives Action Committee (RAC), as well as looking at women's active roles in loyalist and republican paramilitary groups.[17]

When sourcing Irish cinema, one can easily see how the Troubles have been 'the distinctive feature' of fiction and non-fiction films about Northern Ireland for the last forty years, making it difficult to find a film 'that does not deal with the impact of the conflict in some way or other'.[18] Fiction films, in particular, have been mostly focused on the paramilitary struggle (usually the IRA) in a world nearly always portrayed as male territory, while the voices of women have remained, for the most part, marginalised, sometimes virtually absent.[19]

Even on the occasions when women are given a certain prominence in the plot, their involvement in the conflict is often underplayed or their roles are restricted to that of the victim or sacrificial mother or wife, the romantic heroine or the violent femme fatale. Brian McIlroy's quick survey of characters highlights this point: the 'apolitical Dee in *Angel* (1982); terrorist fanatic Jude in *The Crying Game* (1992); mercurial Matron in *High Boot Benny* (1994); victimised Marcella in *Cal* (1984);

anguished Kathleen and Annie in *Some Mother's Son* (1996); and politically passive Maggie in *The Boxer* (1997)'.[20] Therefore, one could argue that these cinematic representations of women have continually reinforced the conventional division between women/private sphere of emotions and men/public sphere of action and politics.

By contrast, female filmmakers have explored women's complex lived experiences and employed 'strategies to disrupt the audience's passive acceptance of the myths surrounding Irish nationalism and, in particular, the symbolic use of women'.[21] Their fiction and non-fiction films reveal a multifaceted portrayal of women and their concerns around nationalism, women's movements, reproductive choice, religious pressures and class structure as well as day-to-day problems.

Pat Murphy's *Maeve* (1982) was one of the first films to tackle representations of Irish nationalist history and is regarded as setting the stage for feminist filmmakers after her.[22] Set in Belfast during the Troubles, the film follows Maeve's return to her native home after a long absence in London, and her political conversations with family members and an old boyfriend who have differing viewpoints. Anne Crilly's *Mother Ireland* (1988) draws on personal interviews and archival footage to explore 'how Ireland is portrayed as a woman in Irish culture and how this image developed as a nationalist motif'.[23] Margo Harkin's *Hush-a-Bye Baby* (1990), about teenage pregnancy during the Troubles, critiques two issues still controversial in Ireland today: female sexuality and reproduction.

Imprisonment – of a loved one and of women themselves – has also been a central issue. Orla Walsh's *The Visit* (1992) centres on a wife's physical (and mental) journey to visit her husband in prison and highlights how women deal with material conditions, such as commuting to the prison, and with sexuality, mainly the expectations of being a prisoner's wife. Maeve Murphy's *Silent Grace* (2004) and Melissa Thompson's *Voices of Irish Women Political Prisoners* (2004) uncover republican women's experiences of imprisonment. By exploring women's relationship with violence and paramilitarism and the specific contexts within which these operate, Thompson's and Murphy's films challenge the view of female prisoners as victims and as apolitical.

While these films have been successful in challenging gender stereotypes, they also highlight how Troubles cinema has been, for the most part, overtly focused on republicanism/nationalism. Subsequently, they raise a further question: why is there a dearth of unionist women making films? In-depth interpretations of such absence are beyond the remit of this chapter; however, it could be suggested that this may be connected to how women have learnt to speak out: while nationalist/republican women have actively participated in protests, unionist/loyalist women have received less community encouragement to speak publicly. As Rosemary Sales notes, the 'public face of the Protestant community is overwhelmingly male, represented by male political and Church leaders', and the ties of this community to the Union 'make it even more difficult for Protestant women to challenge the authority of "their" state and political leaders'.[24]

It was only in the early 2000s that films with more plural female perspectives, particularly non-fiction films, began to emerge. Jolene Mairs and Cahal McLaughlin's *Unseen Women: Stories from Armagh Gaol* (2011) and McLaughlin's *Armagh Stories: Voices from the Gaol* (2015) include stories of women from mixed backgrounds who were imprisoned or worked in the prison and deal with issues such as motherhood, strip-searching and paramilitarism. Similarly, Margo Harkin's *The Far Side of Range* (2012) follows dramatist Teya Sepinuck and a group of women from mixed backgrounds as they develop a play about their experiences of the Troubles.

What is common in all the films analysed here is that they have, within their particular aims and methodologies, challenged the assumption that women are passive bystanders of a male war. By questioning myths about motherhood, sexuality and imprisonment, these films have revealed the multi-layered and complex roles that women played throughout the Troubles. While such questioning is a positive and much-needed development in Troubles cinema, no film has yet offered a thorough exploration of the women's plural experiences of the Maze and Long Kesh Prison. As will be demonstrated, this informed many of my creative choices when editing *We Were There*.

Lessons from making *We Were There*

This context motivated many of my filmic choices when selecting parts from the PMA to make *We Were There*. While watching the twenty-three interviews featuring women, I searched for participants who would enable the film to transcend differences of affiliation – whether political, social or religious – and to privilege the human story over the historical context. The same rationale was applied when selecting parts of participants' recordings to feature in the film. This selection was further negotiated with participants who either vetoed (i.e. asked not to include it), or suggested a different part that they felt was more representative of their story.

Therefore, every cut, every re-arranging of parts, every addition of soundtrack, visuals and texts was motivated by my attempt to show the plurality of female experiences, their active roles in their homes, in the prison and in the Troubles, the effect of the prison in their lives (as workers or as relatives of someone who was there), and how they were not simply victims of the conflict but also important agents of change. This collaborative approach extended the PMA's co-authorship and co-ownership protocols to the editing phase: while the walk/talk approach adopted by the PMA enabled women to decide what stories would be told during the filming process, our meetings between rough cuts gave participants control over how their stories would be re-contextualised and re-told in a linear film during the editing process.

Sharing authorship with participants at the editing stage enabled me to create narratives that were adequately contextualised and deemed respectful by them, and played a significant role in the shaping of the film and in any subsequent meaning that derives from it. It shows that unless a relationship of trust is developed with participants, 'we can have no confidence that our research on women's lives and consciousness accurately represents what is significant to them in their everyday lives, and thus has validity in that sense'.[25]

The collaborative approach was welcomed by all participants as they felt they could take on the role of co-directors and co-editors of their own stories, regaining a significant sense of power and control over their own representation. The approach was cited as a major factor in their decision to take part in the PMA and be actively involved in the editing of We Were There. One prisoner's relative, for instance, found that it 'made a massive difference' as she knew that 'nobody would try to hijack it or depict one side or another, demonise anyone, just to tell stories'.[26] However, it would be naive to assume that sharing authorship automatically means that 'all the perspectives of various contributors can be combined into a kind of composite conglomerate'.[27] We all belong to different socio-economic classes, have certain assumptions and views and when we work together these differences will not necessarily be suddenly overcome.

Differences were visible, for example, when negotiating the representation of the republican hunger strike period.[28] While republican participants believed that the event deserved a long section in the film because of its importance for Irish history, other participants believed that this was just a small fraction of what happened in the prison and thought a brief mention was enough. As the director of the PMA, McLaughlin was particularly concerned with the film over-emphasising the republican narrative if much screen time was devoted to it. I, in turn, was less inclined to offer much attention to this story because the recordings did not offer much detail on how the strikes affected women on a human level. Nevertheless, we discussed these different viewpoints and were able to reach an agreement to offer a brief section which was considered fair by all collaborators. This clearly shows that sharing authorship 'does not require agreement on all things, but a mutual commitment to talk things through, to reach a common understanding, and to respect considered differences.[29]

It is equally important to acknowledge that sharing authorship does not necessarily guarantee equal sharing of tasks, and that people will have different roles and responsibilities throughout the filmmaking process. Our different roles were clear from the beginning and, as a result, there was more a sense of trust rather than a desire to control the editing process. As one participant put it, 'Of course you had the bigger picture in your head in terms of how it is going to work but I felt that you actually listened and talked about things, even if something may not have worked.'[30]

This shows that having the 'expert' (filmmaker) in charge of the process does not undermine the attempt to share authorship, as long as there is an expressed commitment to engage in dialogue and negotiation with a willingness to listen to participants' concerns. If there is no such commitment, then there is always the danger that the filmmaker remains as 'the real author, with the participants being simply brought in to legitimate a collaborative rubber stamp'.[31] This commitment is fundamental when working in places such as Northern Ireland where people have not only been segregated from one another, but also constantly over-researched and misrepresented by the media.

Furthermore, participants pointed out that being involved in the editing process enabled them to develop a critical awareness of how representations are constructed by the media. For women who have previously experienced misrepresentation, this awareness may help restore their trust in the media as they see that filmmaking can be ethical and beneficial. For those who will be recorded again, this awareness could better prepare them to deal with the process and ensure that it will be as beneficial as possible for them.

The participants' close involvement in this project also enabled them to acknowledge their co-authorship of not only the film but also of the history of the prison, which has been hitherto male-centred. As one of the workers noted, 'It was historically a very interesting and important time and the whole peace process was born there and we were part of it … it is a very affirming thing to see yourself.'[32] This acknowledgement was subsequently important when bringing the film to more critical audiences, such as the Belfast Film Festival, where a man complained angrily about the constant demonisation of prison officers and humanisation of prisoners in films about the Troubles. I shared the post-screening discussion panel with seven participants and we all addressed his comment in a calm and respectful tone and highlighted the importance of hearing all stories. Despite the anxieties of not knowing how audiences would react, it was apparent that the collaborative approach contributed in some way to participants' engagement with the audience as they felt confident to stand by the film if it came under criticism.

Speaking nearby

Some film scholars argue that female filmmakers are more likely than their male counterparts to make films where 'women are the heroes'. Janice Welsch, for example, observes that, in most cases, female documentary-makers make films differently from men as they use particular language, film techniques, narrative and visual discourses: 'Not only do the documentaries thematically address issues germane to women, within women-centred contexts, but the structures and techniques employed further punctuate and interrogate the feminist discourse.'[33]

However, it could be misleading to suggest that male directors cannot address issues germane to women. Stephen Burke's *After '68* (1993) can exemplify this point. Burke's film tells the story of teenage Frieda and her mother, who leave Derry/Londonderry at the start of the Troubles. The film is narrated by Frieda, but within the diegesis we only hear male British voices speaking through the media. As Debbie Ging notes, '[i]t is only in retelling her story that Frieda's voice assumes acoustic authority over the intra-diegetic events' and her voice offers 'a striking counterpoint to accepted and naturalised accounts of the Troubles'.[34]

This example highlights the fact that not only gender, but also age, nationality, language, class and so forth are all factors that can be influential when making films about women. However, it could still be argued that because of the low numbers of female directors when compared to their male counterparts, a female signature is essential as it constitutes an act of agency in itself where women and their marginality become visible and male history writing is regendered so that it can no longer claim universality.[35]

As important as the filmmaker's identity is his/her ability to 'speak nearby', as suggested by filmmaker Trinh T. Minh-ha. Speaking nearby is to talk about someone without objectifying or claiming him/her, without pointing 'to an object as if it is distant from the speaking subject or absent from the speaking place ... Every element constructed in a film refers to the world around it, while having at the same time a life of its own.'[36] Women become the subject of the film's *actions and events*, and not merely the subject of *narration*, the one the story is about. For Minh-ha, speaking nearby instead of merely speaking about someone is challenging because it is more than a 'technique or a statement to be made verbally. It is an attitude in life, a way of positioning oneself in relation to the world. Thus, the challenge is to materialise it in all aspects of the film – verbally, musically, visually.'[37]

One way of 'speaking nearby' is by letting subjects narrate their own stories on-screen and off-screen. Two approaches to on-screen narration inspired my decision-making: Connie Field's in *The Life and Times of Rosie the Riveter* (1980) and Byun Young-Joo's in *The Murmuring Trilogy* (1995–9), who both eschewed an authoritarian narrator and focused on the participants' multiple voices. Field drew on archival footage and music to support the participants' own voices to critique the military discrimination of women during the Second World War. In this manner, these women's different truths were 'established against the lies of the official propaganda'.[38] *The Murmuring Trilogy* is the result of a collaborative effort between Byun Young-Joo and her former Korean 'comfort women' participants. Unlike Field, Young-Joo refused to use official documents or archival photographs as she believed these would objectify and depersonalise her participants. In this manner, she drew attention to the fact that 'what is at stake in the writing of history is not simply reclaiming facts and figures, but rather identifying and recognizing the repercussions, the traces, and the scars extant in the present order to reach a better-informed interpretation of the past'.[39]

For *We Were There* I combined Young-Joo's and Field's approaches: I enhanced the participants' own voices by letting them narrate their own stories and used extra material, such as visuals of the prison, text and soundtrack, minimally, to support the women's own voices and to offer a visual and aural journey through the prison. In this manner, the focus was on prioritising women's direct testimony and plurality of stories through their own voices and body language. Audience responses to my editing strategy show that hearing stories from people's own voices humanises the conflict and allows an emotional engagement with narratives which could be more effective than written accounts or statistics. One particular response, which was emailed to us by writer and lecturer Dr Sophie Hillan after a screening, illustrates well the responses we received from audiences in Ireland and abroad:

> Their voices, their stories told without ornament or embellishment, recorded in the bleak shell of what was once a formidable jail, show more effectively than the most dramatic account not only the grim, punishing conditions endured by the prisoners, but also the humiliations and privations shared by their families and visitors, and by the families of the prison guards. The film makes no distinction between political affiliations or religious convictions: all involved in the life of the prison are shown to have suffered, to a greater or lesser degree, the constraints of prison life. That the conclusion of those who were there is that it became impossible to consider the prisoners or their guards as anything but fellow-humans trying to survive a situation of extreme difficulty, speaks to the success of this restrained, respectful and, ultimately, deeply moving film.[40]

Responses such as this, and the many others we received, suggest that films such as *We Were There* can potentially contribute to a 'coexistence of plurality' which enables people to 'transcend their differences as private individuals, families and households, and create, as in rituals of initiatory rebirth, a public sense of "sheer human togetherness"'.[41] Films, thus, can be a powerful tool to break the mental and physical segregation that persists in post-conflict Northern Ireland.

Another way of 'speaking nearby' is through off-screen narration which enables participants' own voices to continue being heard in post-screening discussions. As Miller and Smith note, 'It is often precisely at the distribution phase that participants recognize both their sense of self and their potential to access power both on a personal and a collective level.'[42] In my research, taking part in post-screening discussions enabled participants not only to see how their stories impacted audiences and to interact with them, but also to maintain control over the framing of their stories and claim a space within discussions on the prison history that for a long time had been off-limits for many women. This was particularly important for prison workers, who at the start of this project saw their stories as less important than the relatives' stories.

Furthermore, their engagement in post-screening discussions enabled them to create a two-way dialogue with the audience and triggered in most participants a desire to continue attending screenings or to further document their experiences. For one of the probation workers, 'having thought that through and talked it through with other people, I've had quite an interesting working life and I've actually started now to take notes and think about maybe put something on a paper'.[43] This shows that a collaborative process with a sensitivity to gender may have the potential to broaden the possibility beyond individual empowerment goals.

Opening up to more dialogues

As Michelle Moloney observes, 'What is present but not always visible in all communities in Northern Ireland is an available resource in the project of conflict transformation, that of women as agents of change.'[44] The blending of a collaborative method with a gender concern enabled me to shift the emphasis from 'I am making a film about the women of the Maze and Long Kesh' to 'I am making a film to strengthen debates on women's experiences of this prison and also of the Troubles and war in general.'

As gender represents 'an essential theme to understand virtually all social relations, institutions and processes' as well as 'conditions of dominance, inequality, stress and conflict',[45] it could be argued that films with a gender perspective can contribute to opening up to a wider debate on these matters. In this model, where research outcomes are used to open up spaces for public dialogue and political action, process and product become one. By being deeply involved in all stages of filmmaking and distribution, participants were able to think about their sense of self and how personal journeys can promote much-needed debates not just on women's life experiences but also on places and times and on filmmaking frameworks. As one of the participants rightly put it, the film 'is not just about women, it is about the place, the time, about the history of this place, how people deal with things, maybe there are better ways of dealing with things'.[46]

Indeed, during the screenings in Northern Ireland the film led to discussions about other marginalised voices, such as prison officers, as well as about how children are engaging with stories from the past. In Montreal, Manchester and Stockholm the post-screening debates focused on the filmmaking process and the different levels of reception. In Belo Horizonte one of the discussions focused on prisoners' and families' experiences of imprisonment, with a particular focus on the deteriorating situation in Brazil.

Therefore, taking *We Were There* to mixed audiences, in terms of age, political and religious affiliations, and geographical locations, and to mixed venues such as film festivals, universities and community groups was an important step in bringing underrepresented stories to the public. Indeed, the audience scope (e.g. attendance numbers and diversity of venues) and their reactions to *We Were There* have shown that there is a wide interest in women's stories. Moreover, audience engagement illustrated how far women's stories can go in opening up to other pressing discussions. This supports Miller and Smith's view that a documentary's success in fulfilling a potential is not necessarily determined by how far it goes in terms of audience numbers and distribution distance, but by who sees it and what they do with it.[47]

Conclusion

I indicated throughout this chapter that collaborative filmmaking to-gether with a sensitivity to gender can help address the gap between women's real lives and their filmic representations. It is only by under-standing the different ways in which conflicts are gendered that film-makers become more likely to really comprehend the plural experiences of women and adopt approaches to make films in which women are the de facto heroes of their own stories. Without this gender inquiry, even that which appears 'natural' can be constituted by gender stereotypes and myths.

It is only when 'we tear the web of women's texts' that we 'discover in the representations of the writing itself [and I would add media in general, including film] the marks of the grossly material, the sometimes brutal traces of the culture of gender'.[48] This enables us, filmmakers, to capture the actual experiences of people from all genders and their existing representations, to understand the contexts within which they are embedded, and to extract from it alternatives for potential changes. Otherwise, if there is not such a conscious effort, the end result is likely to be a stereotypical image in which the women suffer and the military men dominate.

Text and Context: Documentary, fiction and animation

Dearbhla Glynn: Documenting war and sexual violence

EILEEN CULLOTY

Introduction

Over the past ten years, Dearbhla Glynn has emerged as a distinctive voice in Irish documentary filmmaking with a body of work that challenges dominant modes of representing human rights abuses. Her most notable work in this area explores the phenomenon of wartime sexual violence in the Democratic Republic of the Congo (DRC). Over a three-year period, Glynn filmed and directed two short films – *The Value of Women in the Congo* (2013)[1] and *War on Women* (2014)[2] – and the feature-length *War in Eastern Congo* (2016)[3]. This chapter examines the significance of the latter in the context of humanitarian filmmaking. In so doing, it highlights how Glynn positions herself on the margins of Irish filmmaking by largely working alone on personal projects that are developed outside the typical routines of documentary commissioning and production. As such, Glynn is somewhat atypical of the women filmmakers interviewed by Anne O'Brien in this volume. However, there are evident overlaps in Glynn's experience as a woman filmmaker and the views of the filmmakers interviewed by O'Brien. Namely, Glynn believes that documentary is favourable to women in that it affords the opportunity to work outside the hierarchies and tensions of larger productions.[4] Moreover, she believes her status as a woman has facilitated access to authority figures who perceive women as non-threatening and to victims of violence who perceive women as more emotionally sensitive than male filmmakers. Although mindful of essentialising her gender, these perceptions have enabled Glynn to develop a filmmaking process grounded in the fostering of relationships with her subjects; prior to any filming, she spends time with her subjects, getting to know them and their daily routines. As argued below, this process contributes significantly to her nuanced portrayal of the disturbing phenomenon of wartime sexual violence. Specifically, it allows her to contextualise individual stories of trauma within a broader understanding of life in the DRC.

Wartime sexual violence in the DRC has been the subject of much human rights advocacy. However, this advocacy is heavily criticised for perpetuating colonial stereotypes about the 'savagery' of African men[5] and for imposing the paradigm of (white) Western feminism onto the local contexts of the DRC.[6] Consequently, critics argue that human rights advocacy has largely failed to understand the myriad of causal factors that contribute to wartime sexual violence and inhibit its eradication. At the same time, human rights filmmaking is criticised for its simplification of complex issues and its reliance on affective narratives, which encourage 'a strategic emotional relationship between the Westerner and a distant sufferer'.[7] Against this background, Glynn grounds the human rights film in an act of understanding over and above the emotional identification typical of contemporary advocacy. Without falling into moral relativism, *War in Eastern Congo* asks viewers to recognise the multiple forms of gendered suffering and structural inequalities that shape daily life in the DRC and contribute to the continuation of sexual violence. Ultimately, Glynn argues that addressing sexual violence requires a holistic view of the multiple forms of violence endured by men, women and children in the DRC. In so doing, she makes a valuable contribution to the international narratives of wartime sexual violence and champions a form of human rights filmmaking in which documentary is less about advocacy than 'a resource for understanding the world'.[8]

Dearbhla Glynn

A graduate of Limerick College of Art and Design, Dearbhla Glynn began making documentaries in 2001. Her early films are notable for their striking visual flair and explorations of artistic creation across borders. For example, music is the primary focus of her 2008 documentary *Dambé: The Mali project*,[9] which follows traditional Irish musicians Liam Ó Maonlaí and Paddy Keenan as they travel to a North African music festival. This film represents a turning point in Glynn's work as it goes beyond artistic themes to explore the marginalisation and oppression of indigenous people. Glynn explains that after witnessing the scale of poverty in Mali, she wanted to highlight the social, economic and environmental issues that drive suffering in regions of conflict and instability. Such human rights themes are the explicit focus of subsequent films about Gaza, Iraq, Liberia, the Ivory Coast, Haiti, and the Democratic Republic of Congo (DRC).

These films have received funding and support from a network of aid agencies and NGOs. For example, the short documentary *Gaza: Post-operation cast lead* (2010)[10] won the Irish Council for Civil Liberties (ICCL) Human Rights Film Award while Action From Ireland (Afri) commissioned Glynn to make a short film about the use of depleted uranium in Iraq. Financial support for Glynn's DRC films is credited to numerous NGOs, including the Simon Cumbers Media Fund, Feminist Review Trust, Mary Raftery Journalism Fund, Trócaire, Oxfam, Afri, and Christian Aid. However, Glynn is conscious of maintaining her distance from NGOs because they can have a negative impact on perceptions of a filmmaker's independence. For this reason, Glynn chose to avoid the pre-established networks of NGOs by travelling alone to the DRC and negotiating access to subjects herself. She believes this independence, coupled with the perception that women are non-threatening, enabled her to gain access to military personnel and to document an underexplored aspect of wartime sexual violence: the perspective of the perpetrators.

In addition, working alone allows Glynn to develop strong relationships with her subjects. In the DRC, she travelled with soldiers through the countryside and worked with women in their homes. The process of building relationships is essential, she believes, to accurately convey the experience of her subjects. Of course, it is the lack of a pre-defined production deadline that affords Glynn the freedom to do this. In conflict and disaster zones, the typical production process requires filmmakers to work with urgency to find dramatic stories that fit a pre-defined narrative.[11] Thus, the freedom of her production process is an essential part of Glynn's nuanced and frank exploration of sexual violence in the DRC.

Stylistically, *War in Eastern Congo* tends towards the expository mode of documentary filmmaking as Glynn relies on voiceover and intertitles to provide background context. However, there are strong observational elements and, contrary to the didacticism typical of expository documentaries, the argument Glynn presents is more tentative than authoritative. This hesitation stems in part from Glynn's uncertainty about how to approach the subject of wartime sexual violence, including concerns about the ethics of contextualising sexual violence and interviewing the perpetrators of rape. In this context, this chapter examines the thematic and stylistic ethics of *War in Eastern Congo* to argue that it represents an important break in the dominant media representations of sexual violence in the DRC. Thematically, Glynn attempts to move beyond simplistic narratives of sexual violence – whereby Congolese women are victimised by brutal Congolese men – to include a more nuanced understanding of gender roles and gendered violence in the region. Thus, while media narratives about distant suffering have come to play a significant role in determining 'which violences are redeemed and which remain unrecognized',[12] Glynn grounds her filmmaking in the act of questioning who may be recognised as a victim. In addition, Glynn's stylistic and narrative strategies attempt to overcome some of the major limitations of filmic representations of distant suffering – specifically, the reduction of distant others to objects of pity[13] and the reduction of complex issues into simplified narratives that Western audiences can easily understand.[14]

Representing conflict and sexual violence in the DRC

The DRC has been embroiled in a protracted conflict since 1996. The immediate origins of the violence stem from the 1994 Rwandan genocide when Hutu *génocidaires* fled to the eastern DRC. Known as Africa's Great War, the DRC conflict engaged military forces from nine countries as well as multiple regional and local militias in disputes arising from population movements, territorial claims, and shifting ethnic identities.[15] Although the war officially ended in 2003, the eastern DRC continues to experience severe instability and outbreaks of violence. In a conflict characterised by sudden attacks on villages and ethnic communities, sexual violence against women and girls has been widespread. It is estimated that several hundred thousand women and children have been subjected to conflict-related sexual violence and that victims often endure additional atrocities such as mutilation, gang rape and sexual slavery.[16] Such extreme sexual violence earned Goma, the principal city of the North Kivu province, its reputation as 'the rape capital of the world'.[17] Unsurprisingly, the scale of the sexual violence has prompted much reflection on causal explanations and preventative measures. Much of the high-profile work in this area has been undertaken by the international community of transnational organisations and aid agencies. However, their work is inhibited by disagreements about definitions and best practice.[18]

A major criticism of the international response to sexual violence in the DRC concerns the narratives of rape that circulate in Western media and policy sectors. Many scholars identify traces of racist, colonial stereotypes in efforts to represent wartime sexual violence as the brutalisation of African women by African men. From this perspective, the interventions spearheaded by the international community seek to rescue 'the exploited, helpless, brutalised, and downtrodden African woman from the savagery of the African male and from a primitive culture symbolized by barbaric customs'.[19] In the process, international narratives tend to represent rape victims as 'submissive receptacles of violence' and to decontextualise or ignore the significance of local issues such as community displacement and broader sociocultural dynamics such as the gendered division of labour.[20] Baillie Bell argues that such local and cultural contexts are essential to understanding the roots of sexual violence in the DRC and that insufficient attention to these issues partially explains why international interventions have failed to eradicate sexual violence.[21] In recounting her experiences over three years of filming, Glynn echoes this view. Although she initially set out to make a film about sexual violence against women, her experience on the ground led her to a broader, more nuanced understanding of the multiple forms of gendered violence in the DRC.

Feminists and human rights advocates have long called for greater recognition of wartime sexual violence. A major achievement of this work was the 2002 Rome Statute of the International Criminal Court, which recognised rape, sexual slavery, enforced prostitution, and other forms of sexual violence as a crime against humanity when committed in a widespread or systematic way. With this legal framework in place, wartime sexual violence could no longer be dismissed as an inevitable, if unfortunate, consequence of war.[22] Moreover, the successful prosecution of military leaders for using rape as a military strategy during the Bosnian Wars appeared to signal the end of impunity for wartime sexual violence.

The criminalisation and successful prosecution of wartime rape in the early 2000s created the framework for the international community's response to the DRC conflict. However, the frameworks that apply to one conflict are not necessarily suitable for another. Moreover, there is growing recognition that it is necessary to look beyond 'militarised masculinity' – the assumption that male combatants share universal characteristics – to examine the region-specific nature of sexual violence and the social structures and norms that enable this violence.[23] It is in this context that Glynn's work marks a significant development in the representation of wartime sexual violence in the DRC as she attempts to link the prevalence of rape to wider sociocultural issues while adopting a broader, more inclusive view of the gendered impact of war on a population.

Documentary representations of suffering

In parallel to criticisms about international narratives of conflict in the DRC, there is a growing body of literature critiquing the use of film and video to document the distant suffering of human rights abuses. The use of film and video for the promotion of human rights has grown significantly since the 1990s when NGOs such as WITNESS and Human Rights Watch championed the use of visual media to 'bear witness' to human rights abuses. As 'technologies of witnessing', film and video are 'mechanisms of publicity through which claims are translated into a human rights framework and circulated in the international area'.[24] However, the practice of human rights filmmaking raises substantial concerns about the simplification of complex issues and the ethical and affective implications of representing distant suffering.

The simplification of complex issues arises in part from the need to translate the experiences of local actors into accessible human rights frames for international, typically Western, audiences.[25] However, in making local stories accessible for international audiences, there is an inherent tension 'between presenting contextualised stories and sight bites' that strip local stories of their meaning and nuance.[26] In other words, filmmakers often rely on familiar narrative tropes or media templates that fail to capture the specificity of human rights abuses.[27] Consequently, within much media coverage of human rights there is 'a lack of awareness of the scope of human rights, which means that social, economic, and cultural rights are almost entirely absent from the human rights discourse of the media'.[28] Moreover, such simplified media reduce the range of interpretations or analyses that can be applied to the documented events.[29]

Similarly, the portrayal of distant suffering in Western media is heavily criticised for engaging a 'politics of pity' that fails to interrogate the status quo and often fails to recognise the agency of those who suffer.[30] Representations of distant suffering primarily rely on emotional affect, which affords viewers the pleasure of 'vicarious suffering', but are 'cruelly ineffective' in terms of working towards change.[31] For Lauren Berlant, such representations are exercises in 'cruel optimism' that give viewers the self-satisfaction of wishing to do the right thing without a corresponding understanding of what needs to be done.[32] While in agreement with this view, Lilie Chouliaraki argues that there are possibilities for representing distant suffering in a way that is compassionate towards victims and respectful of their individual agency. Advocating that filmmakers adopt 'proper distance' from their subjects, Chouliaraki contends that ethical representations of distant suffering engage a search for knowledge and understanding of another person or culture and that this understanding is a prerequisite for engaging with suffering rather than merely responding emotionally to the representation of suffering.

Clearly, there are significant overlaps in the arguments put forward by critics of international narratives of wartime sexual violence in the DRC and the arguments put forward by critics of media representations of distant suffering. Both identify a tendency towards de-contextualisation as a major flaw that inhibits an ethical understanding of suffering and renders local contexts invisible. Both question whether there is ethical value in the emotional engagement derived from the politics of pity that typify representations of distant suffering. Finally, both share an explicit criticism of the Western perspective, which assumes a normative role in defining human rights abuses and articulating those abuses internationally.

In the DRC, Western NGOs and filmmakers have played a significant role in raising awareness of wartime sexual violence by working within the operational spaces created by development and security initiatives. For example, the documentary *Weapons of War: Confessions of rape in the Congo* (van Velzen and van Velzen, 2009) exposes the atrocities of wartime sexual violence through the voices of militia men and some female survivors.[33] The film is about a Dutch-based educational programme, the Mobile Cinema Tool, which invites Congolese soldiers to watch films about sexual violence and to reflect on its consequences. In *The Greatest Silence: Rape in the Congo* (2007) the Western filmmaker Lisa Jackson inserts herself into the narrative by framing her solidarity with Congolese women in terms of her own experience of rape.[34] However, such interventions are criticised for imposing Western concepts of gender onto non-Western contexts[35] and for representing Congolese women as 'objects of advocacy' rather than as individual subjects.[36] In contrast to Jackson, Glynn primarily remains off-camera and there is no explicit reference to her personal interest in the subject or to her feminist perspective on sexual violence. Nevertheless, Glynn acknowledges that her status as a white Western woman afforded her privileged access to the subject, including access to government officials, military officials and prisons. Thus, while this chapter argues that Glynn makes an important contribution to human rights filmmaking, it is important to recognise that her work remains embedded in the privileges of Western filmmaking or what Susan Sontag derisively calls the 'specialised tourism' of journalists and filmmakers.[37]

Film synopsis

War in Eastern Congo opens on a stormy sky over Lake Kivu with the sound of thunder engulfing the scene. The accompanying intertitle sets a philosophical tone: 'Nothing is truly clear, everyone exists in the moment.' A series of shots embeds the viewer in the perspective of the Congolese national army. The camera tracks heavily armed soldiers through the jungle and it sweeps over villages as soldiers peer out from army helicopters. An unattributed voiceover explains: 'Alarming levels of sexual violence [are] committed by Congolese army soldiers, by rebels, by civilians … despite increased international attention, the rapes continue.' Filmed in their homes and villages, rape survivors give voice to this situation in which women 'are considered as weapons' and 'everybody rapes'.

In these opening scenes, Glynn briefly introduces herself with a black and white photograph. It depicts her sitting with a Congolese soldier, her camera tilted upwards mirroring the soldier's gun. In voiceover, she explains, 'I had heard about the high level of rape and violence that had been going on in Congo and I wanted to go there to talk to both the survivors and perpetrators to find out what happened to communities.' The ensuing film is presented as what Glynn 'witnessed over the course of three years'.

The documentary largely follows an episodic structure. Aerial shots reveal the jungle landscape of the eastern DRC, with villages dotted in remote clearings. Glynn travels to these villages to piece together local experiences of war and sexual violence. The testimony of rape survivors is intercut with archive footage of combat and original interviews with former combatants. In these interviews, Glynn traces the varying circumstances of rape survivors and the contexts which led combatants to commit rape. Among rape survivors, we hear stories of women who are suicidal and hopeless as well as stories of women who are defiant and campaigning for change. Among combatants, we hear stories of men who were instructed to rape by their superiors and men who committed rape because they 'felt worthless'.

A key argument that is developed in the film concerns the culture of rape among combatant groups and the impunity given to military and rebel leaders. The persistence of sexual violence in the eastern DRC is attributed, in part, to corruption within the national army. A popular and successful national army colonel, Mamadou Ndala, vows to eradicate sexual violence by establishing greater discipline among his troops. However, when Colonel Ndala is killed in an ambush, community activists suggest that his military superiors may be responsible because they feared Ndala's reforming intentions and popularity. Through the story of Colonel Ndala, Glynn highlights the deep divisions within the Congolese military that inhibit efforts to eradicate sexual violence. However, the film goes on to suggest wider contexts for the persistence of the conflict and this sexual violence. Specifically, Glynn highlights the gendered impact of conflict on men, women and children and the broader structural inequalities that exist in a resource-rich country. Ultimately, viewers are invited to conclude that sexual violence cannot be eradicated without also addressing these broader inequalities.

War in Eastern Congo presents little hope for change in the immediate future. Rather, the film articulates the complex nexus of factors that conspire to sustain the phenomenon of sexual violence. In so doing,

Glynn moves beyond the dominant international narrative of the DRC and introduces a more nuanced understanding of violence and victimisation. As outlined in the following analysis, this is achieved in part by Glynn's emphasis on the collapse of communities and on the individuality of suffering within the war.

The collapse of community

The dominant international narrative of the DRC conflict presents mass rape as the major consequence of regional violence. In contrast, *War in Eastern Congo* presents the collapse of communities as the major consequence of war and situates sexual violence within the context of broken community structures. This concurs with Bell's analysis of the DRC, which finds that insufficient attention has been given to the role of ethnic communities and the gendered division of labour within these communities, which leaves women and girls particularly vulnerable to attack.[38] In *War in Eastern Congo*, the collapse of community relations is neatly encapsulated in an early scene. An elderly woman stares directly at the camera while she works in the communal centre of the village. Her thoughts are relayed in voiceover and subtitles: 'We are treated as weapons.' The reverse shot reveals a young village man staring back at her/the camera, flanked on either side by his peers. This eyeline match cut is held momentarily, establishing a sense of threat and unease within an everyday encounter between two village inhabitants.

This pervasive sense of threat is echoed by many of the interviewed women, who describe being attacked in their village homes. Later, a similar sense of threat is articulated by village men, who describe the sudden attacks, mass murder and land seizures committed by militias. As such, the film presents the claim that wartime sexual violence in the DRC is inseparable from the violence perpetrated on remote villages and that this violence is exacerbated by social and gender inequalities that pre-date the conflict.

Throughout the film, Glynn presents observational scenes of community life in the villages of the eastern DRC. Thus, while much of the film is expository in format, it also attempts to narrate the conflict 'from below' by observing everyday life.[39] In these scenes, Glynn conveys the gendered division of labour for men, children, and especially women. In the eastern DRC, familial gender divisions dictate that women are responsible for daily household chores such as gathering firewood, collecting water, and cultivating fields.[40] One community activist, Marie-Therese, explains that 'women are objects of work for the men'. Her analysis is intercut with footage of women tilling the hard clay soil while civilian men and soldiers linger, unhelping in the background. Many of the women Glynn films are shown working in some way and they describe how the trauma and fear of rape obstructs their ability to work. In addition, the cycle of violence forces their male relatives to flee their villages or join militias, which leaves women and girls more vulnerable to attack. Consequently, when Marie-Therese describes women as 'the hope of the family', we are encouraged to understand mass rape as an attack not just on Congolese women but on the Congolese family and community.

There is little hope and few positive stories among the film's portrayal of community life. However, the film indicates that it is ordinary Congolese civilians, rather than Western aid agencies, that provide relief to communities. Moreover, by focusing on community activists, Glynn makes it clear that Congolese women are not 'in need of a Western vehicle to make their voices audible'.[41] For example, an extended sequence introduces Mama Masika, a rape survivor whose husband was killed by rebels. She now runs women's shelters and orphanages for the unwanted children of rape. With the camera engulfed by the inquisitive faces of small children, Mama Masika explains that the pregnant women she helps 'often go back to husbands who don't want the babies'.

The corruption of children is a dominant theme throughout the film. While the war in the DRC is often described as a war on women, it clearly has a horrifying impact on children. In addition to the unwanted children of rape, the film documents a litany of abuses suffered by children: young girls are raped because some combatants believe virginal blood will protect them from harm while young boys are forced to join militias and to participate in mass murder and rape. The brutalisation of children leaves villagers in despair. In one village, a group of dazed, older men guide Glynn through the aftermath of a machete attack. A series of stark photographs portrays the survivors and their vicious wounds. The men list the ages of their own murdered children and report that 'children carried out these massacres … men were giving orders to children'. A sense of total defeat by the war is palpable. One man stands in the centre of the village and gestures with his arms that there is nowhere safe to go: 'There is war in every corner around us.' In this and similar scenes, Glynn expands the dominant narrative of sexual violence into the wider sphere of violence that engulfs communities.

Understanding individual suffering

Unsurprisingly, the on-screen testimony of rape survivors is shocking in the trauma and viciousness it reveals. Yet the film is not overwhelmed by the horror and misery of victimhood. In his analysis of video advocacy, WITNESS programme director Sam Gregory criticises filmmakers' reliance on visual evidence, which holds 'a deceptive immediacy and tends to overwhelm purely verbal arguments' as it 'lends itself more easily to the creation of outrage, horror, and indignation'.[42] Gregory argues that such emotional responses overwhelm the potential for bearing ethical witness to suffering because there is no room for understanding the causes of suffering. Glynn cleverly circumvents this tendency by combining separate instances of a survivor's visual and verbal testimony. For example, one rape survivor shakes her head, unable to speak; she repeatedly shields her eyes as if thinking about her experiences is too much to bear. Yet in voiceover we hear her stark testimony in a clear, measured voice: 'They rape our mothers, they rape our sisters, they rape our little girls, they rape everyone.' This simple juxtaposition has the powerful effect of endowing victims with the opportunity to speak at their most forceful and eloquent without concealing the emotional and mental impact on the interviewee.

An interest in the interviewees as individuals is evident throughout the film. Glynn often lets the camera linger on the faces or gestures of interviewees to capture a sense of their individuality. Consequently, we are not presented with a procession of rape survivors and perpetrators, but a collection of individuals whose lives have been impacted by the war in different ways. We meet rape survivors who are variously stoic, defiant and defeated, and we meet men who are unrepentant and remorseful about their crimes to varying degrees. This approach further humanises the male perpetrators and often reveals possibilities, however small, for change. In one interview Glynn asks a former combatant if he raped women. With his calm and thoughtful demeanour, the young man's response is quietly shocking: 'I don't know if you could say it was rape … if the girl didn't say yes, I took her by force.' The camera lingers on his distant gaze, appearing to capture a flicker of doubt about the integrity of his statement.

Perhaps the strongest testament to Glynn's 'proper distance' from all her subjects is the absence of accusation in the scenes in which rape perpetrators attempt to contextualise their actions, which include the use of guns and knives for sexual torture. Rather, within the cycle of violence, Glynn questions whether these combatants should also be recognised as victims of the war. Research indicates that the way combatants are inducted into military factions can have a significant influence on the perpetuation of rape and sexual violence.[43] As outlined in the film, the collapse of local economies pushed men and children into a complex nexus of militaries and armed factions while military authorities normalised a culture of sexual violence by turning a blind eye to rape and by forcing new recruits to commit rape. In this way, sexual violence serves multiple functions for militarised groups: it destabilises 'enemy' communities, it humiliates 'enemy' men for failing to protect their communities, and it binds combatants together in acts of transgression. Moreover, once sexual violence is established in one armed group, it spreads to other groups who retaliate on behalf of their own communities.[44]

Many former combatants describe their mental states in terms of dissociation and extreme isolation: 'We didn't see ourselves as human. It was like we were dead already', and 'I had nothing. My parents were dead. My home was gone.' Other former combatants describe their personal anguish to explain their participation in rape: 'We needed it. We felt better', and 'I did it because of my suffering.' In these interviews, combatants confirm the loss of humanity that accompanies conflict, and while Glynn does not ask viewers to excuse sexual violence, she does present the weaponisation of women as a consequence of the gendered impact of war on men.

If a natural implication of the presented testimony is the recognition that men are also victims of the war, then the consequent challenge is to accept the multiple forms of victimhood without slipping into moral equivalency or relativism. As Bell argues, narratives that fail to acknowledge the gendered experience of conflict by men and boys leave a large part of the conflict unanalysed.[45] In this regard, it is notable that male-on-male violence is normalised within narratives of war while male-on-female violence is considered exceptional. Yet it is primarily men and boys who are susceptible to forced recruitment into armed groups, which necessarily complicates the distinction between male combatants and male civilians, a key distinction in international law. Moreover, male non-combatants are highly susceptible to brutal assault and murder, as exemplified in the gruesome catalogue of dead and injured victims following the machete attack.

In its conclusion, the film pushes deeper into the structural dynamics that sustain the conflict and enable the seemingly intractable problem of sexual violence. The key structural context for sexual violence in the DRC, as identified by the international community, is the struggle for resources between competing regional and national forces. In *War in Eastern Congo*, Glynn suggests that there are powerful, private interests who benefit from the violent chaos and the decline of traditional social structures. In place of education and fair labour, much of the civilian population spend their days meeting basic needs of food and water. The threat of massacres causes farmers to abandon their lands and villages. Many end up as forced labour, digging for coltan in 'artisanal mines', while young girls in Goma spend their days collecting water from a lake because there is no water infrastructure. Amid the crowd collecting water at Lake Kivu, one interviewee laments: 'They say our country is rich, but we don't get that wealth. We get nothing.' Taking this broad view, Glynn suggests that government neglect dehumanises the population of the eastern DRC and leaves them vulnerable to exploitation by armed groups, which in turn sustains the culture of sexual violence. In terms of combating sexual violence, Glynn does not engage in the 'cruel optimism' identified by Lauren Berlant. There are brave and heroic figures in the film, but it is ultimately pessimistic that the required structural changes will be enacted in the near future. As viewers, we are not asked to empathise with the victims of the DRC so much as we are asked to understand why the violence is happening. As Régine Michelle Jean-Charles says, 'The pursuit and achievement of empathy have limitations when viewed in relation to wartime sexual violence.'[46]

Conclusion

While working on the margins of the Irish film industry and developing a highly personal process of filmmaking, Dearbhla Glynn has made a significant contribution to the human rights documentary. Embedded in the funding and promotional structures of NGOs, human rights documentaries typically betray an underlying belief in the capacity of visual images to inspire action and effect change. Such films are entangled in ethical concerns about the representation of distant suffering and the simplification of complex issues into easily understood and emotionally affective narratives. In this context, Glynn's work is notable for moving beyond the 'politics of pity' to ground the human rights film in an act of understanding. Glynn's approach to documentary-making is one in which documentary is 'part of the media that can help us understand not only our world but our role in it, that shape us as political actors'.[47] This is especially significant at a time when the very concept of documentary is being redefined by the ubiquity of factual digital media and the ideal of documentary as a 'discourse of sobriety' appears outmoded as a consequence.[48]

War in Eastern Congo exemplifies the ethical call for 'proper distance' between human rights filmmakers and their subjects. Drawing on Roger Silverstone's work, Chouliaraki and Orgad argue that proper distance is an ethical imperative which 'must reflexively assert the irreducibly distinct quality of the other whilst, against the logic of difference, it must sustain an empathetic sense of the other as a figure endowed with her own humanity'.[49] By largely working alone and developing projects over an extended time period, Glynn has cultivated a filmmaking process that affords proper distance to her subjects. In the case of wartime sexual violence, it allows Glynn to interweave highly individual and local stories of suffering into a sociopolitical understanding of the contexts that enable and perpetuate this suffering and to use documentary as a means of cultivating a cosmopolitan moral disposition.[50] There are, however, significant drawbacks to Glynn's approach to documentary filmmaking. By avoiding the routine structures of documentary commissioning and production described in Anne O'Brien's essay, Glynn remains outside the collaborative networks and industry contacts that might sustain a career in documentary filmmaking. For her part, Glynn perceives documentary as just one component of her work on human suffering and resilience.

In the future, she aims to integrate her work as an artist and yoga instructor into the process of filmmaking to create a more collaborative process that gives back to communities.

Pat Murphy: Portrait of an artist as a filmmaker

LANCE PETTITT

I used to think of myself as an artist, but I didn't like how the art scene worked ... Sometimes I miss the immediacy of painting, but I have simply moved away from that way of thinking.[1]

This essay offers a retrospective analysis of the films of Pat Murphy and the creative contexts in which they were produced. Speaking in 1984 – as the quotation above indicates – Murphy was aware of a pivot point in her creative development. Turning away from the individual endeavour of painting to embrace the collective processes of making films, she understood the consequences that follow from aesthetic decisions. This consideration of her work reflects on her status as an artist who chose to work in the medium of film. Elected to Aosdána in 'visual arts', Murphy's creative arc has included four feature-length films but has eschewed the usual marker-posts of a cinema industry 'career'. Wary also of the 'art scene' as she experienced it in the 1970s and '80s, she followed her own pathway, evolved her practice, and has been true to her creative and spiritual impulses over four decades. Despite some long periods of filmmaking inactivity across Murphy's life, she has produced a small but significant body of work of such quality to merit consideration as one of Ireland's foremost female film directors, from an earlier generation of artist film and video makers like Vivienne Dick and Margot Harkin.

Revisiting her work for a volume such as this is a timely enterprise in itself, coming as it does in the wake of the Irish Film Board's report (2015), its Six Point Plan, and other initiatives to promote gender equality in the film business. But it is given sharper focus by the coincidence of events and resurfacing of debates in Ireland and beyond its shores that echo the formative decades of Murphy's development as an artist. In early 2018 Murphy was in South Africa researching a new film; in London, the Irish embassy hosted an inaugural Lá Fhéile Bríde/St Brigid's Feast Day event (1 February) celebrating women's creativity, culture and enterprise. In March the MeToo campaign, to end the silence about the abuse of women and younger men in the screen industries, continued to exert its presence at its showcase awards events like the Oscars, the BAFTAs and the IFTAs. In Ireland, the government worked through its options about the terms and date of the Referendum on the Eighth Amendment on abortion. March 2018 also saw the news that Film Base in Dublin had gone into liquidation. It had been founded in 1986 as a grassroots organisation to support, train and facilitate low-budget filmmaking in all its technical and production aspects. One of its co-founders, Pat Murphy, the subject of this essay, was then an emerging talent with two feature-length films to her name and had been actively involved in the campaign to establish an Irish Film Board (1981). Finally, April 2018 saw the twentieth anniversary of the Good Friday Agreement, which marked a turning point in the fortunes of Northern Ireland, the gendered politics of which had been the subject of Murphy's debut feature film, *Maeve*, back in 1981.

In the context of the events, occasions and debates referred to above and Susan Liddy's editorial rationale for this present volume, this essay identifies a number of patterns and themes that emerge from a consideration of Murphy's creative work, where she has done it and what she has produced. She is a woman who has remained restlessly on the move and I want to argue that her mobility and location in certain places at certain periods, along particular axes of creative energy, have produced a series of preoccupations in her work. These revolve around feminist creative responses to power, position(ing) and identification, oppositional processes of history, memory and exile, and organising alternative ways to create.

Origins and journeys

Born in 1951 in Dublin, Murphy's early childhood was shaped by the pre-Vatican II mores of that decade of Ireland's development: a traditional Catholic schooling, taught by nuns, where nationalist politics remained intact and rarely challenged, and where a wider social deference to authority was maintained until well into her teenage years. In 1967, aged fifteen, a year after the fiftieth anniversary of the Easter Rising was commemorated and the seeds of revisionist questioning were sown, Murphy's father accepted a job in Northern Ireland and the family moved to Belfast. This first journey – on a south/north axis – *within* Ireland but crossing a border proved to be highly provocative. Her idea of what constituted Irish history was challenged by her new environment and the school curriculum. Here, on another part of the island of Ireland, as she recalled, things presented themselves differently:

> I had never visited the North of Ireland before my family moved there in 1967, so my concept of the place was based on entirely nationalist rhetoric taught in Dublin schools … At school in Belfast I learnt about the Fenians and the 1916 Rising from the completely opposite position of English textbooks.[2]

In this recollection from a treatment for *Maeve*, a film then called 'Belfast', written around 1980, Murphy offers a political analysis of Ireland that deliberately uses the shifting terminology of 'Six Counties', 'English', 'North of Ireland', 'a 32-county Republic', 'the South', 'Ulster' and 'Northern Ireland'. Her conclusion is the realisation:

> I saw how *Northern Ireland* functions as the negative focus of both *Irish and English* propaganda … *Ulster* represents the desire-image projected by the *Southern Irish* politicians … For *Britain*, *Ulster* is the focus of a displaced configuration of *colonial/imperialist* symbols.[3] [my italics]

It is, however, an analysis in retrospect and written with the detachment of physical distance, the result of a politicisation that took place in London and New York during the 1970s. How did such a politics become fused with a creative vision? Murphy had begun her art education at Ulster College of Art and Design (now part of the University of Ulster), where she studied between 1969 and '70, but the onset of widespread violence and the militarisation of Northern Ireland meant that she picked up her training in London with a year at St Martin's School of Art (1972–3) before taking a BA in Fine Art at Hornsey College of Art (1976) and then an MA at the Royal College of Art (RCA).[4] These were radicalising hotspots for self-expression and collective action. This period provided a crucible of experiences, influences and experiments for an artist finding her medium. Through this period, Murphy was living and learning on an east/west axis, outside of Ireland itself. However, the lines between London and New York, connecting via Ireland, carried particular cultural and creative charges for the artist. It was at the RCA that she engaged with film and with the structural mode of filmmaking under the tutelage of New Yorker Steve Dwoskin and also Laura Mulvey, who practised a theorised filmmaking that was personal but deeply imbued with the politics of gender. As Alice Butler has shown, Murphy was involved with art performance and installation in the 1970s and showed little interest in mainstream commercial cinema.[5]

Indeed, she had been part of an art collective called 'The Ting: Theatre of mistakes' from 1974 that devised art performances/exhibitions which included venues like The Slade and Goldsmith's College ('Two Journeys'), The Roundhouse ('Free Sessions'), Cambridge International Poetry Festival ('Preparation for Displacement') and at the Artist's Meeting Place in Covent Garden.[6] The 'Two Journeys' was a devised piece, setting up performers in a space of the Slade portico to be seen by an 'audience' who witnessed the actions, sequence, repetition and change (in body movement, voice, sound) of two groups of figures on journeys but whose outcome was unpredictable and lacked a script-generated narrative. This was an avant-garde event, 'structural' theatre practice akin to the 'structural film' that became vogue in alternative and experimental circles between London and New York in the late 1960s and 1970s and where, according to Deke Dusinberre, the stress was on 'the subordination of any "content" to "form" (more precisely, the subordination of "image-content" to "image-production") and the decisive rejection of narrativity'.[7] Murphy commented in retrospect that:

> although the work manifested as formal/abstract/structural, I feel that there was in fact a narrative element in the way audiences, understanding the structure, anticipated conflict or projected a narrative onto the performance. The piece worked with tensions around the perception of the mistake before it actually happened.[8]

Some events took place in purpose-built or more informal spaces, but one performance, called 'The Street', a community project in conception, took place on a whole street in Kentish Town, mixing artists, performers and residents. This time, she did not refer to herself as a filmmaker as such, rather as an artist who used different media to express herself, including film. Her RCA final project, 'Rituals of Memory' (1977), was not a film initially. Its genesis exemplifies these different strands of her early practice perfectly, comprised as it was of photography, Xerox reproduction, slideshow and soundtrack, in an installation that became a 16 mm film. Murphy's exposition of the work's creation is instructive in understanding her practice and the emerging aesthetic. Described as 'a continuing' work in a programme note that is worth quoting at length, she says it

> is concerned with the relationship between memory and its expression in language and image. The act of remembering is similar/akin to the act of imaging/construction of an image … One element of an image implies its completion, just as one element of memory triggers the reconstruction of a whole pattern.
>
> The photo-etchings come from fragments of letters and First Communion photographs. 'The Muybridge Solo' is a Xerox book based on the degeneration of mechanic memory. As a performance, its progress was contingent on the interdependence between a series of movements and the recitation of a sequence of words.[9]

One can see here the formal and structural concerns of image-production and the time-based 'liveness' of performance that were at the heart of her creative process. The final piece was consolidated into a film that was exhibited in galleries and at film festivals in London, Dublin and New York among other venues, with the soundtrack. Donated to the Irish Film Institute (IFI) in Dublin, it exists now only as a water-damaged reel of 16-mm celluloid that lacks the voiceover and is partially discoloured, obscuring some sequences of frames. The film begins with no titles on a lava-lamp image that slowly dissolves through a series of photographs – each framed by black side bars – that document the memory of a family, focusing on the growing up of one of the daughters, her sisters and mother. Murphy pointed out in her programme note that the long dissolves used 'are extended beyond their conventional "film function"' to represent the passing of time, asserting that 'Memories are static configurations. It is we who change our positions in relation to the memory image', once again suggesting a link between mobility, perception and memory.[10]

In fact, Murphy used photographs from her own family album, images that punctuate a collected life with its marking-post moments – Christmas meals, weddings, Communion, christenings, new schools, holidays and so on – to compile the ritual memories of a family as it grows up, ages, and brings new life into the world. It ends on a portrait shot of a middle-aged woman that slowly fades to black. We know from her own account that the film's soundtrack consisted of 'disjointed readings from my sister's letters and fragments of conversations' and that Murphy's sister had read her own letters to Pat in this process. So, *Rituals of Memory* exists as an intensely autobiographical art work on film, a testament to a family past, to sisterly and maternal affection under the pressure of the artist's physical distance from home, and hence a poignant filmic expression of Irish migration. But it is also an art work about 'the degeneration of mechanical memory', as Murphy put it, the workings of the mental processes and expression of what we term 'memory'.

Some of these aesthetic concerns were carried over into what became *Maeve*, discussed in the next section, but the next two years (1978–80) took Murphy from London to New York, where she lived while studying on the prestigious Independent Study Programme as an artist at the Whitney Museum of American Art. She met and worked with filmmakers, actors and artists including Lizzie Borden, Kathryn Bigelow (then an actor), Becky Johnston, and fellow Irish migrant Vivienne Dick, who was already making low-budget experimental films within the city's punk art scene, and generally absorbing the intellectual and political activist thinking of the moment. If, in London, Murphy was conscious of working 'in a politically determined alternative way' through her structural film, performance and involvement in film cooperatives, it was in New York that she began to define her practice in overtly feminist terms.[11] As a 'second-step' migrant in New York, too, she began to view examples of what at that time was emerging as the elements of an indigenous 'new wave' of Irish filmmaking, including work by Bob Quinn, Joe Comerford and, operating between London and Ireland, Thaddeus O'Sullivan.[12] This had emerged in Ireland based partly on the Arts Council funding that had become available from 1973 and a growing activism to establish a state-funded film board. The creative displacement in New York had the effect of focusing Murphy's practice. She consciously adopted a feminist aesthetic and began to look with some critical distance at her relationship with Ireland. She recalled that she 'had a strong feeling that fiction or fictionalizing work was the only way, at that stage, that one could deal with the north [of Ireland] because of the kinds of documentaries that were being made'.[13] She had begun writing a script called 'Belfast' in this period but because of the paucity of funding in Ireland looked to London and the BFI Production Fund to help finance it. *Maeve* (as it became) and the film that followed it, *Anne Devlin*, took Ireland as their subject.

1980s oppositional filmmaking: *Maeve* (1981) and *Anne Devlin* (1984)

Murphy's first two feature-length films were created and released in a period of growing confidence within Ireland's filmmaking community and represent a significant achievement set against, as they are, a turbulent decade in Irish politics, economically and socially. Although they differ in setting – one set in the Belfast of its day, the other distanced by history in the Wicklow and Dublin of 1798–1806 – they share an attitude to politics and filmmaking, although Murphy consciously chose different creative strategies for each film. Viewed in 2018, both films offer a way into the cultural politics of the 1980s that saw a retrenchment of authoritarian, conservative ideas and policies that halted the promise and potential in Murphy's art. This section will explore the origins of *Maeve*, analyse the script, and re-examine the reception of the film on its release based on materials held in the IFI. It will then move on to compare and contrast the handling of her material in *Anne Devlin* and its distinctive visual style. It concludes with a brief noting of her other creative activities and an analysis of the film she made on the Famine for Strokestown Museum (1992), a film work that encapsulates in some sense a return to her earlier 'fragmented and diaristic' aesthetic of *Rituals of Memory* though now infused with notions of public, communal memory rather than individual experience of personal or family memory.

Both *Maeve* and *Anne Devlin* use cinema to critique Irish nationalist history, republican politics in particular, and practise 'herstory' through the medium of film. *Anne Devlin* is a historical drama that acts to make women's contribution to history central, not marginal, and provide an alternative view of a popular Irish narrative (of 'Emmet's rebellion') where the feminine is not a passive, suffering figure to rouse male action or console other women but has autonomous agency in political analysis and direct action. The closing on-screen dedication makes this explicit: 'To the women forgotten by history: The women who worked for freedom and are imprisoned for their beliefs'. In revising the historical account of the part played by women in the United Irishmen's failed uprisings in 1798 and 1803, the film – in an Irish context – also aligned itself with the struggles of republican women prisoners on protest in Armagh Prison in the late 1970s and 1980s. Murphy made this 'authentication' and link quite clear in interviews at the time: 'The film is a tribute to the women I know right now who do see themselves as feminists but are working within the Republican movement. There is an analogue between the two.'[14] *Maeve*, too, engaged critically with Irish myth and Irish republicanism through its titular fictional character's return to Belfast, as we will see. But Murphy set about this challenge by adopting a radically different aesthetic that was devised and written to resist conventional structures of viewing identification.

Maeve exists as a fully fledged shooting script, completely story-boarded with 52 scenes/293 shots, to reassure its London funders that, as a debut feature film, Murphy possessed the required skills and discipline to direct a crew.[15] Back in London she worked with John Davies and Robert Smith to put together a cast and crew, and planned the production. With the action set in contemporary Belfast, featuring scenes with British soldiers, harassment and the security routines of a militarised city, Murphy was committed to filming it on location. This was a bold but challenging decision given the heightened tension during the republican prison protests. Armed as she was with film spectatorship theory from the RCA, her performance and cooperative film distribution experience from London, and a body of feminist theory developed in New York, Murphy's conception of the film and the treatment she gave to the material made for an ambitious debut feature. As we will see, it achieved a considerable profile for a film shot on 16 mm, attracted a lot of critical attention, and was widely screened internationally, including the BFI screening it at Cannes.

Maeve follows what happens when a young Irish woman returns from London to her native Belfast and confronts her family, her boyfriend, her own nationalist community, the British military and the history of her mother city by revisiting particular locations. This narrative of return, encounter and critique comes to some kind of resolution in a scene of seaside sisterhood on the Giant's Causeway but the film resists offering its viewers a conventional identification with the 'heroine'.[16] Maeve's personal memory of her childhood, provoked by her return home, is structured into the film as a series of 'unmotivated' flashbacks that counterpose the dominant stories of family and home controlled initially by her father and the narratives of republican nationalism represented by Liam, her boyfriend. These episodes break the conventional homogeneity of the film text and its viewing pleasures: characters become types, dialogue becomes deliberately non-naturalistic and the effect is that the audience, as Murphy noted, 'experience uncertainty. Contradictions are set up which are not resolved in the narrative.' The film's closing shot is of Maeve's father, Martin, who began the film writing to his daughter with the news from home, talking to himself. As Janet Hawken points out, 'a great deal of the film's pleasure lies in its various modes of storytelling' – family stories, fairy stories, republican history, local history, incidents recalled, and so on – and foregrounding the filmic techniques by which past events are presented: dialogue 'between characters (on- and off-screen), direct address to camera, voice-over and visual representation'.[17] The film attracted a significant amount of critical notice in the press and associated magazine reviews and interviews. It annoyed some local groups, including feminists who argued: 'No contact was made with any women's groups here. I think it is evident in the film, as it fails abysmally at portraying feminism or its role in the present situation.'[18] Murphy took on board aspects of the criticism but the film's critique of women and traditional forms of republicanism did not enamour it to many reviewers in the British press, notoriously by Alexander Walker at its Cannes screening whose review was inaccurate invective.[19] Many other reviewers in Ireland, Britain and further afield struggled with the film's challenging formal properties, but several identified Murphy's considerable talents and promise for future work. Murphy already had the idea for her next film under development.

In writing *Anne Devlin* she derived great power from using Devlin's own journal account, letters and other diary sources from the period, allowing her 'voice' to come through the film in dialogue exchanges but more dramatically in the actions and attitude of her silent defiance during her detention, torture and interrogation at Dublin Castle and Kilmainham Gaol. Murphy commented on the journal as a source for screenwriting:

I was astonished by how strong her voice was, and how simple and basic it was. And how she saw things in a totally imagistic way, as a camera would … I'm really feeling my way into her journals and I've staged things accordingly.[20]

Brid Brennan as Anne, present on-screen in every scene bar one, gave an extraordinary performance in using gesture, body posture and looks to visualise the historical 'voice' of her character in a film characterised by its slow pace, spare dialogue and striking visual qualities both in its art design (sets, costume) and cinematography (lighting, framing, long 'takes' and careful sound editing). This, according to Kevin Barry, meant 'picturing the action in a way which hesitates between the painterly approach of late eighteen century landscapists and a grainy sense of surfaces and textures'.[21] Murphy explained her counter-history thinking in an interview with Patsy Murphy:

You have to remember that history as one receives it has been codified and falsified toward a male bias. What I've done is use her diaries and the other materials that exist to create as accurate a portrait of that period as possible. I wanted to have people actually feel they were there. I wanted that illusion.[22]

While the film in some ways resembles a more realist aesthetic and puts Anne's character firmly within the narrative – for an audience to follow and respond to – it retains a restrained, measured quality. But Murphy wanted to create a 'tension' within the film, as she explains: 'So I had very naturalistic acting. [But] there are tensions between that and how the rest of the film is staged.'[23] Luke Gibbons argues that the lighting and framing of scenes progressively shifts perspective from an outer world to Anne's imprisonment, an inner world focused on her body and a resilient silence, but that the cinematic device of her 'voice over' towards the end becomes her conscious thoughts, an 'inner voice'.[24] The film is not without moments of ironic humour, as in the exchange between Anne and Emmet when he enters a room to find her looking at herself in the mirror holding his United Irishman uniform against her body. She dislikes uniforms, she tells him, continuing: 'they look like green versions of the redcoats [i.e. yeoman soldiers supporting the British in Ireland]. We are *ourselves*, we should rebel as *ourselves*' (my emphasis) and she points out they are impractical for fighting in the streets. She neatly expresses her doubts that the rebellion might merely mirror the regime run by the British and her words anticipate 'sinn féin', the 'ourselves' of the modern republican nationalist mantra that first became a political party in 1905. Murphy's play with the mirror image and clothing in this scene also visualises the feminist theory that the power underlying gendered relations is a kind of masquerade, contingent upon repeated performance, including the subversive role as Emmet's 'housekeeper'.[25] As a film, the viewing pleasures of *Anne Devlin* are derived from an austere beauty, a recognition of a visual iconography of the feminine being framed and displayed, e.g. in the pieta shot of Anne cradling her dead brother, that leads to a contemplative critique of how traditions in visual culture serve particular kinds of politics such as patriarchal nationalism and property ownership.

The period between the release and circulation of *Anne Devlin* and what became Murphy's next film included various kinds of teaching posts in Dublin's art colleges and institutes that offered the beginnings of an art education in Ireland. Murphy also continued to serve on the board of Film Base, an organisation of which she had been a co-founder, during the brief period of the new Irish Film Board (1982–7), and was also a founder member of Circles Women's Distribution Collective. In conversation with Patsy Murphy in 1984, she outlined the need to develop alternative networks for distributing feminist and experimental films to address an audience in formation. 'Circles,' she pointed out, 'doesn't even intend to take on the big cinemas. It sees its circuits as art colleges, alternative venues, festivals', adding: 'That's why feminist filmmakers are not producing films, they are also producing audiences.'[26] In the same interview she called for the state to force RTÉ to relinquish a proportion of its funding for independent production in Ireland and discussed the idea of the trade union organisations supporting film. This, and Murphy's engagement in public art of protest such as the 'Parade of Innocence' event in Dublin in 1989, show a critical awareness and opposition to the structures of political/legal power and that of the screen media industry, particularly its training and employment gender inequalities.[27] Murphy continued working on film, notably in the late 1980s in collaboration with her partner Tiernan MacBride in his documentary about his father, Sean, an IRA revolutionary who became a notable international lawyer, co-founder of Amnesty International, a

UNESCO Nobel Peace Prize winner, a government minister and public intellectual and a huge figurehead for old school republicanism. It became a two-part film funded by RTÉ, *Sean MacBride Remembers* (1988), whose cause Murphy championed directly with RTÉ.[28] But Murphy's collected papers indicate that from Aeon Films (her company based in Dublin) she continued to try to develop feature film projects as *Anne Devlin's* wider release progressed beyond Ireland. Murphy had secured the rights to *Moon Eyes*, a children's 'ghosts story' by Josephine Poole, with whom she corresponded and outlined her concept for adaptation.[29] Other sources clarify this further; it would be a 'horror film, but Victor Erice's *The Spirit of the Beehive* and the imagery of Tarkovsky's films are closer to what I am trying to get at [rather] than the *Omen/Exorcist/Shining* genre of "weird child" movies', she argued in an application to the Arts Council Script Fund. She explained that she wanted to develop *Moon Eyes* 'in a more flexible, open-ended way than the manner in which my other films were written', describing her script development as featuring:

> the production of related drawings, paintings and photographs and would include a short film experimenting with methods of colour saturating and bleaching the print. In this way, the visual design of the film would proceed at the same time as the screenplay and work on one would affect the other.[30]

This gives a fascinating insight into her practice at this point but the envisaged ninety-minute feature (with an outline budget of £0.5 million) did not come to fruition.

In fact, her next project on film was a site-specific piece, commissioned by Luke Dodds, Director of the Irish National Famine Museum at Strokestown Park in 1992. Based on excerpts from reports, diaries and letters from the period of An Gort Morda (1845–7), the short film was created to be screened as part of an exhibition display on TV screen monitors to help museum visitors interpret the space, the location and the historical import of the Famine as it was experienced in this part of Ireland – Roscommon – using the location of the estate but also the workhouse at Castlerea. Visually, the film adopts a slow, meditative pace of shots, transitions, close-ups of bricks, crumbling wall, flaking paint, ironmongery, slow tracking shots 'searching' through corridors and room space, exploring the grassy, outlying surroundings. Accompanying this is a kind of narration, or commentary, based on the different period documents voiced off-screen by a male and a female narrator. These weave the impersonal, sometimes graphic and the acutely intimate together in a powerful reflective process for the viewer of memorialising the past. Murphy spent much of the rest of this decade of her life carrying out commissioned film curation work for IMMA/IFC and teaching film in Ireland, the UK and US. This work took place as she continued to develop what would become her own next feature about Nora Barnacle, Galway-born partner, then wife, of the novelist James Joyce. It demonstrates again how, as the subject matter moved and dealt with lovers in exile out of Ireland, so Murphy's practical stance and creative aesthetic responded to the material she had chosen to work with.

An Irish European art film: *Nora* (2002)

With *Nora*, Murphy's axis of creative production extended eastward, southward and out into Europe. The times and the topic dictated it so. Based on Brenda Maddox's biography *Nora: The real life of Molly Bloom* (1988), there was 'a certain rescuing, a recuperation taking place in the film. But I really don't think it's a feminist film in the sense that *Anne Devlin* or *Maeve* are,' Murphy argued.[31] The project endured a long gestation as Murphy was bereaved of her partner Tiernan McBride in 1995 and the film struggled to secure finance in the changing climate of film funding. Post-1993, with the re-launch of the Film Board, producing art film was more tricky and yet also held out more opportunities for creative work within the context of the EU's Eurimages support programme. Although based on Maddox's book, the action of a feature-length film – in dealing with the relationship that Nora had with Joyce – had necessarily to telescope and focus its scenario. In fact, for practical purposes, Murphy and Gerry Stembridge's screenplay found its subject by dramatising the lovers' early life together in Trieste, an Italian coastal city then part of the Austrian empire, where they had eloped to from Dublin in 1904, raised a family and where Joyce wrote *Dubliners* (1914) and *A Portrait of the Artist* (1916). In its subject, location, production values and crewing *Nora* epitomises the best of what European collaboration can produce in creative work. Jean-Francois Robin's cinematography, the art direction of Stephano Maria Ortolano and Consolate Boyle's costume design ensured that the film looked superbly sumptuous beyond the necessities of 'period accuracy'. In fact, Joyce was a notorious spendthrift and the couple were frequently penniless in Trieste, but Nora shared his enjoyment of sartorial elegance and, as she says in the film, 'They say that living well is the best revenge.'

With *Nora*, too, Murphy produced a film that explored a rich sensuality and the emotional landscape of a relationship of a very modern couple in the opening years of the twentieth century. As well as on-screen sex, the film featured the complex psychodrama of the intimate sexual fantasies that are shared between a couple of open-minded, independent Irish exiles breaking the convention of marriage. The infamous, frank and scatological correspondence between the two when they were apart could not – because of the restrictions of the Joyce Estate – be used so the two screenwriters wrote their own 'dirty letters' for the script. As with her earlier work, Murphy's approach had the effect of reframing our ideas of Joyce's creativity and demonstrating Nora's qualities as a partner, mother and muse to Joyce. Woven into the backdrop of the writing of *Dubliners* and their letter exchanges ('I knew I'd always best him at this writing game,' Nora says to Stanislaus Joyce at one point), the film highlights the importance of Irish song and music to the couple in their lives in Ireland but more importantly when they are abroad: the film is dotted with scenes of songs being shared and Stanislas Syrewicz's film music provides an acoustic backdrop that evokes the European period. But *Nora* was notable for two art forms that became powerful narrative conceits in the film: painting and cinema, both arts notable for their scopophilic dynamic. In one episode in the film, Nora is sitting for a painting commissioned by Joyce but his friend and editor Bruni drops by at the house and is seen to be admiring her. This is picked up on by the insecure, jealous Joyce and it becomes part of an elaborate, paranoid questioning of Nora's fidelity. Visualising the dramatisation of the shared emotional vulnerabilities of the couple is one of the strengths of Murphy's direction, a considerable maturation from the exchanges of Maeve and Liam in *Maeve*. But it is cinema as an art form, Nora's act of looking at a screen and the emotional memory of a previous love that it evokes (prefigured in the opening shots of the movie), that proves a pivot point for the film. As Murphy has explained, she was conscious of the enmeshed Joycean and Irish cinematic traditions as she devised the fictional sequence of Nora at the cinema in Trieste with its arresting shot of Nora's direct gaze out at us.[32] So affected, she tells Joyce of her younger love, and this becomes the material at the heart of Joyce's 'The Dead' which closes *Dubliners*. Critically, the film was warmly received, attracted festival awards and had perhaps the widest appeal of all Murphy's films to date. She resists interpretations that the film is, or was, in some way 'post-feminist', which 'ignores the very real issues of power and gender that drove my films in the first place, issues which have not been satisfactorily resolved'.[33] Although, the following year, Murphy produced a short, three-minute piece, *What Miro Saw* (2002),[34] much of her time until her next film, *Tana Bana* (2015), was spent engaged in teaching film. This included stints in Galway, at Queen's in Belfast and, from 2010 to 2015, as an Associate Professor in Graduate Film in Singapore, the base for New York University Tisch Asia. Pushing along the axis beyond Europe to this location, travelling, teaching and learning in Asia, especially India, led Murphy to her next film, which forms an appropriate conclusion to this essay.

Tana Bana: The warp and weft of 'living history'

Tana Bana (2015) is an extraordinary film about the traditional weavers of Varanasi, a centuries-old centre for Muslim artisans under jeopardy from multinational competition in an increasingly globalised and modernising India. India was a country that was confronting the continued incidence of sexual assaults on women in public, child labour exploitation and one of the largest democracies with a caste system and heightened inter-religious conflicts. Taking its title from the 'warp' and 'weft' of weaving, *Tana Bana* seems a far cry from Murphy's films of the 1970s and '80s, but the patient assembling of people's occluded stories, the focus on women's narratives within the culture, the careful attention to the particularity of the historical context of her subject and the mesmerising visual impact that the film achieves all evidence the journey and aesthetic maturing of Murphy's practice. Discussing its evolving story structure, Murphy pointed out that she filmed in 2008 and then returned in 2010, exploring location and interviewing people, but added that 'as the editing process took shape the day in the life [of the city] structure emerged again naturally and organically'.[35] She wanted to avoid the topical, immediate, news story approach to the situation, to explore people's lives and work with Indian crew, to avoid as far as possible a Western eye and attitudes being exerted on the subject matter. After one screening a member of the audience referred to the viewing experience as watching 'living history' unfold.

Conclusion

Early on in her development, we observed how Murphy understood what is given up and what is gained as an artist when the film camera is adopted as your chosen medium of expression. In that interview from the mid-1980s in *Iris* with which we opened this essay, we recall that, forsaking the lone individuality of the fine art practitioner, Murphy understood the lasting collaborative benefits and wisdom that comes from film production:

> In film making, you have to include so many people in every part of the process – bar writing the script – that the insight becomes communal because the final product is shaped by so many. What you have is a tension between your original ideas and their expression, and then how the audience responds to that.[36]

With the unscripted, organically structured and collaboratively produced *Tana Bana*, Murphy returned to her artistic instinct for trying to create things differently, taking on Western feminist notions of Muslim women, exploring the capacity for Hindu and Muslim coexistence and questioning professional conventions of the news media and filmmaking. As she said herself,

> It's important to challenge boundaries, not to accept the limitations and to somehow create a contested space within the false certainties of all these issues.[37]

In stating this, Murphy demonstrates that she has retained the underpinning of a feminist concern for gendered inequalities of power as they intersect with the politics of nationality, religion and ethnicity, that she developed over four decades ago. The challenge for her as an artist remains: of finding the right way with the materials at hand to express her vision of a world yet to be.

Juanita Wilson:
A crusading Irish filmmaker

ISABELLE LE CORFF

The Irish postcolonial context in filmmaking

Like many other decolonised countries, Ireland has had to face the difficulties of developing a postcolonial identity at a time of globalisation, when senses of home and community were being called into question. In such a context, any elements that did not share a specific identity constructed from the inside were marked as not belonging to the constructed nation.

The search for specific criteria, the need to determine what is Irish and what is not, has prevailed in Irish film studies for years, with a persistent difficulty to define Irish cinema from a national as well as from a universal perspective. The assessment of Irish cinema includes the achievements of Irish people (filmmakers, actors, etc.) abroad but often tends to exclude what is being made in Ireland by non-Irish filmmakers or actors. While giving an overview of Irish films in 2014, Tony Tracy insisted that *Frank* could be considered an Irish film because of

> its production company (Element), significant IFB development/ production funding, the directorial presence of Lenny Abrahamson and 'Irish' stars Michael Fassbender (Irish-German playing American) and Domhnall Gleeson (with an Irish accent) ... but it can ultimately be seen – in different ways – as of a piece with both Abrahamson and Gleeson's respective bodies of work ... *Adam & Paul* and *Garage* were located within recognizable Irish settings and socio-spatial contexts.[1]

The very fact of arguing in favour or in disfavour of the Irishness of a film is indicative of the prevailing insecurity of a postcolonial film culture, its genesis being linked to historical forms of hegemony. The concept of nation remains fundamental, no matter how far Ireland has been incorporated into the process of globalisation. Frontiers may be permeable and much cultural life may supersede geographical boundaries across the globe but the question of what counts as an Irish movie remains crucial.

Another argument in favour of a postcolonial reading of the Irish film industry is the preponderant gender imbalance. Postcolonial feminism argues that women living in postcolonial countries are misrepresented. Analysis has shown that after independence was won, the postcolonial countries did not push for gender equality in public life, defining women's place in society in a restrictive way. In Ireland it was reinforced by the church, which played an important ideological role in the formation of Irish nationalism, the construction of Irishness depending on establishing a difference between Protestant and Catholic beliefs. The model characterised by a special devotion to the Virgin Mary implied a female ideology of self-denial. It is well-acknowledged that in twentieth-century Ireland women were silenced and excluded within the process of nation-building.[2]

The position of women in cinematic representations, but equally as filmmakers, has remained minimal and liminal. As stated in the programme of the 28th Galway Film Fleadh (2016), 'A male-dominated industry leads to male-focused films, leaving women not only under-represented amongst directors but under-represented in the art and stories themselves.'[3] Financial concerns have been and continue to be a principal stumbling block, and for women it is a particularly challenging area. As Megan Sullivan argues, 'Beset by the peculiarities of a patriarchal, (post) colonial history, seditious religious ideologies, and a complex relation to multinational capitalism, women have always had to work with and against oppressive structures, thus making it more difficult for them to get films made.'[4] The first film made by Pat Murphy during the first wave era, *Maeve*, was all the more important as it challenged the male gaze on the female body and on women's status in the history of Ireland. None of Murphy's three major films, *Maeve*, *Anne Devlin* and *Nora*, got the public acclaim they deserved, despite being included in the *Sunday Times* 'list of the top 100 Irish films of all time'. Apart from *Nora*, the films have not yet been released on DVD. Since then, Pat Murphy has made the short film *What Mira Saw* (2002). She has worked for television and taught film. Her documentary film *Tana Bana* was released in 2015. Yet it seems that she has not been able to face the difficulties of making another feature film. And she is no exception. Quite a few talented women have made films in Ireland: Margo Harkin, Mary McGuckian, Liz Gill, Carmel Winters, Aisling Walsh, Kirsten Sheridan, among others. Yet they all have short filmographies. As Liz Gill made clear, 'No matter how good and successful your film was, when it comes to finding money for the next film, the producer will always ask you who is the first lead, and he wants a male director.'[5] The liminal status of women filmmakers is still unfortunately the norm in postcolonial Ireland. As a result, most of the films made by Irish women in the 1980s and '90s are set in Ireland and address female issues of repression in religion, politics and sexuality, thus responding to the necessity of telling one's own stories.

Belonging to a long literary tradition

Dublin-born writer and director Juanita Wilson, selected as one of the ten European 'directors to watch' by *Variety* in 2012, occupies a marginalised position on the national scene in the way that she has addressed universal issues from her directional debut. With a body of only three films (one short and two feature films) she has consolidated her position as a worldwide auteur. The purpose of this chapter is to highlight the specificities of a unique cinematographic work in the country's filmic landscape while unravelling the influences of the cultural and social context in which the filmmaker lives and works. It develops Wilson's originality in being inspired by written texts far from the conventions of adaptation. It then provides an analysis of the films' aesthetics, exploring the tenuous links between factual testimonies and fictional representations. A close exploration of Wilson's work proves the filmmaker's engagement in creating filmic devices devoid of melodrama and sensationalism, yet documenting with great finesse the human tragedies in a twenty-first-century world saturated with images.

The first point to be observed is Wilson's quality as a reader and transmitter of foreign prose, thus offering what Bluestone defined as 'representing a different mode of experience, a different way of apprehending the universe'.[6] Theorist François Jost deprecates the language of criticism dealing with the film adaptation of novels for entertaining the illusion that spectators are readers who watch a film with the novel on their lap, constantly interrupting the film in order to check its conformity with the book.[7]

In Wilson's films the issue of adaptation is not based on whether the dialogue corresponds to the source, whether it retains the integrity of the source book or how faithful the film is to the original novel or short story, but on the profound exchange established with the creator. As she declared, 'Reading certain books for the first time, I instantly know that I am gripped by a desire to put this story on a big screen for an audience.'[8] Her talent consists in perpetrating and disseminating major works of world literature unknown to the public at large; inversing the process through which foreign filmmakers adapted Irish stories to the screen at a time when Ireland did not have the means of a film production industry,[9] Wilson follows her predecessor John Huston's footsteps in the way her deep attraction to the experience of reading informs her approach to filmmaking, each film offering the audience a journey into a foreign space.[10] Walking the way of the master, she is an astute reader of literature who relates to a wide variety of writers from different parts of the world.

The short film *The Door* (2008) is based on the 'Monologue About a Whole Life Written Down on Doors, the testimony of Nikolai Fomich Kalugin' by Svetlana Alexievich, from her book *Chernobyl Prayer: A chronicle of the future*. 'An unfamiliar name to many English-speaking readers' according to *The Guardian*, even after winning the 2015 Nobel Prize for literature,[11] Alexievich has also been a major female artist concerned with issues of transmission: 'I've been searching for a literary method that would allow the closest possible approximation to real life. Reality has always attracted me like a magnet, it tortured and hypnotised me, I wanted to capture it on paper.'[12] The journalist and novelist dedicated her work to the people of the post-Soviet society after the collapse of the USSR. In *Voices from Chernobyl: The oral history of a nuclear disaster* (1997), she explores the consequences of the Chernobyl catastrophe through the voices of numerous witnesses over ten years. Although the book belongs to fiction, its style is characterised by its closeness to reality, and testimonies are injected into the stories according to Ales Adamovich's method.[13] *The Door* is set in the Ukrainian radioactive wasteland surrounding Chernobyl, and tells of a man who slips into the apartment he used to occupy with his wife and daughter to steal his own front door. He does so in a deserted quarter by night, crossing barbed wire next to a Ferris wheel reminiscent of happy days, the complete silence resonating in a snow-covered landscape. A feeling of fear is fuelled by the multiple points of view on the man, who keeps running and hiding in the dark. After loading the door onto his motorbike baggage-carrier, a long shot shows him from a distance, riding his motorbike in the snow. A male voiceover saying 'That day, we didn't just lose a town, we lost our whole world' informs the spectator that the story is told from the father's point of view. After the four-minute prologue, the flashback structure sheds light on how the inhabitants of the contaminated land were displaced and the children diagnosed with radioactive disease. At the end of the story, the door, being part of a traditional ritual of the grieving process, is used during such a ceremony. What may have seemed an incongruous robbery turns out to be heartbreaking when one realises that the door is being used as a stretcher for the funeral of the little girl who has succumbed to radioactive contamination. The disaster that has struck the town of Chernobyl is told through the fate of a single child, yet it takes on a universal dimension.

Resilience and surviving are major components of Wilson's cinema, as though centuries of distress in Ireland still permeated her social imagery. For her first feature film she adapts the work of Croatian novelist Slavenka Drakulic, one of Europe's foremost women writers, and the resulting work succeeds in having the nature of rape in war recognised by the international community.

Drakulic's novel *As If I Am Not There* tells of the brutalities of the Yugoslav Wars. Founded on atrocities that were perpetrated in Bosnia and Herzegovina during the Balkan war between 1992 and 1995, Drakulic testified:

> I was living in Zagreb when the first women were exchanged for imprisoned soldiers and the first camps for refugees were set up in Zagreb neighborhoods. Many journalists and women's groups started to collect documentation about these rapes. Immediately there was awareness that they should be documented. Very soon it became clear that the numbers were on a huge scale. To be sure, rapes happen in every war, but the scale of these ones, once they were discovered, was extraordinary. What was remarkable, too, is that, although many of these women were from remote areas (and you would not expect that these women would speak openly about these kinds of things), it turned out to be a political issue for them. These women felt instinctively that it was their revenge to say who the perpetrators were.

As If I'm Not There opens on a close-up of a naked baby whose eyes are wide open and looking at the camera. The next shot reveals the face of a young woman on a white hospital bed, a lost look in her eyes. Even though the editing implies that they are mother and child and facing each other, their eyes do not meet. A door slamming and the baby's cries have no impact on the young woman's sad expression. The following long shot includes mother and child, but shows a profile of her face stuck gazing into infinity while the baby is desperately seeking her attention. The second scene shows the young woman under the shower. She is obviously going through a lot of pain and trying to alleviate her suffering. A close-up on her feet discloses that she is bleeding. The red blood contrasts with her unsettling paleness and the whiteness of the bath. The opposition also breaks with the usual happy representation of a young mother with her baby in a maternity hospital. The thus described prologue is followed by a ninety-minute flashback during which we follow the life of this young Muslim woman from Sarajevo called Samira (Natasa Petrovic), who goes to teach in a rural village and is captured with all the other women of the village by soldiers who keep them in a prison camp to torture and rape them.

When three of the opening shots – the baby, baby and mother, mother under the shower – are repeated in an identical fashion at 1 hour 32 minutes of film, the audience has become deeply acquainted with the young woman's story of displacement, hatred and rape by the enemy. The silent takes of the prologue repeated at length in the ending make the viewer understand the heroine's dilemma of giving birth to the enemy's child, a pain reinforced by her own status as an orphan. Again, the filmic adaptation reveals a thorough understanding of the deepening human tragedy of the original literary narrative set in the context of the Balkan war, while taking on a broader meaning.

Wilson, when asked about her third film *Tomato Red*, confirms her interest in singular tragedies 'and how we respond as human beings trapped in difficult circumstances and what we do to try and preserve our sanity and humanity'.[14] Following the seminal work of filmmaker Neil Jordan in *Angel* (1982) and *The Crying Game* (1992), she explores violence and its effect on helpless individuals. *Tomato Red* (2016) is based on Daniel Woodrell's eponymous novel. Most of the American writer's stories are set in the Missouri Ozarks, a powerful landscape that has attracted other filmmakers to adapting his works.[15] What Wilson says drew her to telling the story of *Tomato Red* was the first sentence of the novel, a long, breathtaking sentence lifting the reader's senses to the highest level.[16] She found Sammy's voice 'immediately arresting in its honesty and humour' and imagined how to shape the novel into a cinematic experience. Yet if the first words are kept unchanged, immediately bringing to life Sammy's voice thanks to the stylistic device of a voiceover, the literary dimension of the tale is also brought to the fore: 'You're no angel. You know how this stuff comes to happen. It's a long story and I'm sure you heard it all before …'

The first words bring grist to the mill of a theory of free adaptation, an adaptation not in terms of conformity of length, dialogues, and accretion of details. The immediate deviation from the original text reveals Wilson's concern for the reader's experience. When opening a book we are fully aware that we have heard of the tale many times before but we still enjoy reading it once more. Wilson's films have a novelistic quality in the sense that they transform the raw material of a novel into a visual experience. Rhythm, metaphors and images are recreated within the cinematic text.

The prologue is another key feature of the literary dimension that is present in her three films. In *Tomato Red* the three-minute prologue opens on a still shot of Sammy smoking a cigarette while sitting on the bonnet of an American car at dawn. A mountain scenery appears in the dimness of the background. A train passes, briefly illuminating the man's face. A voiceover accompanies the plaintive warning cry of the train in the darkness, suggesting an analogy between stories and trains passing by. As railcars follow one another, the voiceover soon makes it clear that 'one wrong turn leads to another' and that the story will end badly, echoing Woodrell's two epigraphs:

'Anybody possessing analytical knowledge recognizes the fact that the world is full of actions performed by people exclusively to their detriment and without perceptible advantage, although their eyes were open'. (Theodor Reik)

'It's not all peaches and cream.
But I haven't learnt that yet.' (Oil Can Boyd)

The first still shot gives way to a second extreme long shot of a mountainous landscape, an establishing shot that serves as a spatial frame of reference but is soon to be contradicted by a close-up of Sammy in custody in a police cell. The contrast with the visuals is ironic. The hoarse-voiced narrative monologue informs the viewer he 'ended up here, on the wrong side of things, as always'. Sammy's release with an extra-diegetic music and the flight of a bird may close the prologue on a positive note but the off-screen narration gives the opening an air of predestination. With the use of interior monologue, Wilson establishes an intimate link with the spectator, who has access to Sammy's thoughts. Yet the story is being narrated by an anti-hero who admits his wrongs from the very opening of the film.

The repeated use of the technique of the prologue in the three films is profoundly significant, as the works are consequently structured in flashbacks, their main interest being not what happened, but how and why.

A reduced aesthetic hyperbolism

The filmmaker has obviously experienced the thirst for strong stories and enjoyed not knowing what would happen next when reading Woodrell's *Tomato Red*.[17] Yet her films testify of her absolute refusal of melodrama for the benefit of truth.[18] Taking the substance out of her own readings, she offers a narrative that is cleared of melodramatic scenes. Far from the Irish tradition of the emotional representation of the family in films like *My Left Foot* (1989), *The Field* (1990) or *In The Name of the Father* (1993),[19] Wilson's aesthetic of film establishes a distance with the protagonists of the narratives through the temporal dislocation produced by the prologue and flashback; she avoids orchestrating the emotional ups and downs of the intrigue according to Thomas Elsaesser's definition of melodrama.[20]

In *The Door*, the flashback consists in identifying the context in which the man stole the door and the reason why he did it. The protagonists have no names except for the little girl Lena. The concise monologue told by an off-screen narrator whom we understand to be the father punctuates the visuals with literary distinction.[21] It is chanted over different scenes in the film, and its juxtaposition with sparse dialogues contributes to producing a distance and to extending the meaning of each scene. Only in the final credits do we learn of the testimony of Nikolai Kalugin to which the film is dedicated. Yet every contemporary viewer who knows of the 1986 Chernobyl nuclear catastrophe can easily reactivate his/her background knowledge of the subject. The fifteen-minute film produces a clear-cut awareness of the singular as well as the universal dimension of the catastrophe. Cutting short the spectacle of suffering, the story brings up no surprise, no tears. A sense of sadness and fate emanates from the blue coldness of the images. Conventional melodramatic elements such as shots of the young girl's agony, or close-ups on the parents' cries at their daughter's death, are absent in a willingness to reduce aesthetic hyperbolism. The funeral procession exudes a mood of dignity. Far from satisfying the urge to indulge in the scopic drive, the short film acts as a sign of deep respect towards the victims.

The same goes for *Tomato Red*. In the scene during which the police take Dev, Sammy and Jamalee to the place where the deceased body of Jason is pulled from the water, a bird's eye view close-up on Jason's face (1.52) is the only close-up on the victim. Dev and Jamalee are then seen crying, and when Dev holds her dead son in her arms, an extra-diegetic music covers her cries, setting the scene of the unbearable loss at a distance and thus preventing spectators from identifying with the bereaved mother. The film also finishes abruptly on a fade to black after Sammy has nervously lifted his crowbar and smashed it into Tim Lake's head. In the original screenplay on which the film is based, Sammy was dragged to his feet, put into the back of the police car and driven away, sirens going. This classical aspect of film narrative was omitted in the final version to the benefit of a non-linear storytelling structure. Similarly, the closing scene pictured Jamalee getting off a bus in Florida and stepping forward into the sea, the cello and violin music starting to swell. Ending on an optimist note would have weakened the film considerably. The omission of the scene leaves the question of Jamalee's fate open even though the viewer cannot possibly hope. The non-conventional ending avoids the victims becoming figures of conservative propaganda and reflecting a Manichean view of the world. Instead it provides a cultural critique that an optimistic ending would have made impossible, fitting Wilson's constant compulsion to denounce unsustainable injustice.[22]

An international engagement through fictional representations

The Irish filmmaker's formal challenge is nourished by the world of contemporary events. Ireland was not shaped around the common experience of European colonisation and in that sense postcolonialism, when applied to Ireland in the 1980s and '90s, did refer to the postcolonial conditions of countries subordinated to European empires. Yet the consequences of colonialism in Ireland have been very different from those of countries affected by colonisation outside Europe. Different forms of colonisation have given rise to different forms of de-colonisation. In the case of Ireland, its cultural and geographical closeness to other European countries, its people's mastery of English, its European Union membership and its dynamic people and diaspora have given rise to unparalleled economic growth. Such cultural challenges as the search for national identity expressed in the films of the 1970s to the 1990s do not dominate national production in the twenty-first century.

Globalisation has hit Ireland in its modes of thought as it has in the other Occidental and Western-oriented societies. According to Ulrich Schmid, 'A sense of being part of world history has weakened considerably since 1991, with a depletion of historical narratives that might locate cultural identity in a historical temporality.'[23] Different generations relate to images otherwise. In his recent works Jean-Luc Godard extensively denounced the failure of cinema to document the horrors of the Second World War. The issue of how to document the terrors of the twenty-first century remains essential, and with it the difference between factual and fictional representations.

Juanita Wilson is clearly on the side of fictional representation. She even pushes further the movement that goes from the real to the narrated by adding a second level of narrative (adapting novels) in order to digest the horrors and clear them of their pathos, just as Samira in *As If I'm Not There* has to dissociate herself cognitively from the events that she went through in order to survive. The director's creative treatment of facts goes through the filters of fiction to come closer to accuracy and broadcast a truth that may either be obfuscated by darkness or threatened to sink into oblivion.[24] She is possibly the only European filmmaker who has tackled foreign policy problems exclusively in her works. In each film she opts for a single point of view, each time dealing with major society issues with the purpose of reaching a large public.[25] Man is victim of his environment. Warning us not to forget nuclear catastrophes, mass rape of women during wars or hidden collective murders of gay young men, she focuses on one character's experience and brings us close to it while resisting pity. Each situation refers to a specific period and place, which Juanita Wilson expresses thoroughly, in a restrained way, thanks to a creative symbolic framework.

Whatever the storyline, Wilson's use of outdoor settings produces a powerful sense of place. The Ferris wheel in the abandoned playground of Prypiat, the deep-focus shot of a man driving a motorbike in the snow through the forest at night with a stolen door on the baggage-carrier, give a sense of actual location and also convey symbolic extensions of coldness, solitude and tragedy (*The Door*). Real locations are thus exploited to create a formalistic effect. The same goes for the opening shot of *Tomato Red*, or for the spectacular shots of landscapes that Samira is going through at the beginning of *As If I'm Not There*. The numerous extreme long shots give the viewer an understanding of the distance that the young woman has to cover before getting to the village where she is going to practise as a teacher; they also depict the aesthetic beauty of a country that is going to be torn apart. In *Tomato Red*, truck stops and trailer parks are captured in their deterioration and Jake Weary's magic tone of voice matches the combination of such sites with the wide-open spaces of America. To convey messages larger than the stories themselves, fiction needs to be based on true stories and actual locations exploited to create an artificial and formalistic effect.

On the same issue, Wilson's need for accuracy made her cast Ukrainian actors and have them speak in their native tongue for *The Door*, and she shot in the most radioactive Ukrainian cities, Kiev and Prypiat.[26] Likewise, *As If I'm Not There* was shot in Macedonia and stars Macedonian actresses Natasa Petrovic and Jelena Jovanova and actors Feda Stukan and Miraj Grbic, both from Sarajevo.[27] Casting Natasa Petrovic for Samira was crucial to the film. The lead character is constantly on-screen and the horrors she endures are expressed through the use of edited juxtapositions of her framed body. The female body has lost identity and become a major concern in terms of possession.[28] A metaphor for the divided country, it is constantly framed, sometimes framed within the frame, rarely in full shot, most often in close-up. One shot is particularly striking. Preceding the collective rape scene, Samira is seen through the blown frosted glass of a door and her body appears cut up in pieces, as if predicting the scene of rape during which the camera remains on her face for most of it while we know exactly that it is the part of her body that is negated by her aggressors. A POV shot of a fly interrupts on two occasions. The insect seems to be glued to the wall, imprisoned in the same way as she is, her only escape being her mental capacity to escape from her body, as suggested by the silence that accompanies these shots.[29] The slow pace of the men's undressing and walking towards her is in complete opposition with the brutality of the moments of actual rape happening off-screen. Preventing the fascination for repulsive images, a distance is brought by rhythm breaks, an abrupt silence in opposition to the men's roars of sexual enjoyment, and a POV framed shot of men in slow motion playing football that depicts male dominance as a universal and collective game. The out-of-body experience Samira goes through when the three men urinate on her after the triple rape is not only true to her traumatic experience, it also adds to the necessary distance imposed on the viewer of a rape scene. Samira is the victim and the viewer, and being spectators we may also be the victim, no matter who we are or where we live.[30]

Resorting to distortion of time and space and to sound effects also serves symbolic functions. The crackle of footsteps on snow (*The Door*), the whistling of an oncoming train (*Tomato Red*), or the silence of an entrapped fly (*As If I'm Not There*) work on a subconscious level that the spectator may not be fully aware of. Juanita Wilson pays particular attention to all the elements of the soundtrack. I previously mentioned Jake Weary's voice timbre and interposed diction in *Tomato Red* as a major component of localisation. In *As If I'm Not There*, music acquires a concrete content from the opening credits. Following the prologue, the soundtrack precedes the film images and its ethnic overtones serve as a kind of overture to grasp the place and spirit of the film as a whole. Yet it is neither omnipresent nor overtly dramatic. Kiril Dzajkowski's composition epitomises the young contemporary urban woman from Sarajevo. It accompanies her and replaces the words she is unable to pronounce after what she has endured. The scarcity of the dialogues is also extremely significant. It tells of the victims' incapacity to articulate what they have been through and how they feel and enlarges the visual power of the glacial photography, saying much with minimal words. The woman's wordlessness echoes the numerous testimonies devoid of any details or feelings. The main dialogue in the film is the captain's.

One may associate the captain's attitude with the men's incapacity to evaluate their crime in the 'Fo a case', but paradoxically in the film he is portrayed as though being with Samira permitted his humanity to be restored.[31] He is attracted to her. While abusing her he treats her kindly and the sex scene is in opposition to the rape scene, suggesting that the way he hurts her is more profound and long-term, as will be revealed by her pregnancy.[32]

Conclusion

The study of Juanita Wilson's work confirms that it clearly belongs to a culture with a long tradition of literature. An alert and discerning reader, Wilson adapts stories that have an emotional impact on her and engages in major international causes, so that a body of work of three films suffices to assert the inseparability between the artist and the world. Avoiding melodrama while tackling hard-hitting subjects through the telling of deeply personal stories, she has developed a film aesthetic with absolutely minimal dialogue. The structure of her films takes the circular pattern of memory. Yet the treatment of memory is not concerned with the Irish national consciousness as the works of her predecessors were, but with emotions stemming from Western civil societies. In that matter, placing the film *As If I'm Not There* in the context of an Irish history of cinema, the case study of the conflict in the Balkans is reminiscent of the films of the 1980s and '90s that dealt with the situation in Ireland. As with Irish director Neil Jordan before her, Juanita Wilson makes it obvious that national identity is a construction and that pure ethnicity is nonsense. She has committed herself to the women's cause by condemning the unspeakable nature of war rape and having such suffering recognised by the international community. Going counter to the assertion that only victims have the right to tell their own stories, she contributes to denouncing the horrors of her time by bearing witness to the victims' traumatic experiences, which has become one of the most fundamental ethical imperatives of the West in the twenty-first century. Her choice of non-national issues and her conceptual approach to filmmaking prove that Ireland has moved on from its postcolonial past and that Irish women fully play their role on the international scene.

Irish Cinema and the Gendering of Space: Motherhood, domesticity and the homeplace

RUTH BARTON

Contemporary Irish cinema has struggled to respond to changing expectations around the positioning of women in society. In particular, as I explore in this chapter, it has found itself faced with new discourses on women's relationship to the home and to motherhood that have troubled its films but seldom been their focus. One explanation for this is the continuing thematic focus on issues of masculinity, inevitably in crisis. Not only are Irish films most often about male dilemmas, Irish filmmakers are overwhelmingly male. Whether male domination of the Irish film industry is solely to account for this is another matter. However, what is undeniable is that Irish cinema has not thrown up its own Maeve Binchy, Eavan Boland, Anne Enright, Eimear McBride or Edna O'Brien, to name just a few of the influential Irish women writers (and writers about women) of this and the previous century. Of course, there are Irish women filmmakers and this volume's chapter on Pat Murphy pays tribute to one of the most highly regarded directors of her generation. However, and this is a discussion I will develop further below, her work has always existed outside of the mainstream, as has the work of Vivienne Dick. It is the space women filmmakers occupy in the Irish production landscape, as well as the spaces that Irish female characters occupy, that I consider here.

It is beyond the scope of this chapter to discuss why women have not been attracted to working in film in the same numbers as they have to creating literary fictions. Nor am I discounting the possibility that men can make women-centred films. In Hollywood, for instance, directors such as Paul Feig have made careers out of female-led dramas – *Bridesmaids* (2011), *Spy* (2015), *Ghostbusters* (2016) – while Kathryn Bigelow is equally well-known for action pictures and other works centred around male leads, notably *Point Break* (1991) and *The Hurt Locker* (2008). The selection of recent films that I discuss below is largely the product of Irish male directors, although two are made by women. Both these latter films are responsible for intensely traumatic images of motherhood and the home, and it may well be that this is as a consequence of their directors' gender. At the same time, I don't want to dwell too much on the identity of any one director but consider more how Irish cinema of recent years has reflected on the gendering of place, and specifically the place of women. I have chosen the time period of the Celtic Tiger and its aftermath because it has been such a provocative one in terms of social discourses on gender, and also because it has witnessed significant changes in how women's 'place' in Irish society has been conceptualised. My critical approach, therefore, is influenced by how Irish cinema and society interrelate, not so much in the older understanding of cinema constituting a mirror to society, but more as a way of discussing how and why films construct their social worlds. Although my discussion concerns films made since the turn of the century, I want to start with a brief overview that situates contemporary Irish filmmaking, and specifically discourses around women and the home, within a wider historical background.

Cultural constructions of Irish women and the home

It is a truism that Irish post-revolutionary society was founded on an understanding that a woman's place was in the home, and the words of Article 41.2 of the Constitution (often referred to as the 'woman in the home' clause) are routinely cited to illustrate this history. Archaic as that wording now seems, it still speaks to certain very valid concerns in today's culture, particularly the idea that women should not be economically obliged to work outside the home. Even more pertinent than the arguments around whether mothers should or should not go out to work, now in any case an option restricted to those with substantial economic privilege, is the fundamental understanding that a woman should have a home. As the housing crisis continues, it is particularly the homeless mother in emergency accommodation who dominates news imagery. At the same time, the recessionary era introduced new concerns around male insecurity and these, as I discuss below, often expressed themselves in a longing for older configurations of the domestic space as the locus of a comforting image of the caring female.

Feminist writing has long been divided on this relationship between woman and home. It is worth reminding ourselves here of Brandon French's celebration of the actions of Mary Kate Danaher (Maureen O'Hara) in John Ford's *The Quiet Man* of 1952. French proposed that it was Mary Kate's 'battle for status in her marriage' that defined her and challenged the 'bases of conventional femininity'. Thus, the sequence in which she throws away the stick handed to her husband, Sean Thornton (John Wayne), by a woman of the village to 'beat the lovely lady' is a rejection of 'her husband's mastery, to which the older woman has obviously acquiesced'.[1] For French, it was not Ford's appropriation of the narrative of *The Taming of the Shrew* that was so revelatory but the triumph of the strong woman. Yet my own experience of discussing Ford's treatment of Mary Kate with students in the classroom seldom throws up a chorus of admiration. In particular, the sequence in which Thornton drags his resistant wife by the hair through the fields and home, an act signalled as appropriate within the film's diegesis, is hard to claim for a positive image of marital relations.

In an influential essay on the 'homeplace', bell hooks has argued for the domestic space as one where the black woman could be free from racist oppression. In her vision, the black mother in the home was, in creating a homeplace, 'making home a community of resistance' against white, supremacist societies.[2] While hooks is evidently writing to a very specific history of oppression, one that the white Irish woman did not experience, it is still useful to recognise the claim that the home was a space where women could exercise a level of authority denied to them in the wider culture. This conflation of the home with maternal power has a long tradition in Irish society and in cultural representations, though one that is treated with some considerable ambivalence. In particular, it is the binaries that have developed around this historical gendering of space that are problematic. Thus, Patricia Neville has argued that 'Film has played an active role in perpetuating the meta-narrative of Irish femininity as dominant and nurturing figures in the life worlds they inhabit, but powerless in society.'[3]

Genre and the city space

In many Irish films, even today, that inability to conceive of women as being defined other than as mother, wife or mother-to-be retards any real development in images of femininity. Take, for instance, the popular *Intermission* (John Crowley, 2003). Made in the style of the moment, as a set of interweaving narratives, the film follows the stories of a set of young suburban working-class Dubliners. Foremost amongst these are John (Cillian Murphy) and Oscar (David Wilmot). A crisis erupts when John's girlfriend, Deirdre (Kelly Macdonald), breaks it off with him to date a middle-aged married banker, Sam (Michael McElhatton). In cahoots with local wild boy Lehiff (Colin Farrell), they decide to kidnap the banker but the scheme soon falls apart. Meanwhile, Sam's wife, Noeleen (Deirdre O'Kane), has launched herself into a compensatory relationship with Oscar based on his willingness to indulge her new pleasure in S/M sex. What seems like an upending of older tropes of Irish identities soon demonstrates its limitations. Deirdre's sister, Sally (Shirley Henderson), is recovering from an abusive relationship, her trauma signified by a lapse in personal grooming that has seen her grow a 'ronnie' or facial hair. The one constant in her life is her mother, Maura (Ger Ryan), a homemaker and widow. When Sally realises what she looks like, she rushes to her mother for reassurance. How could she have let herself go like this? As Maura comforts her daughter, Sally asks her why she never remarried. Maura explains why not: 'Who could ever give me what he gave me anyway … his love, for one thing, my home, the times we had … the children he gave me.' The scene ends with Sally confessing how lonely she has been (without a boyfriend), a situation that will soon be rectified as she enters a new relationship with sensitive bus driver Mick (Brían F. O'Byrne). By the conclusion of *Intermission*, Noeleen has returned to Sam and as the end-credits play, we see her take her revenge on him by withholding his access to the television remote control and forcing him to change channel manually at her whim. Even as the film announces itself as an ironic play on old stereotypes, so scenes such as these reinforce those most enduring gender tropes, particularly of marital loyalty, the primacy of the domestic space in women's lives, and the revenge of the scorned wife.

Intermission's off-setting of problematised masculinity against stable configurations of femininity/domesticity is consistent with its origins as a crime or caper movie. This genre has come to dominate Irish cinema, particularly its city-set films, and has certainly contributed to the sidelining of female-centred narratives within the national cinematic corpus. To take another example, a director who has consistently worked within this generic framework is Mark O'Connor (*Between the Canals* (2010), *Stalker* (2012), *King of the Travellers* (2012), *Cardboard Gangsters* (2017)). The last of these was the top grossing indigenous Irish production of 2017 and speaks to many of O'Connor's thematic preoccupations. For the purposes of this argument I want to focus here on the central character Jason Connolly's (John Connors) relationship with his mother, Angela (Fíonna Hewitt-Twamley). Connolly is one of the titular cardboard gangsters, a fundamentally decent man who becomes embroiled in criminality in an attempt to settle his mother's debts to a local loan shark. She in turn dotes on him and is willing to accept his protestations of innocence when faced with hints about his new occupation. O'Connor likes to reference classic Hollywood and European cinema in his productions and in this film this tendency is articulated through his gangster son/blindly adoring mother dyad. Thus, when Jason confesses to his 'ma' that he has killed a man, she cradles him like a baby, shushing him and consoling him in a pose that recalls the classic mother-of-the-gangster in films such as *The Public Enemy* (William A. Wellman, 1931) or *White Heat* (Raoul Walsh, 1949). There is something disconcerting about encountering such regressive cinephile referencing in a contemporary production, and far from drawing attention to the redundancy of this kind of maternal configuration, *Cardboard Gangsters* works to affirm it.

Of course, not all Irish cinema of the period under discussion was genre-driven and not all genre films were crime films. The early 2000s saw the making of a number of romcoms, including *About Adam* (Gerard Stembridge, 2000), *When Brendan Met Trudy* (Kieron J. Walsh, 2000) and *Goldfish Memory* (Elizabeth Gill, 2003). The genre fell into abeyance after this, most plausibly because of its inappropriateness as a model for critiquing societal inequality in the Celtic Tiger and subsequently the recession. As I have discussed elsewhere, productions such as *About Adam* are interesting for their celebration of the new sexual freedom on offer in post-Catholic Ireland.[4] Yet even this film returns to the home as a space of comforting domesticity, one controlled by the domineering but loving matriarch, Peggy (Rosaleen Linehan). As much as it celebrates female desire, in this case the fantasies of its family of sisters and their construction and reconstruction of the titular Adam as sexual object, *About Adam* ends with marriage and the affirmation of the heterosexual family.

Discussing new configurations of masculinity in Celtic Tiger Dublin, Conn Holohan has written of Lenny Abrahamson's *Adam & Paul* (2004) that the two heroin addicts, the eponymous Adam and Paul, are denied a 'homespace', and are condemned to live on the streets, where they are othered by those whom they encounter, whether it is their former friends, the shopkeepers, or the brother of an old girlfriend, Janine (Louise Lewis), whose apartment they enter looking for items to steal.[5] Developing this argument, Tony Tracy has further considered the place of the home in this film and specifically Janine's apartment as 'a "dream house" of physical and psychological shelter'.[6]

Even in this highly lauded art film, therefore, the home is unproblematically associated with domesticity and motherhood while it is the relationship between masculinity and the public space that is insecure. With the exception of *Cardboard Gangsters*, the productions discussed above share Celtic Tiger settings and are defined by their characters' accession, or otherwise, to the material well-being that was allegedly on offer to the people of Ireland during this period and which is configured through the stable homeplace. This meant that when the Celtic Tiger crashed and the recession took hold, the thematic concerns of Irish cinema changed little. Its emblematic male characters continued to suffer from exclusion from the comforts of home, but now for different reasons. The 2011 release *Parked*, for instance, directed by Darragh Byrne, stars Colm Meaney as Fred, a middle-aged single man who has been forced to live in his car. Parked on the seafront at Sandymount, on the outskirts of Dublin, he makes friends with a young drug-taker, Cathal (Colin Morgan), and, more importantly for the purposes of this chapter, an attractive single woman, Jules (Milka Ahlroth), living nearby. Meaney's lengthy career in Irish cinema has seen him emerge as a screen everyman, that honest, slightly put-upon middle-aged male to whom unfortunate things happen, but whose inherent generosity of spirit guarantees that he will ultimately prevail over adversity. In *Parked*, his Fred has returned from England and can offer Irish society something it has lost, not just his decency of character but specific artisan skills (as a watchmaker) that were rendered obsolete in the boom years. In the recession, these skills identify him as a positive contributor. This is one of the reasons tacitly offered to the audience for accepting him as the film's deserving hero (unlike Cathal with his drug problem); another is that he maintains bourgeois standards of cleanliness, and much is made of the makeshift plumbing he has rigged up in his car. His reward, the film posits, ought to be a home. It also ought to be his acceptance in Jules' home. Cathal, by contrast, is thrown out of his home by his own father when he turns up looking for money and responds by stealing from his wallet. In this manner, the male/paternal homeplace is rendered as unforgiving (and aesthetically unremarkable) while Jules' home is warm, well-appointed and welcoming.

Good mothers and sensitive strangers

In a trope that runs through the films of this era, Jules has come to Ireland from continental Europe. While there is a mundane explanation for this in *Parked* – Ahlroth is Finnish and casting her thus satisfies the requirements of Finnish co-production funding – it also alters the narrative. She, like the immigrant Czech 'girl' (Markéta Irglová) in *Once* (John Carney, 2006), is a professional pianist. Both women thus represent an older European cultured identity that offers the lost Irish male not just the promise of physical affection but also a reawakening of the senses through their playing of classical music. By contrast, Ondine (Alicja Bachleda), in Neil Jordan's 2009 film of the same name, is a Romanian drug mule, yet she too is associated with an eerie musical ability that touches the emotionally dead Syracuse (Colin Farrell), who falls in love with her. In this film Ondine's sensitivity is contrasted with Syracuse's estranged wife, Maura's (Dervla Kirwan), aggression. The latter's poor mothering skills are explained by her alcoholism but also contrasted to Ondine's easy relationship with Syracuse and Maura's daughter, Annie (Alison Barry). Ondine will thus ultimately replace the bad mother, Maura, and take up her rightful place in the home Syracuse inherited from his own mother.[7]

One of the most popular evocations of female domesticity during this period was Ken Wardrop's documentary *His & Hers* (2009). Wardrop's feature cost €100,000 to make and was the most successful domestically released Irish documentary of its day, taking in more than €300,000 at the Irish box office.[8] It is constructed around interviews with a selection of women who speak to camera of their relationships with their fathers, husbands and sons. In all, Wardrop features some seventy interviewees (this number includes a baby, a toddler and an older woman, none of whom speaks). All are from the Irish midlands and, excepting those who are too young or too old, they discuss their relationships with the men in their lives to camera and as voiceover. Each interviewee is older than the last so that by the end of the film many of the women are widowed, as is Wardrop's mother, who appears in the film.

Released in 2009, at the start of the period of the economic crash, part of the local success of *His & Hers* can be ascribed to its affirmation of unchanging gender roles and its depiction of the enduring bonds of male/female relationships. As Neville notes, 'It proposes that women's relationships with men are harmonious, with the interviewees celebrating, one way or another, heterosexual love.'[9] Small children confide how much they love and are loved by their fathers; teenagers discuss boyfriends, brides husbands, and older women the losses of widowhood. In a similar vein to Neville, Sinéad Molony argues that the film 'frames an ordinary female body that achieves universality not by what it shows but by what it excludes, namely masculinity, sexual and class alterity, and the sociocultural histories of the public sphere'.[10] Any critique of *His & Hers* needs to take into account its seductive shooting style as well as its affirmative mood. By keeping the production team to a bare minimum and making use of natural light, the film ensured that its interviewees were comfortable speaking to camera, or more often looking slightly off-screen, as if their thoughts were on the absent male figures they were describing. Consistently framed through doors, corridors and stairwells, and with very few close-ups, the women busy themselves with domestic chores, making up beds, laying the table, ironing a dress, folding clothes, scrubbing a pan.

It is not so much the use of the home as a space to film the interviewees that is problematic, but that it is the only space the women occupy. On the few occasions when they are seen engaging in outside activities, wheeling in a child's bicycle or driving a tractor, for instance, the camera remains in the home, as if it were just letting them out the door for a moment. So seamless is *His & Hers* that the viewer might be forgiven for thinking that all Irish homes are essentially the same, and all Irish womanhood follows the same trajectory, from cradle to grave (or at least to nursing home, where the film ends).

Traumatic maternity and the troubled homeplace

What the above films share is an association between womanhood, comfort and the homeplace. Not all Irish women are deemed fit to occupy this space, though few reject it as a statement of defiance. Janine in *Adam & Paul*, for instance, evidently still has some considerable reservations about living in her apartment, and one might question how much she has acceded to the responsibilities of motherhood given that she has left her baby unattended there. Maura's mothering and domestic skills in *Ondine* equally leave much to be desired. Yet these acts of rebellion against the assumptions of motherhood and domesticity are not positioned within these productions as liberating, rather more they point to the diminishment of the social fabric. If one solution to the challenge of depicting new social iterations of motherhood and domesticity is to replace the failed Irish mother with the more desirable foreign woman, another is simply to rewrite Irish maternal narratives so as to exclude the Irish mother completely.

This trope entered Irish filmmaking with two not . dissimilar productions, *Patrick's Day* (Terry McMahon, 2014) and *Glassland* (Gerard Barrett, 2015). Both feature 'bad mothers', whose inadequate life skills extend to failed marriages and poor parenting of their male offspring. In McMahon's film, New Zealand actor Kerry Fox plays Patrick's (Moe Dunford) mother, Maura, as a tough single parent, who obsessively protects her special needs son. The latter is institutionalised but still manages to meet an English flight attendant, Karen (Catherine Walker). She suffers from suicidal tendencies and these two social outsiders fall in love. Incensed by this, Maura enlists local policeman John Freeman (Philip Jackson) to help her retrieve Patrick. She and Freeman are attracted to each other, but he is ultimately unable to cope with her obsessive need to control her son's life. This extends to pressurising Karen to have an abortion when the latter finds herself pregnant with Patrick's baby. The viewer is reminded on several occasions that Karen is older than Patrick and she is positioned as at once his lover and mother. This leads to the central tension of the film revolving around two competing modes of mothering, with Maura justifying her continuous interventions as necessary for Patrick's wellbeing, and insisting to Karen that he is capable of violence and delusional fixations.

One of the film's strengths is its ability to sow doubt in the minds of the viewer as, for instance, to whether Patrick is actually being abused by his institutional carer or whether these scenes are projections of his mental disorder. This raises the further possibility that 'both' mothers are also creations of his paranoia, dividing into the classic maternal dichotomies of castrator and lover. The dreamy final sequence, shot in home-movie style, in which Karen returns from England to 'play' with Patrick, their child in her arms, while Maura looks on lovingly, thus unites both mothers in a fantasised act of completion.

McMahon's direction is elliptical and disorienting; characters communicate in riddled dialogue, and Patrick's emblematic relationship with Ireland is hinted at without ever being fully realised. Not only is his name symbolic, key sequences take place on St Patrick's Day and the film opens with John F. Kennedy's famous speech ('We need men who can dream of things that never were …'). In addition, Maura gives Patrick a jigsaw map of Ireland, which we later see completed. Given these visual cues, one might ask how the film speaks to Irish womanhood, particularly given that none of the key characters or actors – Maura, Karen (and John Freeman) – is Irish. The answer seems to be rather that *Patrick's Day* finds itself in a representational void, unable to imagine new configurations of Irish motherhood that will speak to contemporary times and, in any case, more focused on the implications of how differing modes of mothering affect the male offspring.

Something similar occurs in *Glassland*, Barrett's follow-up to his debut *Pilgrim Hill* (2013). Here, Tallaght taxi driver John (Jack Reynor) is trying to cope with an alcoholic mother, Jean (played by Australian actor Toni Collette), and his younger Down Syndrome brother, Kit (Harry Nagle), whom Jean has placed in a care home and seldom visits. 'Sometimes a mother just doesn't bond with her child,' as she explains to John. John has inherited the taxi from his no-good father, who, rather as did Patrick's father, walked out on the family upon realising that Kit was a special needs baby. When Jean is diagnosed with imminent liver failure, it falls on John, as ever, to come up with a financial solution for her care needs. The film's star is Reynor, who is the bearer of a moral authority denied his mother or any of the film's other characters. As *Glassland* opens, we hear his voiceover: 'It's been a long night. Had a few difficult clients. Worked a lot of hours.' But the second time he delivers these lines, close to the conclusion of the film, he adds in: 'I can't do this anymore. I can't.' In this manner, the viewer is cued to empathise with the young man and his excessive duties of care. Their home is disorderly and unkempt, the sink overflowing with dirty dishes. John spoon-feeds Jean and comforts her as she lies whimpering on her bed. By contrast, his good friend, Shane (Will Poulter), has abdicated his role as father and is heading to London. Shane's mother is the classic Irish 'mammy', her name, Bridie, a throwback to an older Ireland. Before his departure for the airport, she sprinkles Shane with holy water, reminding him that, 'There's no shame in a mother's love.' By the film's conclusion, John has brought Shane together with his ex-partner and child and rescued a young foreign immigrant from the sex industry. *Glassland* plays out over images of Jean, now in rehab, touching knuckles with Kit while John looks on, and, finally, of the young Chinese woman gazing at her rescuer.

Both *Patrick's Day* and *Glassland* retain some sympathy for their 'bad' mothers, emphasising that both are victims of circumstance. Yet neither displays any particular investment in exploring female subjectivity, particularly, as I have noted, Irish female subjectivity. It is to the work of directors Rebecca Daly and Carmel Winters that we need to turn to locate the most traumatic images of motherhood and the most complicated rendering of the home in contemporary Irish cinema. Of these, Daly's *Mammal* is the most disturbing, with Winters' *Snap* its only rival. *Mammal*'s central character, Margaret (Rachel Griffiths), is a divorced woman living on her own in a small apartment in Dublin from where she runs a charity clothing shop. Her leisure activities consist chiefly of swimming in the local indoor pool and she has few, if any, friends. As the film starts, her ex-husband, Matt (Michael McElhatton), appears and informs her that their eighteen-year-old son, Patrick, is missing. The exchange between them reveals that she has had nothing to do with the boy since birth, and later when he is discovered drowned in the canal, Matt warns Margaret not to attend the funeral and cause a scene. Meanwhile, one night, she finds a bruised teenager, Joe (Barry Keoghan), lying in the alleyway outside her home, takes him in, and patches him up. He is one of a gang of socially disadvantaged teens whose pastimes include luring older men into wasteland spaces with the promise of sex before beating them up. Constantly scrapping, Joe is almost as emotionally blank as Margaret, and wastes little time in robbing her purse after she has given him a bed for the night. So starts an odd relationship. Where in another film, Joe would simply substitute for Patrick, as Matt suspects he is doing, here he seems to be a mirror to Margaret's own anomie, acting out behaviour that she has repressed. Thus, he confesses to having engaged in erotic asphyxiation, and later she too will lie in the bath and wind a scarf tentatively around her neck. Finding her there, Joe slips into the water with her and they have sex.

Mammal – the title suggests the reduction of motherhood to its biological essentials – is a cold, detached film. The minimalist soundtrack is interspersed with howling, feral cats and the interiors are shot in dull greys, slate blues and browns, with the camera lurking behind doors studying the characters. Most of all, images of water dominate, from the swimming pool, where Margaret curls up into a foetal position and submerges herself on the bottom for minutes on end, to the lake where she and Joe swim, to her constant showering, and the sequences of intimacy in the bathtub. These watery settings suggest a return to the womb or a longing for a safe, enclosing world before the trauma of birth. Margaret will ultimately give birth twice, to the son she has rejected and to Joe, but her own relationship to motherhood is fraught. She may nurture – cats, the lost boy, a baby temporarily abandoned in a stroller – but her emotional reticence inhibits her from forming any real bonds. This psychological isolation is further reinforced by the film's disconcerting topography. The co-production requirements that resulted in the scenes in Margaret's home and in the pool being shot in Luxembourg no doubt contributed to this, providing a strange effect of Dublin/not Dublin throughout. Once again, the central female role is taken by a non-Irish actor (here Australian), and once again, this remains unexplained within the plot. The consequences of this thematic and visual estrangement are to void *Mammal* of Irish cultural identifiers. This may well be intentional – an authorial statement of the need to make a thematic break with those ingrained images of motherhood and explore universal, rather than nationally specific, concerns.

Snap, on the other hand, speaks unambiguously to Irishness, as much through casting as its fierce deconstruction of the myth of Irish motherhood. A faux documentary, Carmel Winters' film consists of a series of interviews with Sharon (Aisling O'Sullivan), who talks to camera about a traumatic event that took place three years ago. This is revealed to be her teenage son Stephen's (Stephen Moran) kidnapping of a toddler, whom he holds in her old parental home. A third strand of footage, home movies shot by Sharon's father, is interwoven into the film. Stephen also films the child before and after he has kidnapped him. Where *Mammal* is defined by its cool minimalism, *Snap* is a chaotic mélange of imagery, its multiple shooting formats and styles creating semantic disjunctures that point to the film's real crisis – the unassimilated act of abuse.

Writing on the film, Eileen Leahy has argued that *Snap* is in 'dialogue with the prevailing cultural stereotypes of Irish femininity', notably the Irish mother.[11] The casting of O'Sullivan reinforces this argument, given her iconic role as Francie Brady's (Eamonn Owens) mother in Neil Jordan's *The Butcher Boy* (1997). As Leahy illustrates, Sharon believes that she can control the camera's gaze even as it is trained on her, but, ultimately, she must confront the reality that she is powerless to dictate how her image is projected. Winters' creation is rebellious and foul-mouthed, constantly asserting her contempt of those neighbours and the anonymous letter-writers who target her with abuse for her son's crimes. In this way, and through the 'documentary', she engages with the public sphere in a manner that Margaret in *Mammal* refuses to. The latter's cognitive disengagement, to the point of sitting on the floor of the swimming pool submerged in water, her refusal to speak to her neighbours, her exclusion of her husband, enable her to hold herself together. It is this strategy more than any particular emotional adherence to the homeplace – which is anodyne and comfortless – that allows Margaret to survive in a manner denied Sharon. The final revelations of *Snap* are particularly cruel, locking Sharon into a circularity of home movie images and a history of incestuous abuse. Even as, in the closing shot, she sits on a park bench in a summer dress, so the dim footage of her childhood closes in around her with the homeplace revealed as the source of her and Stephen's emotional trauma.

Conclusion

In comparison with the mainstream, male-centred films that comprise much of recent Irish cinema, the narratives discussed here are at pains to distance themselves from traditional associations of motherhood, plenitude, and the maternal homeplace. By voiding themselves of recognisable signifiers of place and of identity, these works, particularly

Mammal, display a desire to move away from the old gendered – for which read regressive – tropes that have framed Irish cultural discourse. Distinguishing between the gendering of time and place, Doreen Massey has argued that:

> It is ... time which is typically coded masculine and space, being absence or lack, as feminine. Moreover, the same gendering operates through the series of dualisms which are linked to time and space. It is time which is aligned with history, progress, civilization, politics and transcendence and coded masculine. And it is the opposites of these things which have, in the traditions of western thought, been coded feminine.[12]

We can see this observation at work in much of what has been discussed above. Time, notably a sense of character development and movement towards a different future, is coded as masculine and attainable, while place, the woman's place, is repeatedly conceived of as stasis.

What is regrettable is that all the films discussed in this final section also have found themselves on the margins of the body of Irish cinema, most of all *Mammal*, which is unavailable for commercial viewing in any format. As I mentioned in my introduction to this chapter, women filmmakers have historically occupied a peripheral position within the landscape of Irish filmmaking and there are strong connections to be made between narratives of outsiderdom and the reality of life on the fringes of the industry. It is thus to one final Irish release, one of the most successful of recent years, that I turn to conclude this chapter and end on a positive note. The adaptation of Colm Tóibín's *Brooklyn* provided a showcase for Saoirse Ronan's stardom and saw her gain an Academy Award nomination for her role as Eilis Lacey, the young Wexford woman who leaves Ireland in the 1950s for work and new opportunities in Brooklyn. The period drama has long been viewed as a woman's genre and one with the potential to open up new avenues to discuss the desiring female, and in particular, her relationship to the domestic.[13] While the viewer would be misguided to expect any radical upending of the status quo in such a production, the adaptation of *Brooklyn*, directed by John Crowley and written by Nick Hornby, follows Tóibín with reasonable fidelity. Thus, Eilis and her sister, Rose (Fiona Glascott), both assume that they will follow careers. On Rose's death, Eilis takes on her fiscal responsibilities, albeit from the distance of Brooklyn, signing up for a night class in accountancy that will move her up the employment ladder from assistant in a large department store to clerical worker. The film (and novel) follow the contours of the woman's film, deploying many of its melodramatic tropes, with Eilis finding herself with two men in her life, the dependable Italian-American Tony (Emory Cohen) and socially well-positioned local Enniscorthy suitor Jim Farrell (Domhnall Gleeson), while a secret that will change everything hangs over her head. Having established this narrative structure, the film then plays with it, refusing to punish Eilis in the way a corresponding production from the 1950s might have. Thus, she does not fall pregnant following one night of pre-marital sex, nor does she have to pay for finding herself in love with two men. The film's ending is somewhat altered from the novel's, but both insist that Eilis will make of her life the best she can within the parameters of social convention. In this the film is enormously aided by Ronan's performance and her undoubted star power. Her Eilis grows in emotional strength as the film develops, a trajectory indicated, in true women's film manner, by her increasingly confident demeanour and clothing. On her return to Enniscorthy, she steps out into the public spaces of the town in her vibrant American colours in a way that her self-effacing mother would never have dared. Eilis speaks to a new younger generation of women for whom marriage is a dubious blessing. It is, as Tony recognises in demanding that she wed him before leaving for Ireland, a tie that binds.

Paradoxically, the popular *Brooklyn* is a more thoughtful film than its costume drama formula suggests, while the arthouse productions discussed above are more limited in their exploration of female screen identities than one might predict. As I hope this discussion has demonstrated, the burden of tradition still hangs heavily over Irish screen images of women, specifically in their treatment of the maternal and the domestic. The edgiest of the arthouse productions were directed by women, which may account for the intensity of their narrative focus. However, as *Brooklyn* shows, a strong female star can radically alter the dynamic of a film and speak to domestic audiences in a manner that is nationally specific. The star power of Irish male actors is undeniable and in part it is this that guaranteed the visibility of films such as *Intermission* and *Parked*. Alongside, then, the employment of more women directors and writers, Irish cinema needs stronger roles for women that will encourage

Irish female actors to develop their screen identities. These measures, alongside improved cultural awareness of changing gender roles and aspirations in Irish society, should bring a greater complexity to films for and about women in the national cinema.

Authority to Speak: Assessing the progress of gender parity and representation in Irish animation

CIARA BARRETT

This chapter aims to provide an overview of the progress of gender parity in the Irish animation industry by qualitatively assessing the link between female creative authorship at the directorial level and the manifestation of a progressive politics of gender representation on-screen. As such, it interprets evidence of gender representation in the industry as well as from the texts themselves, which may variably indicate – or not – female authorial input.

Up until recently, feminist criticism of the Irish film industry has been focused largely on analysis of live action features. However, this has somewhat overlooked the recent critical success and rise to international recognition of Irish animated films. Within the last ten years, Irish animation has expanded enormously, from estimates of less than 100 full-time professionals in the early 2000s to 1,600 workers today.[1] According to Animation in Ireland, the trade association for animation studios in Ireland, there are currently twenty-five such studios in the country.[2] Clearly, animation is a rapidly expanding sector of the Irish film industry, with animation benefiting firstly from the establishment of a number of specialised training programmes in Irish colleges and secondly from the proliferation of digital technology.

Indeed, the vast majority of imagery in Irish animated releases is computer-generated. However, the most high-profile Irish animated films to date have been animated in the traditional, 2D, hand-drawn style. Out of these, *The Secret of Kells* (Tomm Moore and Nora Twomey, 2009), *Song of the Sea* (Tomm Moore, 2014), and *The Breadwinner* (Nora Twomey, 2017) from Cartoon Saloon collectively represent the entirety, to date, of feature-length releases by homegrown Irish animation studios.[3] (Other major Irish animation studios like Brown Bag Films are primarily focused on TV and short film production.) They are also some of the most recent and high-profile full-length Irish films made with significant female creative input and even, in the case of *The Secret of Kells* and *The Breadwinner*, authorial control under the co-direction and direction, respectively, of studio co-founder Nora Twomey. I will return to an analysis of gender representation in these films – centring ultimately on *The Breadwinner* as the most progressive – but first it will be necessary to provide a fuller context for the pertinence of assessing gender parity in Irish animated films.

The Irish film industry has come under particularly heavy fire in the last few years for its evident hesitancy to address its blatant under-representation of women both on-screen, in lead acting roles, and off-screen in lead creative roles.[4] Elsewhere, I have argued that the man-ifest disembodiment of 'woman' throughout the history of Irish visual culture, due to a combination of religious and political factors, has led to the relative dearth of Irish female stars.[5] (This is as weighed against the contrastively large number of Irish male performers who satisfy the criteria for stardom, and notwithstanding the recent international suc-cess of Saoirse Ronan.) Moreover, Screen Ireland has recently published figures that admit to the lingering underrepresentation of female protag-onists in Irish films: between 2011 and 2017, less than half of Irish film productions, at 40 per cent on average, had a female protagonist.[6]

It should be noted that average female representation has even been skewed *upwards* in this respect by records from 2017, which show that 69 per cent of completed Irish films in that year had a female protagonist. This statistic is a considerable outlier to data from the previous six years, in which female protagonist representation was on average 33 per cent.[7] Nor does this data from 2017 (or indeed from earlier years) speak to the palpable underrepresentation of women in major – if not, strictly speaking, 'protagonist' – roles more generally, or the perceived quality of such roles. Substantial roles for women in the Irish live action film industry remain relatively few and far between – a fact that film producer Ed Guiney has even admitted likely contributes to the Irish film industry's poor record of retaining female acting talent.[8]

Irish cinema is hardly unique for its lack of gender parity within the industry, as this is the case in Hollywood, Britain, and across the European film industries generally. More surprising, though, is that it is only since late 2015 that Screen Ireland (previously called the Irish

Film Board) has officially acknowledged the retardant effect gender imbalance has had – and will continue to have, if not rectified – on the development of 'a distinct Irish cinematic voice'.[9] It has been well-documented that in male-dominated industries – particularly where women are underrepresented as writers and directors – there are less female characters, more nudity and sexual objectification of women, and more violence in their filmic output.[10] As Susan Liddy has pointed out, in the case of a national cinema like Ireland's, which aims for an output of films reflective of the collective/national character and perspective, it is impossible for such a national cinema to develop a reliable 'voice' for itself when half its voices are underrepresented, and as such, effectively *mis*represented.

On the other hand, as Liddy points out in her own chapter in this collection, the Irish film industry is progressive in having made gender parity a priority of its current Strategic Plan. Yet Irish animation, as a distinct sector of the Irish film industry, quietly rising in capital and critical value for two decades, has already developed a particular reputation for progressiveness in gender representation. This begs two questions: Why might the Irish animated film industry be more progressive in its culture of gender politics? And if it is, can this be measured in any sort of way, through filmic output, that suggests a trend or representational model for the rest of the industry to follow?

Putting national/industrial contexts to the side for the moment, it may be the case that animated film is, in general, less beholden to the traditionally gendered politics of viewing and representation that live action cinema has made paradigmatic. Indeed, the politics of star discourse and the literal/physical ramifications of character embodiment are theoretically irrelevant to animation. Because the female body is not 'really' seen in the (fully) animated film, in the sense that it is not photographed, it does not (in)form the fetish object/image that, Mulvey tells us, conventional live action cinema presupposes it to be.[11] Of course, theorisation of mainstream Western animation shows that the paradigmatic practice of gender representation in animation has been to re-mediate the sexist, gendered politics of representation familiar to classical (live action) cinema.[12] As Paul Wells argues, 'Masculinity ... is often played out through the universalizing concept of "everyman", in which male figures, or figures which are assumed to be male, become the symbolic embodiment of humankind.'[13] And this is to say nothing of the 'Boopist' representation of women, by which female protagonists are visually rendered in such a way as to heighten their secondary sex characteristics, caricature their femininity and simultaneously make them 'cute', with proportionally oversized round heads and huge eyes.[14] As an analysis of recent Irish animated films will show, it is manifestly possible for the animated film to render gender – like any other image/concept/object – in a more 'plasmatic' fashion (as fluid, metamorphic).[15] This is by virtue of two facts: 1) the animated image need not be an index for images already extant in the 'real world' *or* live action cinema, and 2) female directorial influence upon – indeed 'authorship' of – an animated film closely correlates with a progressive politics of gender representation.

Indeed, since the release of *The Secret of Kells* in 2009, Irish animated features have made significant strides towards re-balancing a gendered politics of representation, at the same time as the industry has seen an increase in female representation at the level of (studio) ownership and (film-creative) authorship. Out of the twenty-five animation studios listed by Animation in Ireland, seven (just under a third) are owned or co-owned by women. And in 2014, Deirdre Barry, a board member of Animation in Ireland, founded the Irish chapter of Women in Animation (WIA), which has since been actively invested in developing female representation at the creative and, more specifically, directorial levels.

Barry estimates that, in the last ten to fifteen years of rapid growth in the animation industry, and as a direct result of an increase in female ownership, female creative representation (in non-authorial roles such as story development, background animation, etc.) has risen close to fifty-fifty. Nevertheless, female authorial control is still underrepresented. As Barry says,

> There is still a lack of female directors. There's a lot of female creatives, like a lot of scriptwriters. I'd work with probably more female scriptwriters than I would with male. ... And I like working with both, but I feel female scriptwriters would bring certain, I guess, I don't know, additional sensitivity in stories. ... But I do feel in general collaboration with both males and females works really well.
>
>   ...
>
> What we did focus on with WIA is, OK, how do we change [the lack of female directors], like I've had a couple of projects where I really

wanted to give it to a female director, and I couldn't find them: they're just not there. … OK, why? We've got fifty-fifty representation in a lot of colleges, you know? … At least fifty per cent female. What happens to them? Why don't they become directors or go into bigger and stronger roles? … They go into production roles and things like that.[16]

Barry poses a question here, concerning the evident incongruity between women pursuing training in animation and women assuming authorial roles therein – a problem that has as yet gone unsolved (though is valuably explored at further length by Susan Liddy in her chapter in this collection). What *is* encouraging is that, from Barry's anecdotal evidence, it appears the culture within the Irish animation industry may be positioned better to foster gender parity in the workplace than, comparatively, the live action industry. Barry references her and her colleagues' willingness to collaborate with female creatives who might have to work from home due to the necessity of childminding, and the fact that she has only felt a positive reaction from male colleagues in relation to the establishment and efforts of Women in Animation. Yet the issue is one of teaching women not just the technical skills of animation, but how to 'speak out' and assume authority (or, perhaps even more complexly, to expect that they will be 'heard'). Towards this end, Women in Animation is currently involved in rolling out an initiative to make presentations to secondary school-age children – particularly aimed at girls – to encourage not just creative ideation from a young age, but a confidence to assume their leadership in creative roles is expected. In such a way, Barry and Women in Animation Ireland hope to see the manifestation of that 'additional sensitivity' – a sensibility, perhaps, in storytelling that would round out the – so far – male-centric image of the 'cinematic voice' of Ireland.

A qualitative analysis of gender representation in the Irish animation industry

Thus far, however, we largely have anecdotal evidence – valuable though it is – on the progress of gender parity and its cultural causes and effects in the animation and broader Irish film industry. In order to make the case that the animation sector is generally more progressive – or perhaps, more reliably, 'promising' – in terms of its internal culture and filmic output, I have attempted therefore to take a broader survey of opinion within the Irish animation industry, beyond analysis of discourse with certain key industry professionals.

In response to feminist outcry at the lack of female representation in the Irish performing arts, led by the 'Waking the Feminists' movement and bolstered by journalistic and academic criticism, Screen Ireland has, in the last two years, made records of gender representation available to the public online. The evidence, however, is grim: between 2011 and 2017, 21 per cent of completed films to which Screen Ireland granted funding had a female writer; 17 per cent had a female director; 60 per cent had a female producer; and 40 per cent had a female protagonist. Out of these four categories, only instances of female protagonists on-screen have overall gone up between 2011 and 2017 – and at that, female protagonist representation dipped considerably below 50 per cent in 2012, 2013, 2015 and 2016.[17] The prognosis for female representation in the Irish film industry is therefore not good.

It should be noted that Screen Ireland has, since 2016, listed as part of its Strategic Plan the challenge to 'embrace diversity and gender equality in all its forms and ensure the participation and representation of the full range of diverse voices in Ireland', with gender parity in 2020 the intended outcome.[18] Thus far, Screen Ireland's attempt to meet this challenge has manifested in a Six Point Plan, part of which is to collect and publish data on gender inequality (accomplished and ongoing), and the rest of which has to do with the promotion of training and mentorship of women. There have been minimal efforts to promise funding to female creatives, with the exception of the POV scheme, which has only just (as of 2018) offered production funding of up to €400,000 to three successful female writer/producer/director teams of live action features.[19] Therefore it remains to be seen – for a number of years at least – whether Screen Ireland's strides towards gender parity in live action filmmaking will manifest into a generally more progressive politics of gender representation in Irish live action features.

However, in looking towards Ireland's animated film output over the last decade, we can see that increased female representation at the authorial/creative level already correlates with a textual de-phallo-gocentricisation of film style and narrative tendency (that is to say, a move away from the traditionally gendered politics of representation on film, which is narratively male-centric and [im]balanced towards the gratification of heterosexual male viewing pleasure). While there are as yet few feature-length Irish animated films to analyse, a qualitative analysis of the progress of gender parity in Irish animation, as compared to its representational manifestations, can provide an interesting counterpoint to the comparatively slow progress of gender parity in the broader film industry.

In order first to gain a sense of how gender balance in the Irish animation industry stacks up against that of the larger Irish cinema, both qualitatively and quantitatively, I sought survey responses from professionals in the industry by targeting social media and emailing individual members of Women in Animation and Animation Ireland. The survey could be taken by anyone, male or female, working in some capacity in the animation industry, asking for respondents' impressions of gender representation on- and off-screen in Irish animated versus live action films. I received seventy responses, representing approximately 4 per cent of the population of people currently working in animation in Ireland. As such, statistics from these results fall outside a 10 per cent margin of error and will not be taken as empirically predictive. Nevertheless, a quantitative analysis of results may be taken as indicative of trends within the industry, while their qualitative analysis will provide context for a textual analysis of Irish animated films' progressiveness in gender representation.

Out of seventy respondents, thirty-six were female (53 per cent), thirty-one were male (46 per cent), and the remaining respondents opted not to answer (two) or identified as gender-fluid/non-binary (one). Regardless of gender, 79 per cent of respondents felt gender parity to be an issue in the Irish film industry, with 53 per cent identifying it as a 'particularly pressing' issue. 11 per cent thought there already was gender parity, and a further 10 per cent claimed it not to be an issue either way. Comparatively, 67 per cent of respondents felt gender parity is an issue in the Irish animation industry specifically, with only 40 per cent identifying it as particularly pressing, 13 per cent less than felt the same about the larger Irish film industry. 25 per cent thought there was gender parity – an increase of 14 per cent compared to Irish cinema overall – and 8.5 per cent felt it not to be an issue either way. Thus, in response to this survey, professionals within the animated film industry rated gender parity as less of a pressing issue in animation specifically and perceived themselves to be working in a relatively more gender-balanced work environment.

It is not without significance, however, that a couple of respondents qualified their answers in support of the animation industry by noting that women were better represented at lower-level jobs and in production roles than at ownership level:

> It is usual [sic] a case of gender being a factor in certain roles. Generally production staff, HR and pay role [sic] are more likely to be women. Where camera people, editors and directors more like likely to be male. This is true in both film and animation.
>
> – Male respondent, working in animation for four years after five years in live action

And:

> [I]n general, there is a gender balance in the animation and film industry from what I've experienced. The only area where I think it is unbalanced is the actual ownership and running of companies where I think it is male dominated. I can only think of one company owned and run by women.
>
> – Male respondent, working in animation for twelve years

These responses therefore corroborate Deirdre Barry's statement that the Irish animation industry is relatively gender-balanced in terms of its overall personnel, and as such, the culture is progressive; yet ownership and creative authorship are still predominantly male-dominated.

When asked about their impressions of gender representation *on*-screen, respondents had a markedly more favourable opinion of animated films, with two particularly outstanding differentials: 56 per cent of respondents found there to be noticeably more male protagonists than female protagonists in live action Irish films, while only 28 per cent found this in relation to animated films. Additionally, 7 per cent of respondents found Irish films in general to be particularly progressive in terms of their representation of gender, whereas a substantial 44 per cent found animated films, specifically, to be progressive.[20]

What is more telling, though, is an analysis of gender breakdown in relation to particular responses. At 64 per cent, versus 45 per cent for men, women in Irish animation were more likely to view gender parity in the Irish industry as a pressing issue. Women's responses were somewhat more levelled out regarding gender parity in the animation industry, with 44 per cent of women viewing it as a pressing issue and 38 per cent of men agreeing. On the other hand, only 19 per cent of women reported that gender parity had been achieved in the animation industry, while 29 per cent of men viewed gender representation as balanced. Indications are, not surprisingly, that men are likelier to perceive gender parity within a company that is *not* actually gender-balanced if that company nevertheless appears to be *better* balanced than others.

As Tamsin Lyons, female producer and owner of TV-based Irish animation studio Ink & Light, comments:

> On our last project we had almost 50/50 but that is rare and I heard a comment 'we are surrounded by women' which spoke to how rare it is given women were still technically in the minority. I would like to think that the industry is more welcoming than live-action. We work predominantly in content for children and in this area more of the commissioners tend to be women. Also given the content, the working atmosphere is more positive and encouraging. So it is an area where women can feel more comfortable. It is still a challenge, however. … We are still woefully short of experienced female writers and directors.[21]

In terms of gendered response to perceptions of on-screen representation, both male (70 per cent) and female (68 per cent) respondents were fairly evenly in agreement that Irish live action films feature more male protagonists than female. Interestingly, women within the industry were considerably *less* likely than men to find an imbalance of gender roles in Irish animated films (at 35 per cent versus 44 per cent) and somewhat *more* likely than men to report that animated films were particularly progressive (at 44 per cent versus 38 per cent). As borne out by these results, it is likely the case that women working in animation are more actively invested in female representation and characterisation on-screen, and thus they are more attuned to the relative progressiveness of the industry in which they work.

Tamsin Lyons again reports of her experience in the industry:

> ... the animation industry has become more aware in the last few years and is trying to rectify the situation. ... Unfortunately, with the Irish projects, animation takes so long that it's not going to happen overnight. Certainly, I realized that because I usually work with a male writer and director, the characters were coming through as default male. ... I am ... actively recruiting more female writers and directors, as well as female candidates for other roles. Until we do this, the level of representation on screen will not change.[22]

Such a willingness to actively recruit women in authorial, creative roles on projects that have already gone through development and into production presents a different strategy to that of Screen Ireland, which regards gender parity as something that will probably – that is, without testing or proof – eventually be achieved through an emphasis on training. Again, the animation industry – specifically, the action group Women in Animation – has taken this strategy further to address not just the issue of training in technical skills, but the social and psychological factors that impact upon women's pursuit of directorial roles in particular (factors substantiated as such in Susan Liddy's chapter here). Even better, the industry also has seen the rise to prominence of a successful female director – Nora Twomey – whom Deirdre Barry credits with fostering a culture of inclusiveness and positivity within the animation industry:

> Nora is one of the most positive people ... The way she talks about working with women who may go on to have a family and all that ... It's just a new way of working.[23]

Indeed, Cartoon Saloon, under the leadership of Twomey alongside Tomm Moore and Paul Young, represents an innovative model for business, production and storytelling that nurtures progressiveness and gender equality. Cartoon Saloon was founded in 1999 by Young, Moore and Twomey, all graduates of the Irish School of Animation at Ballyfermot College of Further Education. Up until 2009, the studio was best known for producing children's animated TV shows *Skunk Fu!* and *Puffin Rock*, but they have since attracted widespread critical attention for the release of three feature-length films. Beyond the fact that the studio is co-owned by a woman who has solo-directed a major international feature, it is significant that the feature is also overtly politically engaged from a feminist standpoint. With a gender balance of personnel at Cartoon Saloon reportedly at fifty-fifty, and anecdotal evidence suggesting the company employs women at a particularly high level of leadership, Cartoon Saloon is thus uniquely progressive for a high-profile Irish film production company – though in the context of Irish animation, specifically, it is perhaps more exemplary of a trend.

Overall, as borne out by the results from my cursory survey, the following trends may be observed:

Gender representation at the creative level is likelier to be more balanced in the production of an Irish animated film than it is in the production of a live action feature, though there remains an underrepresentation of women at the directorial level.

As a result, the working culture within animation in Ireland is perceptibly more progressive – if not perfectly so – with regard to gender than the live action industry.

Irish animated films are likelier to be regarded as progressive in terms of textual gender representation than are live action Irish features.

Yet it remains to be seen from critical analysis of Cartoon Saloon's feature-length films – which also represent the entirety of homegrown, Irish feature-length animated films to date – if there is a similarly direct correlation between female creative authorship and the representation of female agency and narrative centrality in Irish animated films. And so, finally, I wish to turn to a textual analysis of *The Secret of Kells*, *Song of the Sea*, and *The Breadwinner*, in order to relate current trends in gender representation within Irish animated films back to the impact of female creative authorship.

A textual analysis of gender representation in Irish animated cinema

The Secret of Kells, co-directed by Moore and Twomey and released in 2009, effectively announces the animated feature film as a loudspeaker for the 'distinct Irish cinematic voice' that is Screen Ireland's mission to disseminate. Centring on a child protagonist and hand-drawn in a fantastical manner – evocative simultaneously of the fluidity of watercolour paintings and the intricate line drawings of the illuminated book from which it takes its name – the film is aimed, ostensibly, at children. The narrative follows a young (male) monk, Brendan, as he helps in the completion of the Book of Kells during the time of Viking raids, aided by supernatural forces including a (female) forest spirit named Aisling. The film thus interpellates a young Irish audience, while opening the film up to visual pleasures and significations that make it interesting to mature Irish – and international – viewers. As Maria O'Brien has argued, the film thus aims to surpass (or even transgress) the Catholic-specific connotations of its subject matter to represent a 'post-Celtic Tiger era Ireland, at once able to exploit its Irishness and simultaneously able to interrogate ideas of the nation as fluid and hybrid'.[24]

An emphasis on the inherent hybridity of the film here is apt. In analysis of the film, O'Brien has invoked Homi Bhabha's theory of the postcolonial hybrid being 'less than one and double'.[25] Though, with *The Secret of Kells* as a sort of post-postcolonial text, it is perhaps more appropriate to read it as simultaneously 'one and double', not 'less than' (in that it is the product of a globalised nation relatively accepting of diversified cultural identity, i.e. less self-conflicted by culturally reductive debates of, for instance, indigenous versus colonising identity, Catholic versus Protestant, etc.). Indeed, the film in its one form is doubly authored in being co-directed, and the contrastively gendered perspectives of each 'author' are internalised in the text at a narrative level.[26]

In featuring a male protagonist with a female sidekick, the film abides by the filmic representational paradigm Diane Negra has observed, by which 'Irishness is correlated with depictions of male centrality and ancillary femininity'.[27] On the level of characterisation, Brendan, the young monk, is more complexly rendered with a distinct psychological progression, to which Aisling is merely an aid. On the other hand, the film's overall narrative is framed by Aisling, who – though she has considerably less screen time and thus less bodily manifestation (moreover her bodily form is in fact split between human and wolf) – opens the film in voiceover. Her face – though as yet unrecognisable as a familiar character – is also the first glimpse of a (semi-human) person's seen in the film.

Aisling speaks:

> I have lived through many ages … I have seen the dark men invading Ireland, destroying all in search of gold. I have seen suffering in the darkness. Yet I have seen beauty thrive in the most fragile of places. I have seen the book – the book to turn darkness into light.

Thus in whispers, Aisling's voice implicitly speaks of/to a revisionist history of Ireland in which women and girls not only bear witness to conflict but are granted the authoritative powers of narrativisation and reflection. In narrative theory terms, the *fabula* (or story) may be Brendan's, but the *syuzhet* (its form and mediation) is Aisling's.

In echoing the film's directorial co-authorship, or doubling, the film is thus split between offering up a subjective female voice, which is representative of a feminist – if not necessarily *female* – authorial voice, and falling back on the traditional representational paradigm of Irish cinema, by which the female's ancillary nature is telegraphed through her association with a general sort of mysticism or spiritual function. Again, this is a holdover from the repressive regime of the Catholic Church in Ireland, which until the twentieth century largely limited the visual representation of the female body to Marian imagery in post-monastic Irish visual culture, and which has been carried over into the palpable disembodiment of human women on Irish screens.[28]

The film is thus caught between a 'feminine aesthetic' of animation, which Paul Wells has theorised manifests in the work of feminist-inclined animators, and a conventionally phallogocentric paradigm of representation.[29] Admittedly, applying an overall gender(ed) identity or quality – specifically such as 'feminine' – to this film (or any) risks propagating a theory of gender binarism and narrowing – rather than expanding – the range of qualifications for female authorship. Nevertheless, the style in which Aisling is drawn is significant in its departure from the 'Boopist' blueprint for drawing female protagonists generally followed by mainstream Western animators (Disney and Pixar being exemplary). While Aisling has a conventionally round face, her nose is unconventionally sharp, her brow is heavy, and her feet are disproportionately large. Despite being a fairy, her image connotes neither daintiness nor cuteness – euphemisms for passivity in women – but rather self-expressivity and readiness for action. Of course, this is imagistically conveyed in relation to her human female form only part of the time, in that she intermittently shape-shifts into a wolf – thus re-invoking clichéd associations in Irish visual culture between femininity and otherworldliness.

In other words, the film's conventional narrative phallogocentrism – in being centred primarily on a male protagonist – is undercut, if not entirely subverted, throughout by various narrative and formal strategies of asserting female subjectivity. Of course, analysis of one film alone will not be enough to prove that the progressiveness of a single film is directly proportional to the input of a female authorial voice, represented here by director Nora Twomey. But when contrasted with an analysis of Cartoon Saloon's second feature, *Song of the Sea*, this theory begins to take shape.

Song of the Sea was directed solely by Tomm Moore, and while it does not actively practise a regime of female objectification, it does regress somewhat from *The Secret of Kells*' efforts to establish female subjectivity both narratively and stylistically within the film. I posit that this is a direct result of *Song*'s having less of a female (or feminist) directive – that is, creative/authorial – voice in production. Consequently, the film furthers the association of female characters with disembodiment (which *Kells*, we have seen, flirts with, vis-à-vis Aisling's animality) – and further, even, literal voiceless-ness – throughout much of its narrative. Again, we have a boy protagonist, Ben, whose psychological maturation provides the primary narrative arc, centred on his forging a protective role over his sister, Saoirse. She is revealed to be a selkie, a magical half-seal/half-human creature, on whom depends the survival of the rest of the fairy folk of Ireland. Thus, again, we have an ancillary female character, but this time drawn even more in the Boopist/Disney princess style (rounded face, button nose, huge eyes), whose femininity correlates with otherworldliness, and indeed a propensity for human disembodiment.[30] Even more strikingly, Saoirse is entirely voiceless throughout the first three-quarters of the film: it is a plot point that she cannot speak without first learning how to sing the selkie song, the eponymous 'song of the sea'. As such, the one solely male-directed Cartoon Saloon feature film to date is also that which de-centres female subjectivity most thoroughly in terms of the visual, vocal and overall narrative rendering of its main female character.

I do not suggest that Moore's direction is inherently or manifestly sexist – it is not – but rather that his authorial stamp does not correlate as strongly as Twomey's with a prioritisation of female subjectivity. Interestingly, *Song*'s representational gender dynamics are flipped in Twomey's solo directorial debut, *The Breadwinner*. Out of the three films considered here, *The Breadwinner* most consistently invokes female subjectivity and narrativity: indeed, it is *about* creating female authorship. Adapted from Deborah Ellis's young adult novel of the same name (the screenplay is also co-authored by Ellis), it tells the story of Parvana, a girl living in Afghanistan who has to cross-dress as a boy in order to provide for her family after her father is arrested by the Taliban. The linear narrative of the film is interspersed with fantasy sequences, which are drawn in a more overtly stylised, cardboard cut-out manner than scenes from the metanarrative, which is rendered in a comparatively Disney-formalist, or 'realist', style. These narrative sub-sequences illustrate the ongoing story that Parvana tells to her infant brother throughout the film in order to comfort him. It gradually becomes apparent that Parvana is, in fact, imagining/narrating the story of Sulayman, her older brother whom, she reveals in the climactic sequence, was killed by a grenade when he was out playing. Thus, beyond even prioritising the subjective viewpoint and narrative capabilities of a female protagonist, the film hinges on Parvana's framing of her brother's story-within-the-story. As a girl who, politically, has no voice, Parvana nevertheless comes to 'speak for' her silenced male relative over the course of the film.

Indeed, the film may overall be read as a narrativisation of the female struggle to establish author-ity (in the sense of having power to narrate). The film opens in a marketplace with Parvana's father relating to her the story of Afghanistan's conflict-ridden history. As her father speaks in voiceover, his narration is simultaneously imaged on-screen. So far, so seemingly typical: a male authority figure's words being privileged to illustration, and as such establishing a subjective viewpoint from which to view the objective narrative. However, under Twomey's direction, the film quickly shifts its subjective viewpoint to that of Parvana: as her father closes his story on the rise of the Taliban regime, the image also cuts to a close-up of a woman behind bars, expressionless for the burqa that covers her entire face. Shifting out of the sub-narrative mode and back into the 'real world' of the story, the film cuts to close-up on Parvana, whose face is partially obscured by a hijab, thus creating a visual simile between the two shots. After her father asks Parvana to tell him about the history of their nomadic ancestors, she begins to speak of a 'Bactrian princess wearing a crown of gold', to which image the film gradually fades in. She, and the image, are abruptly interrupted by members of the Taliban, thus emphasising the transgressive nature of her assumption of narrative subjectivity. In such a way, the film establishes Parvana as successor to her father's narration: the power of storytelling is passed on to the female protagonist, who – in the ultimate proof of successful female author-ity – comes to lend her voice to her dead brother before re-assuming narrative subjectivity: she is not just framed; she *is* the frame.

The remarkable climax of *The Breadwinner* takes place in parallel sequences: in the 'real' story world, Parvana anxiously awaits her father's release from prison as war rages outside; in the story-within-the-story, the boy of Parvana's imagination finally encounters the evil Elephant King from whom he seeks to retrieve stolen seeds. Parvana is seen gazing out a window, whispering 'Sulayman … Sulayman …' before the image cuts back to the boy on a mountainside, facing down the roaring Elephant King. In a boy's voice, he cries, 'I have not come to kill you!' Parvana speaks directly to the character of her imagination:

Sulayman! Soothe him with your story – the one Papajan cannot speak of! Tell him what happened! Tell him your story!

As the Elephant King gallops towards him, Sulayman (in a boy's voice) declares,

My name is Sulayman. My mother is a writer. My father is a teacher. And my sisters always fight each other. One day I found a toy on the street. I picked it up. It exploded. It was the end.

He repeats the story, the male and female voices of Sulayman gradually layering over each other. As the Elephant King yields to the boy, Sulayman's voice fades out, and Parvana's voice reasserts itself to finish the story with the boy/Sulayman's triumph. In such a way, Parvana revises an imagined history of her brother's life into a narrative that serves her, emotionally, and gives closure to a shared family trauma. In parallel, Twomey fashions a tale of female author-isation – unconventional both in form and narrative – that nevertheless satisfies a conventional need for catharsis or emotional gratification. In terms of the narrative progression from each of Cartoon Saloon's three films to the next, *The Breadwinner* thus ultimately represents the achievement of a female authorial voice both within and without its text.

Conclusion

Indications are, as seen from *Song of the Sea*, that if Nora Twomey, as a female director, had *not* taken the helm of *The Breadwinner*, its subtle invocation of a female authorial voice might not have been so effectively and *affectively handled. It is textual evidence of the effect gender parity – and particularly female authorship as a balance to conventional phallogocentrism – in the workplace can have on artistic output, and the diversification of the 'Irish cinematic voice'. As discursive and textual analysis has shown, the Irish animated film industry, as spearheaded by Cartoon Saloon, provides a model for gender parity in the creative workplace with proven results of eliciting a progressive politics of gender representation on-screen. It will remain to be seen what the release of Tomm Moore's upcoming *Wolfwalkers*, Cartoon Saloon's next feature, might or might not do in terms of form and narrative to carry on the legacy of *The Breadwinner*. Certainly, the fact that *Wolfwalkers* is promised to have two female protagonists indicates that balanced gender representation and female subjectivity are a storytelling priority in Cartoon Saloon features to come – regardless of the gender of their directors. Animation is thus a crucial platform for the female authorial voice in Irish film, providing a model, both in terms of production planning and narrative development, that Screen Ireland might wisely follow in its efforts to secure gender parity.

Conclusion

Concluding Remarks:
The road ahead

SUSAN LIDDY

Gender inequality in the film industry has become a pressing political issue across the world. This collection offers a critical inquiry into the significance of gender in the Irish film industry, a sector that has been male-dominated, and unchallenged, for very many years. Exploring female presence and absence, it provides a compelling contribution to ongoing national and international debates, touching on a range of pertinent issues: visibility, vision and voice, inclusion and marginalisation and new horizons. Chapters highlight the work of individual female filmmakers; collaborative filmmaking; the industry experiences of screenwriters, directors and producers; the importance of developing gender-aware film education formally in schools and colleges; the contribution of Irish women to non-traditional and emerging fields such as cinematography and animation; an analysis of the roadblocks many female practitioners continue to meet, and the ongoing struggle to survive in an often unwelcoming and, until recently, gender-blind industry.

Celebration and caution must co-exist in any assessment of progress in the Irish film industry. Both Screen Ireland (SI) and the Broadcasting Authority of Ireland (BAI) are now forthright in their stated commitment to gender equality, as has emerged in previous chapters. There have been notable achievements over a four-year period – a credible shift from a 'gender-neutral' position in which there was little or no awareness of gender equality, to a proactive engagement with equality issues.[1]

It is generally acknowledged that, since December 2015, with the introduction of the Six Point Plan, Screen Ireland has made a serious attempt to transform the gendered landscape of Irish film production, albeit, initially, quite tentatively. The greatest change can be seen in the increased number of female filmmakers being funded through the short film schemes: in 2017, 70 per cent of shorts in the 'Short Stories' and 'Frameworks' schemes had a female director attached; in 2018, 60 per cent of shorts in the 'Focus Shorts' and 'Real Shorts' schemes were female directed.[2] It is possible to argue that short films are a gateway to the making of feature-length films, and to see the increased number of female writer/directors being funded as positive, relevant and a pointer to a more equitable future. However, it could equally be argued that supporting female short filmmakers, and heralding that support as evidence of Screen Ireland's commitment to '5050 x 2020', is providing a limited and less risky investment in Irish female talent.

Statistical information spanning 2011–17 suggests there is much still to be done to increase the number of funded female directors on feature-length projects.[3] While the first half of 2018 is impressive, with a number of female-led feature-length projects coming through to production, there is insufficient data at this stage to point to long-term, sustainable change. Interestingly, in the light of the issues that emerged in Liddy's chapter, concern at the 'relatively low' number of funding applications with female writers and directors attached prompted Screen Ireland to introduce a range of initiatives, announced in mid-2017 and rolled out in 2018, to incentivise female creative talent. These include enhanced production financing, where up to €100,000 in additional funding is available for female-led projects, and POV, a female-led, low-budget, film production and training scheme after which three projects will be selected for production, with a budget of up to €400,000 each.[4] The success of these incentives has yet to be established so it is difficult, at the time of writing, to determine with any confidence what the outcome will be.

Screen Producers Ireland have not published a gender policy to date and, as a body, they do not appear to have engaged to any great extent with the process. For gender equality to be embedded in the industry the support of production companies is vital. Anecdotally, Screen Ireland has practised a softly-softly 'wait and see' response to the problem, arguably not wishing to fracture relationships with the big Irish production companies. However, the *Screen Ireland Production Catalogue, 2019* appears to signal a change of approach, stating: 'There is a responsibility on those who are in receipt of public funding from Screen Ireland to ensure gender equality, diversity, and inclusion are at the heart of their productions.'[5] This was followed, in April 2019, by a statement from the Department of Culture, Heritage and the Gaeltacht outlining new guidelines for Section 481, the Irish tax incentive for the film, television and animation industry. Among the requirements in the Skills Development Plan are 'details on gender equality initiatives, diversity and inclusion initiatives together with a sustainability plan'.[6] Although it is too early to assess the impact of these changes, if indeed there will be any significant impact at all, it may be that, going forward, production companies will be called to account, something that representative bodies have lobbied for over the last few years.

In April 2018, the BAI published its Gender Action Plan, which supports the collection of data and addresses gender balance on-screen and behind the camera by introducing a requirement, at the strategic assessment stage, that women will be represented in key creative roles.[7] The BAI have moved towards a 'points system' in the strategic assessment stage; projects that demonstrate greater gender inclusivity, when all else is equal, will be favoured over those that do not, in funding decisions. Not only must the gender of the proposed producer, writer and director be specified at the application stage but, according to Stephanie Comey of the BAI, they must later report on the gender of those who occupied the key creative roles when the project was produced 'in order to draw down the final tranche of payment'.[8] It will be interesting to evaluate the extent to which these policies and initiatives have impacted on applications and funding decisions during its first year. Speaking in December 2018, CEO Michael O'Keeffe stated that the initiative 'has resulted in more funding being awarded to projects that have women in a leadership/creative role', but the details have yet to be publicised.[9]

There are also welcome indications that the resistance to female protagonists, discussed at length previously (Liddy chapter), could be on the wane. For example, Screen Ireland's gender statistics, 2011–17, identifies the completion of ninety-eight films within that time period, 40 per cent of which had a female protagonist. It is perhaps noteworthy that 69 per cent of films produced in 2017 had a female protagonist compared with 22 per cent and 36 per cent in 2016 and 2015, respectively. In a similar vein, the BAI has recently announced that, under the Sound and Vision 3 Broadcasting Funding Scheme 2019, it is introducing a 'women's stories' initiative in order to 'widen the narrative, present new female characters, real or fictional, and generally promote different stories and different voices'.[10]

The contribution of voluntary organisations and representative bodies continues to be significant in terms of advancing gender equality in the industry through advocacy, education and the promotion of female filmmakers and their work. As a consequence, there is an awareness of the issues within the film community and beyond. For instance, debates on gender equality are the subject of dedicated seminars and panels in third-level institutions, at film festivals around the country and as part of *Spotlight*, the Irish Film Institute's annual review of the year in Irish film.[11] At the time of writing, WFT Ireland, in partnership with the 5050 Cannes Collective,[12] is working with a number of Irish film festivals that have signed up to the 'programming pledge for parity and inclusion' – an important step for gender equality in the film industry nationally and internationally.

However, increased awareness does not necessarily mean inevitable progress, as lessons from other countries have demonstrated. For instance, in UK television, there has been an overall decline of 2.98 per cent in the share of television episodes directed by women from 2013 to 2016.[13] Similarly, in Hollywood, during 2018, women accounted for just 8 per cent of directors, a decrease of 3 per cent from 2017. The triumphant arrival of a female Captain Marvel in 2019 (Brie Larson), with Anna Boden and Ryan Fleck co-directing, signalled, for many, a significant breakthrough. Yet while there are a number of female-led projects currently in development, 'studios continue to rely on men overwhelmingly to lead productions'.[14] Despite the prevalence of impassioned equality discourses in the media, the enthusiastic and sometimes flamboyant endorsement from high-profile celebrities, and the emergence of movements like Time's Up, Lauzen urges against over-optimism. Her data 'provides no evidence that the mainstream film industry has experienced the profound positive shift predicted by so many industry observers. This radical underrepresentation is unlikely to be remedied by the voluntary efforts of a few individuals or a single studio. … The distance from 8% to some semblance of parity is simply too vast.'[15]

The slow pace of change, the possibility of losing momentum, and the very real likelihood of gender fatigue over time underpins the decision by the Writers Guild (WGI), the Screen Directors Guild (SDGI), and Women in Film and Television (WFT) to argue for the introduction of 'managed' quotas, phased in over a three-year period, to fully embed the progress achieved to date.[16] Quotas, it is contended, would accelerate the rate of change in the industry and cultural change will follow. They are a means to capitalise on work already done and ensure that Screen Ireland reaches its own target by 2020.

The research here is timely and pertinent. However, it represents merely the tip of the iceberg. Future research could include, for instance, intersectionality and broader issues of diversity and inclusion; gender and film criticism; non-traditional employment for women; motherhood and the film industry; gender and opportunity in the advertising industry; and short films as a gateway to Irish feature-length film production.

What this collection illustrates is that gender is, and should always be, a crucial lens for the analysis of film, filmmakers and the film industry. The picture emerging from the research presented here suggests there is some way to travel before gender equality is embedded in the Irish film industry, but a laudable start has been made. It is hoped that this body of work will provide a baseline for future research and will help foster a cohesive and focused research community.

Notes

Setting the Scene: Women in the Irish film industry

1. For example, A. Acker, *Reel Women: Pioneers of the cinema, 1896 to the present* (New York: Continuum Publishing, 1991); C. Beauchamp, *Without Lying Down: Frances Marion and the powerful women of early Hollywood* (Berkeley and Los Angeles: University of California Press, 1997); S. Stamp, *Lois Weber in Early Hollywood* (Oakland: California University Press, 2015).

2. S.L. Smith, M. Choueiti and K. Pieper, 'Gender Bias Without Borders: An investigation of female characters in popular films across 11 countries', p. 4, https://seejane.org/wp-content/uploads/gender-bias-without-borders-full-report.pdf [accessed 21 September 2019].

3. N. Wreyford and S. Cobb, 'Towards a Feminist Methodology for Producing Historical Data on Women in the Contemporary UK Film Industries', *Feminist Media Histories*, vol. 3, no. 3, 2017, pp. 107–33.

4. N. Baughan, 'The Invisible Woman: Films gender bias laid bare' (BFI, 22 June 2018), https://www.bfi.org.uk/news-opinion/sight-sound-magazine/comment/invisible-woman-film-gender-bias-laid-bare [accessed 21 September 2019].

5. S. Cobb, L.R. Williams and N. Wreyford, 'Calling the Shots: Women and contemporary film culture in the UK, 2000–2015', https://www.southampton.ac.uk/cswf [accessed 21 September 2019].

6. H. Aylett, *Where Are the Women Directors in European Films? Gender equality report on female directors, 2006–2013 with best practice and policy recommendations* (Strasbourg: EWA, 2016), p. 3.

7. Screen Australia (2015), 'Gender Matters: Women in the Australian screen industry', https://www.screenaustralia.gov.au/getmedia/f20beab8-81cc-4499-92e9-02afba18c438/Gender-Matters-Women-in-the-Australian-Screen-Industry.pdf [accessed 21 September 2019].

8. S.L. Smith, K. Pieper and M. Choueiti (2017), 'Inclusion in the Director's Chair? Gender, race, and age of film directors across 1,000 Films from 2007–2016', p. 7, https://annenberg.usc.edu/sites/default/files/2017/04/06/MDSCI_Inclusion%20_in_the_Directors_Chair.pdf [accessed 21 September 2019].

9. For example, S. Liddy, 'Look Who's Talking! Irish Female Screenwriters', in J. Nelmes and J. Selbo (eds), *Women Screenwriters: An international guide* (London: Palgrave Macmillan, 2015), pp. 410–33; Smith et al., 'Inclusion in the Director's Chair?'; M. Lauzen, 'It's a Man's (Celluloid) World: Portrayals of female characters in the top 100 films of 2018', https://womenintvfilm.sdsu.edu/wp-content/uploads/2019/02/2018_Its_a_Mans_Celluloid_World_Report.pdf [accessed 15 August 2019].

10. G. Tuchman, 'Introduction: The symbolic annihilation of women by the mass media', in G. Tuchman, A. Daniels Kaplan and J. Benet (eds), *Hearth and Home:*

Images of women in the mass media (New York: Oxford University Press, 1979), pp. 3–38.

11. A.E. Lincoln and M.P. Allen, 'Double Jeopardy in Hollywood: Age and gender in the careers of film actors, 1926–1999', *Sociological Forum*, vol. 19, 2004, p. 611; Lauzen, 'It's a Man's (Celluloid) World'; S. Liddy, 'Older Women and Sexuality On-Screen: Euphemism and evasion?', in C. McGlynn, M. O'Neill and M. Schrage-Fruh (eds), *Ageing Women in Literature and Visual Culture: Reflections, refractions, reimaginings* (Basingstoke: Palgrave Macmillan, 2017), pp. 167–80.

12. Lauzen, 'It's a Man's (Celluloid) World', p. 6.

13. S. Smith, K. Pieper and M. Choueiti, 'Exploring the Barriers and Opportunities for Independent Women Filmmakers, Phase I and II, 2014, p. 3, https://www.sundance.org/pdf/artist-programs/wfi/phase-i-ii-research---exploring-the-barriers.pdf [acccessed 21 September 2019].

14. A. Coles, *What's Wrong With this Picture? Directors and gender inequality in the Canadian screen-based production industry* (Toronto: Canadian Unions for Equality on Screen (CUES), 2016).

15. Telefilm Canada, 'Telefilm Canada releases its latest gender parity statistics for feature film production funding', https://telefilm.ca/en/news-releases/telefilm-canada-releases-its-latest-gender-parity-statistics-for-feature-film-production-funding [accessed 21 September 2019].

16. EU and Irish Women/Ireland-European Commission, https://ec.europa.eu/ireland/node/684_en [accessed 21 September 2019].

17. I. Bacik, 'Legislating for Article 40.3.3', *Irish Journal of Legal Studies*, vol. 3, no. 3, 2013, p. 22.

18. National Women's Council of Ireland (2015), 'Better Boards, Better Business, Better Society', https://www.nwci.ie/images/uploads/Better_Boards_PDF.pdf [accessed 21 September 2019].

19. National Women's Council of Ireland, *No Small Change: Closing the gender pay gap* (Dublin: NWCI, 2017).

20. National Women's Council of Ireland, 'We need the appropriate resources and political will to restore and advance women's rights and equality in Ireland', 16 February 2017, https://www.nwci.ie/learn/article/we_need_the_appropriate_resources_and_political_will_to_restore_and_advance [accessed 21 September 2019].

21. K. Walsh, J. Suiter and C. O'Connor, *Hearing Women's Voices? Exploring women's underrepresentation in current affairs radio programming at peak listening times in Ireland* (Dublin: NWCI, 2015).

22. B. Donohue et al., 'Gender Counts: An analysis of gender in Irish theatre, 2006–2015', https://learning.educatetogether.ie/mod/resource/view.php?id=12781 [accessed 21 September 2019].

23. Liddy, 'Look Who's Talking!'

24. T. Tracy and R. Flynn, 'Quantifying National Cinema: A case study of the Irish film board, 1993–2013', *Film Studies*, vol. 14, no. 1, 2016, pp. 32–53.

25. U. Barry and P. Conroy, 'Ireland in Crisis, 2008–2012: Women, austerity and inequality', https://researchrepository.ucd.ie/handle/10197/4820 [accessed 21 September 2019].

26. H. Davies and C. Callaghan, 'All in this Together? Feminisms, academia, austerity', *Journal of Gender Studies*, vol. 23, no. 3, 2014, p. 227.

27. Ibid., pp. 227–32.

28. National Women's Council of Ireland, 'We Need the Appropriate Resources and Political Will To Restore and Advance Women's Rights and Equality in Ireland', https://www.nwci.ie/learn/article/we_need_the_appropriate_resources_and_political_will_to_restore_and_advance [accessed 21 September 2019].

29. M.P. Murphy, 'Gendering the Narrative of the Irish Crisis', *Irish Political Studies*, vol. 30, no. 2, 2015, p. 230.

30. Ibid., p. 233.

31. R. Lysaght, 'Sounding Off: Rachel Lysaght asks "Where my ladies at?"', http://filmireland.net/2013/02/20/sounding-off-rachel-lysaght-asks-where-my-ladies-at-issue-144-spring-2013/ [accessed 21 September 2019]; S. Liddy, 'Missing in Action: Where are the Irish women screenwriters?', http://filmireland.net/2015/04/20/missing-in-action-where-are-the-irish-women-screenwriters/ [accessed 21 September 2019].

32. S. Liddy, '"Open to All and Everybody"? The Irish Film Board: Accounting for the scarcity of women screenwriters', *Feminist Media Studies*, vol. 16, no. 5, 2016, p. 904.

33. Ibid.

34. Ibid.

35. E. O'Toole, 'Waking the Feminists: Re-imagining the space of the national theatre in the era of the Celtic phoenix', *Lit: Literature Interpretation Theory*, vol. 28, no. 2, 2017, p. 144.

36. Ibid., p. 137. Maeve Stone, associate producer of Pan Pan Theatre Company, coined the hashtag #WakingTheFeminists (#WTF).

37. U. Mullally, 'Abbey Theatre Celebrates 1916 Centenary with Only One Woman Playwright', *Irish Times*, 2 November 2016, https://www.irishtimes.com/opinion/una-mullally-abbey-theatre-celebrates-1916-centenary-with-only-one-woman-playwright-1.2413277 [accessed 21 September 2019].

38. B. Donohue, 'Women and the Abbey Theatre', https://www.irishtimes.com/opinion/letters/women-and-the-abbey-theatre-1.2415780 [accessed 21 September 2019]; S. Liddy, 'Women and the Irish Film Industry', https://www.irishtimes.com/opinion/letters/women-and-the-irish-film-industry-1.2424444 [accessed 21 September 2019].

39. Murphy, 'Gendering the Narrative of the Irish Crisis', p. 233.

40. E. Turley and J. Fisher, 'Tweeting Back When Shouting Back: Social media and feminist activism', *Feminism and Psychology*, vol. 28, no. 1, 2018, pp. 128–32.

41. B. Cammaerts, 'Social Media and Activism', in R. Mansell and P. Hwa (eds), *The International Encyclopaedia of Digital Communication and Society* (Oxford: Wiley-Blackwell, 2015), pp. 1027–34.

42. P. Gerbaudo, *Tweets and the Streets: Social media and contemporary activism* (New York: Pluto Press, 2012), p. 7.

43. O. Dawe, 'Hearing Women's Voices', conference paper delivered at Women's Voices in Ireland, Women's Studies, UCC, 10 June 2017.

44. O Toole, 'Waking the Feminists', p. 138.

45. D. Clarke, 'Irish Film Board Issues Statement on Gender Inequality', http://www.irishtimes.com/blogs/screenwriter/2015/11/12/irish-film-board-issues-statement-on-gender-equality/ [accessed 21 September 2019].

46. Liddy, '"Open to All and Everybody"?'

47. Women in Film and Television, https://wft.ie/ [accessed 21 September 2019].

48. Broadcasting Authority of Ireland, BAI Gender Action Plan, 2018, https://www.bai.ie/en/media/sites/2/dlm_uploads/2018/04/20180423_BAI_GenderActionPlan_vFinal_AR.pdf [accessed 21 September 2019].

49. The first WFT group emerged from an informal meeting organised by Rachel Lysaght and held in Dublin's Odessa Club. The first WFT board comprised Lysaght, Neasa Hardiman, Lindsay Campbell, Aoife Kelleher, Emer Reynolds, Ailish McElmeel and Katie Holly.

50. The Equality Action Committee was suggested by Marian Quinn and first met formally in early November 2015. Founder members were Liz Gill, Susan Liddy, Lauren Mackenzie and Marian Quinn. The CEOs of the SDGI and the WGI, Birch Hamilton and David Kavanagh, respectively, were also members.

51. For example, *Women in the Irish Film Industry: Moving from the margins to the centre*, Susan Liddy, MIC, Limerick, 2016; *New Horizons: Women in the Irish film and television industries*, Susan Liddy, MIC, Limerick, 2017; *See It – Be It! Putting women in the picture*, EAC, Galway Film Fleadh, 2016; *Building Momentum: The road to gender equality*, WFT and EAC, Galway Film Fleadh, 2017; *Balancing the Industry: The European perspective*, Creative Europe Ireland and WFT Dublin, 2017; *Accelerating Gender Equality: Time for quotas?* EAC and WFT, Galway Film Fleadh, 2018.

52. T. O'Regan, *Australian National Cinema* (London and New York: Routledge, 1996), p. 294.

53. V. Mayer, M. Banks and J.T. Caldwell (eds), *Production Studies: Cultural studies of media industries* (New York: Routledge, 2009), p. 2.

54. M. Banks, B. Conor and V. Mayer (eds), *Production Studies: The sequel!* (New York: Routledge, 2016), p. xi.

Ellen O'Mara Sullivan and Her Role in Early Irish Cinema

1. D. Casella, 'Women and Nationalism in Indigenous Irish Filmmaking of the Silent Period', in M. Dall'Asta, V. Duckett and L. Tralli (eds), *Researching Women in Silent Cinema: New findings and perspectives* (Bologna: University of Bologna, 2013), pp. 53–80.

2. https://journal.historyitm.org/v5n1/staff-herstory-biography/ [accessed 21 September 2019].

3. Ibid.

4. https://wfpp.cdrs.columbia.edu/pioneer/ellen-omara-sullivan/ [accessed 21 September 2019].

5. Casella, 'Women and Nationalism', pp. 53–80.

6. Ibid., p. 53.

7. https://journal.historyitm.org/v5n1/staff-herstory-biography/ [accessed 21 September 2019].

8. M. Leigh, 'Reading Between the Lines: History and the studio owner's wife', in J. Knight and C. Gledhill, *Doing Women's Film History: Reframing cinemas, past and future* (Champaign, IL: University of Illinois Press, 2015), p. 42.

9. Ibid., p. 43.

10. https://journal.historyitm.org/v5n1/staff-herstory-biography/ [accessed 21 September 2019].

11. D. Mukherjee, 'Scandalous Evidence', in Knight and Gledhill, *Doing Women's Film History*, p. 30.

12. https://journal.historyitm.org/v5n1/staff-herstory-biography/ [accessed 21 September 2019].

13. http://humphrysfamilytree.com is the genealogy website of Mark Humphries, a descendant of the O'Maras. This site is a very useful resource for building the history around Ellen O'Mara Sullivan in terms of her family background, her husband and other relatives. However, details of her life itself need to be established from other sources.

14. Ibid.

15. M. McCloskey, 'O'Maras of Limerick and Their Overseas Businesses', *The Old Limerick Journal*, no. 37, Summer 2001.

16. http://humphrysfamilytree.com/OMara/jim.sullivan.html [accessed 15 April 2018].

17. M. Felter and D. Schultz, 'James Mark Sullivan and the Film Company of Ireland', *New Hibernia Review*, vol. 8, no. 2, Summer 2004, pp. 24–40

18. Ibid., p. 27.

19. From a letter dated 6 May 1965 in the Irish Film Institute Archive.

20. Felter and Schultz, 'James Mark Sullivan and the Film Company of Ireland', pp. 24–40.

21. After the 1916 Rising James was arrested and held briefly in Dublin Castle and possibly Arbour Hill Jail and, according to Felter and Schultz, is described as the life and soul of the prison, a lively American full of stories.

22. K. Rockett, L. Gibbons and J. Hill, *Cinema and Ireland* (New York: Routledge, 1987).

23. Felter and Schultz, 'James Mark Sullivan and the Film Company of Ireland', pp. 24–40.

24. Casella, 'Women and Nationalism in Indigenous Irish Filmmaking of the Silent Period', p. 5.

25. *Clonmel Chronicle*, 2 February 1918, p. 5.

26. Felter and Schultz, 'James Mark Sullivan and the Film Company of Ireland', p. 4.

27. B. Ó Cathaoir, 'An Irishman's Diary', *The Irish Times*, 11 September 2006.

28. C. Clutterbuck, quoted in Ó Cathaoir, 'An Irishman's Diary'.

29. Ibid.

30. Casella, 'Women and Nationalism in Indigenous Irish Filmmaking of the Silent Period'.

31. Ibid.

32. In a letter dated 22 July 1918 in Mary Rose Callaghan's private papers.

33. In a letter dated 14 July 1918 in Mary Rose Callaghan's private papers.

34. In a letter dated 14 August 1918 in Mary Rose Callaghan's private papers.

35. In a letter dated 19 December 1918 in Mary Rose Callaghan's private papers.

36. Ibid.

37. In a letter dated 4 December 1918 in Mary Rose Callaghan's private papers.

38. https://journal.historyitm.org/v5n1/staff-herstory-biography/ [accessed 21 September 2019].

39. Felter and Schultz, 'James Mark Sullivan and the Film Company of Ireland', p. 6.

40. https://wfpp.cdrs.columbia.edu/pioneer/ellen-omara-sullivan/ [accessed 21 September 2019].

Feminist Reclamation Politics: Reclaiming *Maeve* (1981) and *Mother Ireland* (1988)

1. M. McLoone, *Irish Film: The emergence of a contemporary cinema* (London: BFI, 2000), p. 149.

2. *Hush-a-Bye Baby* is a production that sought to deal with the experience of being a Catholic Irish woman living in Derry during the Troubles in the 1980s. It did not

have the explicit intention to examine the relationship between the 'struggles' for an Irish identity for women. Brian McIlroy's *Shooting to Kill: Filmmaking and the 'troubles' in Northern Ireland* (Richmond, BC: Steveston Press, 2001) offers an overview of the issues that led to the film's making: the 1983 defeated abortion referendum in the south of Ireland, the death of fifteen-year-old Ann Lovett giving birth alone in a field in County Longford and the case of Joanne Hayes, falsely accused of infanticide.

3. See M. Sullivan, '*The Visit*, Incarceration, and Film by Women in Northern Ireland: An interview with Orla Walsh', *The Irish Review*, no. 21, Autumn–Winter 1997, pp. 29–40.

4. This is not intended as any kind of judgement.

5. See K. Crenshaw, *On Intersectionality: The essential writings of Kimberlé Crenshaw* (New York: The New Press, 2015).

6. C. Weedon, *Feminist Practice and Poststructuralist Theory* (Cambridge, MA, and Oxford, UK: Blackwell, 1987), explains that 'Feminism is a politics. It is a politics directed at changing existing power relations between women and men in society.'

7. Exemplified in media coverage of the case against Harvey Weinstein, among others, and the subsequent online #MeToo movement/campaign.

8. There are other feminist movements within the UK and Ireland; however, I am concentrating here on those being profiled by the news media.

9. See R. Gill, 'Empowerment/Sexism: Figuring female sexual agency in contemporary advertising', *Feminism & Psychology*, vol. 18, no. 1, 2008, pp. 35–60.

10. While these women of wealth and success may continue to project this slightly modified role, women from other areas of culture, particularly those connected to working-class culture, are removed from their jobs. http://www.independent.co.uk/sport/general/darts-walk-on-girls-pdc-masters-milton-keynes-tv-itv-a8180876.html [accessed 21 September 2019].

11. 'Patriarchy refers to the power relations in which women's interests are subordinate to the interests of men.' Weedon, *Feminist Practice*.

12. A. Kuhn, *Women's Pictures: Feminism and cinema* (London and New York: Routledge, 1982), p. 3.

13. Ibid., p. 5.

14. J. Wolff, *Feminine Sentences: Essays on women and culture* (Cambridge: Polity Press, 1990), p. 121.

15. J. Fiske, *Television Culture* (London: Methuen, 1987), p. 160.

16. C. Coulter, 'Feminism and Nationalism in Ireland', in David Miller (ed.), *Rethinking Northern Ireland* (London and New York: Longman, 1998), p. 160.

17. Ibid., p. 161.

18. Citing E. Longley, 'From Cathleen to Anorexia', in E. Boland et al. (eds), *A Dozen Lips* (Dublin: Attic Press, 1994), among others.

19. See J. Hill, 'Images of Violence', in K. Rockett, L. Gibbons and J. Hill, *Cinema and Ireland* (London: Routledge, 1988), pp. 247–93.

20. This has also been identified in the writing of theorists such as bell hooks, *Feminist Theory: From margin to center* (1984), second edition 2000, sometimes described as a shift from second-wave essentialist feminism to third-wave (postmodern) feminism.

21. Pamela Clayton explains, 'A term frequently used in the Northern Ireland context is "sectarianism", used to mean mutual dislike between Protestants and Catholics. That the hostility in the religious sphere, where it exists, is mutual is not in doubt; but the term suffers from the handicap that the inferior social, economic and political state of the members of one sect, Catholics, is not obvious from the term.' P. Clayton, 'Religion, Ethnicity and Colonialism as Explanation of the Northern Ireland Conflict', in D. Miller (ed.), *Rethinking Northern Ireland* (London and New York: Longman, 1998), pp. 40–1.

22. In 1994 I co-organised a conference, Gendered Narratives, one of the first conferences to address the place of feminist theory and the cultural identity of Irishness. In a session titled 'Political Divisions and Aspects of Cultural Identity', Anne Crilly and Margo Harkin both openly discussed the feminist intention for *Hush-a-Bye Baby* and *Mother Ireland* as one that 'grew out of a need for us to express our particular experience'. They both noted how the negative interpretation of these works as Irish nationalist and thus un-sisterly, or even anti-feminist, impacted on how they moved forward with other films with such content.

23. I did publish some work in this area at the time: 'Women Are Trouble, Did You Know That, Fergus?'; Neil Jordan's *The Crying Game*', *Feminist Review*, no. 50, Summer 1995; and 'Representing Gender and National Identity', in D. Miller (ed.), *Rethinking Northern Ireland* (London and New York: Longman, 1998), pp. 211–28.

24. In my attempt to raise academic debate on *Mother Ireland*, my own research fell quickly into this interpretive framework. When giving a paper in 1994, the chair of the panels turned his back to me in protest while I spoke.

25. See essays in L. Pettitt, *Screening Ireland: Film and television representation* (Manchester: Manchester University Press, 2000); McIlroy, *Shooting to Kill*; McLoone, *Irish Film*; K. Rockett and J. Hill (eds), *National Cinemas and World Cinemas* (Dublin: Four Courts Press, 2005 and 2006).

26. In 1990 it was described as being 'at odds with the perspective of feminism internationally'. M. McLoone, 'Lear's Fool and Goya's Dilemma', *Circa*, vol. 50, nos. 54–8, p. 57. In 1993 K. Nutt suggested that these films needed 'to start to respond to the problems of more than one group of women in society' to be feminist. 'Time for a real change', *Fortnight*, no. 320, 1993, pp. 42–3.

27. H. O'Brien, *The Real Ireland* (Manchester: Manchester University Press, 2004), p. 205.

28. McLoone, *Irish Film*, p. 145.

29. See L. Gibbons, 'Lies that Tell the Truth: *Maeve*, history and Irish cinema', *The Crane Bag*, vol. 2, 1983, pp. 148–55; Claire Johnston, '*Maeve*', *Screen*, vol. 22, no. 4, 1981, pp. 54–71; L. Pettitt, *Screening Ireland: Film and television representation* (Manchester:

Manchester University Press, 2000); see essays in Rockett and Hill (eds), *National Cinemas and World Cinemas*.

30. McLoone, *Irish Film*, p. 145.

31. Gibbons, 'Lies that Tell the Truth', p. 151.

32. Ibid., pp. 148–55. Reading this is very useful in offering a sustained and detailed feminist examination of these visual strategies and the complexities of the history of the land and storytelling from an Irish feminist perspective as achieved in the film.

33. Johnston, 'Maeve', pp. 54–71.

34. Ibid., p. 54.

35. Ibid., pp. 54 and 61. I am not sure of the validity of such a reading of English feminism. As an English feminist living in England in the 1980s and part of the 'Troops Out' movement, I saw little to no support for Irish republicanism from other feminist groups in this period. This was acknowledged to a point by *Feminist Review*, no. 50, Summer 1995, special issue 'The Irish Issue: The British question', which sought to address the lack of attention 'British' feminists had given to Northern Ireland.

36. Derry Women's Aid, 1980, cited in Johnston, 'Maeve', p. 54.

37. Johnston, 'Maeve', p. 55.

38. Ibid., p. 65.

39. Hill, 'Images of Violence', pp. 247–93.

40. Ibid., p. 70. Pat Murphy uses the terminology of the period and is sensitive about the accusations of excluding other types of women that carried a quite specific meaning in the historical context I have rebuilt of being 'sectarian', which it would not have done in another context, for example class differences between women.

41. Richard Kearney still describes it as a film about a 'Belfast girl suffering from the tribal conflicts of male aggression', *Navigations: Collected Irish essays, 1976–2006* (Dublin: Lilliput Press, 2006), p. 293.

42. Drawing upon Laura Mulvey's call for an avant-garde cinema 'which is radical in both a political and an aesthetic sense and challenges the basic assumption of the mainstream film'. L. Mulvey, 'Visual Pleasure and Narrative Cinema', *Screen*, vol. 16, no. 3, 1975, pp. 7–8.

43. C. Gledhill, 'Pleasurable Negotiation', in J. Story (ed.), *Cultural Theory and Popular Culture: A reader*, 4th edition (Harlow: Pearson Education, 2009), p. 98.

44. L. Mulvey, 'Notes on Sirk and Melodrama', in C. Gledhill (ed.), *Home Is Where the Heart Is: Studies in melodrama and the woman's film* (London: BFI, 1987), p. 75.

45. Johnston, 'Maeve', p. 67.

46. Ibid., p. 70.

47. An issue Murphy was aware of at the time when she notes, 'The problem of the audience will change and go on over the years whenever the film is shown.' Johnston, 'Maeve', pp. 68–9.

48. Ibid., p. 66.

49. See C. Holohan and T. Tracy (eds), Masculinity and Irish Popular Culture: Tiger's tales (London: Palgrave Macmillan, 2014).

50. J. Kristeva, Revolution in Poetic Language (New York: Columbia University Press, 1984).

51. While writing this chapter I came across a text that draws similar conclusions to my own. See J. Scarlata, Rethinking Occupied Ireland: Gender and incarceration in contemporary Irish film (New York: Syracuse University Press, 2014).

52. J. Lesage, 'The Political Aesthetics of the Feminist Documentary Film', Quarterly Review of Film Studies, vol. 3, no. 4, 1978, pp. 507–23, at p. 507.

53. A. Kuhn, Women's Pictures: Feminism and cinema (London and New York: Routledge & Kegan Paul, 1982), pp. 148–9.

54. Ibid., p. 152.

55. McIlroy, Shooting to Kill, dedicates a chapter to Mother Ireland that is both unusual and commendable. He makes similar formal points to the ones given here.

56. Ibid., p. 177. Lance Pettitt's Screening Ireland: Film and television representation (Manchester: Manchester University Press, 2000) also takes issue with this, suggesting that 'rather than a kind of spurious inclusivity it might be a more valuable project for a group of Protestant/unionist women to make a video about their attitudes to female figures produced in Irish and British culture', p. 212.

57. J. Hill, Cinema and Northern Ireland: Film, culture and politics (London: BFI, 2006), pp. 171–2.

58. This is an important historical fact ignored in writings on the group and their productions. See R. Flynn and P. Brereton, Historical Dictionary of Irish Cinema (Lanham, MD: Scarecrow Press, 2007).

59. I have used an online interview with Anne for information: http://www.tallgirlshorts.net/marymary/anne.html [accessed 21 September 2019].

60. M. Ward, Unmanageable Revolutionaries: Women and Irish nationalism (Dingle: Brandon Publishing, 1983), p. 1.

61. Ibid., p. 3. She cites the 1980s debates around whether the demand for political status for women in Armagh should be regarded as a feminist issue and the betrayal that women in Sinn Féin felt due to the lack of support from the wider Irish feminist movement.

62. Ibid., p. 3.

63. McIlroy, Shooting to Kill, p. 175.

64. This drew upon existing Irish legislation (Section 31, Republic of Ireland Broadcasting Act 1971), which banned the broadcasting of groups such as Sinn Féin. (It ran until 1994.)

65. With the following cuts: Christy Moore's song 'Unfinished Revolution' was removed, as was some archive footage including that of Emma Groves being shot with a plastic bullet. A dissolve was removed from Pat Murphy's film *Anne Devlin* which showed a woman defying British Redcoats 200 years ago, that dissolved into contemporary masked women. Some of the contemporary photographs were also removed. http://www.tallgirlshorts.net/marymary/anne.html [accessed 21 September 2019].

66. http://www.tallgirlshorts.net/marymary/anne.html [accessed 21 September 2019].

67. This is clearly revealed in the re-watching of *Mother Ireland* in a post-ceasefire context and within the now widely recognised need to acknowledge differences between women.

68. Edge, 'Women Are Trouble', p. 176. This article was based on a reading of the character Jude in a contemporary context (1992), but my findings are as relevant to historical reclamation politics as well as the reception of these two productions in the 1980s.

69. http://www.tallgirlshorts.net/marymary/anne.html [accessed 21 September 2019].

70. Pat Murphy located her subsequent productions within feminist/nationalist reclamation politics with *Anne Devlin* in 1983 and *Nora* in 2000, while Anne Crilly used post-ceasefire Northern Ireland as a backdrop for her challenging drama *Limbo* (2001), and more recently her work *The Maiden's City: A herstory of the walled city*, to reclaim Derry City's missing female past.

Where Are the Women? Exploring perceptions of a gender order in the Irish film industry

1. For example E. Kelan, 'Gender Fatigue: The ideological dilemma of gender neutrality and discrimination in organizations', *Canadian Journal of Administrative Sciences*, vol. 26, no. 3, 2009, pp. 197–210; J. Handy and L. Rowlands, 'Gendered Inequality Regimes and Female Labour Market Disadvantage within the New Zealand Film Industry', *Women's Studies Journal*, vol. 28, no. 2, 2014, p. 1; D. Hesmondhalgh and S. Baker, 'Sex, Gender and Work Segregation in the Cultural Industries', *Gender and Creative Labour: The sociological review*, vol. 63, S1, 2015, p. 24; B. Conor, R. Gill and S. Taylor, 'Gender and Creative Labour: Introduction', *The Sociological Review*, vol. 63, no. 1, 2015, p. 7.

2. S. Liddy, 'Look Who's Talking!'; Screen Australia, 'Gender Matters: Women in the Australian screen industry', https://www.screenaustralia.gov.au/getmedia/f20beab8-81cc-4499-92e9-02afba18c438/Gender-Matters-Women-in-the-Australian-Screen-Industry.pdf [accessed 21 September 2019].
3. L. French, *Women in the Victorian Film, Television and Related Industries: Research report* (Melbourne: RMIT University, 2012), p. 42.

4. S. Liddy, '"Open to All and Everybody"? The Irish Film Board: Accounting for the scarcity of women screenwriters', *Feminist Media Studies*, vol. 16, no. 5, 2016, p. 902.

5. A. Doona, *Spotlight*, Irish Film Institute, 27 April 2018.

6. S. Harding, 'Feminist Standpoints', in S.N. Hesse-Biber (ed.), *The Handbook of Feminist Research: Theory and praxis* (Thousand Oaks, CA., London, New Delhi and Singapore: Sage, 2012), p. 49.

7. C. Enloe, *The Curious Feminist: Searching for women in a new age of empire* (California: University of California Press, 2004), p. 220.

8. J. Sprague, *Feminist Methodologies for Critical Researchers: Bridging differences* (Walnut Creek, CA: Altamira Press, 2005), p. 5.

9. S.N. Hesse-Biber and P. Leavy, *The Handbook of Feminist Research: Theory and praxis* (Thousand Oaks, CA., London, New Delhi and Singapore: Sage, 2007), pp. 2–26.

10. M.L. DeVault and G. Cross, 'Feminist Qualitative Interviewing: Experience, talk and knowledge', in Hesse-Biber (ed.), *The Handbook of Feminist Research*, p. 224.

11. A discussion of motherhood and familial/domestic responsibilities was also included but is outside the scope of this paper because of space restrictions.

12. H. Aylett, *Where Are the Women Directors in European Films? Gender equality report on female directors, 2006–2013 with best practice and policy recommendations* (Strasbourg: EWA, 2016), p. 5.

13. L. French, 'Gender Then, Gender Now: Surveying women's participation in Australian film and television industries', *Continuum: Journal of Media and Cultural Studies*, vol. 28, no. 2, 2014, p. 194.

14. W. Fry. 'Age in the Workplace: Lessons and Guidance for Employers', *Industrial Relations News*, vol. 34, no. 21, September 2017.

15. M. Lauzen, 'It's a Man's (Celluloid) World: Portrayals of female characters in the top 100 films of 2018', p. 3, https://womenintvfilm.sdsu.edu/wp-content/uploads/2019/02/2018_Its_a_Mans_Celluloid_World_Report.pdf [accessed 15 August 2019].

16. L. Wing-fai, R. Gill and K. Randle, 'Getting In, Getting On, Getting Out? Women as career scramblers in the UK film and television industries', *Gender and Creative Labour: The sociological review*, vol. 63, S1, 2015, pp. 50–65.

17. Liddy, 'Look Who's Talking!', p. 911.

18. N. Wreyford, 'Birds of a Feather: Informal recruitment practices and gendered outcomes for screenwriting work in the UK film industry', *Gender and Creative Labour: The sociological review*, vol. 63, S1, 2015, p. 84.

19. P. O'Connor, 'Feminism and Politics of Gender', in M. Adshead and M. Millar (eds), *Public Administration and Public Policy in Ireland: Theory and methods* (London and New York: Routledge, 2003), pp. 2–3.

20. J. Lantz, *About Quality: The film industry's view of the term quality* (Stockholm: WFT Sverige, 2007), p. 7.

21. Ibid., p. 31.

22. Liddy, 'Look Who's Talking!', p. 909.

23. Smith et al., 'Gender Bias Without Borders', p. 2.

24. Lauzen, 'It's a Man's (Celluloid) World', p. 1.

25. H. Jacey, *The Woman in the Story: Writing memorable female characters* (Studio City, CA: Michael Wiese Productions, 2010), p. 6.

26. Lauzen, 'It's a Man's (Celluloid) World'.

27. S. Liddy, 'Older Women and Sexuality On-Screen: Euphemism and evasion?' in C. McGlynn, M. O'Neill and M. Schrage-Fruh (eds), *Ageing Women in Literature and Visual Culture: Reflections, refractions, reimaginings* (Basingstoke: Palgrave Macmillan, 2017), pp. 167–80.

28. I. Whelehan and J. Gwynne (eds), *Ageing, Popular Culture and Contemporary Feminism: Harleys and hormones* (Basingstoke: Palgrave Macmillan), p. 8.

29. Hesmondhalgh and Baker, 'Sex, Gender and Work Segregation in the Cultural Industries', p. 33.

30. D. Jones and J.K. Pringle, 'Unmanageable Inequalities: Sexism in the film industry', *The Sociological Review*, vol. 63, S1, 2015, p. 39.

31. B. Grummell, K. Lynch and D. Devine, 'Appointing Senior Managers in Education: Homosociability, local logics and authenticity in the selection process', *Educational Management, Administration and Leadership*, vol. 37, no. 3, 2009, p. 333.

32. A. Fels, *Necessary Dreams: Ambition in women's changing lives* (New York: First Anchor Books, 2005).

33. P. O'Connor, 'Where Do Women Fit in University Senior Management? An analytical typology of cross-national organisational culture', in B. Bagilhole and K. White (eds), *Gender, Power and Management* (London: Palgrave Macmillan, 2015), p. 169.

34. R. Kanter, *Men and Women of the Corporation* (New York: Basic Books, 1993), p. 152.

35. Higher Education Authority, 'HEA National Review of Gender Equality in Irish Higher Education', p. 14, https://hea.ie/assets/uploads/2017/06/HEA-National-Review-of-Gender-Equality-in-Irish-Higher-Education-Institutions.pdf [accessed 15 August 2019].

36. National Women's Council of Ireland, *Better Boards, Better Business, Better Society*, p. 10.

37. O'Connor, 'Where Do Women Fit in University Senior Management?', p 180.

38. P. O'Connor, 'Ireland: A man's world', *The Economic and Social Review*, vol. 31, 2000, p. 97.

39. National Women's Council of Ireland, 'Better Boards', pp. 13–19.

40. McKinsey and Company, 'Women in the Workplace 2016', p. 1, https://www.mm-foundation.org/sites/mmf/files/2016_McKinsey_LeanIn_Women-in-the-Workplace.pdf [accessed 21 September 2019].

41. M. Grace, M. Leahy and J. Doughney, 'Response to Striking the Balance: Women, men, work and family', https://www.humanrights.gov.au/sites/default/files/content/sex_discrimination/publication/strikingbalance/submissions/114.doc [accessed 21 September 2019].

42. C.J. Taylor, 'Occupational Sex Composition and the Gendered Availability of Workplace Support', *Gender and Society*, vol. 24, 2010, p. 192.

43. Higher Education Authority, *HEA National Review*, p. 14.

44. N. Edley and M. Wetherell, 'Jekyll and Hyde: Men's constructions of feminism and feminists', *Feminism and Psychology*, vol. 11, no. 4, 2001, p. 450.

45. S. Budgeon, *Third-Wave Feminism and the Politics of Late Modernity* (Basingstoke: Palgrave Macmillan, 2011), p. 24.

46. I. Kamberidou (2011), 'Gender Devaluation and Gender Fatigue: Getting women on the glass escalator', Presentation at the European Commission's Digital Agenda Assembly, 'Every European Digital', European Commission, INFSO, Brussels, 16–17 June 2011, p. 5, https://eclass.uoa.gr/modules/document/file.php/PHED269/1._DigitalAgendaPresentatio.Dr._Irene_Kamberidou.2.pdf [accessed 21 September 2019].

47. Higher Education Authority, *HEA National Review*, p. 14.

48. National Women's Council of Ireland, 'Better Boards', p. 33.

49. Kamberidou, 'Gender Devaluation and Gender Fatigue', p. 6.

Irish Production Cultures and Women Filmmakers: Nicky Gogan

1. All quotations from Ms Gogan are taken from an interview conducted with her on 5 December 2017.

2. S. Liddy, 'Where Are the Women?' Exploring perceptions of a gender order in the Irish film industry', *Women in Irish Film: Stories and storytellers* (Cork: Cork University Press, 2020).

3. Irish Film Board, 'Statement from the IFB on Gender Equality: Six Point Plan', https://www.irishfilmboard.ie/about/gender [accessed 22 March 2018].

4. V. Mayer, M.J. Banks and J.T. Caldwell (eds), *Production Studies: Cultural studies of media industries* (London and New York: Routledge, 2009), p. 4.

5. V. Mayer, 'Studying Up and F**cking Up: Ethnographic interviewing in production studies', *Cinema Journal*, vol. 47, no. 2, Winter 2008, p. 146.

6. Along with Chantal Doody and Sue Patterson; Patterson continues to run Sink Digital Media.

7. Both the IFB and Screen Training Ireland also became significant funders of Darklight as the festival established itself.

8. D. Jones and J.K. Pringle, 'Unmanageable Inequalities: Sexism in the film industry', *The Sociological Review*, vol. 63, S1, pp. 37–49.

9. Ibid., p. 39.

10. Ibid.

11. This later became the Short Shorts initiative.

12. Liddy, 'Where Are the Women?'

13. R. Flynn and T. Tracy, 'Waking the Film Makers: Diversity and dynamism in Irish screen industries 2017', *Estudios Irlandeses*, no. 13, 2018, p. 240.

14. And perhaps Erigha's note that women filmmakers may be concentrated 'in areas of work that were less lucrative and profitable relative to men's areas of work … At film festivals, women had greater presence in the documentary film genre than working on narrative feature films. Narrative films have a greater likelihood of wide theatrical releases than do documentary films.' M. Erigha, 'Race, Gender, Hollywood: Representation in cultural production and digital media's potential for change', *Sociology Compass*, vol. 9, no. 1, 2015, p. 85.

15. P. Smith, P. Caputi and N. Crittenden, 'A Maze of Metaphors around Glass Ceilings', *Gender in Management: An international journal*, vol. 27, no. 7, 2012, pp. 436–48.

16. From an IFB statement, as reported by Donald Clarke, 'Irish Film Board Issues Statement on Gender Equality', *Irish Times*, 12 November 2015, http://www.irishtimes.com/blogs/screenwriter/2015/11/12/irish-film-board-issues-statement-on-gender-equality/ [accessed 14 November 2016].

17. R.E. Caves, *Creative Industries: Contracts between art & commerce* (Cambridge, MA: Harvard University Press, 2000), p. 21.

18. B. Conor, R. Gill and S. Taylor, 'Gender and Creative Labour', *Sociological Review*, vol. 63, 2015, p. 10.

19. D. O'Connell, *New Irish Storytellers: Narrative strategies in film* (London: Intellect Books, 2010), p. 28.

20. Ibid.

21. From Jones and Pringle's analysis of the 2008 Skillset report, 'Why Her? Factors that have influenced the careers of successful women in film & television', AFTV & Alliance Sector Skills Councils, UK, http://publications.skillset.org/admin/data/why%20her/why%20her%202009.pdf [accessed 21 September 2019].

22. Conor, Gill and Taylor, 'Gender and Creative Labour', p. 12.

23. The Arts Council have confirmed in correspondence with the author that no decision has yet been taken on the future of the Reel Art programme following Filmbase's closure in March 2018.

24. From a Reel Art scheme funding application document, http://www.artscouncil.ie/Funds/Reel-Art-scheme/ [accessed 22 March 2018].

25. O'Connell, *New Irish Storytellers*, p. 36.

26. From a Reel Art scheme funding application document, http://www.artscouncil.ie/Funds/Reel-Art-scheme/ [accessed 22 March 2018].

27. Ibid.

28. The centre for filmmakers established in 2009 by filmmakers John Carney, Kirsten Sheridan and Lance Daly and casting director Maureen Hughes in a semi-derelict building in Dublin's Barrow Street.

29. American film director and producer Pallotta is perhaps best known for his work on the production and animation of Richard Linklater's *Waking Life* (2001), and *A Scanner Darkly* (2006).

30. T. Tracy and R. Flynn, 'Contemporary Irish Film: From the national to the transnational', Éire-Ireland, vol. 52, nos. 1 & 2, 2017, pp. 169–97.

31. W. Higbee and S. Hwee Lim, 'Concepts of Transnational Cinema: Towards a critical transnationalism in film studies', Transnational Cinemas, vol. 1, no. 1, 2014, p. 9.

32. Such as the variety of studies cited by Jones and Pringle (2015), or Liddy (2020).

33. Liddy, 'Where Are the Women?'

34. Although she had stepped back to a certain extent prior to this, with writer and filmmaker Derek O'Connor acting as director of the festival.

Women Cinematographers and Changing Irish Production Cultures

1. The term 'cinematographer' is generally favoured in the US, and in many European contexts, while 'director of photography' (variously abbreviated as DP or DoP) is more often used in Ireland and the UK, where the role often encompasses additional responsibility for lighting.

2. S. Prince, 'The Emergence of Filmic Artifacts: Cinema and cinematography in the digital era', *Film Quarterly*, vol. 57, no. 3, Spring 2004, p. 25.

3. See IMAGO [European Federation of Cinematographers], 'Guide on Contractual Agreements for Authors of Cinematography', http://www.imago.org/index.php/cinematographers/item/431-imago-model-contract.html [accessed 21 September 2019].

4. C. Greenhalgh, 'Shooting from the Heart: Cinematographers and their medium', in IMAGO, *Making Pictures: A century of European cinematography* (New York: Harry N. Abrams, 2003), p. 151.

5. No specific research sources are cited: http://www.imago.org/index.php/news/item/568-forum-on-diversity.html [accessed 1 June 2018].

6. British Society of Cinematographers, https://bscine.com/bsc-members?category=1 [accessed 1 June 2018].

7. M. Citron and E. Seiter, 'The Perils of Feminist Film Teaching', in P. Steven (ed.), *Jump Cut: Hollywood, politics and counter-cinema* (New York: Praeger, 1985), p. 270. (Originally published as 'The Woman with the Movie Camera', *Jump Cut*, vol. 26, December 1981, pp. 61–2.)

8. Ibid., p. 276.

9. D. Petrie, 'The Development of Film Schools in Europe and North America', in D. Petrie and R. Stoneman (eds), *Educating Film-makers: Past, present and future* (Bristol: Intellect Books, 2014), pp. 70–1.

10. Ibid., p. 100.

11. E. Lieberman and K. Hegarty, 'Authors of the Image: Cinematographers Gabriel Figueroa and Gregg Toland', *Journal of Film and Video*, vol. 62, nos. 1–2, Spring/Summer 2010, p. 33.

12. There are some exceptions. Zoe Dirse draws upon practical experience of cinematography in an article mainly focused on her own films, 'Gender in Cinematography: Female gaze (eye), behind the camera', *Journal of Research in Gender Studies*, vol. 3, no. 1, 2013, pp. 15–29.

13. Lieberman and Hegarty, 'Authors of the Image', p. 33.

14. Prince, 'The Emergence of Filmic Artifacts', p. 29.

15. B. Brown, *Cinematography: Theory and practice. Image-making for cinematographers and directors*, volume 3, 3rd edition (London: Focal Press, 2016).

16. V. Mayer, *Below the Line: Producers and production studies in the new television economy* (Durham and London: Duke University Press, 2011).

17. J.T. Caldwell, 'Worker Blowback: User-generated, worker-generated, and producer-generated content within collapsing production workflows', in J. Bennett and N. Strange (eds), *Television as Digital Media* (Durham and London: Duke University Press, 2011), pp. 283–310.

18. R. Gill, 'Inequalities in Media Work', in P. Szczepanik and P. Vonderau (eds), *Behind the Screen: Inside European production cultures* (London and New York: Palgrave Macmillan, 2013), p. 198.

19. Ibid., p. 200.

20. K. Erbland, 'Female Cinematographers Band Together to Form New Collective', http://www.indiewire.com/2016/05/female-cinematographers-band-together-to-form-new-collective-291265/ [accessed 20 May 2018].

21. M. Ryzik, 'Women Not Content to Hide Behind the Camera', *New York Times*, 2 June 2016, https://www.nytimes.com/2016/06/02/movies/female-cinematographers-not-content-to-hide-behind-the-camera.html [accessed 20 May 2018].

22. In addition to these activities, Kirsten Johnson, a member of CXX, directed and shot a well-received autobiographical documentary feature called *Cameraperson* (2016), reflecting upon her own experience (including her ethical concerns) as a cinematographer.

23. See illuminatrix DOPs press release, 8 November 2016, http://www.illuminatrixdops. com/About-illuminatrix [accessed 21 September 2019].

24. Gill, 'Inequalities in Media Work', p. 199.

25. Video documentation of the discussion, which took place in Dublin on 2 August 2017, can be accessed on the Women in Film and Television (Ireland) website: https://wft.ie/watch-wfts-dop-masterclass-with-kate-mccullough-frida-wendel/ [accessed 20 May 2018]. I am indebted to costume designer Judith Williams for alerting me to this discussion.

26. Wendel is Swedish but working on attached Irish TV productions such as the drama *Striking Out*.

27. These projects include an episode of *Doctor Who*, and *Queers* (2017), a series of eight monologues created by Gatiss, commissioned to mark the fiftieth anniversary of The Sexual Offences Act 1967.

28. In addition to *Divestment*, directed by artist Paul Rowley, Lavelle has shot artworks by Zineb Sedira, Daria Martin, Charlotte Prodger, Rosalind Nashashibi and Nicky Gogan (a producer and director with Still Films, with a background as an artist). McCullough has shot films by Roisin Loughrey, Niamh O'Malley and Sarah Browne.

29. Michael Lavelle chaired the WFT 'masterclass' previously cited.

30. These films include the feature documentary *Jaha's Promise* (dir. Kate O'Callagan and Patrick Farrelly, 2017), which focuses on US-based Gambian activist Jaha Dukureh on a campaign to end the practice of female genital mutilation in her home country.

31. K. McCullough (interview), *Filmmaker Magazine*, 26 January 2017, https://filmmakermagazine.com/101406-i-felt-a-huge-responsibility-to-get-it-right-dp-kate-mccullough-on-its-not-yet-dark/#.WpkvxOfLg2w [accessed 20 May 2018].

32. I discuss McCullough's collaboration with Sarah Browne in more detail in M. Connolly, 'Choreographing Women's Work: Multitaskers, smartphone users and virtuoso performers', in L. Reynolds (ed.), *Women Artists, Feminism and the Moving Image: Contexts and practices* (London: IB Tauris, 2018).

Documenting Documentary: Liberated enclave or pink ghetto?

1. B.A. McLane, *A New History of Documentary Film*, 2nd edition (New York and London: Continuum, 2012), p. 7.

2. M. Cousins, *The Story of Film* (New York: Thunder's Mouth Press, 2004).

3. R. Kilborn and J. Izod, *An Introduction to Television Documentary: Confronting reality* (Manchester and New York: Manchester University Press, 1997).

4. J. Cornor, 'A Fiction Unlike Any Other?', *Critical Studies in Television*, vol. 1, no. 1, 2006, pp. 89–96.

5. J. Greenberg, 'Netflix Wants to Usher in a New Golden Age of Nonfiction TV', *Wired*, https://www.wired.com/2015/05/netflix-original-documentaries [accessed 21 September 2019].

6. P. Bernstein, 'What Does Netflix's Investment in Documentaries Mean for Filmmakers?', http://www.indiewire.com/2015/03/what-does-netflxs-investment-in-documentaries-mean-for-filmmakers-64347 [accessed 21 September 2019].

7. Greenberg, 'Netflix Wants to Usher in a New Golden Age of Nonfiction TV'.

8. Bernstein, 'What Does Netflix's Investment in Documentaries Mean for Filmmakers?'

9. K. Ross and C. Carter, 'Women and News: A long and winding road', *Media, Culture & Society*, vol. 33, no. 8, 2011, pp. 1148–65.

10. M.M. Lauzen, 'More Female Documentary Directors, But Celluloid Ceiling Remains', http://www.thewrap.com/women-representation-documentary-films-grows-celluloid-ceiling-remains-indie-features-53586/ [accessed 21 September 2019].

11. Ibid.

12. S. Liddy, 'Missing in Action: Where are the Irish women screenwriters?', http://film ireland.net/2015/04/20/missing-in-action-where-are-the-irish-women-screenwriters/ [accessed 21 September 2019].

13. Irish Film Board, 'IFB Gender Statistics 2010–2015', http://www.irishfilmboard.ie/files/7.%20Gender%20Statistics%202010%20-%202016.pdf [accessed 21 September 2019].

14. Irish Film Board, 'Statement from the IFB on Gender Equality: Six Point Plan', https://www.irishfilmboard.ie/about/gender [accessed 15 August 2019].

15. Irish Film Board (2018), 'Produced Irish Feature Films Gender Statistics, 2011–2017', https://www.irishfilmboard.ie/images/uploads/general/2011_-_2017_Produced_Films_Overview.pdf [accessed 15 August 2019].

16. McLane, *A New History of Documentary Film*, p. 16.

17. A.H. Eagly, 'Female Leadership Advantage and Disadvantage: Resolving the contradiction', *Psychology of Women Quarterly*, vol. 31, no. 1, 2007, pp. 1–12.

18. C. McKeogh and D. O'Connell, *Documentary in a Changing State: Ireland since the 1990s* (Cork: Cork University Press, 2012), p. 152.

19. Personal communication.

20. P. Yancey-Martin, '"Said and Done" versus "Saying and Doing": Gendering practices, practicing gender at work', *Gender & Society*, vol. 17, no. 3, 2003, pp. 342–66, at p. 362.

21. A. Zoellner, 'Professional Ideology and Program Conventions: Documentary development in independent British television production', *Mass Communication and Society*, vol. 12, no. 4, 2009, pp. 503–36, at p. 505.

22. Ibid., p. 519.

23. Personal communication.

24. Personal communication.

25. Personal communication.

26. Personal communication.

27. Personal communication.

28. Personal communication.

29. Personal communication.

30. European Institute for Gender Equality, *Advancing Gender Equality in Decision-Making in Media Organizations Report* (Luxembourg: Publications Office of the European Union, 2013).

31. Pew Research Centre, *Women and Leadership: Public says women are equally qualified, but barriers persist* (Washington, DC: Pew Research Center, 2015).

32. Personal communication.

33. Personal communication.

34. Personal communication.

35. Personal communication.

36. Personal communication.

37. A. Morfoot, 'Oscars: Examining gender bias in the documentary categories', http://variety.com/2016/film/news/gender-bias-documentary-industry-1201708404/.

38. C. O'Falt, 'Full Frame: Why are women filmmakers finding more opportunities in documentaries?', http://www.indiewire.com/2016/04/full-frame-why-are-women-filmmakers-finding more-opportunities-in-documentaries-21750/ [accessed 21 September 2019].

39. Ibid.

40. Lauzen, 'More Female Documentary Directors'.

41. Personal communication.

42. Personal communication.

43. D. Gipson, 'Ebertfest 2016: Women in film panel', http://www.rogerebert.com/festivals-and-awards/ebertfest-2016-women-in-film-panel [accessed 21 September 2019].

44. Morfoot, 'Oscars'.

45. O'Falt, 'Full Frame'.

46. Personal communication.

47. Personal communication.

48. Eagly, 'Female Leadership Advantage and Disadvantage'.

49. Personal communication.

50. Personal communication.

51. Personal communication.

52. A. O'Brien, 'Producing Television and Reproducing Gender', *Television & New Media*, vol. 16, no. 3, 2015, pp. 259–74.

53. Personal communication.

54. Personal communication.

55. Personal communication.

56. Personal communication.

57. Personal communication.

58. Morfoot, 'Oscars'.

59. Ibid.

60. Personal communication.

61. Personal communication.

62. Personal communication.

63. Personal communication.

64. Personal communication.

65. B. Smaill, 'Interview with Kim Longinotto', *Studies in Documentary Film*, vol. 1, no. 2, 2007, pp. 177–87, at p. 177.

66. Ibid., pp. 179–80.

67. Personal communication.

68. M. Banks and K. Milestone, 'Individualization, Gender and Cultural Work', *Gender, Work & Organization*, vol. 18, no. 1, 2011, pp. 73–89.

69. O'Brien, 'Producing Television and Reproducing Gender'.

70. Ibid.

71. B. Connor, R. Gill and S. Taylor, *Gender and Creative Labour* (Malden, MA, and Oxford: Wiley Blackwell, 2015), p. 62.

72. Zoellner, 'Professional Ideology and Program Conventions'.

73. Eagly, 'Female Leadership Advantage and Disadvantage'.

Educating Gráinne: The role of education in promoting gender equality in the Irish film industry

1. *Looking Back and Moving Forward*, Gender Equality Report 2017, Swedish Film Institute, https://www.filminstitutet.se/globalassets/2.-fa-kunskap-om-film/analys-och-statistik/publications/other-publications/swedish-film-insitute-gender-equality-report_2017_eng.pdf [accessed 21 September 2019].

2. M. Lauzen, 'It's a Man's (Celluloid) World: Portrayals of female characters in the top 100 films of 2018', https://womenintvfilm.sdsu.edu/wp-content/uploads/2019/02/2018_Its_a_Mans_Celluloid_World_Report.pdf [accessed 15 August 2019].

3. S. Cobb, L.R. Williams and N. Wreyford, *Calling the Shots: Women directors and cinematographers in British films since 2003*, Arts & Humanities Research Council, UK, 2016.

4. H. Aylett and F. Raveney, *Where Are the Women Directors in European Films? Gender equality report on female directors, 2006–2013 with best practice and policy recommendations* (Strasbourg: EWA, 2016).

5. www.cao.ie/courses.php?bb=courses [accessed 21 September 2019].

6. *A Strategy for the Development of Skills for the Audio-visual Industry in Ireland*, Screen Ireland/Broadcasting Authority of Ireland, Crowe Horwath, May 2017, https://www.screenireland.ie/images/uploads/general/AV_Skills_Strategy_Report.pdf [accessed 21 September 2019].

7. Ibid.

8. *Creative Capital: Building Ireland's audio-visual creative economy* (A report prepared for the Minister for Arts, Heritage and the Gaeltacht by the Audiovisual Strategic Review Steering Group – April 2011), http://www.crowe.ie/wp-content/uploads/2017/09/Crowe-Horwath-AV-Skills Strategy-Report.pdf [accessed 21 September 2019].

9. *Creative Ireland Programme 2017–2022*, https://www.chg.gov.ie/arts/creative-arts/creative-ireland-programme/ [accessed 21 September 2019].

10. www.screenireland.ie/about/gender.

11. *Film Focus: New Directions in Film and Media Literacy* (IFI/Screen Ireland, December 2012), https://ifi.ie/filmfocus [accessed 21 September 2019].

12. Formal education is used here to refer to education that is classroom-based, provided by trained teachers and generally part of the assessed curriculum. Informal education here refers to activity that happens outside the classroom, in after-school programmes, community-based organisations, museums, libraries, etc.

13. L. Mulvey, 'Visual Pleasure and Narrative Cinema', in L. Braudy and M. Cohen (eds), *Film Theory and Criticism: Introductory readings* (New York: Oxford University Press, 1999), pp. 833–44.

Activism through Celebration: The role of the Dublin Feminist Film Festival in supporting women in Irish film, 2014–17

1. The festival extended the work of one-off screenings, film seasons, and standalone events with a female focus. For example, Cork Feminista launched a Film Collective ('Red'), in 2014. The Irish Film Institute's Alice Butler, always a bastion of the avant-garde, has also run seasons such as 'Beyond the Bechdel Test' in July 2014.

2. M. Barlow, 'Feminist 101: The New York Women's Video Festival, 1972–1980', *Camera Obscura*, vol. 18, no. 2, 2003, pp. 2–39, at p. 13.

3. Based on a numerical analysis of the films listed in the archived programmes at http://www.diff.ie/festival/archive [accessed 21 September 2019]. In 2011, 119 films were shown, of which 20 had a female director (16.8 per cent). In 2012, 25 of 122 films had a female director (20.5 per cent). In 2013, women directors were involved in 19 out of the 126 film sessions (15.1 per cent).

4. S. Liddy, 'Irish Female Screenwriters, 2007–2013', in J. Nelmes and J. Selbo (eds), *Women Screenwriters: An international guide* (Basingstoke: Palgrave Macmillan, 2015), pp. 422–3.

5. Screen Ireland, 'Gender Statistics: Production funding 2018', https://www.screenire land.ie/images/uploads/general/2018_Gender_Statistics_PRODUCTION_TOTAL_ FIGURES.pdf [accessed 8 April 2019].

6. C. Johnston, 'The Subject of Feminist Film Theory/Practice', *Screen*, vol. 21, no. 2, 1980, pp. 27–34, at p. 27.

7. L. Torchin, 'Networked for Advocacy: Film festivals and activism', in D. Iordanova and L. Torchin (eds), *Film Festival Yearbook 4: Film festivals and activism* (St Andrews: St Andrews Film Studies, 2012), pp. 1–12, at p. 4.

8. S. Loist and G. Zielinski, 'On the Development of Queer Film Festivals and Their Media Activism', in D. Iordanova and L. Torchin (eds), *Film Festival Yearbook 4: Film festivals and activism* (St Andrews: St Andrews Film Studies, 2012), pp. 49–62, at p. 50.

9. Johnston, 'The Subject of Feminist Film Theory/Practice', p. 28.

10. Dublin Feminist Film Festival, 'Margarita, with a Straw' (Shonali Bose, 2014, 100 min)', https://www.dublinfeministfilmfestival.com/screenings-2016/2016/11/19/margarita-with-a-straw-shonali-bose-2014-100min [accessed 28 March 2018].

11. S. Mayer, *Political Animals: The new feminist cinema* (London: I.B. Tauris & Co., 2016), pp. 5–6.

12. Barlow, 'Feminist 101', p. 19.

13. A. Juhasz, 'The Future Was Then: Reinvesting in feminist media practice and politics', *Camera Obscura*, vol. 21, no. 1, 2006, pp. 53–7, at pp. 54–5.

14. Ibid., p. 56.

15. M.C. Kearney, *Girls Make Media* (New York: Routledge, 2006), Chapter three.

16. Juhasz, 'The Future Was Then', p. 56.

17. Torchin, 'Networked for Advocacy', p. 2.

18. H. Meany, 'Waking the Feminists: The campaign that revolutionised Irish theatre', *The Guardian*, 5 January 2018, https://www.theguardian.com/stage/2018/jan/05/feminist-irish-theatre-selina-cartmell-gate-theatre [accessed 28 March 2018].

19. Torchin, 'Networked for Advocacy', p. 3.

20. D. Iordanova, 'Film Festivals and Dissent: Can film change the world?', in D. Iordanova and L. Torchin (eds), *Film Festival Yearbook 4: Film festivals and activism* (St Andrews: St Andrews Film Studies, 2012), pp. 13–30, at p. 16.

21. Torchin, 'Networked for Advocacy', p. 3.

22. E. Leahy, '*The Irreducible Difference of the Other*' (Vivienne Dick, 2013)', *Estudios Irlandeses*, vol. 10, 2015, pp. 209–11, at p. 209.

23. J. Hoberman, 'A Context for Vivienne Dick', *October*, vol. 20, 1982, pp. 102–6, at p. 105.

24. K. Kay, 'New York Super-8: Edinburgh Event, 1980', *Idiolects*, vols 9–10, 1980, pp. 7–9, at p. 9.

25. Hoberman, 'A Context for Vivienne Dick', pp. 103–4.

26. Ibid., p. 104.

27. J. Hoberman, 'No Wavelength: The para-punk underground', *The Village Voice*, May 1979, http://www.luxonline.org.uk/articles/no_wavelength(1).html [accessed 28 March 2018].

28. M. Connolly, 'Sighting an Irish Avant-Garde in the Intersection of Local and International Film Cultures', *boundary 2*, vol. 31, no. 1, 2004, pp. 243–65, at p. 244.

29. J. Hoberman, 'The Super-80s', *Film Comment*, vol. 17, no. 3, pp. 39–43, at p. 39.

30. C. Johnston, 'Women's Cinema as Counter-Cinema' [1973], in E.A. Kaplan (ed.), *Feminism and Film* (Oxford: Oxford University Press, 2000), pp. 22–33.

31. A. Lorde, 'The Master's Tools Will Never Dismantle the Master's House' [1981], in *Sister Outsider: Essays and speeches* (Berkeley: Crossing Press, 2007), pp. 110–13.

32. Leahy, '*The Irreducible Difference of the Other*', p. 209.

33. Ibid.

34. See P. Farrelly, 'Lelia's Picture Palace', *Irish America*, January 2013, http://irishamerica.com/2012/12/lelias-picture-palace [accessed 28 March 2017].

35. Ibid.

36. L. Greene, 'Placing the Three Bernadettes: Audio-visual representations of Bernadette Devlin McAliskey', in G. Pearce, C. McLaughlin, and J. Daniels (eds),

Truth, Dare or Promise: Art and documentary revisited (Newcastle upon Tyne: Cambridge Scholars Publishing, 2013), pp. 112–35, at p. 113.

37. J. Whyte, 'Free Radicals', *cineoutsider: beyond the mainstream*, 11 December 2011, http://www.cineoutsider.com/articles/stories/f/free_radicals_1.html [accessed 28 March 2017].

38. Cited in Greene, 'Placing the Three Bernadettes', p. 126.

39. Ibid.

40. L. Greene, 'Music and Montage: Punk, speed, and histories of the troubles', in J.M. Carlsten and F. McGarry (eds), *Film, History, and Memory* (Basingstoke: Palgrave Macmillan, 2015), pp. 169–82, at p. 173.

41. Ibid., p. 174.

42. Greene, 'Placing the Three Bernadettes', p. 114.

43. M. Thompson, 'Interview with Anne Crilly', http://www.tallgirlshorts.net/marymary/anne.html [accessed 28 March 2018].

44. See M. del Campo del Pozo, '"Mother Ireland, Get Off Our Backs": Gender, republicanism, and state politics in prison short stories by Northern Irish women writers', *Estudios Irlandeses*, vol. 9, 2014, pp. 13–23, at p. 21.

45. Cited in F. Farley, *Anne Devlin* (Trowbridge: Flicks, 2000), p. 37.

46. A.K. Martin, 'Death of a Nation: Transnationalism, bodies and abortion in late twentieth-century Ireland', in T. Mayer (ed.), *Gender Ironies of Nationalism: Sexing the nation* (London: Routledge, 2000), pp. 65–86, at p. 67.

47. Iordanova, 'Film Festivals and Dissent', p. 16.

48. Ibid., p. 18.

49. A. Crilly, 'Banning History', *History Workshop Journal*, vol. 31, no. 1, 1991, pp. 163–5, at p. 164.

50. Torchin, 'Networked for Advocacy', p. 1.

51. Ibid., p. 6.

52. Ibid., p. 7.

What If We Had Been the Heroes of the Maze and Long Kesh? Collaborative filmmaking in Northern Ireland

1. S. Thornham, *What If I Had Been the Hero? Investigating women's cinema* (London: Palgrave Macmillan, 2012), p. 4.

2. The term collaborative (or participatory) has been emptied of its meaning and is often overused. Here it refers to a process which allows participants to share control of every phase of the project – from production to editing and dissemination.

3. D. McKittrick and D. McVea, *Making Sense of the Troubles: A history of the Northern Ireland conflict* (London: Penguin, 2001).

4. See L. McAtackney, 'The Negotiation of Identity at Shared Sites: Long Kesh/Maze Prison site, Northern Ireland', *Forum UNESCO University and Heritage 10th International Seminar Cultural Landscapes in the 21st Century*, April 2005; B. Graham and S. McDowell, 'Meaning in the Maze: The heritage of Long Kesh', *Cultural Geographies*, vol. 14, no. 3, 2007, pp. 343–68.

5. L. Miller, 'Building Participation in the Outreach for the Documentary *The Water Front*', *Journal of Canadian Studies/Revue d'études canadiennes*, vol. 43, no. 1, 2009, p. 72.

6. See M.H. Alison, *Women and Political Violence: Female combatants in ethno-national conflict* (London: Routledge, 2009), and C. Cohn, *Women and Wars* (Cambridge: Polity Press, 2013).

7. See L. Dowler, '"And They Think I'm Just a Nice Old Lady": Women and war in Belfast, Northern Ireland', *Gender, Place and Culture*, vol. 5, 1998, pp. 159–76; K. Adie, *Corsets to Camouflage: Women and war* (London: Cornet Books, 2003); E. Jelin, *State, Repression and the Labours of Memory* (Minneapolis: University of Minnesota Press, 2003); R. Ward, *Women, Unionism and Loyalism in Northern Ireland: From 'tea-makers' to political actors* (Dublin: Irish Academic Press, 2006).

8. S. MacDonald, P. Holden and S. Ardener, *Images of Women in Peace and War: Cross-cultural and historical perspectives* (London: Macmillan Education, 1987), p. 1.

9. Adie, *Corsets to Camouflage*, p. 251.

10. Cynthia Enloe, cited in Cohn, *Women and Wars*, p. 19.

11. Cathy Harkin, cited in E. Fairweather, R. McDonough and M. McFadyean, *Only the Rivers Run Free* (London: Pluto, 1984), pp. 131–2. Feminist filmmakers such as Pat Murphy have challenged this myth since Irish men have also posed a real threat to women, for example in domestic violence cases.

12. R. Sales, *Women Divided: Gender, religion and politics in Northern Ireland* (London: Routledge, 1997), pp. 62–3.

13. Dowler, '"And They Think I'm Just a Nice Old Lady"', p. 166.

14. Monica McWilliams, cited in Sales, *Women Divided*, p. 63.

15. See P. Shirlow and L. Dowler, '"Wee Women No More": Female partners of republican political prisoners in Belfast', *Environment and Planning A*, vol. 42, no. 2, 2010, pp. 384–99; F. Ní Aoláin and C. Turner, 'Gender, Truth & Transition', *UCLA Women's Law Journal*, vol. 16, Spring 2007, pp. 229–79; D. Ging, *Men and Masculinities in Irish Cinema* (London: Palgrave Macmillan, 2012).

16. See Fairweather, McDonough and McFadyean, *Only the Rivers Run Free*; C. Coulter, *Web of Punishment* (Dublin: Attic Press, 1991); N. McCafferty, *The Armagh Women* (Michigan: Co-Op Books, 1981); R. Murray, *Hard Time: Armagh gaol, 1971–1986* (Dublin: Mercier Press, 1998); M. Corcoran, *Out of Order: The political imprisonment of women in Northern Ireland, 1972–1999* (Devon: Willan Publishing, 2006).

17. See C. Roulston, 'Women on the Margin: The women's movement in Northern Ireland, 1973–1988', *Science and Society*, vol. 53, no. 2, 1989, pp. 219–36; E. Evason, *Against the Grain: The contemporary women's movement in Northern Ireland politics* (Dublin: Attic Press, 1991); M. McWilliams, 'Struggling for Peace and Justice: Reflections on women's activism in Northern Ireland', *Journal of Women's History*, vol. 6, no. 4 / vol. 7, no. 1, 1995, pp. 13–39; C. Hackett, 'Narratives of Political Activism from Women in West Belfast', in L. Ryan and M. Ward (eds), *Irish Women and Nationalism: Soldiers, new women and wicked hags* (Dublin: Irish Academic Press, 2004).

18. J. Hill, *Cinema and Northern Ireland: Film, culture and politics* (London: BFI Publishing, 2006), p. 242.

19. M.I. Bergquist, 'Mother Ireland and the Gun: Representations of women and violence in the films of Northern Ireland', master's thesis, Queen's University Belfast, 1996, p. 6.

20. B. McIlroy, *Shooting to Kill: Filmmaking and the troubles in Northern Ireland* (Trowbridge: Flicks Books, 1998), p. 73.

21. S. Edge, 'Representations of Women in Films about the Troubles: Gender and nationalism in Northern Ireland', in V. Tolz and S. Booth (eds), *Nation and Gender in Contemporary Europe* (Manchester: Manchester University Press, 2005), p. 154.

22. M. Sullivan, *Women in Northern Ireland* (Florida: University Press of Florida, 1999), p. 85.

23. Anne Crilly in Sullivan, *Women in Northern Ireland*, p. 102.

24. Sales, *Women Divided*, p. 5.

25. M. Alvesson and K. Skoldberg, *Reflexive Methodology: New vistas for qualitative research* (London: Sage, 2009), p. 242.

26. Interview with participant, June 2014.

27. I. Barbash and L. Taylor, *Cross-Cultural Filmmaking: A handbook for documentary and ethnographic films and videos* (Los Angeles: University of California Press, 1997), p. 89.

28. After years of 'Blanket' and 'No Wash' protests for the return of political status, republican prisoners went on two hunger strikes in 1980 and 1981. The last ended with the deaths of ten prisoners.

29. Rouverol, cited in S. Zembrzycki, 'Sharing Authority with Baba', *Journal of Canadian Studies/Revue d'études canadiennes*, vol. 43, no. 1, 2009, p. 225.

30. Interview with participant, June 2014.

31. Barbash and Taylor, *Cross-Cultural Filmmaking*, p. 89.

32. Interview with participant, June 2014.

33. Janie Welsch, cited in G.J. Gibson, 'Identities Unmasked / Empowerment Unleashed: The documentary style of Michelle Parkerson', in D. Waldman and J. Walker (eds), *Feminism and Documentary* (Minneapolis: University of Minnesota Press, 1999), pp. 149–50.

34. Ging, *Men and Masculinities in Irish Cinema*, p. 144.

35. See M. Silverstein, 'New Research Shows a Six-Year Low for Women Directors, 98% of Films Feature More Male than Female Characters', http://blogs.indiewire.com/womenandhollywood/new-research-shows-a-six-year-low-for-women-directors-98-of-films-feature-more-male-than-female-characters-20140731.

36. T.T. Minh-ha and N.N. Chen, 'Speaking Nearby', in E.A. Kaplan (ed.), *Feminism and Film* (Oxford: Oxford University Press, 2000), pp. 327–8.

37. Ibid.

38. J. Corner, *The Art of Record: A critical introduction to documentary* (Manchester: Manchester University Press, 1996), p. 138.

39. H.J. Chung, 'Reclamation of Voice: The joint authorship of testimony in the *Murmuring Trilogy*', in B. Sarkar and J. Walker (eds), *Documentary Testimonies: Global archives of suffering* (New York: Routledge, 2010), p. 143.

40. Sophie Hillan, email message to author, 19 March 2014.

41. Hannah Arendt, cited in M. Jackson, *The Politics of Storytelling: Violence, transgression and intersubjectivity* (Copenhagen: Museum Tusculanum Press, 2002), p. 193.

42. L. Miller and M. Smith, 'Dissemination and Ownership of Knowledge', in E.J. Milne, C. Mitchell and N. de Lange (eds), *Handbook of Participatory Video* (Lanham, MD: AltaMira Press, 2012), p. 345.

43. Interview with participant, June 2014.

44. M. Moloney, 'Reaching Out from the Archive: The role of community oral history archives in conflict transformation in Northern Ireland', PhD thesis, University of Ulster, 2014), p. 296.

45. Alvesson and Skoldberg, *Reflexive Methodology*, p. 237.

46. Interview with participant, June 2014.

47. Miller and Smith, 'Dissemination and Ownership of Knowledge', p. 345.

48. Nancy Miller, cited in Thornham, *What If I Had Been the Hero?*, p. 99.

Dearbhla Glynn: Documenting war and sexual violence

1. *The Value of Women in The Congo* (2013), directed by D. Glynn, Ireland, short documentary film.

2. *War on Women* (2014), directed by D. Glynn, Ireland, short documentary film.

3. *War in Eastern Congo* (2016), directed by D. Glynn, Ireland, documentary film.

4. All views attributed to Dearbhla Glynn are derived from a personal interview with the author on 26 January 2018.

5. R.M. Jean-Charles, *Conflict Bodies: The politics of rape representation in the francophone imaginary* (Columbus: Ohio State University Press, 2014).

6. B. Bell, 'The Wartime Rape Narrative in the Democratic Republic of the Congo', PhD dissertation, Université d'Ottawa/University of Ottawa, 2016; O. Oyewùmí, 'The White Woman's Burden: African women in Western discourse', in O. Oyewùmí (ed.), *African Women and Feminism: Reflecting on the politics of sisterhood* (Trenton, NJ: Africa World Press, 2006).

7. L. Chouliaraki, 'Post-humanitarianism: Humanitarian communication beyond a politics of pity', *International Journal of Cultural Studies*, vol. 13, no. 2, 2010, p. 109.

8. J. Corner, 'Documentary Studies: Dimensions of transition and continuity', in T. Austin and W. De Jong (eds), *Rethinking Documentary: New perspectives, new practices* (New York: OUP/McGraw Hill, 2008), pp. 13–28, at p. 22.

9. *Dambé: The Mali project* (2008), directed by D. Glynn, Ireland, documentary film.

10. *Gaza: Post-Operation Cast Lead* (2010), directed by D. Glynn, Ireland, short documentary film.

11. L. Abdela, '"Anyone Here Been Raped and Speaks English?" Workshops for editors and journalists on gender-based violence and sex-trafficking', *Gender & Development*, vol. 15, no. 3, 2007, pp. 387–98.

12. M. McLagan, 'Introduction: Making human rights claims public', *American Anthropologist*, vol. 108, no. 1, 2006, pp. 191–5, at p. 191.

13. L. Chouliaraki, *The Ironic Spectator: Solidarity in the age of post-humanitarianism* (Cambridge and Malden: Polity Press, 2013).

14. McLagan, 'Introduction'.

15. C. Williams, 'Explaining the Great War in Africa: How conflict in the Congo became a continental crisis', *The Fletcher Forum of World Affairs*, vol. 37, no. 2, 2013, p. 81.

16. OHCHR, *Progress and Obstacles in the Fight Against Impunity for Sexual Violence in the Democratic Republic of the Congo*, UN Office of the High Commissioner for Human Rights (2014), http://www.refworld.org/docid/534b931f4.html [accessed 21 September 2019].

17. M. Wallström, '"Conflict Minerals" Finance Gang Rape in Africa', *The Guardian*, 14 August 2010, https://www.theguardian.com/commentisfree/2010/aug/14/conflict-minerals-finance-gang-rape [accessed 21 September 2019].

18. D.K. Cohen, A.H. Green and E.J. Wood, *Wartime Sexual Violence: Misconceptions, implications, and ways forward* (Washington, DC: United States Institute of Peace, 2013).

19. Oyewùmí, 'The White Woman's Burden', p. 29.

20. Jean-Charles, *Conflict Bodies*, p. 5.

21. Bell, 'The Wartime Rape Narrative'.

22. M.E. Baaz and M. Stern, *Sexual Violence as a Weapon of War? Perceptions, prescriptions, problems in the Congo and beyond* (London: Zed Books, 2013).

23. M.E. Baaz and M. Stern, 'Knowing Masculinities in Armed Conflict?', in F. Ní Aoláin, N. Cahn, N. Valji and D. Haynes (eds), *The Oxford Handbook of Gender and Conflict* (Oxford: Oxford University Press, 2018), pp. 532–45.

24. McLagan, 'Introduction', p. 191.

25. Ibid.

26. S. Gregory, 'Transnational Storytelling: Human rights, WITNESS, and video advocacy', *American Anthropologist*, vol. 108, no. 1, 2006, pp. 195–204, at p. 197.

27. J. Kitzinger, 'Media Templates: Patterns of association and the (re)construction of meaning over time', *Media, Culture & Society*, vol. 22, no. 1, 2000, pp. 61–84.

28. Gregory, 'Transnational Storytelling', p. 197.

29. Kitzinger, 'Media Templates', pp. 61–84.

30. L. Boltanski, *Distant Suffering: Morality, media and politics* (Cambridge: Cambridge University Press, 1999).

31. L. Berlant, 'Cruel Optimism', *Differences: A journal of feminist cultural studies*, vol. 17, no. 3, 2006, pp. 20–36.

32. Ibid.

33. *Weapons of War: Confessions of Rape in the Congo* (2009), directed by F. van Velzen and I. van Velzen, Netherlands, Women Make Movies, documentary film.

34. *The Greatest Silence: Rape in the Congo* (2007), directed by L.F. Jackson, USA, documentary film.

35. Bell, 'The Wartime Rape Narrative'.

36. Jean-Charles, *Conflict Bodies*, p. 260.

37. S. Sontag, *Regarding the Pain of Others* (New York: Picador, 2003), p. 18.

38. Bell, 'The Wartime Rape Narrative'.

39. D. Matar and Z. Harb (eds), *Narrating Conflict in the Middle East: Discourse, image and communications practices in Lebanon and Palestine* (London: IB Tauris, 2013).

40. Bell, 'The Wartime Rape Narrative'.

41. Jean-Charles, *Conflict Bodies*.

42. Gregory, 'Transnational Storytelling', p. 196.

43. Baaz and Stern, 'Knowing Masculinities in Armed Conflict?', pp. 532–45; D.K. Cohen, *Rape during Civil War* (Ithaca, NY: Cornell University Press, 2016).

44. R. Branche and F. Virgili (eds), *Rape in Wartime* (New York: Springer, 2012).

45. Bell, 'The Wartime Rape Narrative'.

46. Jean-Charles, *Conflict Bodies*, p. 205.

47. P. Aufderheide, *Documentary Film: A very short introduction* (Oxford: Oxford University Press, 2007), p. 5.

48. B. Nichols, *Representing Reality* (Bloomington: Indiana University Press, 1991).

49. L. Chouliaraki and S. Orgad, 'Mediation, Ethics and Otherness', special issue in the memory of Prof. Roger Silverstone, *International Journal of Cultural Studies*, vol. 14, no. 4, 2011, pp. 341–5, at p. 344.

50. J. Tomlinson, 'Beyond Connection: Cultural cosmopolitan and ubiquitous media', *International Journal of Cultural Studies*, vol. 14, no. 4, 2011, pp. 347–61.

Pat Murphy: Portrait of an artist as a filmmaker

1. Murphy interviewed by the magazine *Irish*, June 1984. Quoted in K. Barry, 'Cinema and Feminism', *The Furrow*, April 1985, p. 249. Unless otherwise indicated, all references to Murphy's papers come from an archive at the Irish Film Institute, Dublin. Note that the newspaper clippings may not have full details, e.g. page numbers of sources. My thanks to the IFI Research Library and viewing service at the Irish Film Institute, Dublin, especially Felix Meehan, Raelene Casey and Kieron O'Leary and for assisting me in viewing films and accessing the files in preparation for this essay.

2. Murphy, 'Belfast', treatment typescript, IFI 129/PM/1/28, p. 1.

3. Ibid.

4. Murphy, 'CV' typescript, *c.* 1980, IFI. This also indicates that Murphy had been teaching film and video in London and New York at Syracuse University and at UCLA variously during 1976–7.

5. A. Butler, '"Permissions and Contexts": Framing the work of Pat Murphy', in L. Pettitt and B. Kopschitz Bastos (eds), *Maeve* (Florianópolis: UFSC, 2019).

6. Murphy, 'CV'.

7. D. Dusinberre, 'St George in the Forest: The English avant garde', *Afterimage*, vol. 6, Summer 1976, p. 5.

8. Murphy, online questionnaire in 2008, 'An AZ of the Ting: Theatre of mistakes', https://bookleteer.com/api/getPublicationPDF?key=&id=39&pageSize=a4> [accessed 26 March 2018].

9. Murphy, 'Rituals of Memory', exhibition programme notes, item 833, undated typescript, IFI/PM/129/5, IFI, Dublin, n.p.

10. Ibid.

11. Murphy, quoted in P. Murphy, 'Interview – film and feminism', *The Irish Feminist Review*, vol. 84, 1984, p. 74.

12. L. Pettitt, 'In the Crack Somewhere Between Two Cultures': Art, cinema and migrant memory', in L. Pettitt and B. Kopschitz Basto (eds), *The Woman Who Married Clark Gable* (Sao Paulo: USP, 2013), especially pp. 26–50.

13. Murphy, 'Interview – film and feminism', p. 74.

14. D. Will, 'Interview with Pat Murphy', *Framework*, nos. 26/7, 1985, p. 133.

15. Pat Murphy in conversation with author at the IFI, Dublin, 25 February 2016.

16. Pat Murphy in interview with Claire Johnston, *Screen*, vol. 22, no. 44, 1981, p. 67.

17. J. Hawken, 'Maeve', *Undercut*, vol. 6, Winter 1982–3, p. 8.

18. Anon. reviewer in *Outta Control* [Belfast?], 16 August 1981, n.p. This review refers to a screening at Belfast's QFT cinema. It is sourced from the over sixty review clippings on *Maeve* worldwide held in the IFI Research Library. Space prevents me from evaluating the full range of them, but they make fascinating reading. For a full bibliography of these reviews, see Pettitt and Kopschitz (eds), *Maeve* (note 5 above).

19. Alexander Walker wrote in London's *New Standard*, 10 September 1981, that it was 'a tedious celluloid lecture about the Republican cause in Ulster financed with £400,000 of public money', which was wholly inaccurate. Mandy Merck rightfully chastised him in her review, 'Low Standards', *Not…* , 17 September – 8 November, 1981, n.p.

20. Will, 'Interview with Pat Murphy', p. 135.

21. Barry, 'Cinema and Feminism', p. 248.

22. Murphy, quoted in Patsy Murphy, p. 76.

23. Will, 'Interview with Pat Murphy', p. 134.

24. L. Gibbons, *Transformations in Irish Culture* (Cork: Cork University Press, 1996), p. 113.

25. F. Farley, *Anne Devlin* (Trowbridge: Flicks Books, 2000), p. 22.

26. Murphy quoted in Patsy Murphy, p. 78.

27. Murphy quoted in P. Murphy, pp. 79–80. As the interview notes, Tish Barry had authored the *Working Party on Women in Broadcasting: A report to the RTÉ Authority* Dublin: RTÉ, April 1981).

28. See C. Lawlor (ed.), *Sean MacBride: That day's struggle* (Dublin: Currach Press, 2005); correspondence on the development, structure and funding for the TV film may be found in the IFI Dublin, IFI/PM/132/13, 16 February 1988.

29. Murphy to Josephine Poole, 14 May 1985, IFI/PM/113 and 129, Box 132.

30. Murphy to Arts Council, Letter 'Arts Council Film Script Award' (no date, *c*. 1985), IFI/PM/129, Box 132.

31. Murphy, interviewed by Des Bell in *Kinema: A journal for film and audiovisual media*, Fall, 2007, http://www.kinema.uwaterloo.ca/article.php?id=328 [accessed 27 March 2018].

32. Gerardine Meaney analyses this sequence and quotes Murphy's thoughts on how it came about in her concise study of the film, *Nora* (Cork: Cork University Press, 2004), pp. 15–18.

33. Murphy, interviewed by Des Bell in *Kinema*.

34. *What Miro Saw* (2002) is described as a 'brief film diary, a dialogue between Robert Janz, an artist trapped in his Lower Manhattan loft by the disaster of September 11th, who faxes drawings of what he sees through his window to a friend in Dublin', https://www.irishfilmboard.ie/directory/view/247/what–miro–saw/archive [accessed 16 April 2018].

35. Jason Coyle interviewing Murphy for *Scannain*, 8 October 2015, https://scannain.com/irish/tana-bana-pat-murphy/ [accessed 20 April 2018].

36. Barry, 'Cinema and Feminism', p. 249.

37. Murphy, interviewed by Des Bell in *Kinema*.

Juanita Wilson: A crusading Irish filmmaker

1. R. Flynn and T. Tracy, 'Irish Film and Television 2014', *Estudios irlandeses*, no. 10, 2015, pp. 193–4.

2. B. Gray and L. Ryan, 'The Politics of Irish Identity: Feminism, nationhood and colonialism', in R. Roach Pierson and N. Chaudhuri (eds), *Nation, Empire, Colony: Historicizing gender and race* (Bloomington, IN: Indiana University Press, 1998), p. 134.

3. 'Women in Film', programme for the 28th Galway Film Fleadh, 2016, p. 11, https://www.galwayfilmfleadh.com/fleadh/archive/28th/ [accessed 21 September 2019].

4. M. Sullivan, *Women in Northern Ireland* (Gainesville: University Press of Florida, 1999), p. 72.

5. Private conversation, May 2014.

6. G. Bluestone, *Novels into Film* (Berkeley: University of California Press, 1966).

7. F. Jost, 'La Transfiguration du Bal', *Cinémas*, vol. 15, nos. 2–3, 2005, pp. 107–19, https://www.erudit.org/fr/revues/cine/2005–v15–n2–3–cine1032/012322ar.pdf [accessed 21 September 2019].

8. J. Wilson, interview, *Studies in Art and Humanities*, vol. 3, no. 1, 2017, https://esource.dbs.ie/bitstream/handle/10788/3267/j%20wilson%20interview%20vol03_iss01.pdf?sequence=1&isAllowed=y [accessed 21 September 2019].

9. To give but a few examples, Alfred Hitchcock adapted *Juno and the Paycock* (Sean O'Casey, 1924); John Ford adapted *The Plough and the Stars* (Sean O'Casey, 1926), *The Informer* (Liam O'Flaherty, 1925) and *The Quiet Man* (Maurice Walsh, 1935).

10. Born in Nevada (Missouri) in 1906, John Huston renounced American citizenship to become an Irish citizen in 1964.

11. https://www.theguardian.com/books/booksblog/2015/oct/08/everything-you-needto-know-about-svetlana-alexievich-winner-of-the-nobel-prize-in-literature [accessed 21 September 2019].

12. Ibid.

13. Ales Adamovich (1927–1994) was a Belarussian Soviet writer, whose method consisted in describing the horrors of the twentieth century through recording the testimonies of witnesses.

14. Interview, *Studies in Art and Humanities*.

15. Woodrell's novel *Woe to Live On* (1987) was adapted by Ang Lee for *Ride with the Devil* (1999), and *Winter's Bone* was adapted by Debra Granik (2010).

16. 'You're no angel, you know how this stuff comes to happen: Friday is payday and it's been a gray day sogged by a slow ugly rain and you seek company in your gloom, and since you're fresh to West Table, Mo., and a new hand at the dog-food factory, your choices for company are narrow but you find some finally in a trailer court on East Main, and the coed circle of bums gathered there spot you a beer, then a jug of tequila starts to rotate and the rain keeps comin' down with a miserable bluesy beat and there's two girls millin' about that probably can be had but they seem to like certain things and crank is one of those certain things, and a fistful of party straws tumble from a woven handbag somebody brung, the crank gets cut into lines, and the next time you notice the time it's three or four Sunday mornin' and you ain't slept since Thursday night and one of the girl voices, the one you want most and ain't had yet though her teeth are the size of shoe-peg corn and look like maybe they'd taste sort of sour, suggests something to do, 'cause with crank you want something, anything, to do, and this cajoling voice suggests we all rob this certain house on this certain street in that rich area where folks can afford to wallow in their vices and likely have a bunch of recreational dope stashed around the mansion and goin' to waste since an article in *The Scroll* said the rich people whisked off to France or some such on a noteworthy vacation.' In *Studies in Arts and Humanities*, vol. 3, no. 1, 2017.

17. Ibid.

18. Melodrama as defined by James L. Smith: 'In melodrama man remains undivided, free from the agony of choosing between conflicting imperatives and desires. He greets every situation with an unwavering single impulse which absorbs his whole personality. If there is danger he is courageous, if there is political corruption he exposes it, untroubled by cowardice, weakness or doubt, self-interest or thought of self-preservation … It follows that the undivided protagonist of melodrama has only external pressures to fight against: an evil man, a social group, a hostile ideology, a natural force, an accident or chance, an obdurant fate or a malign deity. It is this total dependence upon external adversaries which finally separates melodrama from all other serious dramatic forms.' J.L. Smith, *Melodrama* (London: Methuen & Co., Ltd, 1973), pp. 7–8.

19. See Chapter VI, 'La famille à l'écran: *The Field*, Jim Sheridan (1990)', in I. Le Corff, *Le cinéma irlandais: une expression postcoloniale européenne* (Rennes: PUR, 2014), pp. 113–28.

20. Introduction to S. Loren and J. Metelmann, *Melodrama after the Tears: New perspectives on the politics of victimhood* (Amsterdam: Amsterdam University Press, 2016).

21. 'That day, we didn't just lose a town … we lost our whole world. We left on the third day. Little did we know that everything we smuggled with us … was a time bomb … slowly ticking. That we, ourselves, had become time bombs. We laid her on the door … the door that my father was laid out on … the door that I had to steal from my own apartment. That day we didn't just lose a town … we lost our own world.'

22. 'Daniel's novel was inspired by a vicious murder that happened in the Ozarks of a young gay man, and it is what sparks the events in the story.' Interview, *Studies in Arts and Humanities*.

23. Loren and Metelmann, *Melodrama after the Tears*, p. 29.

24. 'I love the idea that I'm like a torch shining a light on something I believe is important and, through illuminating it, other people can see it and make up their own minds', http://filmireland.net/2012/02/15/interview-juanita-wilson/ [accessed 9 May 2018].

25. The father's in *The Door*, Slavenka's in *As If I'm Not There*, Sammy's in *Tomato Red*, 25, https://www.independent.ie/breaking-newsirish-news/filmmaker-went-toradioactive-city- 26629954.html [accessed 9 May 2018].

26. The situation is slightly different for *Tomato Red*, since the film was shot in Canada. Yet Jake Weary (Sammy), Nick Roux (Jason) and Julia Garner (Jamalee) are American actors.

27. In the book she is called 'S', as in Marguerite Duras's novel *La Douleur*.

28. The fly may also be an allusion to the first group of men, who were tried and sentenced for rape as a crime against humanity in Drakulic's book *They Would Never Hurt a Fly*. These three men couldn't believe what was happening to them. In their culture and in their surroundings, to rape a woman was nothing. They defended themselves by saying that they actually saved the lives of these girls. Interview, *Studies in Arts and Humanities*.

29. It is estimated that between 20,000 and 50,000 women were raped in the war in Bosnia. The victims were mostly Muslim, Bosniak women, but rape was committed on all sides.

30. Fo a is a town in eastern Bosnia-Herzegovina where the first group of men were tried and sentenced for rape against humanity.

31. The relationship between a jailer and a prisoner in a context of civil war evokes *The Crying Game* (Neil Jordan, 1992), in its depiction of Stockholm syndrome.

Irish Cinema and the Gendering of Space:
Motherhood, domesticity and the homeplace

1. B. French, *On the Verge of Revolt: Women in American films of the fifties* (New York: Frederick Ungar Publishing, 1978), p. 18.

2. b. hooks, *Yearning: Race, gender, and cultural politics* (London: Turnaround, 1991), p. 42.

3. P. Neville, 'Mediating between *His & Hers*: An exploration of gender representations and self-representations', in B. Monahan (ed.), *Ireland and Cinema: Culture and contexts* (New York and Basingstoke: Palgrave Macmillan, 2015), p. 97.

4. R. Barton, *Irish National Cinema* (London and New York: Routledge, 2004), pp. 126–7.

5. C. Holohan, *Cinema on the Periphery: Contemporary Irish and Spanish film* (Dublin: Irish Academic Press, 2010), pp. 118–20.

6. T. Tracy, 'A Wandering to Find Home: *Adam & Paul* (2004)', in R. Richman Kenneally and L. McDiarmid (eds), *The Vibrant House: Irish writing and the domestic space* (Dublin: Four Courts Press, 2017), p. 233.

7. For more on the configuration of gender relations in popular culture during the recession, see D. Negra, 'Adjusting Men and Abiding Mammies: Gendering the recession in Ireland', *The Irish Review*, vol. 46, 2013, pp. 23–34.

8. P. Molloy, 'Labour of Love Proves a Box-Office Hit', *The Sunday Business Post*, 12 September 2010, p. 6.

9. Neville, 'Mediating', p. 101.

10. S. Molony, 'House and Home: Structuring absence in post-Celtic Tiger documentary', in D. Negra and Y. Tasker (eds), *Gendering the Recession: Media and culture in an age of austerity* (Durham and London: Duke University Press, 2014), pp. 181–202, at p. 193.

11. E. Leahy, 'Snap (Carmel Winters 2010)', *Estudios Irlandeses*, vol. 6, 2011, pp. 215–17, at p. 215.

12. D. Massey, *Space, Place and Gender* (Cambridge: Polity, 1994), p. 6.

13. See, for instance, C. Monk, 'Sexuality and the Heritage', *Sight and Sound*, vol. 5, 1995, pp. 32–4.

Authority to Speak: Assessing the progress of gender parity and representation in Irish animation

1. 'About the Animation Industry', *Irish Film Board*, 23 April 2018, www.irishfilmboard. ie/about/about-the-animation-industry [accessed 21 September 2019].

2. 'Studios', *Animation Ireland*, 23 April 2018, http://animationie.wpengine.com/studios/.

3. Sullivan Bluth Studios, which created animated feature films such as *The Secret of NIMH* and *The Land Before Time*, was established first in Van Nuys, California, before moving to Dublin for tax-incentive reasons. Sullivan Bluth's presence in Ireland since the late 1980s inarguably spurred growth in the industry, resulting in the establishment of many indigenous animation houses. It will not, however, be considered here as 'homegrown', nor its films as contributing to an 'Irish national cinema'.

4. S. Liddy, '"Open to All and Everybody"? The Irish Film Board: Accounting for the scarcity of women screenwriters', *Feminist Media Studies*, vol. 16, no. 5, 2016, pp. 901–17.

5. C. Barrett, 'Black and White and Green All Over? Emergent Irish female stardom in contemporary popular cinemas', in B. Monahan (ed.), *Ireland and Cinema: Culture and contexts* (London: Palgrave Macmillan, 2015), pp. 59–70.

6. Irish Film Board, 'Produced Irish Feature Films Gender Statistics, 2011–2017', https://www.irishfilmboard.ie/images/uploads/general/2011_-_2017_Produced_Films_Overview.pdf [accessed 15 August 2019].

7. Ibid.

8. Interview by author with Ed Guiney, National Media Conference panel, Trinity College Dublin, 16 November 2013.

9. Liddy, '"Open to All and Everybody"?, p. 904.

10. Ibid., p. 902.

11. L. Mulvey, 'Visual Pleasure and Narrative Cinema', *Screen*, vol. 16, no. 3, October 1975, pp. 6–18.

12. P. Wells, *Understanding Animation* (London: Routledge, 1998), p. 187.

13. Ibid., p. 196.

14. Ibid., p. 199.

15. The 'plasmatic', as Cary Elza explains, refers to the 'utopian promise of animation', which Eisenstein idealised, 'hearken[ing] back to a primal period, in which formless blobs could turn into anything'. C. Elza, 'Alice in Cartoonland: Childhood, gender, and imaginary space in early Disney animation', *Animation: An Interdisciplinary Journal*, vol. 9, no. 1, 2014, p. 15.

16. Phone interview by author with Deirdre Barry, 23 April 2018.

17. 'Produced Irish Feature Films Gender Statistics, 2011–2017'.

18. 'Bord Scannán na hÉireann/Irish Film Board Strategic Plan 2016–2020', Irish Film Board, 23 April 2018, https://www.irishfilmboard.ie/images/uploads/general/IFB_Five_Year_Strategy_2016-1.pdf [accessed 21 September 2019].

19. 'POV', Irish Film Board, 23 April 2018, https://www.irishfilmboard.ie/funding/production-loans/pov-low-budget-production-and-training-scheme-for-female-talent [accessed 21 September 2019].

20. Of course, as this survey was taken exclusively by people working within the Irish animation industry, a bias of viewpoint must be acknowledged regarding respondents' tendency to view gender representation in their own field in a more positive – though overall still critical – light.

21. Tasmin Lyons, survey response, 23 March 2018.

22. Ibid.

23. Phone interview by author with Deirdre Barry, 23 April 2018. Barry is here referring to a series of interactions with director Nora Twomey.

24. M. O'Brien, '*The Secret of Kells*: A film for a post-Celtic Tiger Ireland?' *Animation Studies*, vol. 6, 2011, p. 38.

25. H.K. Bhabha, 'Signs Taken for Wonders: Questions of ambivalence and authority under a tree outside Delhi', *Critical Inquiry*, vol. 12, no. 1, Autumn 1985, p. 158.

26. It should be noted that the screenplay was written by Fabrice Ziolkowski, a French-American male screenwriter, whose authorial stamp and gendered perspective may also be taken into account.

27. D. Negra, 'Irishness, Anger and Masculinity in Recent Film and Television', in R. Barton (ed.), *Screening Irish-America* (Dublin: Irish Academic Press, 2009), p. 280.

28. Barrett, 'Black and White and Green All Over?'

29. Wells, *Understanding Animation*, p. 199.

30. Admittedly, Ben is drawn in a similar fashion. As such, their shared traits of round faces, small noses and big eyes could be seen as more a function of childlike iconicity than a gendered representational trope. On the other hand, Ben's face is overall more expressive throughout, bearing a gap tooth and heavy brow, which are manipulated throughout for the purposes of showing overt emotional reaction. Saoirse is more of a cipher, and her relative lack of emotivity directly indicates the fact that she is not intended to be a point of audience identification.

Concluding Remarks: The road ahead

1. S. Liddy, '"Open to All and Everybody"? The Irish Film Board: Accounting for the scarcity of women screenwriters', *Feminist Media Studies*, vol. 16, no. 5, 2016.

2. Screen Ireland, 'From Shorts to Features: Screen Ireland celebrates leading Irish female directors for International Women's Day', https://www.screenireland.ie/news international-womens-day-2019-female-directed-short-film [accessed 21 September 2019].

3. Irish Film Board (2018), 'Produced Irish Feature Films Gender Statistics, 2011–2017', https://www.irishfilmboard.ie/images/uploads/general/2011_-_2017_Produced_Films_ Overview.pdf [accessed 15 August 2019].

4. Screen Ireland, POV and Enhanced Production Funding, https://www.screenireland. ie/gender-and-diversity/ifb-gender-statistics/enhanced-production-funding-for-female-talent-other-funding-schemes [accessed 21 September 2019].

5. Screen Ireland Production Catalogue (2019), https://www.screenireland.ie/images/ uploads/general/ScreenIreland_ProductionCatalogue_2019_Web.pdf, p. 2 [accessed 14 August 2019].

6. Screen Ireland, 'INDUSTRY NOTICE: Key Changes Introduced to Section 481, Including a New Requirement For a Skills Development Plan' (April 2019), https://www.screenireland.ie/news/industry-notice-key-changes-introduced-to-section-481 [accessed 14 August 2019].

7. Broadcasting Authority of Ireland, 'BAI Gender Action Plan', https://www.bai.ie/en/media/sites/2/dlm_uploads/2018/04/20180423_BAI_GenderActionPlan_vFinal_AR.pdf [accessed 14 August 2019].

8. S. Comey, *Spotlight*, Irish Film Institute, 27 April 2018.

9. Ibid.

10. https://www.bai.ie/en/bai-focuses-on-womens-stories-under-sound-vision-scheme/ [accessed 21 September 2019].

11. Galway Film Fleadh, 14 July 2018; Cork International Film Festival, 15 November 2018.

12. 5050 x 2020 Cannes Collective, http://www.5050x2020.fr/ [accessed 21 September 2019].

13. Directors UK, 'Who's Calling the Shots? A report on gender inequality among screen directors working in UK television' (August 2017), https://www.directors.uk.com/news/who-s-calling-the-shots [accessed 14 August 2019].

14. B. Barnes and C. Buckley, 'As Hollywood Embraces Diversity, Jobs for Female Directors Remain Sparse', *New York Times*, 14 April 2019.

15. M. Lauzen, 'The Celluloid Ceiling: Behind-the-scenes employment of women on the top 100, 250, and 500 films of 2018', https://womenintvfilm.sdsu.edu/the-celluloid-ceiling-behind-the-scenes-employment-of-women-on-the-top-100-250-and-500-films-of-2018/ [accessed 14 August 2019].

16. Galway Film Fleadh, *Accelerating Change: Time for quotas?* 14 July 2018.

Bibliography

Abdela, L. 'Anyone Here Been Raped and Speaks English?' Workshops for editors and journalists on gender-based violence and sex-trafficking', *Gender & Development*, vol. 15, no. 3, 2007, pp. 387–98

Acker, A., *Reel Women: Pioneers of the cinema, 1896 to the present* (New York: Continuum Publishing, 1991)

Acker, J., 'From Glass Ceiling to Inequality Regimes', *Sociologie du Travail*, vol. 51, 2009, pp. 199–217

Alexievich, S., *Chernobyl Prayer: A chronicle of the future* (London: Penguin Classics, 2016)

Aufderheide, P., *Documentary Film: A very short introduction* (Oxford: Oxford University Press, 2007)

Aylett, H. and Raveney, F., *Where Are the Women Directors in European Films? Gender equality report on female directors (2006–2013) with best practice and policy recommendations* (Strasbourg: EWA Network, 2015)

Baaz, M.E. and Stern, M., 'Knowing Masculinities in Armed Conflict?', in F. Ní Aoláin, N. Cahn, N. Valji and D.F. Haynes (eds), *The Oxford Handbook of Gender and Conflict* (Oxford: Oxford University Press, 2018), pp. 532–45

Baaz, M.E. and Stern, M., *Sexual Violence as a Weapon of War? Perceptions, prescriptions, problems in the Congo and beyond* (London: Zed Books, 2013)

Bacik, I., 'Legislating for Article 40.3.3', *Irish Journal of Legal Studies*, vol. 3, no. 3, 2013, pp. 18–35

Banks, M. and Milestone, K., 'Individualization, Gender and Cultural Work', *Gender, Work & Organization*, vol. 18, no. 1, 2011, pp. 73–89

Banks, M., Conor, B. and Mayer, V. (eds), *Production Studies, The Sequel! Cultural studies of global media industries* (New York: Routledge, 2016), p. xi

Barlow, M., 'Feminist 101: The New York Women's Video Festival, 1972–1980', *Camera Obscura*, vol. 18, no. 2, 2003, pp. 2–39

Barrett, C., 'Black and White and Green All Over? Emergent Irish female stardom in contemporary popular cinemas', in Barry Monahan (ed.), *Ireland and Cinema: Culture and contexts* (London: Palgrave Macmillan, 2015), pp. 59–70

Barry, K., 'Cinema and Feminism: The case of *Anne Devlin*', *The Furrow*, vol. 36, no. 4, April 1985, pp. 244–9

Barry, U. and Conroy, P., 'Ireland in Crisis 2008–2012: Women, austerity and inequality', https://researchrepository.ucd.ie/handle/10197/-4820 [accessed 30 June 2018]

Barton, R., *Irish National Cinema* (London: Routledge, 2004)

Baughan, N., 'The Invisible Woman: Film's gender bias laid bare', www.bfi.org.uk/news-opinion/sight.../invisible-women-film-gender-bias-laid-bare [accessed 3 July 2018]

Bayliss, D., 'Ireland's Creative Development: Local authority strategies for culture-led development', *Regional Studies*, vol. 38, no. 7, 2004, pp. 817–31

Beauchamp, C., *Without Lying Down: Frances Marion and the powerful women of early Hollywood* (Berkeley and Los Angeles: University of California Press, 1997)

Bell, B., 'The Wartime Rape Narrative in the Democratic Republic of the Congo', PhD dissertation, Université d'Ottawa/University of Ottawa, 2016

Berlant, L., 'Cruel Optimism', *Differences: A Journal of Feminist Cultural Studies*, vol. 17, no. 3, 2006, pp. 20–36

Bernstein, P., 'What Does Netflix's Investment in Documentaries Mean for Filmmakers?', http://www.indiewire.com/2015/03/what-does-netflixs-investment-in-documentaries-mean-for-filmmakers-64347 [accessed 21 September 2019]

Bhabha, H., 'Signs Taken for Wonders: Questions of ambivalence and authority under a tree outside Delhi', *Critical Inquiry*, vol. 12, no. 1, Autumn 1985

Bielby, D., 'Gender Inequality in Culture Industries: Women and men writers in film and television', *France: Sociologie du Travail*, vol. 51, no. 2, April–June 2009

Bluestone, G., *Novels into Film* (Berkeley: University of California Press, 1966)

Boltanski, L., *Distant Suffering: Morality, media and politics* (London: Cambridge University Press, 1999)

Booth, A., 'Recovery 2.0: Beginning the Collective Biographies of Women Project', *Tulsa Studies in Women's Literature*, vol. 28, no. 1, Spring 2009, pp. 15–35, https://www.jstor.org/stable/pdf/40783472.pdf [accessed 3 April 2019]

Branche, R. and Virgili, F., *Rape in Wartime* (London: Springer, 2012)

Broadcasting Authority of Ireland, BAI Gender Action Plan, www.bai.ie/en/media/sites/2/.../20180423_BAI_GenderActionPlan_vFinal_AR.pdf [accessed 3 July 2018]

Brown, B., *Cinematography: Theory and practice: Image making for cinematographers and directors*, vol. 3, 3rd edn (London: Focal Press, 2016)

Budgeon, S., *Third-Wave Feminism and the Politics of Late Modernity* (Basingstoke: Palgrave Macmillan, 2011)

Butler, A., '"Permissions and Contexts": Framing the work of Pat Murphy', in L. Pettitt and B. Kopschitz Bastos (eds), *Maeve* (Florianópolis: UFSC, 2019)

Caldwell, J.T., 'Worker Blowback: User-generated, worker-generated, and producer-generated content within collapsing production workflows', in J. Bennett and N. Strange (eds), *Television as Digital Media* (Durham and London: Duke University Press, 2011), pp. 283–310

Cammaerts, B., 'Social Media and Activism', in R. Mansell and P. Hwa (eds), *The International Encyclopaedia of Digital Communication and Society* (Oxford: Wiley-Blackwell, 2015), pp. 1027–34

Casella, D., 'Ellen O'Mara Sullivan', *Women Film Pioneers Project*, http://wfpp.cdrs.olumbia.edu/pioneer/ellen-omara-sullivan/ (accessed 15 April 2018)

Casella, D., 'Women and Nationalism in Indigenous Irish Filmmaking of the Silent Period', in Monica Dall'Asta, Victoria Duckett and Lucia Tralli (eds), *Researching Women in Silent Cinema: New findings and perspectives* (Bologna: University of Bologna, 2013), pp. 53–80.

Caves, R.E., *Creative Industries: Contracts between art & commerce* (Cambridge, MA: Harvard University Press, 2000)

Chouliaraki, L., 'Post-Humanitarianism: Humanitarian communication beyond a politics of pity', *International Journal of Cultural Studies*, vol. 13, no. 2, 2010

Chouliaraki, L. and Orgad, S., 'Mediation, Ethics and Otherness', special issue in the memory of Prof. Roger Silverstone, *International Journal of Cultural Studies*, vol. 14, no. 4, 2011, pp. 341–5

Citron, M. and Seiter, E., 'The Perils of Feminist Film Teaching', in Peter Steven (ed.), *Jump Cut: Hollywood, politics and counter-cinema* (New York: Praeger, 1985), pp. 269–76

Clarke, D., 'Irish Film Board Issues Statement on Gender Inequality', 12 November 2015,http://www.irishtimes.com.../irish-film-board-issues-statement-on-gender [accessed 21 September 2019]

Cobb, S. and Wreyford, N., 'Data and Responsibility: Towards a feminist methodology for producing historical data on women in the contemporary UK film industry', *Feminist Media Histories*, vol. 3, no. 3, 2014, pp. 107–32

Cobb, S., Williams, L.R and Wreyford, N., 'Calling the Shots: Women and contemporary film culture in the UK, 2000–2015, https://www.southampton.ac.uk/cswf [accessed 21 September 2019]

Cohen, D.K., Green, A.H. and Wood, E.J., *Wartime Sexual Violence: Misconceptions, implications, and ways forward* (Washington: United States Institute of Peace, 2013)

Coles, A., *What's Wrong With This Picture? Directors and gender inequality in the Canadian screen-based production industry* (Toronto: Canadian Unions for Equality on Screen (CUES), 2016)

Condon, D., *Early Irish Cinema, 1895–1921* (Dublin: Irish Academic Press, 2008)

Connolly, M., 'Choreographing Women's Work: Multitaskers, smartphone users and virtuoso performers', in Lucy Reynolds (ed.), *Women Artists, Feminism and the Moving Image: Contexts and practices* (London: IB Tauris, 2018)

Connolly, M., 'Sighting an Irish Avant-Garde in the Intersection of Local and International Film Cultures', *boundary 2*, vol. 31, no. 1, 2004, pp. 243–65

Conor, B., Gill, R. and Taylor, S., 'Gender and Creative Labour', *Sociological Review*, vol. 63, 2015, p. 10

Corner, J., 'A Fiction Unlike any Other?', *Critical Studies in Television*, vol. 1, no. 1, 2006, pp. 89–96

Corner, J., 'Documentary Studies: Dimensions of transition and continuity', in T. Austin and W. De Jong (eds), *Rethinking Documentary: New perspectives, new practices* (Maidenhead: OUP/McGraw Hill, 2008) pp. 13–28

Cousins, M., *The Story of Film* (New York: Thunder's Mouth Press, 2004)

Crilly, A., 'Banning History', *History Workshop Journal*, vol. 31, no. 1, 1991, pp. 163–5

Davies, H. and Callaghan, C., 'All in this Together? Feminisms, academia, austerity', *Journal of Gender Studies*, vol. 23, no. 3, 2014, pp. 227–32

Dawe, O., 'Hearing Women's Voices', conference paper delivered at *Women's Voices in Ireland*, Women's Studies, UCC, 10 June 2017

del Campo del Pozo, M., '"Mother Ireland, Get Off Our Backs": Gender, republicanism, and state politics in prison short stories by Northern Irish women writers', *Estudios Irlandeses*, vol. 9, 2014, pp. 13–23

della Porta, D. and Diani, M., *Social Movements: An introduction*, 2nd edn (Oxford: Blackwell Publishing, 2006)

DeVault, M.L. and Cross, G., 'Feminist Qualitative Interviewing: Experience, talk and knowledge', in S.N. Hesse-Biber (ed.), *The Handbook of Feminist Research: Theory and praxis* (Thousand Oaks, CA., London, New Delhi and Singapore: Sage, 2012), pp. 206–36

Dirse, Z., 'Gender in Cinematography: Female gaze (eye), behind the camera', *Journal of Research in Gender Studies*, vol. 3, no. 1, 2013, pp. 15–29

Donohue, B., 'Women and the Abbey Theatre', https://www.irishtimes.com/opinion/letters/women-and-the-abbey-theatre-1.2415780 [accessed 21 September 2019]

Donohue, B., Dowd, C., Dean, T., Murphy, C., Cawley, K. and Harris, K., 'Gender Counts: An analysis of gender in Irish theatre, 2006–2015', https://learning.educatetogether.ie/mod/resource/view.php?id=12781 [accessed 21 September 2019]

Donovan, S., 'Introduction: Ireland's own film', www.screeningthepast.com/2012/02/introduction-ireland (accessed 1 October 2016)

Drakulic, S., *As If I Am Not There* (London: Hachette, 2013)

Dusinberre, D., 'St George in the Forest: The English avant garde', *Afterimage*, vol. 6, Summer 1976, pp. 5–19

Eagly, A.H., 'Female Leadership Advantage and Disadvantage: Resolving the contradiction', *Psychology of Women Quarterly*, vol. 31, no. 1, 2007, pp. 1–12

Edley, N. and Wetherell, M., 'Jekyll and Hyde: Men's constructions of feminism and feminists', *Feminism and Psychology*, vol. 11, no. 4, 2001, pp. 439–57

Elsaesser, T., *European Cinema: Face to face with Hollywood* (Amsterdam: Amsterdam University Press, 2005)

Elza, C., 'Alice in Cartoonland: Childhood, gender, and imaginary space in early Disney animation', *Animation: An Interdisciplinary Journal*, vol. 9, no. 1, 2014, pp. 7–26

Enloe, C., *The Curious Feminist: Searching for women in a new age of empire* (Los Angeles: University of California Press, 2004)

Erigha, M., 'Race, Gender, Hollywood: Representation in cultural production and digital media's potential for change', *Sociology Compass*, vol. 9, no. 1, pp. 78–89

EU and Irish Women/Ireland–European Commission, www.ec.europa.eu/Ireland/note/ 684_en [accessed 30 June 2018]

European Institute for Gender Equality, *Advancing Gender Equality in Decision-Making in Media Organizations Report* (Luxembourg: Publications Office of the European Union, 2013)

Falvey, D., 'Yes We Did: Irish theatre's gender-equality revolution', *Irish Times*, 14 July 2018, www.irishtimes.com/.../yes-we-did-irish-theatre-s-gender-equality-revolution-1 [accessed 21 September 2019]

Farley, F., *Anne Devlin* (Trowbridge: Flicks Books, 2000)

Fels, A., *Necessary Dreams: Ambition in women's changing lives* (New York: First Anchor Books, 2005)

Felter, M. and Schultz, D., 'James Mark Sullivan and the Film Company of Ireland', *New Hibernian Review*, vol. 8, no. 2, Summer 2004, pp. 24–40

Flynn, R. and Tracy, T., 'Irish Film and Television 2014', *Estudios irlandeses*, no. 10, 2015, https://www.estudiosirlandeses.org/wp-content/uploads/2015/02/IrishFilmandTV_10. pdf [accessed 21 September 2019]

Flynn, R. and Tracy, T., 'Waking the Film Makers: Diversity and dynamism in Irish screen industries 2017', *Estudios Irlandeses*, no. 13, 2018, pp. 238–68

Follows, S., 'Gender within Film Crews', http://stephenfollows.com/site/wp-content/ uploads/2014/07/Gender_Within_Film_Crews [accessed 15 December 2016]

French, B., *On the Verge of Revolt: Women in American films of the fifties* (New York: Frederick Ungar Publishing, 1978)

French, F., 'Gender Then, Gender Now: Surveying women's participation in Australian film and television industries', *Continuum: Journal of Media and Cultural Studies*, vol. 28, no. 2, 2014, pp. 188–200

French, L., 'Women in the Victorian Film, Television and Related Industries: Research report', RMIT University, February 2012, p. 42

Gerbaudo, P., *Tweets and the Streets: Social media and contemporary activism* (New York: Pluto Press, 2012)

Gibbons, L., *Transformations in Irish Culture* (Cork: Cork University Press, 1996)

Gill, R., 'Cool, Creative and Egalitarian? Exploring gender in project-based new media work in Europe', *Information, Communication & Society*, vol. 5, no. 1, 2002, pp. 70–89

Gill, R., 'Inequalities in Media Work', in P. Szczepanik and P. Vonderau (eds), *Behind the Screen: Inside European production cultures* (London and New York: Palgrave Macmillan, 2013), pp. 189–205

Gipson, D., *Ebertfest 2016: Women in Film Panel*, http://www.rogerebert.com/festivals-and-awards/ebertfest-2016-women-in-film-panel [accessed 21 September 2019]

Grace, M., Leahy, M. and Doughney, J., *Response to Striking the Balance: Women, men, work and family*, https://www.humanrights.gov.au/sites/default/files/content/sex_discrimination/publication/strikingbalance/submissions/114.doc [accessed 21 September 2019]

Greenberg, J., 'Netflix Wants to Usher in a New Golden Age of Nonfiction TV', https://www.wired.com/2015/05/netflix-original-documentaries [accessed 21 September 2019]

Greene, L., 'Music and Montage: Punk, speed, and histories of the Troubles', in J.M. Carlsten and F. McGarry (eds), *Film, History, and Memory* (Basingstoke: Palgrave Macmillan, 2015), pp. 169–82

Greene, L., 'Placing the Three Bernadettes: Audio-visual representations of Bernadette Devlin McAliskey', in G. Pearce, C. McLaughlin and J. Daniels (eds), *Truth, Dare or Promise: Art and documentary revisited* (Newcastle upon Tyne: Cambridge Scholars Publishing, 2013), pp. 112–35

Greenhalgh, C., 'Shooting from the Heart: Cinematographers and their medium', in IMAGO, *Making Pictures: A century of European cinematography* (New York: Harry N. Abrams, 2003), pp. 94–155

Gregory, S., 'Transnational Storytelling: Human rights, WITNESS, and video advocacy', *American Anthropologist*, vol. 108, no. 1, 2006, pp. 195–204

Grughlis, I. and Stoyanova, D., 'Social Capital and Networks in Film and TV: Jobs for the boys?', *Organisation Studies*, vol. 33, no. 10, 2012, pp. 1311–31

Grummell, B., Lynch, K. and Devine, D., 'Appointing Senior Managers in Education: Homosociability, local logics and authenticity in the selection process', *Educational Management, Administration and Leadership*, vol. 37, no. 3, 2009, pp. 329–49

Hallward, P., *Absolutely Postcolonial: Writing between the singular and the specific* (Manchester: Manchester University Press, 2002)

Handy, J. and Rowlands, L., 'Gendered Inequality Regimes and Female Labour Market Disadvantage within the New Zealand Film Industry', *Women's Studies Journal*, vol. 28, no. 2, 2014, pp. 24–38

Harding, S., 'Feminist Standpoints', in S.N. Hesse-Biber (ed.), *The Handbook of Feminist Research: Theory and praxis* (Thousand Oaks, CA., London, New Delhi and Singapore: Sage, 2012), pp. 46–64

Hesmondhalgh, D. and Baker, S., 'Sex, Gender and Work Segregation in the Cultural Industries', *Gender and Creative Labour: The sociological review*, vol. 63, S1, 2015, pp. 23–36

Hesse-Biber, S.N. (ed.), *The Handbook of Feminist Research: Theory and praxis* (Thousand Oaks, CA., London, New Delhi and Singapore: Sage, 2012), pp. 2–26

Higbee, W. and Hwee Lim, S., 'Concepts of Transnational Cinema: Towards a critical transnationalism in film studies', Transnational Cinemas, vol. 1, no. 1, 2014, pp. 7–21

Higher Education Authority, 'HEA National Review of Gender Equality in Irish Higher Education', p. 14, https://hea.ie/assets/uploads/2017/06/HEA-National-Review-of-Gender-Equality-in-Irish-Higher-Education-Institutions.pdf [accessed 15 August 2019]

Hill, E., *Never Done: A history of women's work in media production* (New Brunswick, New Jersey and London: Rutgers University Press, 2012)

Hoberman, J., 'A Context for Vivienne Dick', *October*, vol. 20, 1982, pp. 102–6

Hoberman, J., 'No Wavelength: The para-punk underground', *The Village Voice*, http://www.luxonline.org.uk/articles/no_wavelength(1).html [accessed 28 March 2018]

Hoberman, J., 'The Super-80s', *Film Comment*, vol. 17, no. 3, pp. 39–43

Höijer, B., 'The Discourse of Global Compassion: The audience and media reporting of human suffering', *Media, Culture & Society*, vol. 26, no. 4, 2004, pp. 513–31

Holohan, C., *Cinema on the Periphery: Contemporary Irish and Spanish film* (Dublin: Irish Academic Press, 2010)

hooks, b., *Yearning: Race, gender, and cultural politics* (London: Turnaround, 1991)

IMAGO [European Federation of Cinematographers],'Guide on Contractual Agreements for Authors of Cinematography', http://www.imago.org/index.php/cinematographers/item/431-imago-model-contract.html [accessed 21 September 2019]

Iordanova, D., 'Film Festivals and Dissent: Can film change the world?', in D. Iordanova and L. Torchin (eds), *Film Festival Yearbook. Volume 4: Film Festivals and Activism* (St Andrews: St Andrews Film Studies, 2012), pp. 13–30

Irish Film Board, 'About the Animation Industry', www.irishfilmboard.ie/about/about-the-animation-industry [accessed 26 March 2018]

Irish Film Board, 'Gender Statistics 2010–2015', http://www.irishfilmboard.ie/files/7.%20Gender%20Statistics%202010%20-%202016.pdf [accessed 21 September 2019]

Irish Film Board, 'Gender Statistics 2016', http://www.irishfilmboard.ie/files/Gender%20Statistics%202016.pdf [accessed 21 September 2019]

Irish Film Board, 'Produced Irish Feature Films Gender Statistics 2011–2017', https://www.irishfilmboard.ie/images/uploads/general/2011_-_2017_Produced_Films_Overview.pdf [accessed 21 September 2019]

Irish Film Board, 'Statement from the IFB on Gender Equality: Six point plan', https://www.irishfilmboard.ie/about/gender [accessed 22 March 2018]

Irish Film Board, 'Strategic Plan 2016–2020', https://www.irishfilmboard.ie/images/uploads/general/IFB_Five_Year_Strategy_2016-1.pdf [accessed 26 March 2018]

Jacey, H., *The Woman in the Story: Writing memorable female characters* (Studio City, CA: Michael Wiese Productions, 2010)

Jean-Charles, R.M., *Conflict Bodies: The politics of rape representation in the francophone imaginary* (Columbus, OH: Ohio State University Press, 2014)

Johnston, C., 'Maeve', *Screen*, vol. 22, no. 4, 1981, pp. 54–71

Johnston, C., 'The Subject of Feminist Film Theory/Practice', *Screen*, vol. 21, no. 2, 1980, pp. 27–34

Johnston, C., 'Women's Cinema as Counter-Cinema', in E.A. Kaplan (ed.), *Feminism and Film* (Oxford: Oxford University Press, 2000), pp. 22–33

Jones, D. and Pringle, J.K., 'Unmanageable Inequalities: Sexism in the film industry', *The Sociological Review*, vol. 63, S1, 2015, pp. 37–49

Jost, F., 'La Transfiguration du Bal', *Cinémas*, vol. 15, nos. 2–3, 2005

Juhasz, A., 'The Future Was Then: Reinvesting in feminist media practice and politics', *Camera Obscura*, vol. 21, no. 1, 2006, pp. 53–7

Kamberidou, I., 'Gender Devaluation and Gender Fatigue: Getting women on the glass escalator', Presentation at the European Commission's Digital Agenda Assembly, 'Every European Digital', European Commission, INFSO, Brussels, 16–17 June 2011, http://ec.uropea.eu/digital-agenda/daa. See Workshop 22, Women for smart growth: http://ec.europa.eu/information_society/events/cf/daa11/item-display.cfm?id=6003 [accessed 21 September 2019]

Kanter, R., *Men and Women of the Corporation* (New York: Basic Books, 1993)

Kay, K., 'New York Super-8: Edinburgh event, 1980', *Idiolects*, vols 9–10, 1980, pp. 7–9

Kearney, M.C., *Girls Make Media* (New York: Routledge, 2006)

Kelan, E., 'Gender Fatigue: The ideological dilemma of gender neutrality and discrimination in organizations', *Canadian Journal of Administrative Sciences*, vol. 26, no. 3, 2009, pp. 197–210

Kilborn, R. and Izod, J., *An Introduction to Television Documentary: Confronting reality* (Manchester & New York: Manchester University Press, 1997)

Kitzinger, J., 'Media Templates: Patterns of association and the (re) construction of meaning over time', *Media, Culture & Society*, vol. 22, no. 1, 2000, pp. 61–84

Knight, J. and Gledhill, C., *Doing Women's Film History: Reframing cinemas, past and future* (Champaign, IL: University of Illinois Press, 2015)

Lantz, J., *About Quality: The film industry's view of the term quality* (Stockholm: WFT Sverige, 2007)

Lauzen, M., *It's a Man's (Celluloid) World: 19ᵗʰ Annual Celluloid Ceiling Report 2016* (San Diego: San Diego University, 2018)

Lauzen, M., 'It's a Man's (Celluloid) World: On-Screen representations of female characters in the top 100 films of 2014', https://womenintvfilm.sdsu.edu/files/2014_Its_a_Mans_World_Report.pdf [accessed 12 September 2016]

Lauzen, M., 'It's a Man's (Celluloid) World: Portrayals of female characters in the top 100 films of 2018', ww.womenintvfilm.sdsu.edu/research [accessed 21 September 2019]

Lauzen, M., 'More Female Documentary Directors, But Celluloid Ceiling Remains', *The Wrap*, http://www.thewrap.com/women-representation-documentary-films-grows-celluloid-ceiling-remains-indie-features-53586/ [accessed 12 September 2016]

Lauzen, M., 'The Celluloid Ceiling: Behind-the-scenes employment of women in the top 100, 250 and 500 Films of 2018', www.womenintvfilm.sdsu.edu/wp.../2019/01/2018_Celluloid _Ceiling_report.pdf [accessed 21 September 2019]

Lavelle, P., 'James O'Mara: The story of an original Sinn Féiner' (Dublin: The History Publisher, 2011 [1961])

Lawlor, C. (ed.), *Sean MacBride: That day's struggle* (Dublin: Currach Press, 2005)

Leahy, E., 'The Irreducible Difference of the Other (Vivienne Dick, 2013)', *Estudios Irlandeses*, vol. 10, 2015, pp. 209–11

Leahy, E., 'Snap (Carmel Winters, 2010)', *Estudios Irlandeses*, vol. 6, 2011, pp. 215–17

Le Corff, I., *Le Cinéma Irlandais: Une expression postcoloniale Européenne* (Rennes: Presses Universitaires de Rennes, 2014)

Le Corff, I., 'The Liminal Position of Irish Cinema: Is using the English language a key to success?', *Mise au Point,* no. 5, 2013, https://journals.openedition.org/map/1455 [accessed 21 September 2019]

Levitin, J., Plessis, J. and Raoul, V., *Women Filmmakers: Refocusing* (New York: Routledge, 2016)

Liddy, S., 'Ireland: Irish Female Screenwriters, 2007–2013', in J. Nelmes and J. Selbo (eds), *Women Screenwriters: An international guide* (Basingstoke: Palgrave Macmillan, 2012), pp. 422–3

Liddy, S., 'Look Who's Talking! Irish Female Screenwriters', in J. Nelmes and J. Selbo (eds), *Women Screenwriters: An international guide* (Basingstoke: Palgrave Macmillan, 2015), pp. 410–33

Liddy, S., 'Missing in Action: Where are the Irish women screenwriters?', http://filmireland.net/2015/04/20/missing-in-action-where-are-the-irish-women-screenwriters/ [accessed 21 September 2019]

Liddy, S., 'Older Women and Sexuality On-Screen: Euphemism and evasion?', in C. McGlynn, M. O'Neill and M. Schrage-Fruh (eds), *Ageing Women in Literature and Visual Culture: Reflections, refractions, reimaginings* (Basingstoke: Palgrave Macmillan, 2017), pp. 167–80

Liddy, S., '"Open to All and Everybody"? The Irish Film Board: Accounting for the scarcity of women screenwriters', *Feminist Media Studies*, vol. 16, no. 5, 2016, pp. 901–17

Liddy, S., 'Stories We Tell Ourselves: Writing the mature female protagonist', *Sexuality and Culture*, vol. 19, no. 4, 2015, pp. 599–616

Liddy, S., 'Women and the Irish Film Industry', https://www.irishtimes.com/opinion/letters/women-and-the-irish-film-industry-1.2424444 [accessed 21 September 2019]

Lieberman, E. and Hegarty, K., 'Authors of the Image: Cinematographers Gabriel Figueroa and Gregg Toland', *Journal of Film and Video*, vol. 62, nos. 1–2, Spring/Summer 2010, pp. 31–51

Lincoln, A.E. and Allen, M.P., 'Double Jeopardy in Hollywood: Age and gender in the careers of film actors, 1926–1999', *Sociological Forum*, vol. 19, 2004, pp. 611–31

Loist, S. and Zielinski, G., 'On the Development of Queer Film Festivals and their Media Activism', in D. Iordanova and L. Torchin (eds), *Film Festival Yearbook. Volume 4: Film Festivals and Activism* (St Andrews: St Andrews Film Studies, 2012), pp. 49–62

Lorde, A., 'The Master's Tools Will Never Dismantle the Master's House', in *Sister Outsider: Essays and speeches* (Berkeley: Crossing Press, 2007), pp. 110–13

Loren, S. and Metelmann, J., *Melodrama after the Tears: New perspectives on the politics of victimhood* (Amsterdam: Amsterdam University Press, 2016)

Lysaght, R., 'Sounding Off: Rachel Lysaght asks "Where my ladies at?"', http://filmireland.net/2013/02/20/sounding-off-rachel-lysaght-asks-where-my-ladies-at-issue-144-spring-2013/ [accessed 21 September 2019]

Martin, A.K., 'Death of a Nation: Transnationalism, bodies and abortion in late twentieth-century Ireland', in T. Mayer (ed.), *Gender Ironies of Nationalism: Sexing the nation* (London: Routledge, 2000), pp. 65–86

Massey, D., *Space, Place and Gender* (Cambridge: Polity, 1994)

Matar, D. and Harb, Z., *Narrating Conflict in the Middle East: Discourse, image and communications practices in Lebanon and Palestine* (London: IB Tauris, 2013)

Mayer, S., *Political Animals: The new feminist cinema* (London: I.B. Tauris & Co., 2016)

Mayer, V., *Below the Line: Producers and production studies in the new television economy* (Durham and London: Duke University Press, 2011)

Mayer, V., 'Studying Up and F**king Up: Ethnographic interviewing in production studies', *Cinema Journal*, vol. 47, no. 2, Winter 2008, pp. 141–7

Mayer, V., Banks, M. and Caldwell, J.T. (eds), *Production Studies: Cultural studies of media industries* (New York: Routledge, 2009)

McCloskey, M., 'O'Maras of Limerick and their Overseas Businesses', *The Old Limerick Journal*, no. 37, Summer 2001

McCullough, K. (Interview), *Filmmaker Magazine*, 26 January 2017, https://filmmakermagazine.com/101406-i-felt-a-huge-responsibility-to-get-it-right-dp-kate-mccullough-on-its-not-yet-dark/#.WpkvxOfLg2w [accessed 22 May 2018]

McKeogh, C. and O'Connell, D., *Documentary in a Changing State: Ireland since the 1990s* (Cork: Cork University Press, 2012)

McKinsey and Company, 'Women in the Workplace 2016', p. 1, https://www.mm-foundation.org/sites/mmf/files/2016_McKinsey_LeanIn_Women-in-the-Workplace.pdf [accessed 21 September 2019]

McLagan, M., 'Making Human Rights Claims Public', *American Anthropologist*, vol. 108, no. 1, 2006, pp. 191–5

McLane, B., *A New History of Documentary Film*, 2nd edn (New York and London: Continuum, 2012)

McLoone, M., *Film, Media and Popular Culture in Ireland: Cityscapes, landscapes, soundscapes* (Dublin: Irish Academic Press, 2008)

McLoone, M., *Irish Film: The emergence of a contemporary cinema* (London: BFI, 2000)

Meaney, G., *Nora* (Cork: Cork University Press, 2004)

Molloy, P., 'Labour of Love Proves a Box-office Hit', *Sunday Business Post*, 12 September 2010, p. 6

Molony, S., 'House and Home: Structuring absence in post-Celtic Tiger documentary', in D. Negra and Y. Tasker (eds), *Gendering the Recession: Media and culture in an age of austerity* (Durham and London: Duke University Press, 2014), pp. 181–202

Monahan, B. (ed.), *Ireland and Cinema: Culture and contexts* (Maidenhead: Palgrave Macmillan, 2015)

Monk, C., 'Sexuality and the Heritage', *Sight and Sound*, vol. 5, 1995, pp. 32–4

Morfoot, A., 'Oscars: Examining gender bias in the documentary categories', http://variety.com/2016/film/news/gender-bias-documentary-industry-1201708404/ [accessed 21 September 2019]

Mullally, Ú., 'Abbey Theatre Celebrates 1916 Centenary with Only One Woman Playwright', *Irish Times*, 2 November 2016, https://www.irishtimes.com/opinion/una-mullally-abbey-theatre-celebrates-1916-centenary-with-only-one-woman-playwright-1.2413277 [accessed 21 September 2019]

Mulvey, L., 'Visual Pleasure and Narrative Cinema', in L. Braudy and M. Cohen (eds), *Film Theory and Criticism: Introductory readings* (New York: Oxford University Press, 1999), pp. 833–44

Murphy, M.P., 'Gendering the Narrative of the Irish Crisis', *Irish Political Studies*, vol. 30, no. 2, 2015, pp. 220–37

Murphy, P., 'Interview – Film and Feminism', *The Irish Feminist Review*, vol. 84, Women's Community Press, 1984, pp. 74–88

National Film Board of Canada, 'NFB Releases Its 2017–2018 Results: Parity in action', www.canada.ca-news-2018/03 [accessed 21 September 2019]

National Women's Council of Ireland, 'Better Boards, Better Business, Better Society', https://www.nwci.ie/images/uploads/Better_Boards_PDF.pdf [accessed 14 January 2017]

National Women's Council of Ireland, 'No Small Change: Closing the gender pay gap', www.nwci.ie [accessed 1 July 2018]

National Women's Council of Ireland, 'We Need the Appropriate Resources and Political Will to Restore and Advance Women's Rights and Equality in Ireland', www.nwci.ie [accessed 3 July 2018]

Negra, D., 'Adjusting Men and Abiding Mammies: Gendering the recession in Ireland', *The Irish Review*, no. 46, 2013, pp. 23–34

Negra, D., 'Irishness, Anger and Masculinity in Recent Film and Television', in Ruth Barton (ed.), *Screening Irish-America* (Dublin: Irish Academic Press, 2009)

Nelmes, J. and Selbo, J., *Women Screenwriters: An international guide* (Maidenhead: Palgrave Macmillan, 2015)

Neville, P., 'Mediating between *His & Hers*: An exploration of gender representations and self-representations', in Barry Monahan (ed.), *Ireland and Cinema: Culture and contexts* (New York and Basingstoke: Palgrave Macmillan, 2015)

Nichols, B., *Representing Reality* (Bloomington, IN: Indiana University Press, 1991)

O'Brien, A., 'Producing Television and Reproducing Gender', *Television & New Media*, vol. 16, no. 3, 2015, pp. 259–74

O'Brien, M., '*The Secret of Kells*: A film for a post-Celtic Tiger Ireland?' *Animation Studies*, vol. 6, 2011, pp. 34–9

Ó Cathaoir, B., 'An Irishman's Diary', *The Irish Times*, 11 September 2006

O'Connell, D., *New Irish Storytellers: Narrative strategies in film* (London: Intellect Books, 2010)

O'Connor, P., 'Feminism and Politics of Gender', in M. Adshead and M. Millar (eds), *Public Administration and Public Policy in Ireland: Theory and methods* (London and New York: Routledge, 2003), pp. 54–68

O'Connor, P., 'Ireland: A man's world', *The Economic and Social Review*, vol. 31, 2000, p. 97

O'Connor, P., 'Where Do Women Fit in University Senior Management? An analytical typology of cross-national organisational culture', in B. Bagilhole and K. White (eds), *Gender, Power and Management* (Basingstoke: Palgrave Macmillan, 2015), pp. 168–91

O'Falt, C., 'Full Frame: Why are women filmmakers finding more opportunities in documentaries?', *Indiwire*, http://www.indiewire.com/2016/04/full-frame-why-are-women-filmmakers-finding-more-opportunities-in-documentaries-21750/ [accessed 21 September 2019]

OHCHR, 'Progress and Obstacles in the Fight Against Impunity for Sexual Violence in the Democratic Republic of the Congo', UN Office of the High Commissioner for Human Rights, http://www.refworld.org/docid/534b931f4.html [accessed 21 September 2019]

O'Regan, T., *Australian National Cinema* (London and New York: Routledge, 1996)

O'Toole, E., 'Waking the Feminists: Re-imagining the space of the National Theatre in the era of the Celtic phoenix', *Lit: Literature Interpretation Theory*, vol. 28, no. 2, 2017, pp. 134–52

Oyewumi, O., *African Women and Feminism: Reflecting on the politics of sisterhood* (New Jersey: Africa World Press, 2006)

Petrie, D., 'The Development of Film Schools in Europe and North America' (pp. 15–83) and 'British Film Schools' (pp. 87–180), in D. Petrie and R. Stoneman (eds), *Educating Film-makers: Past, present and future* (Bristol: Intellect Books, 2014)

Pew Research Centre, *Women and Leadership: Public says women are equally qualified, but barriers persist* (Washington: Pew Research Center, 2015)

Prince, S., 'The Emergence of Filmic Artifacts: Cinema and cinematography in the digital era', *Film Quarterly*, vol. 57, no. 3, Spring 2004, pp. 24–33

Reel Art scheme funding application document, http://www.artscouncil.ie/Funds/Reel-Art-scheme/ [accessed 22 March 2018]

Rhyne, R., 'Film Festival Circuits and Stakeholders', in D. Iordanova and R. Rhyne (eds), *Film Festival Yearbook 1: The festival circuit* (St Andrews: St Andrews Film Studies with College Gate Press, 2009), pp. 9–22

Rockett, K., Gibbons, L. and Hill, J., *Cinema and Ireland* (London: Routledge, 1988)

Ross, K. and Carter, C., 'Women and News: A long and winding road', *Media Culture & Society*, vol. 33, no. 8, 2011, pp. 1148–65

Screen Australia, 'Gender Matters: Women in the Australian screen industry', https://www.screenaustralia.go.au [accessed 20 January 2017]

Screen Ireland, 'From Shorts to Features: Screen Ireland celebrates leading Irish female directors for International Women's Day', https://www.screenireland.ie/news/international-womens-day-2019-female-directed-short-film [accessed 21 September 2019]

Skillset, 'Why Her? Factors that have influenced the careers of successful women in film & television, AFTV & alliance sector skills councils, UK', http://publications.skillset.org/admin/data/why%20her/why%20her%202009.pdf [accessed 29 May 2018]

Smaill, B., 'Interview with Kim Longinotto', *Studies in Documentary Film*, vol. 1, no. 2, 2007, pp. 177–87

Smith, J.L., *Melodrama* (London: Methuen, 1973)

Smith, P., Caputi, P. and Crittenden, N., 'A Maze of Metaphors around Glass Ceilings', *Gender in Management: An International Journal*, vol. 27, no. 7, 2012, pp. 436–48

Smith, S.L., 'Gender Oppression in Cinematic Content? A look at females on-screen and behind-the-camera in top grossing 2007 films', http://www.annenberg.usc.edu/ [accessed 19 December 2016]

Smith, S.L., Choueiti, M. and Pieper, K., 'Gender Bias Without Borders: An investigation of female characters in popular films across 11 countries', https://seejane.org/wp.../ gender-bas-without-borders-full-report.pdf [accessed 24 January 2017]

Smith, S.L., Pieper, K., Choueiti, M. and Case, A., *Gender & Short Films: Emerging female filmmakers and the barriers surrounding their careers* (Los Angeles: School for Communication and Journalism, USC Annenberg, 2015)

Smith, S.L., Pieper, K. and Choueiti, M., 'Inclusion in the Director's Chair? Gender, race, and age of film directors across 1,000 films from 2007 to 2016', https://annenberg. usc.edu/sites/default/files/2017/04/06/MDSCI_Inclusion%20_in_the_Directors_Chair. pdf [accessed 24 April 2019]

Sontag, S., *Regarding the Pain of Others* (London: Picador, 2003), p. 18

Sprague, J., *Feminist Methodologies for Critical Researchers: Bridging differences* (Walnut Creek, CA: Altamira Press, 2005)

Staff, M., '"Herstory" and Biography: Recovering the forgotten woman's voice', https:// journal.historyitm.org/v5n1/staff-herstory-biography/ [accessed 3 April 2019]

Stamp, S., *Lois Weber in Early Hollywood* (Oakland, CA: California University Press, 2015)

Sullivan, M., *Women in Northern Ireland* (Gainesville, FL: University Press of Florida, 1999)

Swedish Film Institute, *Gender Equality – Svenska Filminstitutet*, http:www.filminstitutet. se/en/about-us/Swedish-film-institute-gender-equality [accessed 2 July 2018]

Taylor, C.J., 'Occupational Sex Composition and the Gendered Availability of Workplace Support', *Gender and Society*, vol. 24, 2010

Telefilm Canada, 'Telefilm Canada releases its latest gender parity statistics for feature film production funding', https://telefilm.ca/en/news-releases/telefilm-canada-releases-its-latest-gender-parity-statistics-for-feature-film-production-funding [accessed 25 April 2019]

Ten Brink, J. and Oppenheimer, J. (eds), *Killer Images: Documentary film, memory and the performance of violence* (London: Wallflower Press, 2012)

Tomlinson, J., 'Beyond Connection: Cultural cosmopolitan and ubiquitous media', *International Journal of Cultural Studies*, vol. 144, 2011, pp. 347–61

Torchin, L., 'Networked for Advocacy: Film festivals and activism', in D. Iordanova and L. Torchin (eds), *Film Festival Yearbook. Volume 4: Film Festivals and Activism* (St Andrews: St Andrews Film Studies, 2012), pp. 1–12

Tracy, T., 'A Wandering to Find Home: *Adam & Paul* (2004)', in Rhona Richman Kenneally and Lucy McDiarmid (eds), *The Vibrant House: Irish writing and the domestic space* (Dublin and Portland, OR: Four Courts Press, 2017)

Tracy, T. and Flynn, R., Contemporary Irish Film: From the national to the transnational', Éire-Ireland, vol. 52, vols 1 & 2, 2017, pp. 169–97

Tracy, T. and Flynn, R., 'Quantifying National Cinema: A case study of the Irish Film Board, 1993–2013', *Film Studies*, vol. 14, no. 1, 2016, pp. 32–53

Tuchman, G., Daniels Kaplan, A. and Benet, J. (eds), *Hearth and Home: Images of women in the mass media* (New York: Oxford University Press, 1978)

Turley, E. and Fisher, J., 'Tweeting Back when Shouting Back: Social media and feminist activism', *Feminism and Psychology*, vol. 28, no. 1, 2018, pp. 128–32

Wahl, A. and Wahl, O., 'No Sexism, Please – We're Swedish: A study of gender equality in the film industry', Women in Film and Television in Sweden, 2017

Wallström, M., '"Conflict Minerals" Finance Gang Rape in Africa', *The Guardian*, 14 August 2010, p. 14, https://www.theguardian.com/commentisfree/2010/aug/14/conflict-minerals-finance-gang-rape [accessed 28 March 2017]

Walsh, K., Suiter, J. and O'Connor, C., *Hearing Women's Voices? Exploring women's underrepresentation in current affairs radio programming at peak listening times in Ireland* (Dublin: NWCI, 2015)

Wells, P., *Understanding Animation* (London: Routledge, 1998)

Whelehan, I. and Gwynne, G. (eds), *Ageing, Popular Culture and Contemporary Feminism: Harleys and hormones* (Basingstoke: Palgrave Macmillan, 2013)

Whyte, J., 'Free Radicals', *cineoutsider: beyond the mainstream*, 11 December 2011, http://www.cineoutsider.com/articles/stories/f/free_radicals_1.html [accessed 28 March 2017]

Will, D., Interview with Pat Murphy, *Framework*, nos. 26–7, 1985, pp. 132–7

Williams, C., 'Explaining the Great War in Africa: How conflict in the Congo became a continental crisis', *The Fletcher Forum of World Affairs*, vol. 37, no. 2, 2013

Wing-fai, L., Gill, R. and Randle, K., 'Getting in, Getting on, Getting out? Women as career scramblers in the UK film and television industries,' *Gender and Creative Labour: The Sociological Review*, vol. 63, S1, 2015, pp. 50–65

Women in Film and Television, https://wft.ie/statement-from-the-ifb-on-gender-equality-six-point-plan/ [accessed 21 September 2019]

Woodrell, D., *Tomato Red* (New York: Henry Holt & Co., 1998)

Wreyford, N., 'Birds of a Feather: Informal recruitment practices and gendered outcomes for screenwriting work in the UK film industry', *Gender and Creative Labour: The Sociological Review*, vol. 63, S1, 2015, pp. 84–96

Wreyford, N. and Cobb, S., 'Towards a Feminist Methodology for Producing Historical Data on Women in the Contemporary UK Film Industry', *Feminist Media Histories*, vol. 3, no. 3, 2017, pp. 107–33

Yancey-Martin, P., '"Said and Done" versus "Saying and Doing": Gendering practices practicing gender at work', *Gender & Society*, vol. 17, no. 3, 2003, pp. 342–66

Zoellner, A., 'Professional Ideology and Program Conventions: Documentary development in independent British television production', *Mass Communication and Society*, vol. 12, no. 4, 2009, pp. 503–36

Index